John Davison

Discourses on prophecy, in which are considered its structure, use, and inspiration

John Davison

Discourses on prophecy, in which are considered its structure, use, and inspiration

ISBN/EAN: 9783337104818

Printed in Europe, USA, Canada, Australia, Japan

Cover: Foto ©Lupo / pixelio.de

More available books at **www.hansebooks.com**

DISCOURSES

ON

PROPHECY,

IN WHICH ARE CONSIDERED

ITS STRUCTURE, USE, AND INSPIRATION;

BEING THE SUBSTANCE OF

TWELVE SERMONS

PREACHED IN THE CHAPEL OF LINCOLN'S INN,

IN THE LECTURE FOUNDED BY

THE RIGHT REVEREND WILLIAM WARBURTON,

BISHOP OF GLOUCESTER.

BY

JOHN DAVISON, B.D.

LATE FELLOW OF ORIEL COLLEGE, OXFORD.

Οὐ γὰρ ὑπ' ἐμοί συνεσκευασμένοι εἰσὶν οἱ λόγοι, οὐδὲ τέχνῃ ἀνθρωπίνῃ κεκαλλωπισμένοι· ἀλλὰ τούτους Δαβὶδ μὲν ἔψαλλεν, Ἡσαΐας δὲ εὐηγγελίζετο, Ζαχαρίας δὲ ἐκήρυξε, Μωϋσῆς δὲ ἀνέγραψεν.—*Justin Martyr*, p. 194.

A NEW EDITION.

Oxford and London:

JAMES PARKER AND CO.

1870.

PRINTED BY J. PARKER & CO.
OXFORD

CONTENTS.

INTRODUCTION.

1. Of the previous probability of a Divine Revelation.

2. Of the plan and course of inquiry pursued in the following Discourses, p. 1—9.

DISCOURSE I.

On the connexion of Prophecy with the other evidences of revealed Religion, p. 10—24.

2 Peter i. 21.

For Prophecy came not in old time by the will of Man; but holy Men of God spake as THEY WERE MOVED *by the Holy Ghost.*

DISCOURSE II.

On the contents of the Prophetic Volume as distinguished from its Predictions, p. 25—38.

Jeremiah xxv. 4.

And the Lord hath sent unto you all His servants the Prophets, rising early, and sending them; but ye have not hearkened, nor inclined your ear to hear.

Essential principles of Religion and Morals enforced by the Prophets.—Intermediate character of the prophetic Revelation between that of the Law and the Gospel.—Personal office of the Prophets.

PART II.

Same Subject continued, p. 39—49.

The doctrines of Providence and Repentance fully stated in

the Prophetic Volume.—Importance of those Doctrines.—General observations on the Moral contents of Prophecy.—Utility of *an authoritative rule of duty.*

DISCOURSES III. IV. V. VI.
Structure of Prophecy in its several Periods.

DISCOURSE III.

On the state of Prophecy—in its earliest age—from the Fall to the Patriarchal times, p. 50—69.

GENESIS xvii. 7.

And I will establish My covenant between Me and thee, and thy seed after thee, in their generations, for an everlasting covenant, to be a God unto thee, and to thy seed after thee.

Objects of it, at the Fall; after the Deluge; in the Patriarchal Age.

PART II.

State of Prophecy in the Patriarchal Age more distinctly considered.—Twofold promise to Abraham.—Partition of the subjects of Prophecy connected therewith.—Prophecy of Jacob.—Measure of illumination afforded to the Patriarchal Age.—Analogy in the use of Patriarchal and later Prophecy.—Difference between them.—Integrity of the Mosaic Records, p. 70—82.

DISCOURSE IV.

State of Prophecy contemporary with the promulgation of the Mosaic Law.

DEUTERONOMY xviii. 15.

The Lord thy God will raise up unto thee a Prophet from the midst of thee, of thy brethren, like unto me ; unto him ye shall hearken.

Cessation of Prophecy from the Patriarchal Age to Moses.—A true idea of the Mosaic Law necessary to the elucidation of the state of Prophecy concurrent with it.—Institution of that Law.—Its genius.—Its Sanctions, temporal only.—Its Types, and whether understood in their mystical sense, when they were first appointed.—Moral use of them.—Prophecy of Balaam.—That of Moses concerning a future Prophet like to himself.—No clear or copious Prophecy concerning the Gospel given at this period.—The judgment of Michaelis concerning the principle of the Mosaic Law inadmissible, p. 83—118.

PART II.

Prophecy on the temporal subject concurrent with the promulgation of the Law.—True relation between the entire state of Prophecy and the Law, deduced.—Remarks upon that relation, p. 119—126.

DISCOURSE V.

State of Prophecy from Samuel to Malachi.

Acts iii. 24.

Yea, and all the Prophets from Samuel, and those that follow after, as many as have spoken, have likewise foretold of these days.

Cessation of Prophecy from Moses to Samuel.—Continuity of it from Samuel to Malachi: this its *One Principal Age:* various subjects of it.—Particular mission of Samuel.—His regulation of the commonwealth of Israel.—Prediction concerning David, p. 127—137.

PART II.

State of Prophecy in the reigns of David and Solomon.

Enlarged revelation of it.—The Temporal and the Evangelical Prophecy united.—Double sense vindicated.—David the promulger of the chief Prophecies concerning Christ and the Gospel, in this age.—Prophetic Psalms.—Integrity of Prophecy.—Duration of the temporal kingdom in the family of David.—Instability of the reigning families in Samaria.—Termination of the temporal kingdom in the reign of Coniah.—Conspicuous Prophecy announcing it.—That kingdom never restored.—Considerations on the history of the Maccabees.—Temple of Solomon.—State of Prophecy respecting it.—One definite use of Prophecy to foreshew the suspension, or abolition, of the particular ordinances of the first Covenant.—Accomplishment of Jacob's prophecy concerning the pre-eminence of the tribe of Judah, p. 138—167.

DISCOURSE VI.

State of Prophecy from the reign of Solomon to its final
cessation, p. 168—255.

Amos iii. 7.

*Surely, the Lord God will do nothing, but He revealeth His secret unto
His servants the prophets.*

PART I.

Temporal prophecy relating to the Hebrew people, from the
time of *Solomon* to the *restoration* from *Babylon.*—Copiousness
of it.—Division of the kingdom foreshewn.—Jeroboam's idolatry.—Divided custody and evidence of the older prophetic
records.—The respective fortunes of the two kingdoms of Israel
and Judah foreshewn.—Extent and connexion of Isaiah's prophecies on the temporal subject, p. 168—193.

PART II.

Prophecy concerning *Christianity* within the same period,
viz., from the time of *Solomon* to the *restoration* from *Babylon.*
—Intermission of such prophecy for some ages.—Revival of it
traced in the books of the Prophetic Canon.—Amos, Hosea,
Isaiah.—This revival subsequent to the mission of Elijah and
Elisha.—Christian prophecy diffused through the Prophetic
Canon.—Whether any of the prophetic books are entirely
devoid of Christian prediction?—Greatest increase of the pro-
phetic information concerning the Gospel, when granted?—
Adaptation of it, p. 194—209.

PART III.

Prophecy on the *Pagan* subjects within that period.—Its
moral uses, in demonstrating the providence of God, and the
exclusive truth of His first revelation, and in foreshewing the
æra of Christianity, p. 210—221.

PART IV.

Last age of ancient Prophecy, from the *Captivity* to its *final
Cessation.*—Completion of former prophecy.—Second Temple.
—Concluding communications of the prophetic oracles.—Their
Christian import vindicated and explained.—Recapitulation,
p. 222—255.

DISCOURSE VII.

Of the Divine foreknowledge, and its union with the liberty of human action, p. 256—273.

ISAIAH xlvi. 10.

Declaring the end from the beginning, and from ancient times the things that are not done, saying, My counsel shall stand, and I will fulfil all My pleasure.

DISCOURSES VIII. IX. X. XI. XII.

On the Inspiration of Prophecy.

DISCOURSE VIII.

Criterion of Prophetic Inspiration.—Proof of it in the Predictions concerning Christianity, p. 274—295.

ISAIAH lx. 3.

And the Gentiles shall come to Thy light, and kings to the brightness of Thy rising.

DISCOURSE IX.

Predictions concerning the Jewish people, p. 296—311.

DEUTERONOMY xxviii. 59.

Then the Lord will make thy plagues wonderful, and the plagues of thy seed, even great plagues, and of long continuance, and sore sicknesses, and of long continuance.

DISCOURSE X.

Predictions concerning the great Apostasy, p. 312—331.

REVELATIONS xix. 10.

For the testimony of Jesus is the spirit of Prophecy.

viii CONTENTS.

DISCOURSE XI.

Predictions on the subject of Pagan kingdoms; Nineveh,
Babylon, Tyre, and Egypt, p. 332—347.

ISAIAH xiii. 19, 20.

And Babylon, the glory of kingdoms, the beauty of the Chaldees' excellency, shall be as when God overthrew Sodom and Gomorrah. It shall never be inhabited, neither shall it be dwelt in from generation to generation; neither shall the Arabian pitch tent there; neither shall the shepherds make their fold there.

DISCOURSE XII.

Predictions concerning the descendants of Ishmael, and the
succession of the four ancient Empires, p. 348—364.

DANIEL ii. 21, 22.

And He changeth the times and the seasons: He removeth kings and setteth up kings; He giveth wisdom unto the wise, and knowledge to them that know understanding.

He revealeth the deep and secret things: He knoweth what is in the darkness, and the light dwelleth with Him.

INTRODUCTION.

I. *Of the previous Probability of a Divine Revelation.*

II. *Of the Plan and Contents of the following Discourses.*

ANTECEDENTLY to a consideration of the proper Evidences of Revealed Religion, it cannot be said with any show of reason, that it is a thing improbable in itself that a divine Revelation should be made. Nothing that we know of the Attributes of God, or of His Moral Government; nothing that we know of the Nature and Condition of Man, would make it appear unfit for God to bestow upon man an immediate communication of His Will. On the contrary, the most just and rational notions we can frame of the providential care of the Deity would lead us to consider it as entirely suitable to His Attributes and His Designs, that He should at times impart to His reasonable creatures, whose whole existence and destiny are dependent upon Him, supplies of knowledge and direction. And on the side of Man, it is too clear, on a sober review of his condition, that he is not so complete in his own natural resources as to be placed above the Benefit, or even the Need, of such supervening assistance.

And so it has been, that the common Belief of the world has borne witness to the intrinsic *Probability* of a Revelation. Supposed Revelations, or Traditions of them, there always have been; and often they have been such, as, having nothing of merit or excellence in their matter, nor any considerable inducement of evidence to recommend them, have yet obtained credit, and been received, solely,

it should seem, on this ground, of the great reason and
likelihood which men have owned in the first supposal of a
Revelation. And as the principle of Religion itself is
proved to be natural to man, and truly conformable to his
constitution and character, by the fact of his embracing it
under forms exceedingly perverted ; so the gift of a Revelation is shewn to be highly probable, and adapted to his
expectation and sense of things, by his reception of fictitious
systems of it, which in many cases have had in them every
thing to create a positive disbelief, excepting the one presumption, which the judgment and feeling of Nature still
cling to, that the Deity can and will somewhere reveal
Himself to His creatures : a propensity of belief, which can
be referred only to one or both of these two causes,—the
absolute likelihood which men have seen in the hope of a
Revelation, or the traditionary impressions of One actually
given ; a propensity, therefore, which attests either the
Probability or the Fact.   .

It is true, a different view of the matter has been attempted to be given. It has been contended, that a
Revelation is improbable, because unnecessary ; and unnecessary, because Natural Religion can do all that is
wanted in the relation between God and man.

But this notion, besides that it is opposed to the general
Sense and Belief of Mankind, which Sense and Belief I
have already adverted to ; and cannot be reconciled with
the History of the World, which has exhibited the hopes
and principles of Natural Religion, in its best day, labour-
ing and crying aloud for aid to their support ; is, further,
alleged ineffectually to the question. For were it ever so
true, that man could *dispense* with a revelation, as not
strictly *necessary* to him, (which is only supposed, not
conceded,) yet it may be *expedient* for his use, and *highly
beneficial* to him ; and where is the improbability in supposing that God should improve, by confirming, or extending in any degree, the discoveries which man may be
able to make of the Nature and the Will of God, and of

his own Hopes and Duties under the divine Government? This is no more than to think that God may open the doors of heaven for a further communication with His rational creatures, to give them more light; and that the State of Man may, in some important respects affecting his Moral Information, and consequently his Duties and his Happiness, be progressive: neither of them very hard or revolting suppositions. And if, in some future period of his existence, it be reasonable to think, as it plainly is, from the confessed disproportion between his present attainments and his capacities, that he may come to a more enlarged knowledge, both of God and himself, than he can now attain to; and come to this by an act of the divine favour, making the adequate change in his condition; there is the like reason to think that he may now begin to receive any intermediate accessions to his knowledge in the same way. It appears, therefore, that neither the sense of his natural ignorance and deficiency in himself, which are seen and felt to be great, nor his future prospects, so far as he can judge of them, can have any other effect than to favour the hope of some present interposition of God for his better direction.

If this statement be a fair one, the cause of Revealed Religion gains so much by it, as to stand clear of any previous imputation lying against it under the idea of all Revelation being unreasonable or unlikely. It follows, that its positive Evidences will have their force entire: whatever that force may be, it is not diminished or encountered by any adverse objection striking at their root. Those Evidences are to be canvassed and applied; but, such as they are, their application is direct to the great question at issue. And it is material to bear in mind that they do apply in this manner. For if the proof of Religion had to overcome an improbability on the first entrance into the question, as well as to vindicate the particular system of Revelation which rests upon it, no doubt a greater body of evidence, a more commanding proof, might be necessary to satisfy both those requisitions, than is necessary for one of them alone. Whereas the claims of Revealed Religion, in respect of its Evidence, must be understood to stand on neutral ground, or rather to come before us with the presumption in their favour—a presumption arising from the reasonableness of expecting a Revelation to be given: although, in point of fact, they are abundantly sufficient to command a reasonable assent, even without that previous concession.

It will be said, The presumption operates equally in favour of *all* revelation, whether *genuine* or *false*. It cannot be otherwise; for it is in the nature of things, that presumptions founded on a general view of what is likely to take place, shall be indifferent to, and equally serve, the true, and the pretended, instance of the event. But here comes in the use of the proper evidence, to ascertain directly the origin of the professed revelation, and discriminate, by decisive signatures, the True from the False. And I think it may be concluded from the whole tenour of the attestation which God has given to that which we believe to be His revealed Truth, that the intention of the evidence with which He has surrounded it, is not so much to prove it against the improbability of any revelation at all, which improbability we have seen to be small or none, as to vindicate it from a very different kind of thing, the hazard of a mistake and confusion of its character, under the claims and pretences which lie in the way from the spurious religions set up in the world.

With respect to the sufficiency of Natural Religion, as the topic is urged by those who would discredit the expediency, or the necessity, of Revealed, we must take into the account that it is a paradox of modern invention, and the boast of it comes with an ill grace, and under great suspicions, so late in the day of trial. That the principles of Natural Religion have come to be so far understood and admitted as they are, may fairly be taken for one of the effects of the Gospel Revelation; a proof of its actual influence, on Opinions at least, instead of any disproof of its necessity, or use. It were easy to establish this point, to the fullest conviction, by a comparison of the different success which has attended the efforts of human reason in working out the scheme of Religion, with or without the aid of those decisive notices which the introduction of the Gospel has supplied. For it is not to be imagined that men fail to profit by the light that has been shed upon them, though they have not always the integrity to own the source from which it comes; or may turn their back upon it, whilst it fills the atmosphere around them; no, not even if in a higher strain of malice, they address the great luminary, only, as the apostate Spirit once did, "to tell it how they hate its beams." The fact is not to be denied; the Religion of Nature *has* had the opportunity of rekindling her faded taper by the Gospel light, whether furtively or unconsciously taken. Let her not dissemble the obligation and the conveyance, and make a boast of the splendour, as though it were originally her own, or had always in her hands been sufficient for the illumination of the World.

At the same time it ought to be understood, that when we venture to judge beforehand, by views of our own, concerning the probable conduct of the Deity in any instance, and to say what He may be expected to do, or not to do, as in the point of giving a Revelation, it is a question we are not equal to, for any very positive solution of it. Sobriety, and diffidence in the determination of our judgment, will here equally become the believer and the unbeliever. For where the *justice* and the *righteousness* of His administration are not interested, all our first ideas of it must be few and uncertain. When, therefore, I have pressed the opinion, that it is consistent with reason to look for a divine Revelation, I mean it is consistent with the best reason we can discern, with the obvious appearances of Man's condition, and the acknowledged ideas we hold of the Providence and Moral Government of God. But in each of these respects enough may be seen to convince us, that the opposite opinion, which objects to Revelation as a thing strange and incredible, is the wrong and untenable assumption. And herein is contained the view which I have wished to secure to the first consideration of Revealed Religion, viz., that its Evidences offer themselves to us unincumbered by any prejudice or suspicion, attaching to the bare idea of such a gift from God. If they are valid and legitimate Evidences, such as will bear the test in their proper character, they are adduced in an unexceptionable cause, and to a great end; that end being to cement, or restore, by the medium of a well-authenticated religion, the union between man and his Creator—a purpose of such a kind, that I should place the desire and the hope of finding it had been accomplished, in other words, of finding Revealed Religion to be true, among the first elements of moral wisdom and virtue; though we must take another rule, and a more cool, dispassionate judgment along with us, when our object is to examine whether it has been.

The following Discourses treat of one branch of the Evidences of Revelation, the argument of Prophecy. Some investigation is offered of the state of this argument, which forms what may be considered the more complex subject of the Evidences of Religion; belonging at once to the Jewish and the Christian Revelations; more than any other part of the proof, penetrating both; and opening a wide field of discussion in various directions.

Accordingly it has drawn to itself more of speculation and learned research, than the other topics which enter into the same comprehensive subject; not merely as to the interpretation of particular texts or portions of Prophecy; but as to the Use and Intent of the whole, the Principles by which it is to be interpreted, and the Mode in which it is to be applied. The field of inquiry has been rich in its produce, like "one which God had blessed;" for the produce has proved it was first sown and prepared by Him, and that He had "cast the good seed into the ground;" though the inferior cultivators have not always agreed well together; and some few of them, with too forward a zeal, have put in the sickle before the grain was ripe, and so far, by their unskilful husbandry, have discredited the harvest. But the result upon the whole has been, that their learned and successful labours have gathered in the stores, and made the interpretation and the evidence of Prophecy, in most of its material subjects, sufficiently accessible to those who are intent on such information; and if much yet remains to be done in the same province of argument, enough has been done to vindicate most amply by this medium of proof the Truth of Revelation.

What I have endeavoured to do has been to investigate the mixt argument of Prophecy, and to state what it is, as derived from its own records, and submitted to be examined. In this general Inquiry, Two objects have been kept chiefly in view: the One, to consider the State of Prophecy in the several Periods of its dispensation; the Other, to reduce to some definite form the proof of its Inspiration and divine Prescience. The First object has led me to trace the history of prophecy, as it lies at large in the Scripture volume, and thence to propose some illustration of its method and order, and also of its use and design, in respect of the seasons at which it was given. The Second has led me to state in a simple, and, I hope, unexceptionable form, what kind of Predictions will answer to the character of divinely-inspired Prophecies, and consequently will possess a *decisive* and *independent* evidence of their Inspiration; thence to suggest some means of judging of the argumentative evidence of different parts of Prophecy; and to vindicate its perfect authority by examples of its predictions canvassed and examined: the demonstration of its Prescience being the true and appropriate Test of its divine origin.

But besides its Prescience, there are other notices and characters of the like origin, dispersed throughout its records, and these not the less satisfactory in being less formal and prominent. Some of these internal notices I have endeavoured to illustrate and improve; and the inquirer, who will be at the pains of making the study for himself, with any degree of patience and connected attention, will easily add many observations to the same effect.

The method which I have followed may be thus stated:

The First of these Discourses is employed in treating of the Christian Evidences in general, and the Connexion of Prophecy with the rest.

The Second, in considering the Moral Contents of the Prophetic Volume, as distinguished from its Predictions.

In the Four next I have entered into the Structure of Prophecy, and the Course of its Dispensation.

In the Six last, its Inspiration and divine Prescience are examined.

It may be right to premise here, as I have again stated when I come to that part of my inquiry, that, in the Four Discourses allotted to the Structure of Prophecy, the subject is treated on the *assumption* of the general authority of the Prophetic Revelation being granted. For the question there to be discussed is this :—Supposing Prophecy to have been given, what was its use and intent? what the measure and kind of illumination which it afforded? The question is one for believers, wishing to see into the order and frame of that Revelation, of the truth of which they are already satisfied. And what is Prophecy, but a main integral branch of Revelation, as well as an evidence of it ?—to be examined therefore in both of these lights. In tracing, however, the tenour of the prophetic volume, I have adduced by the way some proofs tending to enforce its authority and inspiration, when, in the survey of its structure, materials for that kind of argument occurred. The *assumption*, which I have mentioned, of course is relinquished, when Prophecy comes to be examined by its proper test, which is done in the Six last of these Sermons.

It has fallen within my purpose to take notice of the *congruity* and *adaptation* of Prophecy in its parts, either in relation to each other, or to the seasons of its progressive developement. I hope the reflections brought forward on this head, are made in the spirit of a sober reason, justified in their ground of evidence, and material in their use. If they fail of being so, I wish them retracted. For what is merely ingenious or subtle in the exposition of Prophecy has little chance of being useful or true. Some parts of it demand a sound erudition, and a sounder intellect, to fix their sense; some an accurate historical knowledge, to elucidate their fulfilment; and who can doubt but that the plan of it, if from God, is ordered with such a perfect wisdom, as to exercise, and commend itself to, our highest reason? But nothing which in the last result wears the appearance of intricate or minute speculation, can have much to do with the principles, or the use, of the Scripture Oracles, which, if they are any thing, are the wisdom of God given for the faith and moral instruction of man.— Within these ideas I have wished to confine the observations which I had to offer on the scheme and adaptation of Prophecy in its several parts.

These Discourses, such as they are, are sent forth before I have had the leisure I could wish to prepare them for publication; but they are published at the earliest season when I could withdraw myself from the pressure and exigency of other duties, to give them some enlargement and revision. In plan and substance, and in the general draught of their composition, they are such as they were when preached, with the extension of particular topics which belonged to my argument, but which I wanted the skill to bring within the compass of single Sermons, when they had to be orally delivered. One important division of the Inquiry is still wholly wanting; that is, a View of the Prophecies of the New Testament. My appointed Course of Lectures was completed before I could embrace this branch of my subject, and the defect remains unredeemed in the present publication.

DISCOURSE I.

---

2 PETER i. 21.

*For Prophecy came not in old time by the Will of Man: but
Holy Men of God spake* as they were *moved by the Holy
Ghost.*

THE Christian Religion appeals to Prophecy as one of
its evidences. If we would do justice to the appeal,
we must examine the volume of Prophecy in this light, to
ascertain how far it does, in fact, establish or confirm the
truth and divine origin of the Religion which professes to
ground itself upon it.

But Prophecy is pledged to attest the Jewish, as well as
the Christian Revelation; being offered as an evidence
common to both. The whole scope of it must therefore
be taken to extend to the proof and vindication of the one
and the other. But since the Jewish Revelation is not
only connected with the Christian, but introductory and
subservient to it; for such is the import which the Christian takes upon itself to assign to the other; it will be
seen that whatever evidence establishes the truth and
authority of the prior Revelation, goes, by just inference,
to a verification of the Christian. In this view, though
Prophecy may confine itself, as it does in many of its subjects and immediate uses, to the support of the elder
Religion; yet the apparent economy of God, embracing
the two dispensations, will constrain us to extend the
truth and authority of the one to the defence of the other;
the connexion of their evidence being a consequence of

the connexion of their design. And by such a kind of estimate, applied to the prophetic records, not only "all the Prophets," but all their Prophecies, will be found, according to the conviction they may afford of their inspired and authentic character, to uphold, and recommend to our assent and reasonable acceptance, that which is offered to us as the last and best of God's dispensations, the Religion of Christ.

To this end, in evidence of the truth and divine origin of the two Revelations, but in particular of the Christian, which is our present concern in the world, and which, if true, demands something more than an inert belief, I wish to direct the substance of my inquiry in the following discourses, in which I shall endeavour to open and enforce some of the illustrations and proofs of the inspired authority of Scripture Prophecy.

What I shall attempt to do, in pursuit of this end, will be reduced under three heads, in giving some account, *First*, Of the Structure, and the Contents, of Prophecy. *Secondly*, Of its Use and Design in reference to the several periods in which it was given. *Thirdly*, Of the Proofs which it bears of a distinct Inspiration, manifested in the accomplishment of its Predictions.

It may be observed, however, that the view which I propose to take of it under the Two First of these heads, will be such as to combine with the argument of the Last of them. For Prophecy, in its Structure, and in its Use and Design, if I am able to represent it truly in these respects, contains much to exercise our attention. The fulfilment of its predictions, no doubt, is the one decisive test of its Inspiration. To this test it must be brought; and there the proof, if it hold good, is simple and direct. But yet, upon the use of so much reflection as so great a question requires, and to persons who will take the pains of putting together the notices which there are of a singular wisdom pervading the volume of Prophecy, that wisdom seen, as well in its matter, as in its adaptation to the supposed course of the divine Economy, there is a satisfaction to be had of no small value; a satisfaction which is of the nature of a positive evidence, and which, though it will vary in its degree to different minds, according to their habits or their capacity of judging of things in this way, yet can be inconsiderable to none. If therefore I can contribute to this kind of conviction by some leading ideas, taken from a survey of Prophecy, they will tend, with the other proof, to one and the same result. Indications of design, of fitness, and wisdom, as well as of internal truth, will coalesce with the evidence of predictions fulfilled. Both will support the conclusion sought to be established, the Inspiration of Prophecy, or in the words of Scripture, that " Prophecy came not in old time by the will of man; but Holy men of God spake as they were moved by the Holy Ghost."—The line of investigation thus described, it remains for me to pursue it.

But I must be permitted to clear my way for that purpose by some preliminary observations on one material point, the general state of the Christian Evidences. For Prophecy is but a single branch of them. We must look at them in a collective view, thereby to apprehend the connexion in which that one stands with the rest, and form a more discriminating judgment of the value, and the application to be made, of the results we may obtain from our particular inquiry. To these preliminary observations I shall devote the remainder of my present discourse.

It is possible that in treating of this, and perhaps some other parts of my subject, I shall pass into details of argument which may seem to convey less of the instruction, proper to a Christian discourse, than might be desired by those of my audience who have made a progress in their religion beyond the scope of such considerations. To men already satisfied of the truth, and the importance of the Gospel, few things are less acceptable than to be recalled from the career of their past conviction, to take up again the original proofs of their faith, and resume the principles

of an inquiry which they have had happily answered in the
effect of a well-persuaded reason and a regulated life.   To
such persons the debate with Scepticism is a tedious and
worn-out speculation.   Their life has outrun the question.
They enjoy what we are asking them to believe.   But I
know not how I should acquit myself of the duty of this
Lecture, or to the intentions of the distinguished Founder
of it, if I declined any kind of discussion likely to enforce
a more correct estimate of the real extent of the whole
evidences of our Religion, or of that one of them which
we have more immediately before us.   His designs would
rather point to a track of discussion which the ordinary
tenour of theological discourse would exclude.   With some
regard, therefore, to a special duty so understood, I shall
proceed with what I have to offer upon the connected
state of the Christian Evidences.

Whenever the truth of Christianity is examined, there
is a certain body of evidence, which taken together consti-
tutes the proper and adequate answer to that inquiry;
which evidence, therefore, ought not to be divided, so long
as the inquiry is supposed to be still open.   If it be asked,
what are the constituent parts of this body of evidence,
they include, among other topics, the following most commonly insisted on :—the Miracles of our Saviour and His
Apostles; the series of Prophecy; the extraordinary perfection and sanctity of His Moral Doctrine; His own
Character, as expressed in His Life upon earth; the rapid
and triumphant Propagation of His Religion under the
special circumstances of that event; the singular adaptation
of the Religion itself to the nature and condition of man,
both in its form and in its essential provisions.

These topics, prominent as they are when separately
taken, compose only one subject of connected and harmonizing proof.   However different the ground and principle
of reason in each of them may be, the effect of them is to
be united, and it bears upon one and the same point in
combining to make up that moral evidence by which it

has pleased the Almighty to ascertain His last revelation
to us. And as each of these arguments, supposing the
matter of them to be truly alleged, possesses some force
in concluding upon the question at issue; so it may be
observed of them, which indeed is only a modification of
the same remark, that they are all of a kind which it comes
within the power of our common reason to apprehend;
and they are satisfactory, because they are so intelligible,
and answer entirely to the natural sense and judgment of
our minds, independently of the accidents of previous
study, or of any peculiar modes of thinking. Agreeably
to the design of the religion itself, they carry with them
an universality of application. Prophecy, verified in the
accomplishment of its predictions, attests the authentic
inspiration by which it was given. Miracles, public unequivocal miracles exhibited, bring home to the very senses
of men the intervention of a divine power; competently
witnessed and recorded, they transmit the conviction from
age to age. Unexampled and perfect moral purity of doctrine seems to be, in fact, what it pretends to be, an ema-
nation from the source of all Rectitude and Holiness. The
life and character of the Founder of Christianity have
no prototype in the examples of human virtue. The
fitness of His Religion, in every part of it, to the exigencies
of the Being to whom it is tendered, gives to it a compendious practical authority, which almost supersedes the
labour of deduction, by an intimacy of use and relation,
identifying the very nature of man in his greatest needs,
his best hopes, and his most rational desires, with the
resources of the dispensation tendered to his acceptance.

Such are the force and tenour of the evidences of Christianity, if, as I have said, the matter of them be truly
alleged; that is, if we have well-attested miracles and prophecies, and the other arguments have a ground in fact.
The defenders of Revelation have vindicated these several
arguments; and the obvious state of the case, after it has
been examined, compels us, on the lowest assumption, to
allow a considerable weight to each. But I speak now of

the arguments in their kind, as distinguished from their degree. I wish to insist upon their great simplicity and reasonableness; which are such, that if any person of a candid mind were to lay down beforehand what would be the most prevailing inducements to his belief of a Revelation, he could not, I think, easily mention any other in kind than such as we find we possess. The actual various attestations of Christianity, external and internal; its august apparatus of prophecies and miracles; the excellence of its constitution, in its laws, doctrines, and sanctions; its power in subduing the laboured opposition of the world; with the glory of its Founder, illuminating His Religion by the signs of a divine presence in His own person; these furnish to us whatever our most deliberate judgment could have suggested, had it been permitted to us to choose the grounds of our belief. It now appeals to that judgment, with an integrity of claim which we shall seek in vain to resist, without invalidating the most certain principles of all our knowledge.

This coincidence of the religion, in its evidences, with the natural frame of our reason and principles of judgment, is worthy of notice, as contrasted with the nature of some of its doctrines, which do not so coincide. Some of its doctrines there are which we could not have anticipated, before they were revealed; and now that they are revealed, we cannot say they are such as come within the command and grasp of our faculties. They are of the nature of discoveries, and they are made from a system of things, of which an infinite Being is the author; and our concern in it is, we know not how great; but it must be all which He may choose to appoint; and an implicit belief may be the only possible, or the most expedient, way of access to a part of the present knowledge which our interest in it requires: whereas hereafter our minds may be adapted to another comprehension of the truths so proposed.

But in the mean time the Revelation itself is authenticated to us by modes of reason in which we have a direct satisfaction. The evidence of it meets precisely the faculty of judging which we already have. It rests on media of belief to which no valid or intelligible exception can be made, as unfit in their kind, or inadequate in their principle, to the ends of a rational conviction. And the difference here adverted to, between the proof of Revelation and the doctrines of it, that the one is perfectly level to our reason, and the other, in some particulars, is above it, is no more than agrees with the following reflexion: That a proof would not be such to a mind which could not distinctly apprehend and judge of it; and, therefore, to bring men to the first knowledge of a revelation, they must be addressed on the footing and principles of their nature: but as disciples and converts to live by the religion, it is in course, and altogether in reason, that they accept the revelation itself as an authority for all it contains. They must learn first, by their present power of judgment, to see the religion to be from God; but under the conviction so admitted, the prerogative of faith will follow.

The extent and comprehensiveness of the whole proof of Christianity being thus concisely stated; and also the simplicity and reasonableness of it; I would next observe, that in treating of any single branch of the Gospel evidences, the result of such separate argument must always be taken with a reference to the other proof in reserve; and if the attention is engaged to a limited view of the subject for a time, the greater compass of it must not be forgotten, when we come in the end to apply the inference of our divided inquiry. Otherwise our notions, as to the real force of the evidence, must be erroneous, or incomplete; erroneous, if, upon a part of the proof, we conclude against the whole; incomplete, if we conclude without it. For though some kind of proof be incapable of accession by an extended cumulative reason, the proof of religion is not of that nature, but one which gathers light and strength by the concentrated force of all its moral evidence. The whole of it, therefore, must be laid together, and the aggregate of the concurrent proofs will close the investigation.

In making this point a matter of distinct remark, and laying some stress upon it; *viz.*, that the vindication of our Faith rests upon an accumulated and concurrent evidence; I am far from supposing that any person literally assumes the fact to be otherwise; or that in canvassing any separate portion of the proofs and reasons of it, he ever states to himself, in the way of a positive proposition, that the inference he derives from that portion of them is all that can be advanced in behalf of the religion. But yet something of this kind of misapprehension does seem frequently to make its way into the examination of this great question, as a feeling at least, and an implied reason at the bottom, for expecting a more complete satisfaction than the single topic in hand may be capable of affording. The mistaken feeling, where it is perfectly sincere, is not hard to be accounted for. For the separation of the essential branches of a combined subject is too apt to limit our conception of the whole nature of it, for the moment, to the train of thought which is present before us; especially where a great interest hangs in the scale, and either our wishes or our fears intervene to agitate the judgment. The separation made seems to have the effect of staking the fortune and issue of the whole cause upon the selected ground of argument, narrowing the subject down to the reduced compass within which we are busied in viewing it, and transferring the imperfection of our details of thought to the substance of more enlarged truth.

And it may be, that it is to some such mistake of mind as I have here been describing, rather than to a plain want of candour and integrity, in treating the evidences of religion, that we ought to ascribe some of the most unwarranted and inconsequent insinuations against it, drawn by sceptical writers from the inconclusiveness or defect, as it appears to them, of single and detached arguments for it.

Take the argument from Prophecy, for instance. Let

it be granted that there are parts of prophecy, of which we cannot determine how they ought to be applied; that there are others partially obscure, as not offering any very obvious or explicit illustration of the characters and things to which we apply them; or that sometimes, where the sense of the prophecy is clear, yet the proof of a divine prescience in it is only precarious. When we have supposed these, or similar defects, attaching to some or many of the various contents of the prophetic writings, what shall we conclude upon it? Does it follow that prophecy is not a valid and substantial argument? Shall its obscurity, in whatever degree it may exist in some instances, refute the force of others which want nothing in point of perspicuity or exact application? Or, because we do not perfectly see how all the evidence of prophecy is to be unfolded, shall we be induced to think we have not much actually given?

Or, to go one step further, suppose the entire argument from Prophecy were only of a doubtful kind, amounting to no more than a low degree of probability; which I put merely as a supposition for the moment: will Sceptical reasoners contend that our minds should be made up, upon that supposed deficiency in a single branch of the argument, to the exclusion or prejudice of all that is yet behind; it may be most ample evidence, sufficient, in the combined view, to a perfect conviction? Yet many of the most confident exceptions which have been taken to the validity of the evidence of religion, have nothing better to support them than this narrow principle, that some points in this or that species of evidence are not well ascertained, or that one entire ground of proof taken by itself does not reach the certainty of a complete moral demonstration: a principle of admirable use to fortify error, and furnish an excuse to any latitude of unbelief.

Had their reasoning followed the truer principle which I have suggested, of considering the inference obtained upon distinct topics of the evidence, as an article and ingredient, which it is, in an aggregate of reason, it is quite certain that their writings must have taken another shape, and been very different from what they are. Perhaps the impression on their own belief might have been different also. But, at the least, they ought to have apprised their readers, which they have omitted to do, that no just conclusion could ever be drawn against the truth of Revealed Religion, till it had been looked at from a point of view embracing the full extent of its diversified matter of argument.

It is in the way of the same vicious manner of reasoning to represent any insufficiency of the proof, in its several branches, as so much objection; to manage the inquiry so as to make it appear that if the divided arguments be inconclusive one by one, we have a series of exceptions to the truth of religion, instead of a train of favourable presumptions, growing stronger at every step. The disciple of Scepticism is taught that he cannot fully rely on this or that motive of belief, that each of them is insecure, and the conclusion is put upon him that they ought to be discarded one after another, instead of being connected and combined.

It is to guard against the insinuation of this error, incidental more or less to divided inquiry, that I have touched upon it in the opening of the following Discourses, which confine me to a single branch of the Christian Evidences. The error will soon be obviated, if there be no bad faith to support it. Candid minds will dismiss it. But whether the error come or go, it would be a waste of high words to call it an unphilosophical one, or to say of it, that it does no credit to the pretensions of those who have been indebted to it for much of the importance of their attempts upon the truth of Christianity. It is neither more nor less than a dissimulation of the evidence existing: a disparagement of its value by suppression; a plea for infidelity, inconsistent with the ordinary rules agreed to and established for the examination of truth. And on this account, unless the advocates of unbelief will deal with the question in another manner than it has been their system and practice to do, they will not give us leave to think they are even capable of stating it.

But in conformity with the partial view which such a mistake implies, the great writers on that side have seldom made any considerable efforts, except upon single heads of the argument. Sometimes it has been a treatise[a] against the proof from Miracles; sometimes against that from Prophecy[b]; sometimes the honour of the Gospel Morals has been assailed, as if they had been rivalled by the wisdom of heathen and uninspired Sages; and so on. Now allowing that the remainder of the proof in favour of the Gospel Revelation, upon each of these points, after they have been fairly stated and examined, is only such a probability as any man may choose to admit; for that there is some evidence from each of them in its favour, and not the smallest measure of disproof or actual objection, I take upon me to assert in behalf of every unprejudiced inquirer; when these several inducements to one and the same conclusion of belief are drawn into each other, the joint amount of them, derived as they are from such different sources, is a collection of moral proof which we cannot properly describe as being less than that of a cogent and conclusive demonstration.

Before an audience, many of whom are highly exercised in the application of their minds to a complex evidence, and to the decision of great interests depending upon it, where nothing but a complete conviction will satisfy, I speak with submission to their judgment, but with no fear of that judgment making against me, when I appeal to them, whether they have not had occasion to know how conviction is improved by converging reasons, and the more so as those reasons arise from considerations differing in kind; how the succession of new matter of proof, even light in itself, reduces any supposed uncertainty left in the earlier stage of the inquiry; how the contingency of error is gradually excluded by checks upon the first conclusion, and the conspiring probabilities of a subject

[a] As by Woolston, and in another manner by Hume.   [b] By Collins.

run together into a perfect conviction. Let this reasonable process be applied to the examination of Christianity
by men who challenge it to the proof; and I will not say,
It, but They, have every thing to hope from the trial.

There is one quality or condition comprehended in these
mixed and various evidences of our Religion, which deserves
to be further considered by itself; a condition highly characteristic of its truth, and indeed replete with the strongest
confirmation of it. The condition is this, that its evidences
are so exceedingly dissimilar in their several descriptions.
They are not necessarily connected in their origin; they
are independent in their principle; they do not infer each
the other; they are connected only in the subject which
they conspire to attest. This independence of the component members of the argument is a material consideration. Perhaps it has not been urged in the defences of
Christianity, with the force it is entitled to. It affords,
however, a very decisive criterion of truth, as the following remarks may serve to shew.

If man's contrivance, or if the favour of accident, *could*
have given to Christianity any of its apparent testimonies;
either its miracles or its prophecies, its morals or its propagation, or, if I may so speak, its Founder, there could be
no room to believe, nor even to imagine, that all these
appearances of great credibility could be united together
by any such causes. If a successful craft could have con-
trived its public miracles, or so much as the pretence of
them, it required another reach of craft and new resources,
to provide and adapt its prophecies to the same object.
Further, it demanded not only a different art, but a
totally opposite character, to conceive and promulgate
its admirable morals. Again, the achievement of its
propagation, in defiance of the powers and terrors of
the world, implied a new energy of personal genius, and
other qualities of action, than any concurring in the
work before. Lastly, the model of the life of its Founder,
in the very description of it, is a work of so much originality and wisdom, as could be the offspring only of con-

summate powers of invention; though to speak more fairly
to the case, it seems, by an intuitive evidence, as if it could
never have been even devised, but must have come from
the life and reality of some perfect excellence of virtue,
impossible to be taken from, or confounded with, the fic-
tions of ingenuity. But the hypothesis sinks under its
incredibility. For each of these suppositions of contrivance,
being arbitrary, as it certainly is, and unsupported, the
climax of them is an extravagance. And if the imbecility of
Art is foiled in the hypothesis, the combinations of Accident are too vain to be thought of. The genuine state of
the Christian evidence is this: there is unambiguous testimony to its works of miraculous power; there are oracles
of prophecy; there are other distinct marks and signs of a
divine original within it. And no stock but that of truth
could, in one subject, produce them all, or can now account
for their existence.

The whole compass and system of the Christian Evidence
unquestionably has nothing like it, nor approaching to it,
in the Annals of the World. It is a phenomenon standing
alone. I assert this, on the concession of those who have
exalted it, beside their intention, by the impotent comparisons through which they have sought to slander and
traduce it. For what has been done? Its Miracles have
been forced into a sort of parallel with some wild unauthenticated relations in the cloudy romance of a Pagan
sophist, (in the case of Apollonius Tyaneus;) or with the
vague and insulated pretences of a better history, (in the
case of Vespasian;) or the mask of a detected and defeated
imposture among a Roman Catholic sect. Its Prophecies
have undergone the violence of a similar comparison with
the oracles of Heathenism, long ago put to silence, or the
legends of a more recent superstition. Its divine Morals
have been represented as little better than might be derived
from the philosophy of a Grecian or an Eastern teacher,
Socrates or Confucius. Its wonderful progress and propagation, carried without any of the instruments of human power,
and in opposition to them, have been matched with the suc-

cess of the Mahometan heresy effected by the power of the
sword. Thus all ages, and countries, and creeds, have been
explored, with an industry greater than the success, to furnish the separate materials of such comparisons as the
objectors have been able to produce: whilst the conspicuous and uncontested fact, that Christianity unites within
itself the signs and indications which no other system,
philosophic or religious, does, nor is pretended to do,
leaves it in possession of a character which repels the
indignity of all comparison, by the distant and incommensurate pretensions of the things attempted to be put
in resemblance with it.

1 close these prefatory remarks, which have been intended to connect Prophecy with the other proofs of the
Gospel, and shew the consolidated state of the whole of
them, by noticing two pieces of concise reasoning, in which
the authors have consented to put the defence of our Religion on single points of strong and commanding evidence.
"The Short Method with the Deists[c]," is one: the Tract
upon "the Conversion and Apostleship of St. Paul[d]," the
other. The respective writers have taken different grounds
for the compendious decision to which they offer to leave
the inquiry; the one resting it upon an acute analysis of
the criteria of matters of fact; the other upon an investigation of the principles and motives of human action,
applied to the Conversion of the Apostle. It has not occurred to me to know of any reply having been made to
shake the credit of either of these essays of Christian argument. For any thing that appears, their ground is un-
assailable. But I mention such concise and limited arguments, to remark, where they leave us, whatever conclusive-
ness we may choose to ascribe to them. If either of them
fail to convince, there is much in store to supply the
defect; and if either be adequate to a satisfactory conviction, they only conspire with other multiplied reasons in
supporting the same belief. If the single stone or column

<hr>

[c] By Leslie.   [d] By Lord Lyttleton.

be sufficient to uphold the edifice, we are not to think
that the edifice really presses upon that single support;
when it reposes, and with a far greater security, upon the
broad united strength of the entire range and system of
its fabric; that fabric of Truth, as we believe it to be,
which, in its Proofs, as well as in its Doctrines, is "built
upon the foundation of the Apostles and Prophets, Jesus
Christ Himself being the chief corner stone[e]."

[e] Ephes. ii. 20.

DISCOURSE II.

JEREMIAH xxv. 4.

*And the Lord hath sent unto you all His servants the Pro-
phets, rising early, and sending them; but ye have not
hearkened, nor inclined your ear to hear.*

IN my former Discourse I spoke of the connexion in
which Prophecy stands with the other evidences of
Revealed Religion. Let me recapitulate briefly what was
there said.

It was pressed upon your reflexion, that Prophecy makes
only one component part of the various and extensive
proof by which it has pleased God to ascertain His last
Revelation to us; and consequently, whatever force and
weight we may choose to assign to it, it ought never to be
taken alone, when the inquiry is, what are the grounds of
our belief in that Revelation? Admitting that Prophecy
may contain enough to satisfy the question, which I apprehend to be the fact, and shall endeavour to establish,
still the case does not stand so, that we are left to any
single medium of Evidence. We have a system of proof;
an evidence drawn from testimonies differing in kind, but
conspiring in effect, and combining together to an accumulated demonstration; in which neither the conclusive-
ness of any of the branches of the argument, taken alone,
is charged with the whole weight of the question; nor the
imputed insufficiency of any of them, when so taken, can
touch the validity of the collective inference.

This limitation I premise, not of course to disparage

the argument from Prophecy, which I am to state and
apply, but to ·obviate the erroneous use which might
be made of it; by pointing out to the Unbeliever, that
there can be no safety for him, as assuredly there is none,
till he has satisfied his mind that the supposed failure of
cogent proof under any one head of the Christian Evidences is not compensated by the positive force of the
rest; or that a chain of attestations and inferences, deduced from distinct and independent reasons, ought to
bring us to a disbelief of the common subject in which
they all concur.

Would he put the case that the Miracles of the New
Testament are not completely authenticated; that Prophecy is not luminous enough; the morality of the
Gospel not so extraordinary as to be clearly beyond the
wisdom of man; and the personal character of its Founder
not so much above all example; the propagation of the
Gospel, by such instruments, not incapable of being explained on human principles; its profound adaptation to
the nature of man not unlike an accident; the sincerity
and martyrdom of its first teachers, who attested the facts
of it, possibly a delusion?

Still he is only at the beginning of his difficulties, and
must for ever remain there, till he is prepared to resist
and reply to the reason which arises from these considerations put together, and repel the claims of a religion
which they so strangely conspire, each in some degree,
and all with a more pregnant evidence, to corroborate and
establish.

The dispassionate inquirer will read these evidences in
another sense. In each of them he will trace some real
and substantial testimony; something not to be invalidated. Finding here, on the whole, so much, and in all
the rest of the world so little, to create or fortify a rational
faith, he will recognise in them the discriminating proofs,
which designate the truth and certainty of the Revelation
to which they adhere, and thereby command his assent to
“ the record which God hath thus given of His Son.”

As to the believer in Revelation, he, with respect to this variety of evidence, may observe upon it, not without some confirmation of his faith, how many of the divine attributes are pledged and engaged to him, for the truth of the Gospel. For the evidence of it embodies to his view the very fulness of those attributes; there being no one just idea we can frame of the Supreme Being, which does not find a place in some point of that attestation. The Sovereign Power of God, overruling nature as His creature, is seen in the miracles—His Omniscience in the Prophecies —His Holiness in the laws of the Gospel—His Wisdom in the adaptation of it—His Providence in its propagation— and not one, but many of the divine perfections, illustrated in the life of His incarnate Son; Benevolence, Long-suffering, Wisdom, Holiness. The very evidences, therefore, of the Christian Religion have impressions of the divine nature irradiating them; and thus they coincide with the system of that religion itself, wherein the Divine Being, in the exercise of these His perfections, is proposed to us as the object of faith, with its consequent affections and duties.

From this introductory survey of the general Evidences of Christianity, I pass to Prophecy, the proper subject of my inquiry. In opening which subject, I take for the present the prophetic writings of the Old Testament only; and keeping in view the Use of Prophecy, and its Inspiration, as the two chief points to which I direct myself, I shall begin with some consideration of the Prophetic Volume, as to its general nature and contents.

By examining the actual contents of Prophecy, we shall take the only legitimate method of investigating its *Use*. For our duty is not to assign to it such a character as we might think it ought to have, and to read it to find that character; but to follow its course and reason, and thereby inform ourselves what was the mission of the Prophet, and what the purport of his prophecy. A restriction this, to which we must submit, whatever be our doubts or our be-

lief. To the believer the ways and word of God will best
explain and justify themselves. And with regard to the
other inquirer, his business cannot be to say, beforehand,
what it is that revelation, or any part of it, ought to contain, but seeing it to be such as it is, whether it be not
worthy of his acceptance.

If we take up the Prophetic Volume, we find it readily
distinguishes itself into two parts, which may be called the
Moral or Doctrinal, and the Predictive; and although
these parts were not disjoined in the communication of
Prophecy, or in the design of it, it will conduce to our
purpose to take a view of them separately. I begin with
the first, the Moral or Doctrinal, which I shall go through,
with as much conciseness as I can, in the present discourse; that, this done, we may give an undivided attention to the Predictive, the more eminent branch of the
same Revelation.

I. Prophecy, then, is not a series of mere predictions.
Far from it. It abounds in matter of another kind: I
mean the continued strain of moral doctrine which runs
through it; including under that name the only efficacious
and sufficient moral doctrine, that which is founded upon
a knowledge of God, His attributes, and His will, with a
sense of the personal and responsible relation of man to
Him. Accordingly the most frequent subjects of the prophet are the laws of God; His supreme dominion, and universal providence, the majesty of His nature, His spiritual
being, and His holiness; together with the obligations of
obedience to Him, in the particular duties of an inward
faith and worship; and of justice and mercy to man; the
whole of these duties enforced by explicit sanctions of reward and punishment. These original principles of piety
and morals overspread the pages of the book of prophecy.
They are brought forward, and inculcated, from first to
last. They are often the subject where nothing future is
in question: they are constantly interwoven with the pre-

dictions; they are either the very thing propounded, or connected with it; and all the way they are impressed with a distinctness and energy of instruction which shew it was none of the secondary ends of the prophet's mission to be this teacher of righteousness; insomuch that, if we except the Gospel itself, there can no where be shewn, certainly not in the works or systems of pagan wisdom, so much of decisive and luminous information, concerning the unity, providence, mercy, and moral government of God, and man's duty founded upon His will, as is to be gathered from the Prophetic Volume.

Let the predictions of Prophecy then, for a time, be put out of our thoughts; and the prophetic books be read for the pure theology which they contain. With what feelings of conviction they are read by the religionist, it is not hard to tell. He perceives that he is instructed and elevated by the discoveries made to him of the Supreme Being, and of the kind of worship and obedience required from himself; and these discoveries made with an authority and a commanding power, which argue them to be, what they are given for, a law of life and practice; doctrines, not of theory, but of self-government and direction; the most useful therefore to himself, and the most worthy of the source from which they profess to come. On this head I cite the words of Origen, who does not overstate this persuasive force of the prophetic writings, when he says of them, that "to the meditating and attentive reader they raise an impression of enthusiasm" (a true and rational enthusiasm, like a spark of their own inspiration), "and by his perceptions convince him, as he reads, that these compositions can be none of the works of men which have obtained the credit of being the oracles of God[a]."

The more sceptical reader will see in them something to arrest his attention at least, and excite in him a sus-

---

[a] Ὁ δὲ μετ' ἐπιμελείας καὶ προσοχῆς ἐντυγχάνων τοῖς προφητικοῖς λόγοις, παθὼν ἐξ αὐτοῦ τοῦ ἀναγινώσκειν ἴχνος ἐνθουσιασμοῦ, δι' ὧν πάσχει πεισθήσεται, οὐκ ἀνθρώπων εἶναι συγγράμματα τοὺς πεπιστευμένους Θεοῦ λόγους. Origines περὶ ἀρχῶν, p. 102. ed. Par.

picion, that the teachers of so excellent and virtuous a discipline of life, and the expositors of so rational a theology, are not to be set down for vain pretenders to inspiration, unless it can be proved that other diviners, or sages, in that period of the world, spoke so much to the purpose, or that such was the ordinary march of reason in these subjects, which, more than any other, have tried the rectitude of the human intellect.

There is a judgment of St. Paul's, which I would refer to in this instance. He institutes a comparison between the gifts of supernatural illumination, and describing that kind of prophecy of which I am speaking, viz., which is for the simple exposition of the doctrines of religious truth, of it he says, "If therefore the whole Church be come together into one place, and all its teachers prophesy" in this manner; and "there come in one that believeth not, or one unlearned; he is convinced of all, he is judged of all." "And thus the secrets of his heart are made manifest; and so falling down on his face, he will worship God, and report that God is in you of a truth[b]." Such was the idea the Apostle had of this gift of moral prophecy, that, by its visible subserviency to the instruction and edification of a religious community, he thought it might do much, even convince an unbeliever. Let the prophets of the Old Testament be tried in this manner. Let the whole company of them be heard as they delivered their doctrines to the ancient Church of God, and reasoned on "righteousness, temperance, and judgments to come." What will the unbeliever say? Has he ever fairly read or listened to this promulgation of instructive truth? and does his conviction answer to the appeal? If it does not, how shall we account for the Apostle's judgment? Perhaps in this way :—St. Paul thought of the unbeliever born, one whose sincerity, in his natural ignorance, was open to inquiry and information. Not of the unbeliever made, who has taken his side, and by prejudice, or by the neglect of a serious examination, that is, by a chosen

[b] 1 Cor. xiv. 23—25.

ignorance, warped himself into the more inflexible principles of unbelief.

But when were these essential doctrines of religion and morality taught? They were taught to one separated people, at a time when the popular religion of the rest of the world was gone into idolatry and polytheism, and the principles of morals proportionably gross and imperfect; or where better notions on these subjects had place in the minds of men, they yet had no solid footing, for want of the sufficient authority to enforce them upon the life and conscience; and at the best, the very choice of their notions fell short of the sanctity and integrity of the doctrine extant in the books of the prophets of Israel.—But what these prophets delivered, they delivered as by inspiration: however they spoke, whether to predict, or to instruct, it was not in their own name, "but as the word of the Lord came unto them." This was a high pretension in their doctrine; yet for what greater or better purpose could inspiration be given? The worthiness of the end, and the apparent fruits of the gift, render the gift itself most credible.

For, compare in this light the oracles of Scripture Prophecy with the creeds of Paganism. In the one, the religion is the foundation of the morals. By the pagan creed, the morals were rather perverted and deteriorated. The best resources, indeed, of heathen virtue were in the natural faith of conscience, which a corrupt theology could not wholly obliterate. But in the one case, religion and virtue were united; in the other, they were at variance. And the Philosophy which did the most to reclaim the theory of ethical truth, could not restore the broken union between that truth and religion; and so the whole system, in which man's best fortunes lay, was out of order. Philosophy wanted religion; and oracles and priests cared little for virtue. The teachers of Israel held both in perfect concord together. In that age of the world they were no ordinary persons who did so. None but they are known to have done it.

II. In the second place, I observe that this Moral Revelation, made by the succession of Prophets, holds an intermediate place between the Law of Moses and the Gospel itself. It is a step in progress beyond the Law, and preparatory to the Gospel. It is a step beyond the Law, in respect of the greater distinctness and fulness of some of its doctrines and precepts; it is a more perfect exposition of the principles of personal holiness and virtue; the sanctions of it have less of an exclusive reference to temporal promises, and incline more to evangelical: the Ritual of the Law begins to be discountenanced by it; the superior value of the moral commandment to be enforced; and altogether, it bears a more spiritual, and a more instructive character, than the original law given by Moses. The Law had said, Thou shalt love the Lord thy God with all thy heart, and with all thy soul, and with all thy strength. Nothing can go beyond this commandment in the *extent* of it; but where nothing is to be added to *extend* a law, much may be added to *expound* it, to animate its spirit, and fill up, or direct its practice. The habits of love, and the sentiments of obedience to the commandment, may be further informed, the obligations may be improved, the practical force of the law exalted. It is such an improvement as this, made by the Prophets upon the Law of Moses, whose authority they every where recognise, which the attentive reader is invited to consider. Perhaps I only multiply words to express the simple important fact, viz., that in the prophets there is a more luminous, and more perfectly-reasoned, rule of life and faith, than in the primary Law; and therefore that God's moral Revelation was progressive. It is more perfect in the Prophets than in the Law; more perfect in the Gospel than in either.—Let me specify a few points of the comparison.

In this order of prophecy, I include the Psalms, which of themselves are a great instrument of piety and devotion, and were so much superadded to the legal worship. They are the institute of a service of piety, for which, in the ordinance of the Law, was no such provision.

Again: the Law forebore, in some few points, a perfection of its discipline. It practised an unwilling condescension, in "yielding to the hardness of heart," the gross and refractory temper, of the people to whom it was given. This was seen in its non-prohibition of a plurality of wives, and its permission of divorce. But the Holy Jesus, who came to restore the divine Law to its first integrity, as well as to make atonement for the transgression of it, He, in His Institutes, reformed these temporary concessions. Meanwhile, one of the Prophets[c] had given a clear intimation that God approved not the permission so allowed, but would draw the domestic charities into stricter bonds of union and severity.

Take another case; the Prophets taught the doctrine of repentance with a clearness and certainty which were not admitted into the Law of Moses. This single doctrine, so promulgated as it is by the Prophets, makes a conspicuous distinction between them and that preceding Law.

Let it not be thought that this view of the Prophetic Revelation derogates in the least from the proper perfection or excellence of the ancient law of God. His law at all times, no doubt, has been perfectly adapted to His purposes in giving it; to the state of the persons to whom given; and to the proper exercise and probation of their obedience. But it no more infringes upon the wisdom or holiness of the Lawgiver, or the dignity of His Law, to suppose His revealed Will to be enlarged from time to time, with respect to the sense of His law, than it reflects upon His Wisdom or Truth, that His revelation in any other parts of it should be, as in some confessedly it is, progressive.

Having so extricated the view which I take of the intermediate character of moral prophecy, as standing between the Law and the Gospel, from any evil suspicion, I trust the truth of it will be admitted. The fact presents itself to my own mind upon a comparison of the Mosaic and the

[c] Malachi ii. 14—16.

D

Prophetic books; and if it make the same impression
upon others, they will perceive it to be, first, explanatory
of the scheme of Revelation; and next, an internal mark
of the consistency and proportion of its distant parts, and
thereby of its entire wisdom and its truth.

This fact, moreover, exhibits the parallel which obtains
in revelation between its *Morals* and its *Predictions*. The
line of prediction began at the first with the promise of
a Redeemer; but the promise was general and obscure,
and indeterminate in all its modes and circumstances.
The same word of promise was enlarged from time to
time; it grew in force and clearness till it approached its
consummation. So of other instances of Scripture prediction; they had their enlargements. In like manner, the
divine law was unfolded. The Patriarchal and the Mosaic
covenants do not express so full a model of the law of
righteousness, by which man is to serve his Creator, as
the later revelation given by the prophets. The prophets
carry on that law; they furnish it with new materials, of
sentiment, motive, and duty; and this they do under the
guidance of an original inspiration granted to them, as
they declare, and not as commentators who merely elicit
the sense of the law existing. Hence the sin of Israel was
this, that "they made their hearts as an adamant-stone,
lest they should hear the *Law*, and the words which the
Lord of hosts *hath sent in His Spirit* by the former *Prophets*[d]." Hence Christ acknowledges and confirms " the
Law and the Prophets" as the two connected parts of the
existing moral revelation, which He came not to destroy,
but "to complete," and establish for ever[e].

And it is remarkable, that the prophet, who of all others
is the most full and explicit in delineating the Messiah's
kingdom of redemption, is equally distinguished for the
copiousness and variety of his lessons of holiness. Isaiah
is not more the evangelical Prophet for that which he
foretold, than for that which he taught. And this might
be said, that, although a Christian could not consent to a

<hr>

[d] Zechariah vii. 12. Compare Nehemiah ix. 30.   [e] Matt. v. 17.

surrender of the New Testament itself, yet if any one book of the Old were to be selected as a substitute for that more perfect gift, whereby to direct equally his faith and his obedience, none could be taken so adequate to both those purposes as the volume of this eminent Prophet, to whom it was given to behold the glory of Christ's kingdom with an eagle eye, and drink of the spirit of holiness beyond his brethren.

To conclude this topic, I may add one observation more upon it. One book of the Pentateuch there is, wherein may be found the pathos and sublimities of religion in a strain not to be surpassed in any part of the Old Testament; the book of Deuteronomy. This book embraces a rehearsal and republication of the law by the great Prophet of it himself; with a survey of the wonders of Egypt and the Wilderness; the past acts of God's mighty arm, working in terror and in mercy; the stipulated blessings of obedience, (which I may call the Mosaic beatitudes); and a terrific insight into the future plagues of His apostate people. Of the majesty of the book, and the impressiveness of it in these particulars, a calm and deliberate perusal can alone convey any just idea. Nor are the signatures of authentic truth and inspiration less stampt upon it. But here also may be traced the progressive scheme of Scripture. For this very book, if I mistake not, might, in its doctrinal character and use, be set above the simpler and earlier promulgation of the law as recorded in Exodus. And next, though in sublimity it be inferior to nothing in the Prophets, it may be ranked as only approaching to the practical standard of faith and personal obedience, exhibited in the doctrines, promises, and precepts of the prophet Isaiah. The considerate reader will judge whether this account of the expansion of the divine law by the later prophets be not a just one. If it be admitted, one use and intent of their mission will be better understood; and the remote members of revelation will be seen to compose a consistent whole, not by uniformity, but progression, every part of it silently advancing toward the spirit and perfection of the Gospel.

III. In the last place, the Prophets, beside their communication of doctrine, had another, and a practical office to discharge, as pastors and ministerial monitors of the people of God. To shew "Jacob his transgression and Israel his sin," was a part of the commission they received. Hence their work to admonish and reprove; to arraign for every ruling sin, to blow the trumpet to repentance, and shake the terrors of the divine judgments over a guilty land. Often they bear the message of consolation or pardon; rarely, if ever, of public approbation and praise.

The integrity and fortitude wherewith these holy men acquitted themselves of this charge, is partly known from history, which recites the death of martyrdom which some of them endured. But it lives also in their own writings; not in the praise of their sincerity and zeal, but in the faithful record of the expostulations and rebukes which they delivered in the face of idolatrous or oppressive kings, a degenerate priesthood, and a corrupt, rebellious people. "*Magna fides et grandis audacia Prophetarum*" is their just panegyric[f]. But in this service they betray none of the spirit of turbulent and fanatical agitators, men who step out of order to make the public sin their field of triumph, but a grave and masculine severity which bespeaks their entire personal soberness of mind, and argues the reality of their commission. Isaiah, Jeremiah, and Ezekiel, are eminent examples of this ministerial duty. And if St. Paul could say of Holy Writ, that it "is profitable for reproof, for correction, for instruction in righteousness," as he speaks of the Old Scripture, so to no part of it does that idea more fitly belong, than to the admonitory homilies of the Prophets.

From this particular service of the Prophets results a testimony to their mission. First on their own part. Whatever proof men would give of integrity in their pretensions by willingness to suffer, that proof they gave. The Prophets, like the Apostles, were confessors and martyrs. No confederacy of interest, none of favour, can be

[f] Hieronym. in Ezek. p. 143. vol. v.

imputed to them: Priesthood, Kings, and People, all fell under their reproof; and they were persecuted by all. "O Jerusalem, Jerusalem! thou that killest the Prophets, and stonest them which are sent unto thee;" this is the opprobrium of that infatuated city: but it is the crown and glory of her martyr Prophets. Next, an equal testimony results on the part of the Jewish people, their persecutors. When we consider the austerity of rebuke addressed by these men to the people of Israel and Judah, and the unfavourable light in which their national character is represented by them, almost without an exception, there is no room to think that public vanity, or public credulity, meant to preserve in such writings as theirs an advantageous history to recommend either people in the eyes of the world, or that they could gain by having it believed, or by believing themselves, that they had had prophets among them. But the words of the Prophets are said to have been "graven on a rock, and written with iron." Had they not been so written and engraved, by an irresistible evidence of their inspiration, how could they have withstood the odium and adverse prejudice which they provoked? How could they have survived with the unqualified and public acknowledgment of their inspiration from the Jewish people, who hereby are witnesses in their own shame; and survive too with that admitted character, when every thing else of any high antiquity has been permitted to perish, or remains only as a comment confessing the inspiration of these prophetic writings? And the stress of the argument lies in this; that these writings were not merely preserved[g], but adopted into the public monuments of their Church and nation; strange archives of libel to be so exalted, if their authority could have been resisted. But the Jews slew their prophets, and then built their sepulchres, and confessed their mission. There is but one reason to be given why they did

---

[g] It is obvious to remark, how the equal preservation of these vituperative parts of the prophetic writings helps to accredit the faithful transmission and authenticity of the entire text of prophecy.

so, a constrained and extorted conviction. But such was the promise given in hand to the Prophet. "I do send thee unto them, and thou shalt say unto them, Thus saith the Lord God. And they, whether they will hear, or whether they will forbear, for they are a most rebellious house, *yet shall know* that there hath been a prophet among them[h]." Or more explicitly: And "*when this cometh* to pass; lo it will come; then shall *they know* that a prophet hath been among them[i]." Here we have the explanation of the fact. The actual fulfilment seen, of what their Prophets had foretold, convinced that most unbelieving people; a people to whom their Pagan judges, looking at them and their religion from a distance, and with the fallacy of their own superstitions at home before their eyes, gave a name for credulity; but whom their own interior history shews to have been governed by a very opposite genius, in a slowness and reluctancy of belief, which stood out against the authority of their real prophets, (as against the other divine guidance they had,) till a feeling experience brought them to reason. This "credulous" people "*mocked* the messengers of God, and *despised* His words, and *misused* His Prophets; *till* the wrath of the Lord rose against His people, and there was no remedy[k]."

But Pagan and Jewish belief held a different course, and the difference is instructive. The Pagan first believed what his prophets and oracles told him, and afterwards rejected; the Jew rejected, and afterwards believed. There is every reason to think that the result in each case was equally just; conformable to the deserts of the subjects examined.

b Ezek. ii. 5.   i Ezek. xxxiii. 3.   k 2 Chron. xxxvi. 16.

END OF PART I.

DISCOURSE II.

PART II.

JEREMIAH XXV. 4.

*And the Lord hath sent unto you all His servants the Pro-
phets, rising early, and sending them; but ye have not
hearkened, nor inclined your ear to hear.*

HITHERTO I have considered the contents of Prophecy, which may be called moral or didactic, as
distinguished from its predictive matter. But I must
pursue the statement already given through two topics
which deserve for their importance, under this head of my
subject, a more distinct mention; an importance which
will be acknowledged on every principle of Reason or
Natural Religion. The first of these topics is the doctrine
of Providence, the other the doctrine of Repentance.

I. The Prophets of the Old Testament inculcate with a
remarkable perspicuity and decision, the overruling agency
of God's providence in the affairs of the world. Their
whole prophecy is more or less a commentary upon this
doctrine. Let us attend to the form in which it is expressed. The prediction of prophecy, verified in its fulfilment, attests the divine foreknowledge, and the communication of that foreknowledge. But prophecy combines
therewith the illustration of another divine attribute. It
represents the future event, which it brings to view, as a
part of that system of things in which the Creator is present by the direction of His power, and the counsels of
His wisdom, appointing the issues of futurity as well as
foreseeing them; acting with " His mighty hand and out-

stretched arm," seen or unseen; "ruling in the kingdoms
of men, ordering all things both in heaven and earth."

This doctrine of a controuling and present providence is
not restricted to the Jewish Theocracy, wherein it is displayed by more palpable manifestations. It is extended to
Egypt, to Babylon, and Persia; to Moab, and Ammon; to
the isles of the Gentiles; in a word, to all the nations of
the earth. It is asserted, when the event in question is
brought about with no sensible disturbance of the ordinary
influence of human motives; no derangement of what we
commonly call the natural course of things. Cyrus, for
instance, whom the Greek historian describes, and describes,
no doubt, truly, as pursuing his career of conquest in his
own proper character, was yet an instrument appointed for
purposes of the divine government, which purposes are explained by the prophet Isaiah. Moses was a deliverer
from Egypt, and Cyrus from Babylon: the one acted
under an express legation, clothed with the power of miracles; the other had no such extraordinary power given
to him. Yet the divine providence wrought by both; and
so that providence, in its ordinary course, is yet certain,
active, and universal. This is the account of the present
constitution of things, which the tenour of prophecy goes
to assert and establish.

Agreeably thereto the Prophets deliver their disclosure
of events hereafter to take place, not as if they were announcing the bare truth of the future fact, but a purpose
and a design; dispensing a strain of prediction which
carries in itself the seed of its accomplishment, and declaring themselves sometimes to have been thereby constituted,
as it were, the agents of the divine counsels. "I the Lord
will accomplish it" is subjoined to the event declared.
" Shall there be evil in a city (evil suffered), and the Lord
hath not done it[a]?" "See," saith the oracle to Jeremiah,
" I have this day set thee over the nations, and over the
kingdoms, to root out, and to pull down, and to destroy,
and to throw down, and to build, and to plant[b]." This is

* Amos iii. 6.
b Chap. i. 10.

a figure indeed, for the Prophet himself was not to do these things; but it is plain without a figure who was to do them. Again, "Hast thou not heard long ago, how I have done it, and of ancient times that I have formed it? Now have I brought it to pass, that thou shouldst be to lay waste defenced cities into ruinous heaps[e]." The Assyrian desolater in the utmost exorbitances of his ambition was the unconscious servant of an unseen power; the instrument of the wisdom which rules the world.

This, to the serious religionist, is a doctrine of the greatest moment to his rational satisfaction. It gives to him the assurance of knowing that the system, in which his place and being are cast, is in the hands of God, not only as foreknowing that which it is to be, but as administering the plan and executing the ends of His providential government, (wise and right that government must be,) in the midst of all the tumult of the seeming disorders, the vicissitudes, and wayward course of the world. To know this, to have his mind set at rest upon it, is a first desideratum of his feelings and knowledge. And how was that satisfaction to be obtained? Reason, indeed, must ever lean to the persuasion that the Creator of the world is its controuling Governor; and in the natural world is fully reflected the order of His Government. But in the world of man, where are the signs of His presence? They are not so obvious to the sight. For there God's "way is in the sea, and His path in the great waters, and His footsteps are not known." And who could say, whether, in the freedom of man, and the precarious effects of that freedom, the controul from above was not for a time suspended or excluded?

Hence the perplexed and interminable speculations which have arisen concerning Providence and Fate, Providence and Fortune; speculations these, which grew out of the sense of nature, and only put into form the anxious questions of every thoughtful mind.

Revelation in prophecy speaks to the point, and solves

the inquiry. And this is the disclosure which it makes, that in the present dispensation of God, as it respects man, there are two causes in action, the Divine Will, and the responsible power of will given to man. Of the latter, our own consciousness had been partly a witness; but the Scripture is infinitely the more decisive and eloquent witness of it, by the universal tenour of its laws and promises, directed to men in an accountable capacity, upon motives and reasons which presuppose, and can only act upon, some moral liberty of will and exercise of judgment. But of the former, the present direction of an overruling Providence, it should seem that we could have no sure knowledge of its existence, nor any competent knowledge of its extent, except by a revelation asserting and exemplifying it. For it is a power which veils its interference, and moves so as not to shock the tenour of man's responsible action in his course of trial and duty. What we see in the world is man's agency; and often he seems only to have too much power there. The other greater mysterious power is out of sight. Scripture then has ascertained that which we wanted to know, which we might surmise and hope for, but could never determine with a practical certainty but by an information better than our own. And perhaps they who have pursued the question the furthest on the grounds of natural reason, will be the first to acknowledge, that revelation interposes in season, in the crisis of their inquiry, to give them possession of a truth, which they could neither quite entertain nor quite reject —The present providence of God in the government of the world.

The sense of Conscience which teaches with some effect the expectation of a judgment to come, that is, some state of retribution under the Divine Government, has nothing to say to the world in its order, as it now is. Conscience, and the *present constitution* of things, are not corresponding terms. The one is not the object of perception to the other. It is conscience, and the *issue* of things, which go together. And Experience, which is a more competent judge in the case, is too often disconcerted and wearied in her observations. Revelation gives the whole truth, the appointed retribution, and the immediate Providence ; and Prophecy especially is employed in asserting this last essential branch of the Divine Economy.

As to the difficulty which there may be, of which I shall have to speak hereafter, in reconciling in one scheme of thought the agency of man with the foreknowledge, and the positive appointments, of Providence, it is what it is; though perhaps not greater than exists in other instances which we pass over without scruple. But the practical embarrassment, the only serious evil of the subject, is done away; for both those principles are established; and we are taught by the one to understand our own obligations of duty, by the other to confess the sovereign attributes of God.

Let me pause for a moment, to observe what a basis, by this doctrine, is laid of peace and tranquillity, to every thoughtful and most feeling mind ; and how different the aspect of the world becomes when we have reason to know that all things in it, and every combination of them, whether in the fortunes of kingdoms, or in the more private state, are under the controul of an intelligent and gracious Ruler. Were we in the chains of fate, how gloomy would our case be. Were we in the hands of men, too often how fearful, how humiliating, and afflicting. But the impression of the scene is changed, when we admit into it the direction of an all-wise and perfect Being, in whose rectitude and goodness we may acquiesce through the whole course of His providential dispensation.—Will it be said, after all, this is the value of the doctrine, if true ; but how shall we know its truth? Definitively, by miracles and prophecy. Miracles prove that the order of physical nature is not Fate, nor a mere material constitution of things, but the subject of a free, omnipotent Master. Prophecy fulfilled, proves that neither Fate nor Man are masters of the world. These are final tests of all such

questions; and so the evidences of Revealed put an end
to some of the main questions and difficulties of Natural
Religion.

II. The other doctrine to which I referred is that of the
efficacy of Repentance. This doctrine, stated with great
energy and precision in the prophetic writings, is one than
which in practical religion none can be named of greater
importance. It involves the last alternative in the judgment which man makes of his condition before his Maker.
What has Natural Religion to promise, or declare, upon
it? Natural Religion stands in suspense, fearful and ignorant. And yet he, who has sinned, is concerned to know
whether there be hope for him in reserve : and who is there
that has not his part in that concern? He who has the
justest sense of his demerit in his failure of duty, has the
keenest concern to know it. And he who experiences no
solicitude of apprehension, nor trouble of mind in the
case, seems only the more depraved in his insensibility.
Now had the Prophets of Israel preached no other doctrine than this, " Repent, and live ye;" they would have
been the messengers of a blessing, among the most
needful and the greatest, that man can receive in the
peace so offered to his wounded conscience, and the encouragement supplied to the recovery of his frail and
faltering virtue.

It is argued, and, I think, justly, that the admission to
the benefit of repentance is an act of pure favour, in the
gratuitous goodness of God; on which account nothing
less than His own word could be a warrant for the doctrine.
The fact is, that the best philosophy of paganism was ignorant of it; and so far that philosophy was unfitted to the
condition of man, in supplying the helps and motives to
his duty, or a remedy to the defects of it. But Prophets
taught what Sages did not. Which of the two were the
best friends of man, let every one's own reflection inform
him.

Comparing the Law and the Prophets together in this

article, we mark the difference between them. The Law[d] includes a general promise of pardon to the people when in captivity, in case of their national repentance; the pardon to comprehend a restoration to their land. The Prophets[e] address the individual, and guarantee the promise to every soul "turning from the error of his ways." The Law in this point regards the nation as the object of the grace. The Prophets do more; they descend to the interests of personal religion.

It is true, the grace of repentance is eminently a Gospel doctrine; its foundation lies in the Atonement of the Christian Scheme. But here, as in other instances, prophecy made anticipations of Gospel truth. The prophets were empowered to preach repentance and pardon, before that Altar was raised on which the Atonement was to be offered which gives to the doctrine its consistency in our knowledge of the divine Economy respecting it. And I would observe generally, that in proportion as the predictions concerning the Gospel itself are enlarged, its practical doctrines, at the same time, are more unfolded. The revelation spreads in each point; and Prophecy, as I have wished to make it appear, is throughout an advancement and approximation to the Gospel. Viewed in which light it serves to elucidate not more its own use, than the entire progressive consistency of Revelation.

I have now given a cursory statement of the contents of the Prophetic Volume, taken apart from its predictions. I have noticed the essential principles of Morals and Religion, which Prophecy, after the Law, inculcates afresh, in some points with an expansion and improvement of them: the personal duty attached to the Prophet's mission has also been considered: and lastly, the doctrines of Providence and Repentance; consolatory, efficacious

[d] Deut. xxx. 1—6. Compare Nehemiah, who appeals to this Mosaic promise of national pardon. Chap. i. 8, 9.

[e] See Ezek. xviii.; Isaiah lvii. 15, 16.

doctrines, which it needed, and may I not say, it deserved, a revelation to bring down from heaven.

Whether the moral and didactic truths, which we have reviewed, are exactly the kind of matter which some persons might expect to find filling so large a portion of the prophetic books, is not of moment. They are there; and it is manifest that the Prophet had the inculcating of these truths in his commission. Perhaps it will be granted on a rational estimate, that it is no small recommendation of the absolute authority of those books, to see that they are so full of essential piety and morals, and take so much care of the unchangeable duties of man to God, and that those duties are so powerfully inculcated in them, and so perspicuously expressed.

If we compare them in this character of their composition with other pretended prophetic records, they will rise by the comparison above the suspicion of having proceeded from any similar origin. Read the oracles of Paganism; consult the most revered of the ancient temples and shrines of divination. Where are the pure morals? where the theology? where the incessant and systematic reference in those oracles to the cause of positive virtue and practical religion? Where, indeed, any great and unequivocal concern in such matters? "What is the chaff to the wheat?" is the demand of one of the Prophets of Israel[1]. May the inquirer after truth take the fan in his hand, and make the separation, in giving the chaff to the winds, and gathering the wheat with these inspired men of God.

Upon the whole of this branch of Prophecy which we have hitherto considered, I subjoin some concluding observations.

First, It was wisely ordered that the gift of prediction, and the teaching of material truth, should go together as they did in the ancient Prophets. It took from them the suspicion of being mere instruments to gratify the passion

---

[1] Jeremiah xxiii. 28.

of natural curiosity, in the discoveries of the future which they professed to make. At the same time, what they taught was enforced by the more cogent evidence of their mission. The teacher and the prophet were combined. His predictions, from time to time fulfilled, gave authority to his doctrine. They did so as much as if they had been designed to no further end.

Secondly, We observe that the Prophets of the Old Testament lay the practice of religion and virtue, where the teachers of the New have laid it, upon faith in the revelation of the Divine Will. It is not a formal system, but a rule, of Ethics, which they propose: and it is best for the purposes of life that it should be so; though men do not seem to understand as they ought the advantage of a clear and authoritative rule of moral Truth provided for their direction. If speculatists are willing to grant its use for the imbecility and ignorance of the mass of mankind, for themselves however they would prefer to rely upon their own independent reason, or the deductions of a philosophic system.

But the Truth which is to govern life, though it lose not its essence in whatever way it be obtained, has not in every way the same efficacy and influence. An operose deduction may convince the understanding, without disposing to practice; nay, it often happens that the greater is the success of the intellect in eliciting a principle or rule of duty, the less is its impression upon the springs of conduct; the reason of which may be, that the mind is wearied before it is satisfied, and the spirit of action is gone before the theory of it is settled. Let the same truth be dictated by the word of God, it puts on a new meaning; and if the maxim be true, that "all knowledge is power," the knowledge which is to give the impulse to duty takes its greatest sway and momentum as derived immediately from His paramount wisdom and will; and so it will be found that "the obedience of faith" is better than the philosophic; and that for action, and an efficient principle of it none are more capable of being benefited by Revelation, than the theorists of moral sentiment, the discoursers upon virtue.

Were the business of life, knowledge and speculation, not a particular demeanour, a course of piety and duty; were we born to be moralists, rather than men of virtue; that would make a difference. But as it is, " life is short, and science is slow," and we shall be learning, perhaps disputing, some of our gravest duties when we should be practising the habits of them, unless we are wise enough to sit at the feet of Apostles and Prophets, and take advantage of the inspired Law, which will abridge our studies, only to promote our work.

The last reflection I shall make is this, that when the divine origin of the prophetic, or any other part of Revelation, is argued from the nature of its very genius and doctrine, it is a kind of proof which cannot be expected to operate upon all men alike. It is granted that this internal evidence is not so strong and conspicuous in the prophetic volume, as in the New Testament: but whatever it may be in either, its force turns upon a certain exercise of the moral perceptions, which vary, and upon what men are in their own character. They in whom the sense of religion, the desire of holiness, integrity, and purity, are the highest, and their minds most alive to such objects, will see, by a real intuition, the excellence of a code of doctrine to which others will be feebly attracted by any sympathy of their judgment or feeling; or, it may be, will turn from it with the alienation and distaste of a mind opposed to its whole spirit. It is no more than the admitted principle, that evidence in moral subjects is modified by the mind to which it is addressed.

If, therefore, unbelievers really study the Scripture with attention, and yet see nothing in its genuine character, its sublime or its didactic matter, to command their faith and reverence, this indifference and failure of conviction on their part ought to create no surprise, nor consequently any uneasiness or mistrust in others, who experience a different impression. We know not how far their temper and spirit may have taken the lead of their judgment. This is certain, that unless they are examples of sanctity and virtue in their own lives, their indifference to Revealed Religion on the head of its internal evidence must, by the nature of the case, be of no weight.

It has been justly observed, that Religion and its Evidence may serve equally to the ends of a moral probation to all to whom it is offered, however it may be received[g]. But, perhaps, it is by its *internal* evidence in particular that this trial is most distinctly made, that evidence having the nearest connexion with our personal habits: whereby, whilst we scan religion, its Author, it is plain, may be making His judgment of us. For it is a great and universal truth which is spoken by Christ, "If any man *will do His Will*, he shall know of the doctrine whether it be of God[h]."

And this is a truth which is prior to the question of Revealed Religion, and will remain whether we admit that or no. Only it follows from the same truth, that, if that religion be of God, it cannot be deliberately rejected without a personal fault in some obliquity of will and temper.

[g] Butler's Analogy.

[h] John vii. 17.

DISCOURSE III.

OF PROPHECY IN ITS EARLIEST AGE, FROM THE FALL
TO THE PATRIARCHAL TIMES.

GENESIS xvii. 7.

*And I will establish My covenant between Me and thee, and thy
seed after thee, in their generations, for an everlasting covenant, to be a God unto thee, and to thy seed after thee.*

IF the observations which have been laid together in the
foregoing discourse should have recommended the
authority of the prophetic volume on account of its moral
doctrines, and the emphasis which it lays upon things
of an eternal truth and obligation, *viz.*, the principles of
essential religion; it will be remembered that the direct
and proper evidence of its inspired origin is still untouched,
consisting in the series and the fulfilment of its predictions, by which medium it is that Prophecy bears its most
effectual testimony to the truth of the Jewish and Christian revelations.

This evidence, constituted in the completion of Prophecy,
is of a more coercive kind. It challenges the assent upon
a clear and independent reason. For the prescience of
futurity, in great and remote instances, is confessedly one
of the divine attributes. The giver of Prophecy claims it
for such, and our reason confesses the claim. "*Who*, as
I, shall call and declare it, and set it in order for Me, since
I appointed the ancient people? and the things that are
coming, and shall come, let them shew unto them[a]."

This is one proof whereby God asserts the prerogative of
His name, in opposition to the vanities of idols, and the

---

[a] Isaiah xliv. 7.

ignorance of men. His prophetic revelation He submits
to us as the instrument of our conviction. If the prophetic
revelation so submitted embrace not merely detached
events, but a series and combination of them, the proof of
a divine foreknowledge dictating the whole, will be the
more conclusive. This is the case of Scripture Prophecy.
It is not a collection of insulated predictions; but it is, in
several parts, a connected order of predictive revelation
carried on under distinct branches. Its evidence becomes
thereby proportionably extensive; and also, which is a
different quality of it, more closely combined : and on that
account less open to the imputation of a fortuitous coincidence between its scheme, and the event of things corresponding with it.

But here again is a twofold view to be taken of the Prophetic Volume. We may consider it either in its *structure*,
or in the *verification* of its predictions. In the last, we
must select single prophecies, or concurrent prophecies relating to one and the same event : a comparison of them
with their completion will shew the evidence attaching to
them : and an extension of the like comparison to other
parts of Prophecy will collect the evidence of the whole.
But with respect to its structure, the points to be observed will be, What were the subjects on which Prophecy
was given, what its order, in relation to seasons and purposes. It is this examination of its *Structure* which it will
be expedient to pursue in the first instance, as preparatory
to the examination of it under the second head, in the accomplishment of its Predictions.

In tracing the course of Prophecy as contained in its
own records, we way presume, that, if it be a gift of divine
wisdom, we shall discover in its very structure some indications of the wisdom by which it was given. We may
expect to find, upon the face of its apparent character,
proofs of fitness and design ; because such proofs are seen
in all the other works which we know to come from the
same wisdom. Moreover, this survey of the order of Pro-

phecy will best open to us the uses which it was intended to serve in the several periods of its dispensation. Lastly, after its general frame has been ascertained, single predictions comprehended in it will be ready to be examined with more advantage, inasmuch as we shall see what place they hold in the entire range of Prophecy; whether they are among the greater or the less articles of it, and how far their particular evidence upholds, or affects, the authority of the whole prophetic book.

My intention is, therefore, to treat of the structure of Prophecy in the present and three following Discourses; and, when some idea of its Form and Use shall have been first established, to treat of the direct proof of its Inspiration.

In the earlier inquiry, however, it is to be observed, that the general truth of Revelation will be *assumed*. The argument will be, Admitting the presumed origin of prophecy, what notices does it supply of wisdom, fitness, and design; what illumination did it afford, in reference to the times when it was given, or the times to which it was to be applied? Upon this ground I shall be allowed, for a time, to speak in the person of a believer, who would follow Prophecy by its own light as it illustrates the divine economy. Incidental proofs of its inspiration will be suggested by the way. But the formal discussion of those proofs will be reserved to its place hereafter, when the Order of Prophecy shall be confronted with its Truth, and its predictions put to a test in their completion.

This survey of ancient prophecy will include its greater documents, wherever they may be found. Books not avowedly prophetical, at least not commonly so named, contain the recorded text of predictions, as the Pentateuch, the Psalms, and others, which therefore must contribute their information to the inquiry in hand. For though Prophecy had its one principal age *subsequent* to the Mosaic Law, when it spoke with a fuller voice and clearer communications, and so the Law and the Prophets are sometimes taken for the divided oracles of Holy Writ; yet it has never been silent in any period of the world, but has been the herald and messenger of Divine Truth, from the first fall of man, to his redemption under the Gospel, and there it continues to speak, if we will hear it, "with the voice of the archangel, and with the trump of God," through futurity, to the final consummation of all things.

I. The date and origin of the predictions of prophecy are with the earliest history of man. The earliest history of man, when he had come from his Maker's hands, and passed into his own, is that of his Sin and his Fall. But no sooner had he lost his original ground of acceptance with his Maker, than prophecy began to intimate the hope of his recovery and restoration. The first prediction was given in mercy: it was given in a promise adapted to man's forfeited condition—the promise of a Redeemer, who, in some way not then explained, was appointed "to bruise the Serpent's head," that is, to take away the Tempter's triumph, which could only be by repairing the loss suffered by transgression, and cancelling or mitigating, the interdict of the divine sentence laid upon it.—This original promise of mercy is the dawn and dayspring of prophecy. Man was not excluded from Paradise, till Prophecy had sent him forth with some pledge of hope and consolation.

But this First Prediction may serve to point out something of the general aim and design of all the rest. At the least it opens to us one comprehensive subject, in which the whole human race was concerned, and their concern in it not less than their state of relation with God. And since this subject was the first that introduced the revelations of Prophecy, we may reasonably suppose it was a principal one always in view; and also that other predictions, when they did not specifically relate, might yet be subservient, to it, by promoting nearer purposes, which purposes, however, centred in that chief design. For Prophecy having begun with the prospect of man's redemption, could be directed in its aftercourse to nothing greater.

And such the fact will appear to be, when we draw to a point the dispersed and multiplied predictions of the Old Testament. The intimation of a scheme of divine mercy given at the Fall, is the prelude to further and more precise discoveries of it, through every subsequent age and æra of revelation. Intermediate predictions there are, and of another kind, interposed from time to time. But the original subject is resumed and prosecuted through the whole body of ancient prophecy: in the Patriarchal, in the Mosaic, in the later age, it is still kept in sight. The frequency of its presence, in union with other subjects, indicates its paramount plan in the order of prophecy.

I would not here apply the technical name of a system to the course of these combined predictions, lest I should seem to measure by conceptions taken from the standard of human works, the order and method of any part of the divine dispensations. Howbeit, it is no more than a strict account of the fact to say, that the nature and objects of the Redemption, as well as the advent, and character of the Person by whom it was to be wrought, were revealed further and further in numerous predictions; the word of promise grew in force and clearness, as it approached to its close; and it was successively enriched with new particulars of information; till at last they embodied within them all the chief lineaments of the dispensation which was subsequently made known in the actual accomplishment of it, and the Advent of the Redeemer was but the visible appearance of the divine light with which the radiant cloud of Prophecy had long been ready to break forth.

The limits and range of Prophecy were indeed as extensive at the first as they were afterwards. To Adam was given a hope of the Redemption of his race. This was the primitive promise; and the last of the Prophets cannot go beyond it. For man's redemption, begun in his present state of being, and hereafter to be completed, is a work which extends itself to the whole duration of his existence, and runs out into the infinitude of the divine mercy. The scope of Prophecy was therefore as large from the first as in later ages. And He "unto whom all his works are known from the beginning," never left man in ignorance of this His design of mercy. But though the horizon of the prophetic sight was thrown open at once to this extent, it was dim, and the vision of it was but the image of a cloud—the objects were shewn darkly, and the mirror of Faith was obscured by the shadows which rested upon the gates of Paradise, from which man was made an exile.

But since religion cannot so much as exist without hope, the earliest intimation of Prophecy we see was adapted to the support of that essential feeling in the heart of man. It was clearly a promise of relief, an antidote to perfect despair. It contained the prediction, that some one should be born of the seed of the woman who "should bruise the head of the Tempter," by whom therefore the penal effect of man's transgression should be in some way reversed. With all its uncertainty as to the mode in which this end should be effected, the promise had within it a principle of hope and encouragement, and the materials of a religious trust fitted to keep man still looking to his Maker. And such was the immediate moral use of this great original prophecy.

II. From the Fall it is but a short step in man's history to the Flood; the interval comprehending but few generations. The Flood is the execution of God's first general judgment upon sin; one of His mysterious doings, in defacing, in punishment of the wickedness of man, the excellent work of His own hands, which at its creation He had pronounced to be good; an æra dividing the old world and the new; the second birth of the fortunes of the human race.

So great a crisis of the world was not permitted to pass without the intervening warnings of prophecy. To the One righteous man and his family, appointed to preservation, the impending deluge was foretold whilst it hung yet within the sealed windows of heaven[b]. The Ark, which

<hr>

[b] Genesis vi. 17.

he was instructed to build, was itself a second, a visible prophetic warning, to the rest of the world, if an obstinate wickedness, which had resisted God's Spirit[c], might be alarmed by the signs of His judgment.

In this instance, Prophecy served to exercise and sustain the faith of the righteous elect Family. It spoke the long-suffering of God, in the intermediate opportunity of repentance, to others[d]: both of them purposes of religion, expressive of the righteous and gracious government of God.

The Renovation of the World had also its auspices of prophecy. God set His bow in the cloud, and prophecy reflected her beams of light from the retiring waters. The predictions which follow the Flood are simple and explicit, and they contain a covenant of mercy conveyed to the second progenitor of our race. But what is the nature of this covenant? The memorable character of it is this, that it is framed in a complete relation to the recent overthrow of the Deluge.

It is a charter of *Natural* mercies and blessings[e], comprehending a second grant to man of dominion over the creatures, and over the earth; the promised multiplication of his species; and the pledge of an orderly succession and return of the seasons: "While the earth remaineth, seedtime and harvest, and cold and heat, and summer and winter, and day and night, shall not cease;" with one specific stipulation added of God's mercy, that He would visit the earth with a Deluge no more. "And I will establish My covenant with you; neither shall all flesh be cut off any more by the waters of a flood; neither shall there be any more a flood to destroy the earth[f]."

Here Prophecy, as we see, re-established the peace and order of Physical Nature, which had undergone so great a

---

[c] Genesis vi. 3.   [d] 1 Peter iii. 20.

[e] See Genesis viii. 21, 22; ix. 1—17.

[f] Genesis ix. 11. "This," says Bishop Taylor, "was the World's covenant, not the Church's."—*Christian Consolations*, chap. v.

convulsion. Its promises were adapted, and with a special fitness, to the occasion : for to the relics of the human race newly escaped from the terrors of the great Deep, the wreck of the world, and the general extirpation of their kind, what other engagements of the divine favour could there have been more seasonable, or more instructive at this time, than that God had recalled His wrath with the flood, and restored the earth to them again, secured to their peaceful use and dominion?

The distinctive and most opportune promise, that this ruin of waters should be the last, is itself a signal monument of prediction. For who will say that a recurrence of the like catastrophe of destruction, a second deluge, was not then to man his most natural fear, or even his most reasonable calculation? But that word of promise took him out of his own fears and notions; and hitherto Four Thousand years have confirmed its truth. At this day we live under this Covenant, coeval with the renewal of the world, and appointed, for so it is expressed, to be commensurate with its duration. This covenant, though not always so thought of, is our tenure; it gives the law to the Elements and the Seasons; till the second change shall come, ordained to be, not by the waters of a deluge, but by the instrumentality of another Element, which in its turn will be the minister of God's purposes.

But here a question occurs, whether the promises respectively given to Adam and to Noah have any thing in common. It has been argued, that the earth after the deluge was *relieved* in its primitive curse; the seasons tempered; the sterility and unkindliness of the ground abated; and therefore, that God having taken off the malediction in this kind, the Natural curse, thereby confirmed the hope of His greater mercy yet in suspense, with respect to the Moral Evil.

This union of the two subjects, if it were well founded, would add an elucidation to the tenour of ancient pro-

ᵉ 2 Peter iii. 7.

phecy. But I am unwilling to build any thing upon
dubious interpretations of the letter, or sense, of Scripture. It admits of a doubt, whether the Scripture text,
in this point, can be so understood, as to exhibit any difference between the Old world, and the New, in respect
of the seasons and natural state of the earth, and thereby
a remission of the primitive curse; or whether the blessing
to Noah be nothing more than a promise of the deliverance
and future exemption of the earth from its recent disorder:
in a word, whether that blessing were opposed to the original evil, or only to the deluge. The former of these two
interpretations is acutely and ably supported by Bishop
Sherlock[h], who has written with so much probability of
reason on his side, that it would be wiser to embrace his
judgment, in the point, than easy to undertake to refute
it. But I shall do neither; for in pursuing the structure
of Prophecy, I wish to impose upon myself the rule of distinguishing between what is *clear*, and what is *justly liable
to question* or *exception*. Under this rule, I forbear to
urge, in the prophecy which is before us, a sense of it,
which yet has no small evidence in its favour, and would,
if received, improve the apparent connexion of early prophecy in its several parts.

So much however is clear, that any one considerable
instance of God's promises brought into a course of fulfilment, becomes a pledge for the completion of others yet
depending; and therefore the safety and security of the
Earth, and of the Natural System, which were witnessed
subsequently to the deluge as mercies in possession, and in
virtue of the promise made to Noah, would furnish an
argument of religious trust in the faithfulness of any other
mercies which might yet be only in prospect. So far the
promises of the Fall, and after the Flood, may be safely
connected.

And in truth it is a distinguishing point of these chief
revelations instant after the Flood, that they are peaceful
and cheering. It is a display of God's mercy and good-

---

[h] Fourth Discourse on Prophecy.

ness, without any admixture of another nature: His placability, His present acceptance of man, His future favour, are the things signified; all encouragements to faith and obedience. So that when God "renewed the face of the earth," He revived the stock of religion too: the fairest part of the change was in these discoveries of mercy, when prophecy rose in an orb of light on the restored world, and shed in the hearts of men hope and consolation. This was a service to religion suited to its exigency. For the gloom of the Fall, and the fate of the old world, which had gone down in the darkness of the Deluge, were now before men's eyes; and if we carry ourselves back to their state and feeling, so placed as they were, we shall see it was of God's wisdom, as well as His goodness, that He was pleased to temper and qualify to them the terrors of His past dispensations, and make prophecy at this time the messenger of reconciliation, and peace, and an immediate hope.

III. The next epoch of Prophecy is the Call of Abraham. He is the Father of the Faithful; and in him Prophecy began to make its larger revelations of the objects of faith. Among the predictions, often repeated, with which he was favoured, two are distinguished among the rest, and they nearly include the sum of the whole; the possession of the land of Canaan by his family, being the subject of the one; the universal blessing of Mankind, "the blessing of all families of the earth in his seed," that of the other[1]; and a solemn pact, or covenant, founded upon these promises, and accompanied with large assurances of God's favour and protection to him and his posterity, being ratified to him.

This *mixed subject* requires to be distinctly noticed. We have here the first point of union, in Prophecy, of the two dispensations, the Jewish and the Christian: and from this æra Prophecy takes up and preserves a twofold cha-

---

[1] Genesis xii. 3; xiii. 14, &c.

racter, related to them both. The possession of the land
of Canaan by Abraham's offspring, now promised, identifies
itself with the establishment of the Hebrew people; thereby it leads us into that dispensation which includes the
law of Moses; the extraordinary superintendence of the
Theocracy over that people; with the authentic transmission of the divine promises and revelations in one line,
by their hands down to the æra of the Gospel. This is the
one part of the divine economy resting on the promise of
the land of Canaan.

With regard to the second, and greater, the universal
blessing of the human race, it is the original promise made
to our First Parents, repeated and confirmed, with this
provision annexed, that the blessing of the human kind,
the blessing "of all nations of the earth," should spring
from the succession of the Jewish Patriarch. And as our
Saviour explained the faith of Abraham, when He said,
"Abraham rejoiced to see My day, and he saw it, and was
glad," no doubt we are to understand that the Patriarch
beheld that day of Christ through the medium of this same
promise which we are now considering; perhaps in other
ways; but unquestionably by this prediction, that "in his
seed all nations of the earth should be blessed."

That we do right in connecting the promise given to our
First Parents with that of the universal blessing made to
Abraham, the common direction of both, which we know
to be to the person of Christ, the promised Seed, sufficiently
shews. This, however, is an interpretation deduced from
the event. But the relation of the two seems to result
also from the very purport of the promises as they were to
be understood when given. It was too plain, in the time
of Abraham, that "the serpent's head" had not been
broken; there were no signs in the Flood, nor in any
thing before it, or after it, that the worst evil of the Fall
had been done away. The moral interdict, the primeval
sentence, therefore, remained; and when a general blessing
to extend to all the nations of the earth was revealed, it
could not be understood otherwise than as applying to the

redemption of man from the state of condemnation into which he had passed. The *Evil* and the *Blessing* would explain each the other.

I. With respect to the promises given to Abraham, I repeat again, that one of them was exclusive and particular to his family; the other extended to all the nations of the earth. The possession of Canaan clearly could not be the universal blessing. They are, therefore, exceedingly distinct, in their extent, and in their kind; and their distinction was marked from the beginning. Further, I assume it as a principle, which indeed has been sufficiently established upon Scripture evidence, and vindicated by learned divines, that we are to consider the selection and appointment of a separate people to have been made for the custody and transmission of the divine promises of that more general nature. It is not affirmed that the sense of Scripture, on this head, directs us to think that such was the only purpose to be served by the selection and appointment of the Jewish people; or that other great and material ends were not thereby promoted: but that the leading and most comprehensive design of the appointment was to introduce the Gospel, by connecting and preserving the several revelations of God, till they merged in the last, to which the whole Jewish economy is declared to have been subservient; the Law, being described as "an elementary teacher to bring men to Christ," in respect of the imperfect knowledge of the Gospel, and the preparatory discipline for it, which it contained; or "as being the shadow of the good things to come:" and the Prophets, who were sent to that separated people, having it as an eminent part of their mission to "bear witness to Christ," and announce His religion. For the benefit and privilege of the Israelite consisted in this, "chiefly because to him were committed the oracles of God;" and those oracles were a perpetual witness of the better dispensation. So that the hopes of the ancient believer may be said to have been always in a state of pilgrimage, travelling onward through successive periods of revelation, and finding no rest, till they had crossed the barrier flood, which divided the law and the gospel, the first dispensation and the second.

The accomplishment, then, of the First of the promises made to Abraham, when God brought in His people by signs and wonders, "to the land which He had sworn to their fathers to give them," laid the foundation of the Jewish polity, under their separate law, and with the privileges of their distinctive character: whereas the Second of those promises remained yet to be accomplished. But if it was deferred, the fulfilment of the first was made to be one conspicuous proof of *its* equal certainty, and also the fulfilment of the first, we see, was in order to *its* completion.

2. Next, the whole order of Prophecy bears a visible reference to this twofold design of the divine economy communicated to Abraham. Take the Prophecies in their several periods, it will be found they all grew out of the one design, or the other. They have their connexion either with the Gospel, or the Jewish people. Their subjects coincide with the promulgation, or progress, of the first, or with the history of the last; at least, the exceptions to this determinate reference of Prophecy are inconsiderable. But the prophecies directed to the history of that people, since they existed as a people principally for the sake of the Gospel, will bear their share in giving evidence to the Gospel itself. Every prophecy which served to uphold the faith of that people; every prediction which passed through their hands, whether relating to themselves, or to the nations with whom their fortunes connected them, as it consolidated the authority of the dispensation under which they lived, was instrumental by a plain and necessary consequence, first, to the introduction of the Gospel, and secondly, to the proof of it for ever.

I have been the more anxious to state precisely the twofold character of prophecy in respect of its subjects, and to fix the sense in which we ought to understand the proper subserviency of the whole of it to the attestation of the Christian Faith, on several accounts. First, By this partition of the subjects of prophecy, we shall simplify our view of its structure, and be carried to a truer idea of the use and intent of its several chapters of prediction, as they may hereafter come to be examined. Secondly, we shall exclude a mistaken principle which has infinitely warped the interpretation of it, in the hands of persons of an excellent piety, but an ill-instructed judgment; the principle of endeavouring to expound almost every prophecy, either immediately, or typically, in a Christian sense. This mode of explication, after all arts and temperaments have been applied to it, fails; and the credit of divine prophecy loses by the detected unskilfulness of the interpreter. The error is one of an early origin in the Christian Church; and the reproof of it followed; for it was soon observed to do disservice to the cause of truth; the adulterated interpretation of the Old Testament prophecies, which did not express any thing of Christ, or His religion, throwing doubt and suspicion upon the genuine sense of those which did[k]. The prophecies which unquestionably relate to the Gospel are numerous, full, and explicit; and they require no support from equivocal or forced expositions to be put upon others. There are also mixt or typical prophecies, which combine the Christian with some other analogous subject. But, besides both of these, there are portions of prophecy which must be granted to stop short in their proper Jewish, or other limited subject, without any sense or application beyond it. Thirdly, we shall perceive at the same time, how unnecessary it is to the honour of the Gospel, to have recourse to that mistaken principle; since after all, it is most true, that the Holy Jesus is the Lord of the Prophets: for they spoke by His Spirit, and all that they spoke was but in subserviency to Him. For when they ministered to the First dispensation, which had its appendant services of prophecy, yet that dispensation

---

[k] Οἱ πᾶσαν τὴν παλαιὰν διαθήκην εἰς τὸν Χριστὸν μεταφέρειν πειρώμενοι, οὐκ ἔξω αἰτιάσεως εἰσίν, ἔπειπερ καὶ Ἕλλησι, καὶ τοῖς μὴ ἐγκρίνουσιν αὐτὴν αἱρετικοῖς, ἰσχύειν ἐν τῇ καθ' ἡμῶν δίδασι μάχῃ—τὰ γὰρ μὴ εἰς αὐτὸν εἰρημένα ἐκβιαζόμενοι, καὶ τὰ ἀβιάστως εἰρημένα ὑποπτεύεσθαι παρασκευάζουσι. Isidorus Pelusiot. lib. ii. epist. 195.

and all its evidences are subordinate to His, and thereby Moses and Elias are witnesses and servants to His proper glory.

3. Lastly, I observe that the twofold design of the divine economy was never divided, but there is an unity in it throughout. It was not the divergent course of two unconnected and independent dispensations; but there was a temporary disposition of things made in the one to prepare the way for the second and greater; that which comprehends in it the constant design of the counsels of God towards man; that which had been the first disclosed, and was often confirmed; and which having been variously prefigured in the veil of types, or expressed in the clearer delineations of prediction, was finally brought to light by Him "who is the Author and Finisher of our faith," and of the faith of all who have known Him by the several communications of prophecy from the beginning.

Antecedently to the time of Abraham, our chief epoch of Prophecy, the predictions properly evangelical are few: being one or two at the most, so far as they are preserved. Whether there may have been others of the like nature, the record of which has been withdrawn, it is impossible to say; but from an allusion made in the Epistle of St. Jude to the "prophecy of Enoch," which has not been preserved in its place in the Old Scripture, it is clear that some predictions were originally given beyond those which we possess; and it is also probable that, of those others, some might be of a nature to keep alive the expectation of the future deliverance of mankind. This idea is favoured by the tenour of that prophecy of Enoch's, of which we owe the notice we have of it to St. Jude. "Enoch also, the seventh from Adam, prophesied of these, saying, Behold *the Lord cometh* with ten thousand of His saints, to execute judgment upon all[1]." Since Enoch foretold of the *Judicial* Advent of *Christ*, it is not unreasonable to think that he might speak also of His Advent of *Redemp-*

---

[1] Jude 14, 15.

tion. And it is to be observed, that his is a signal history in the antediluvian age. We see he was a Prophet; we know also that he was an eminent Saint, and God gave a sign to the world in the miracle of his translation. "Enoch walked with God, and he was not. for God took him[m]." I argue, that this sign and exhibition of his singular end, besides being a reward to the Saint, had its use in commanding the faith of others to his prophecy, whatever that might be : and whilst his removal to blessedness was itself some presage of the general hope of a future immortal state, such a specific miracle causing "that he should *not see death*," would plainly be a fit counterpart, or confirmation, to any prophecy of his, if such there were, of *Christ's* coming "to dissolve the *Power of death*" over the human race.

But though these ideas be exceedingly reasonable, there is no material consequence depending upon them. For if Enoch was the example and the prophet of the old world, yet since his predictions have not been transmitted in a distinct form to a later age, it is clear that they were meant for the Faith of the times in which they were better known, not of ours to which they have not descended. His translation to reward has been a perpetual motive of hope, and will be so, to the end of the world; but how far it was interpreted and explained by collateral notices, we have the less occasion to inquire, since we want the means to decide.

Reverting then to the state of Gospel prophecy prior to the time of Abraham, I have no desire to make the written contents of it appear to be other than they are, or to suggest by implication any apology for them, as though they needed to be anxiously vindicated, because they are not more full and expressive. We have only a brief memorial of the state of Prophecy and of Religion at the first. But the fewness, as well as the indefiniteness, of the older discoveries of prophecy will soon be forgotten, in the copious-

[m] Genesis v. 24.

F

ness and circumstantial delineations of those which follow
in their proper age. For my own part, I think we ought
rather to perceive and admire the perfect order of written
Prophecy, as it now stands, taken in conjunction with the
known order of the Divine Economy. For when God
began, by the Call of Abraham, to make the *first visible
disposition* and *determination* of things in the world, towards the accomplishment of His intended mercy, prophecy began also to unfold the scheme of that mercy.
The free communication of the Gospel promises, bears
date with the commencement of that system of Providence, in the appointment of a family, a nation, and a
temporary covenant, out of which the completion of those
promises, in the fulness of time, was ordained to spring.
The event was at a distance: but in the first step taken
towards it, there is a disclosure made, ascertaining the
distant design: and the Patriarch, who is the original
Heir of the promises, is made the depositary of those
chief informations which convey them. The Father of
the Faithful is put in possession of the oracles of Faith.
There is a harmony and consistency here which cannot
be denied.

Moreover, in the general simplicity of the earlier records of prophecy, we have a pregnant evidence (that I
may take notice of that also) of the veracity and good
faith of the sacred Historian. For with respect to the
Antediluvian period, who does not see that room was
given, by the defect of permanent authentic memorials
of that time, and by the opportunities of a broken tradition, intercepted in many of its channels by the ruin of
the deluge, to cast back upon that period more favourable and prominent revelations of prophecy, than are now
to be found in the Pentateuch ascribed to so early an
origin? For example, some monument of prophecy to
bear upon the history of the Jewish people, or any other
subject incident to the time of Moses, or his own purposes,
might have been carried to that remote age, more safely,
than the *later* predictions, which do actually occur, could

be submitted to scrutiny with the more distinct checks of a recent evidence pressing upon them. But there is an absence of all such remote and well-accommodated predictions; and whilst the scantiness of early prophecy, in its actual records, is no impeachment to the completeness of the Mosaic Scriptures for every end of our faith and instruction, it is one of the many palpable indications of the truth and integrity wherewith they were written.

One other *supposed* evidence there is, which I must not pass by without a particular notice, since it is sometimes so much insisted on, of a specific revelation having been made to the primitive race, concerning the Christian Redemption; that supposed evidence is the use of Sacrifice. If the rite of Sacrifice conveyed to the Antediluvian race that kind of information which some Christian divines have assigned to it, it would be one of the greatest of prophecies. But whether we are justified in constructing the proof of a prophetic revelation, in any degree, out of that rite of primitive worship, is yet a question: for the case is, that both the *primary fact*, and the *explication* of it, are precarious in the argument. By the primary fact, I mean, whether Sacrifice was a Divine appointment; and if it were, the next question is, whether it were explained, in any degree, to the sense of the Christian Atonement. All prophecy must be of God : and a type, or prophetic fact, can come into the census of prophecy, only by His ordinance of that type, or prophetic fact. If we admit others not known to be so positively ordained, we shall have nothing but uncertainty in our deductions. That the first Sacrifice was by divine Institution, is more than the text of Scripture will permit us to say. Its silence, in such an article, an article connected with the very life of religion, suggests the contrary opinion. But be that as it may; in default of the direct information, whatever the reasons of probability may be, it is wiser to forbear to treat of primitive Sacrifice as a prophecy, or an evidence of one, lest we forget the great difference there is between the known positive ordinances of the Jewish Covenant, and the uncertain authority of an earlier usage, on which the stamp of a special appointment is not clearly set. In truth, unless we have the certain datum of the Type having been instituted, or the Prophecy delivered, we shall be joining materials of our own to the sacred edifice, presuming to *make* the prophecy as well as *interpret* it; and all such speculation, whatever else it may be, is not fit to be committed with the solid evidences of our Faith and Religion, or with the history of them.

I conclude by resuming the authentic testimonies of Prophecy. The dispensation of it was not confined to Abraham. It reached through the Patriarchal age, and the whole body of its predictions belonging to this age easily combine together. The oracles of God became to the Patriarchs a bond of personal religion. His name and His worship were invested with authority and honour among them, whilst Idolatry[n], and Corruption[o] of life and practice, polluted the nations around them. Their faith was directed by multiplied promises of His favour, but still involving the same specific objects which were contained in the revelation to Abraham, the blessing of mankind, and the possession of Canaan. But prophecy deigned to take these early disciples of it by the hand. We see their personal fortunes, and in many particulars their life and conduct, were guided by it[p] : this was a present pledge, a sensible evidence, of the faithfulness of God in all His promises; and so the supports of their faith grew with the enlarged duties of it : reserved and distant hopes acquired a footing to rest upon, and drew strength from the conviction which they had, not only of His revelation, but of His experienced providential care and goodness. "They drank of the brook in the way." Immediate mercies guaranteed the greater in prospect. Such was the service rendered to religion by prophecy in the patriarchal age, which was the first æra of its more copious promulgation.

[n] Joshua xxiv. 2.   [o] Genesis xv. 16; xix.
[p] Patriarchal History passim.

In closing our survey of this period, I would bring together once more the original promise made after the Fall, and the evangelical promise to Abraham. The first was given when the state of primitive blessedness in Paradise was newly lost; the other, when the land of Canaan was first promised. The former of these prophecies supplied some hope that the forfeited blessedness was not wholly gone for ever; but the second, the Gospel promise given to Abraham, is set by the side of the earthly promise of Canaan, to shew that Canaan was not Paradise restored, nor the seat of man's expected recovery. The Gospel promise being coincident in the time of its revelation with the Temporal, we shall be justified in considering it as a corrective to mistaken views of the Temporal: a timely evidence of God's ulterior dispensation.

DISCOURSE III.

PART II.

----•----

GENESIS xvii. 7.

And I will establish My covenant between Me and thee, and thy seed after thee, in their generation, for an everlasting covenant, to be a God unto thee, and to thy seed after thee.

RESUMING the investigation of Prophecy in its predictive matter, I shall follow it in its course: and shall combine throughout such observations as may tend to illustrate the scope and aim of the predictions themselves, in regard to the seasons at which, or the persons to whom, they were delivered. For the word of Prophecy, as the examination of it will shew, always had its *twofold* use, to instruct by its promulgation, as well as by its accomplishment. It directed the eye of one age to look forward to the opening designs of God: it offered to convince another by the work of His Providence exhibited in their completion.

After we shall have seen what it is upon the whole which Prophecy communicated, we shall be the better prepared to judge of its use and intent in the system of the divine Government: and also to seek the proper proof of its inspiration in the fulfilment of its predictions. In the earlier stage of the inquiry we consider what it is to which Prophecy asks our attention: in the second, we examine in what degree it satisfies it. In the first, we have to explore a history: in the second, to weigh an evidence. Only if it shall appear from the very scheme of Prophecy, and upon the face of its records, that there is something in it which manifests an extended wisdom, under a coherence and aptitude of design, which is one point I shall endeavour to establish; in that case it will be reasonable to carry such visible character of it to the side of evidence, and admit it as a presumption, that there was some great origin of that internal wisdom of design which is discernible in the Prophetic Volume; and which, at the least, will command our attention as a fact to be accounted for.

It has been stated that the Call of Abraham is the æra from which Prophecy takes a double, though not a divergent, course; and that, from that time, it is occupied in two general subjects, first, in predicting the history of his Family, the Hebrew people, or of the nations with whom they were connected: secondly, in developing the Gospel Dispensation. This partition of it is complete; for either the Hebrew, or the Christian subject, embraces the whole of what there is of the Pagan: Pagan history being included only as it fell within the range of Jewish observation, or was connected with the origin or the interests of the Gospel. Prophecy did not extravagate into remote subjects, beyond the Jewish, or the Christian pale.

Further I observe, that the promises granted to Abraham, those promises of God so often referred to throughout the Scripture, are, in fact, the fundamental points, which (as we may presume) have fixed and determined, in the divine plan of Prophecy, the tenour of its subsequent traditions. For in Abraham were united both the temporal and the evangelical promises—the possession of Canaan by his offspring being the object of the one, the universal blessing of Mankind, ordained to originate also in his offspring, that of the other. Prophecy, therefore, by pursuing the divided course which I have specified, only adhered to, and completed, the mixt revelation made to him at its beginning.

And here it is remarkable that God hath pleased to make this Patriarch to be the head and root of the succession and derivative order of Revelation. From his

time began that line of the divine oracles, which, first
being preserved in his family, and afterwards secured in
record, has never been broken nor lost, but having successively embraced the Law, the Prophets, and the Gospel, is now completed, to remain the lasting and imperishable monument of Revealed Truth in the world.
We know not what reception the older oracles of divine
truth had, nor how far they were preserved, from Adam
or from Noah downwards, till the later inspired Prophet,
a descendant of Abraham, fixed the memory of them in
part, perhaps restored it, in his volume of the Pentateuch.
But from Abraham the authentic tradition of Prophecy
and of Revelation is perfect. With this Patriarch we
enter the visible church which God began to build upon
earth, and in that sanctuary the light of Revelation has
been fixed in its sphere, and has never ceased to burn.
Hence it is that the inheritance of God's revealed promises in the world is traced in Scripture to Abraham,
not to the elder progenitors of the Jewish, or the human
race, Noah, or Adam: as in that emphatic and sublime
invocation of Isaiah, " Hearken to me, ye that follow after
righteousness, ye that seek the Lord; look unto the rock
whence ye are hewn, and to the hole of the pit whence
ye are digged. Look unto Abraham your father, and
unto Sarah that bare you; for I called him alone, and
blessed him, and increased him[a]." In the New Testament the like reference to Abraham is constant.

That we do not mistake in classing the predictions of
Prophecy under the two general heads, and giving to
them the application, which I have described, is obvious
from the text of the Prophecies themselves, without assuming either their inspiration, or their fulfilment. For
from Abraham to Malachi, the language in which they
are conceived is so far clear and explicit as that we perceive, and every hearer or reader of them, when first they
were given, might perceive the same, that they foreshewed

<hr>

[a] Chap. li. 1, 2.

the fortunes and condition of the Hebrew people, their
Church and country, whether of good or evil; or the condition of the states with which they were most connected
by vicinage, league, or hostility: or that they foretold the
establishment of a new dispensation of things, to be effected
by the advent of an extraordinary Person, for ends of a
religious nature, particularly of Mercy and Redemption;
which is the complex account of the Gospel Dispensation.

Keeping, therefore, this partition of the subjects of Prophecy in view, and reverting to it as a principle of their
order and connexion, we may go on to examine Prophecy
in its progress; taking with us the observation which has
been made, that the rational exposition of it requires that
we attend to the seasons and circumstances under which
it was given, and endeavour to take some measure of it
by its adaptation to *them.* For it was never given to be
an insulated phenomenon, nor merely to demonstrate the
prescience of its all-wise Author; but by Him it was ingrafted upon the exigency of times and persons, and made
to serve as a light of direction to the attentive observers
of it, before the event had set the seal to its truth. Let
this reflection be borne in mind, if I seem to be intent
on keeping the line of Prophecy and of History united
together. I must add also, that a certain acquaintance
with the contents of Scripture must be presumed on the
part of my hearers in this branch of our inquiry: without which I could not expect the general view proposed
to be given, to be admitted as a just and faithful one; nor
is it possible, by quotation made on the moment, to supply
the materials for an adequate judgment in this case, which
materials can be derived only from the knowledge or examination of the chief document itself, the Scripture volume. Nor is this the only instance wherein our satisfaction, and even our means of judging of the Truth, or
Use of Revelation, are made to depend upon some personal study of it. There is cause to think that scepticism
itself is often no more than a form of very unreasonable

enthusiasm, demanding conviction without the pains of inquiry.—But I must proceed.

I. The descendants of Abraham, whilst as yet he had no offspring, were constituted into a distinct people by the word of the divine prediction. For He "who seeth the things that are not as though they were," by granting to the progeny of the childless Patriarch the possession of the land of Canaan, a grant implying an exclusive dominion of occupation, thereby circumscribed His promise, and, as a consequence, separated the people, to whom it was conveyed, from the rest of the world. But this people, so constituted in the designs of God, was yet to be formed, and to be formed and reared to maturity in another country, in Egypt. When therefore the patriarch Jacob was driven thither by the casualty of a famine, combined with the seemingly fortuitous elevation of one of his sons to be lord of that country, he received by the way the interpretations of Prophecy upon the designs of providence. "God spake unto Israel in visions of the night; and said, I am God, the God of thy father: fear not to go down into Egypt. For I will *there* make of thee *a great nation.* I will go down with thee *into Egypt;* and *I will also surely bring thee up again*[b]."

This prophecy in part repeats, in part fills up, a former given to Abraham. To Abraham it had been foretold, "Thy seed shall be a stranger in a land that is not theirs, and shall serve them; and they shall afflict them four hundred years...... But in the fourth generation they shall come hither again: for the iniquity of the Amorites is not yet full[c]." The addition made in the prophecy to Jacob, is to shew that *Egypt* was to be the land of the last intermediate abode, and increase, of his race: a particular which had not been specified before, but was now supplied at the crisis when Jacob was carried thither, under the uncertainties of a momentary occasion; "not knowing

<hr>

[b] Genesis xlvi. 2, 3.   [c] Genesis xv. 13.

whither he went;" nor to what further ends, till they were so explained of God.

"Three score and ten persons," composing the family of Jacob, were the beginnings of this people, Famine and Exile the preparatives of its greatness. But the seed of a nation, thus sown in weakness, was raised in power. Consider by what steps it was so raised. The men were Shepherds; "they were all men of cattle;" and "every shepherd was an abomination to the Egyptians." It is of moment to observe this historical fact; because the circumstance in it which looked most adverse to the fulfilment of the divine prediction, did eventually conduce to, and almost prepare the way for it. First, their occupation and habits of life, as Shepherds, were a reason for a separate place being given them to inhabit, the land of Goshen, the best fitted to their use. Next, the prejudices and antipathy of the Egyptians to their pastoral character, acted as a constant principle of separation to preserve the selected race in union with itself, and unmingled with the mass of their indigenous, but to them alien, fellow-subjects. The land of Goshen, covered with its cattle, in a country principally devoted, as Egypt always has been, to the labours of tillage, and the inhabitants of that pastoral Oasis, fenced in, like their own flocks, within a separate pale and fold, by the very hatred of the people who had given them a reception, wore a character of their own, and gave signs of the purposes which the almighty Shepherd was preparing to bring out of such beginnings, when He should "lead His people forth like sheep," as He afterwards did, "by the hand of Moses and Aaron;" and bring them, according to His promise, to their land of rest. Prophecy, therefore, seems to have entered into a course of preparation to its accomplishment, though with adverse and contradictory appearances, from the instant of the settlement in Egypt, which began with clear and distinct predictions of its *long period* of continuance, of the *bondage* of the adopted race, of their *increase*, of their *deliverance*, and their *restoration* to Canaan in the power of a *great* people.

II. The death-bed of Jacob, the founder of this sacred colony, was visited with a further effusion of prophecy. He was enabled to predict to his sons distinctively some striking points in the future condition of the Twelve Tribes which were to spring from them; points exceedingly unlike in their kind, and comprising a variety of determinate particulars. The general scope of his prophecy, however, is this, that it is directed to the land of Canaan, and distributes the Tribes there with a peculiarity of lot, under a geographical restriction; which makes it clear that the land of Canaan is the field of the prophecy, even if the explanation were not subjoined; " Behold, I die: but God shall be with you, and bring you to the land of our fathers."

The prophecy bears one circumstance included in it, which demands a separate notice. It foretold, that these twelve sons of Jacob should be the founders of so many *Tribes,* by a perpetuation of race and lineage to each. This itself was a great *undertaking* of prophecy. The common calculation of human life would not have warranted such a promise, at least in any times of the world with which we are acquainted. For if an inheritance of territory were to be apportioned upon the contingency of a several male offspring in a numerous and multiplied distant issue, to twelve sons of a family, I believe it will be allowed to be an event highly improbable that such a disposition of the inheritance should in all its branches take effect. But here the grant was from the almighty Disposer, and Prophecy relied upon intentions not to be defeated[d].

---

[d] The succession and increase of the human race, however, are among those phenomena which we shall not be justified in subjecting to the calculations of any *fixed immutable* laws, for the *ordinary* state of things, in all seasons of the world. God has kept the system of nature in this great instance in His own hands; witness the disparate longevity of man in different periods

Again : Observe the season when this disclosure, so full
and circumstantial, is made, confirming, for the third time,
the promise of the return from Egypt, with an accession
of particulars against a time still far off. Jacob, under
the divine command, had planted his family in Egypt;
he had given them a home there, and a fixed possession.
Lest, therefore, the force of the antecedent predictions
with regard to Canaan, should be obliterated or obscured
by the interposed abode and domestication in this other
foreign country, the most specific disclosure is made to
them as to their subsequent enjoyment and partition of
their proper inheritance, which had been originally assured to their fathers, and which was still shewn to be ·
the immutable object of the divine donation; whilst the
distribution of this patrimony held forth to be made among
twelve tribes, gave to the heads and founders of these tribes
an immediate personal hope and interest in the promised
land, and thereby turned their minds the more distinctly
and forcibly to the object of God's promise. I need not
stay to remark how seasonable the Patriarch's prophecy
was to bespeak his own faith. His death-bed was full of
hope, and he departed like one of those who "died in faith,
not having received the promises, but beheld them afar
off." But we see it furnished a new and signal instruction to the hopes and views of his family, and led them
on to God's further purpose. At the crisis of time, and

since the Creation. And if the term of human life have varied from seven
hundred to seventy years, what a multitude of other phenomena connected
with the succession and increase of the species may have partaken of a similar
variation!

Perhaps the descent of twelve numerous tribes from as many sons of one
family was not so extraordinary in those days, as it would be in our own
under any circumstances whatever of society or life. The same obtained in
the line of Ishmael. We want the sufficient data from which to draw any
certain conclusions in the comparison we make in this point, between those
primæval times and any others. It is a precarious hypothesis in like manner to assume, without limit, a perpetual uniform action, retrospectively, for
the *general* system of the world. Since man, in his physical constitution,
has undergone such a change, what may not have happened to other parts of
the Natural System?

in the conjuncture of things, when the course of Providence appeared to be making a different order for them; when they seemed to be taking root in Egypt; their faith is recalled to the primitive blessing secured to them by the veracity of the God of their Fathers.

But this prophecy contains something more: it opens to us one distinct view towards the Advent of Christ. This it does in the memorable designation which it makes of the tribe of Judah, and of the perpetuity, or prolonged continuance, of the sceptre with that tribe, appointed to extend to the Gospel æra. "The sceptre shall not depart from Judah, nor a lawgiver from between his feet, until Shiloh come; and unto Him shall the gathering of the people be." The critical investigation of this prophecy in all its parts is not necessary to my purpose. But after all that has been written upon it, I may treat it as a prominent revelation of two things: the prolonged duration of some public power of the tribe of Judah, as distinguished from the rest; and the cessation of that power on the coming of Christ;—to whom "the gathering of the people should be;" who should rule by a new sceptre, or polity, that of Judah being then to be taken away.

Now, although the evangelical prophecies during these early times could never be out of place or season, yet I think we must confess a singular aptitude of season for the union of this one Christian prediction with the other branches of the Patriarch's prophecy. For his prophecy, be it observed, is the first place in Scripture[e] which exhibits or implies, the constitution of the twelve tribes under which their state was afterwards to be moulded and wholly governed. As soon as prophecy recognised this division and arrangement of tribes, it set the mark also upon that one tribe which was destined to have the pre-eminence of duration, and the privilege of a nearer

---

[e] His prophecy is followed by this significant comment upon it: "All these are the *twelve tribes of Israel:* and this is it that their father spake unto them, and blessed them; every one according to his blessing he blessed them."— *Genesis* xlix. 28.

union with the Advent of Christ. When the form of
tribes began to be seen at all, the Christian subject, in
relation to those tribes, is immediately introduced. And
so this one design of God is disclosed under each other
view of the intentions of His Providence. It was joined
with the first general promise of Canaan; it is now joined
with the partition of that promised land, and specifically
with the tribal constitution.

III. The remaining predictions belonging to this age
come under the same scheme of exposition with those
which have been considered. They laid a basis of religion grounded on Faith, in which the temporal and the
Gospel promises were combined together. But the more
distinct and the more copious revelations of prophecy,
those which gave the most determinate objects of hope,
and the clearest guidance to the life, by an immediate
reliance upon the understood purposes of God, were the
temporal. It is not to be denied that the nearer purposes
of the Divine Economy are in this period the most explicitly unfolded. The fact is so. And in reason we shall
see it accords most perfectly with the visible work and declared order of God's providence, that it should be so.
For it is no more than this, that men's duty, and their
conformity of hope and action to the divine will, were in
the first instance guided by prophecy through that instant
course of things which God made to be the sphere of their
faith and trial, as it was of His own first dispensation;
" He having provided some better thing for us, that they
without us should not be made perfect[f]."

IV. Concerning the measure of illumination afforded to
the Patriarchal, and the next ensuing age, by the other,
the Evangelical, Prophecies, we have no criterion whereby
we can judge, so safe and exact as that of the recorded
predictions themselves. No disclosure of prophecy can be
without its use in furnishing a guidance to the minds of

[f] Heb. xi. 40.

men, according to the light which it conveys. It may also have another direct use, in exciting inquiry, and hope, and a desire of further knowledge; and these are exercises of the habit and disposition of religion; and they are as much so as the principles of a more resolved, and more instructed faith. The evangelical prophecies therefore, in whatever measure they were given, were a direction to faith in its views, and an inducement to the further exercise of its habit, where the prospects of it were less clear. It was an act of religion in Prophets, and in Patriarchs, "to desire to see the things which yet they did not see," or were permitted to see only " as through a glass, darkly." At the same time, by the actual communications made, it is right to think that some were more enlightened than others, and taught to see further into the truths partially revealed. For these degrees of knowledge are relative to the minds and apprehensions of men, which differ, or to the gift and favour of God's illuminating Spirit, not subject to be measured.

But upon the whole, we shall take our opinions of the comparative illumination of prophecy, in that time, most judiciously and truly, if we think of it as shedding its greater light upon the first, the Temporal promise, the nearer in its approach; whilst whatever discoveries it made of the better promise of God's mercies, would be cherished and improved with a zeal according to the piety of particular men, whose aspirations after those greater mercies would cause them to love the promise itself more, and instruct them to draw from it a support to their desires and hopes, proportioned to the cravings of their own exalted piety. In the actual contents of Patriarchal prophecy, however, the temporal subject takes by far the precedence, in the copiousness, and the strict delineation, of the predictions relating to it.

Hence we discern that Patriarchal prophecy was plainly a preparative to the Covenant of Canaan. And because it was so, there is on this account a great analogy seen to subsist in the distribution of the light of prophecy, and the succession of the Mosaic and the Christian covenants. For patriarchal prophecy is to the covenant of Canaan the same beacon of light which later prophecy is to the Christian covenant. Not only the promise of Canaan in the antecedent prophecy is most explicit, but the years are numbered to the commencement of the possession of it. The term of four hundred years foreshewn to Abraham corresponds with the period of years numbered to Daniel[g]. There is a definite period of time prefixed in each case. The many varied predictions of Patriarchal prophecy still tend to Canaan, as the predictions of later prophecy centre in the Gospel. The general analogy therefore which I have stated, and which I think will be acknowledged to obtain in the *structure* of Prophecy in its two chief periods, the one preceding the Law, the other subsequent to it, as related to the two Covenants, may contribute to fix our judgment in each case of its use, and to illustrate also the accordance and harmony of revelation in its most essential branches.

One great difference, however, we perceive in these two principal members of prophecy. The later is full of predictions, not merely of the Gospel Covenant, but of the Messiah, His person, His nature, His works, and every note of His character. In short, Prophecy delineates the second covenant, and the Founder of it. Not so in Patriarchal prophecy; it knows nothing of Moses, the destined legislator of the first. There is no provision made for his honour. It is simply the promise of Canaan, with a profound silence as to the legislator, or the mediator, of the covenant in question. Such testimony is there given to the eminent glory of the mediator of the better covenant, no less by the silence of the older prophecy, its silence concerning Moses, than by the full utterance of the later, concerning Christ. This distinction we know to be due to Him; for He was Lord over all, and Moses was "but faithful as a servant[h]." But the point in hand is, that Prophecy has adequately expressed this distinction.

[g] Genesis xv. 13.   [h] Heb. iii. 5.

It would be obvious to insist here again on the integrity of this first divine Messenger, "who was faithful indeed in all his house," but who was not deemed worthy to be an object of prophecy. For if, in the exact and luminous predictions concerning the land of Canaan, which he has pre-fixed to the history of his law and ministry, not a word of prophecy be found calculated to draw attention to his own person, character or mission, no auxiliary oracle to aid his pretensions or office, we shall be obliged to acknowledge his abstinence from the use of an advantageous opportunity of representation, which any principle short of Truth could scarcely have rejected. But it is too little to speak of the veracity of this great Prophet, when we should rather be impressed with the divinity of the oracles which he has delivered.

But finally, Patriarchal Prophecy, whilst it was silent as to Moses, was not so of Christ. It cast its prediction forward to Him who was ordained to be "the Seed of Abraham," and the consummator "of the sceptre of Judah." Ancient Prophecy, therefore, predicted Canaan; but it penetrated beyond, to the Redeemer; which anterior notices of Him, preceding the Law, shew the constant and pre-eminent designation made of Him from the beginning. When He came into the world, He had His signs before Him. He came only as God had "spoken by the mouth of His holy Prophets, which have been since the world began[i]."

<hr>

[i] Luke ii. 70.

DISCOURSE IV.

———— ◆ ————

DEUT. XVIII. 15.

*The Lord thy God will raise up unto thee a Prophet from
the midst of thee, of thy brethren, like unto me : unto him
ye shall hearken.*

HAVING brought the consideration of Prophecy in the
Patriarchal times to a close, we may pass to the next
epoch of it, which is coincident with the promulgation of
the Mosaic Law.

The deliverance from Egypt being the step of God's
Providence preparatory to the institution of that Law, and
to the possession of Canaan connected therewith; and
being also the accomplishment of one principal part of
antecedent prophecy; I will take a brief view of that event
of deliverance, and of the ordinary and miraculous Providence combined, by which it was brought to pass. After
which, I will speak of the Law, and the accompanying
prophecies which were joined with its promulgation.

But on moving upon this line of the prophetic history,
I shall find it necessary to enter into some discussion concerning the Mosaic Law itself: for, except upon some
clear and definite ideas of its nature and constitution, it
will be impossible to treat sincerely of the state of prophecy concurrent with it. The principles of that Law
therefore, its Sanctions, and its Types, will come under
consideration; and some of the questions which have been
raised on these points will be examined. And, as the

result of such preliminary discussion, I propose to deduce
the true and determinate relation subsisting between Prophecy, in each of its parts, and the Mosaic Law, and shew
what was the state of Faith and Religion under which men
were placed by those connected members of Revelation.
Craving, then, a patient indulgence to a course of argument, which in some points may appear digressive, but is
in truth directed throughout to the single object of elucidating the state of Prophecy, and its use, I go on with the
prophetic subject.

I. Four hundred years had been foretold to Abraham,
as the term of the abode appointed to his family in a
foreign land; during the latter half of which period, from
the death of Jacob to the Exodus, there is a pause in the
communications of prophecy. When " the time of the
promise drew nigh which God had sworn, the people grew
and multiplied[a];" nor did the persecution of their Egyptian masters impede the progress of their increase and
greatness; but, as it is written, "the more they afflicted
them, the more they multiplied and grew[b]."
This persecution of bondage, which was enforced with
an unsparing hand, because with the rigour of a declared
policy[c], was an instrument which furthered the purposes
of Providence to their liberation. It did not succeed to
the diminution or decay of the people upon whom it was
inflicted; it did succeed in disposing them to wish for
their deliverance out of a land which was become, throughout its coasts, their prison-house. Nor was it more than
sufficient to break off their growing attachment to their
present home—that home was a seat of plenty, and had
won them, under all their sufferings, by the gratification
it afforded to the meaner appetites, which under the de-
basing influence of slavery are so apt to gain in strength,
and prevail upon the character. When therefore Moses,
their deliverer, had brought them out into freedom, but
set before them only the table of Providence in the desert,

<hr>

[a] Acts vii. 17.   [b] Exod. i. 12.   [c] Exod. i. 10.

we have their manner of spirit significantly described : " in their heart they turned back into Egypt; starting aside like a broken bow[d]." They turned back to the fruits and plenty they had left behind, and started aside from their great directing marksman's aim. In no material instance did they promote, scarcely did they follow, the high things proposed to be done for them. But as they were unwilling agents in the cause of prophecy, they are efficient witnesses to it in the same degree. It had foretold that which they would have defeated, had the fulfilment been left simply to their obliquity of action.

Their redemption from Egypt, which had been the subject of Prophecy, was the work of miracles. God's mighty arm verified His own oracles. The judicial plagues inflicted upon Pharaoh and his people, were the vindication wrought by the God of Israel in His own cause : first, in pursuance of His covenant of mercy to His people, to which covenant a constant reference is made through this scene of His doings ; secondly, to the confusion of " the gods of Egypt," and the impieties of false religion in the person of His idolatrous enemies, and to the overthrow of that obstinate pride of Unbelief which defying His commands, given in behalf of His people, opposed itself to the most sufficient evidence of a divine power, enforcing those commands. " Who is the Lord that I should obey Him ?" was the impious demand of Pharaoh. The reproof of his obduracy was in plagues and death upon him and his people. Tyrannic oppression, unbelief, pride, false religion, were arrayed on the one part. On the other, miracles, which had failed to convince, were multiplied to subdue ; and the issue of these miracles was in the fulfilment of an engagement of prophecy, in the *judgment* of the oppressor, and the consequent rescue of the chosen people from their ignoble captivity and affliction of bondage. For so to Abraham it had been foretold, " Know of a surety that thy seed shall be a stranger in the land

<hr>

[d] Psalm lxxviii. 57.

that is not theirs, and shall serve them; and they shall afflict them four hundred years. And also *that nation* whom they shall serve *will I judge*, and afterwards *they shall come out* with great substance[c]."

II. Subsequently to the departure from Egypt, but before the entrance into Canaan, the promulgation of the Law was interposed. The rescued people were at large; they were disengaged, as much as men could be, from the holdings of local or civil connexion; in that sense they were ready to receive an entire body of civil laws and polity, if there should be an adequate authority to impose it: but they were placed in a state which has not been known, I believe, to produce any other second instance of the like phenomenon. When did a migration through a desert ever besides produce a new and complicated Polity, exempted in its *principles* from the impieties of a surrounding dominant superstition, framed on the reverse model, and opposed to an assimilation with them; fully digested in the detail, and wrought into the public choice of the migratory people? A desert does not supply the *matter* upon which a great part of such a system could attach, and which usually serves to mould the frame of it; in fact, well-ordered Politics in the common experience of the world grow up out of their first essays of administration, and do not precede it. But, as I have said, the moral capacity of this sequestered people was ready for such a system to be imposed, because their minds were so far unoccupied and detached; though the taint of corruption they had imbibed in Egypt was never wholly purged away; and God, without doing violence to their moral state, supplied what else was wanting, the wisdom of framing their law, and the authority of imposing it: the very reception of which law, under such circumstances, would itself have been the great miracle, had others been wanting to attest that law, and to enforce it.

But the preceding miracles of Egypt ushered in the act

of divine Legislature. They were its credentials; they established it in its principle, and in its whole authority. Its principle was the confession of the Unity of God, and of His Sovereignty, as the exclusive object of obedience and of worship. The miracles of Egypt were the direct and sensible vindication of this His Sovereign character, and they clothed His delegated Messenger and Prophet with the authority required for the admission of His law. Those works of power were therefore to the children of Israel the palpable proofs of the One true God whom they were to serve, and the credentials of the law under which they were to serve Him. What had been fire to consume their enemies was light to them. And such, perhaps, we may infer to have been the adequate and ultimate purpose of those signs and wonders, which, being simply neither for destruction nor deliverance, but including both, were intended to consign in indelible characters, and with an irresistible force, the truth and divine origin of the dispensation about to be revealed. For the signs of God have a bearing upon some law of faith, or doctrine of obedience. He works Miracles to give force to Truth. So it was in the wonders of Egypt, the prelude to His Law; so it was in the wonders of the Wilderness, which crowded round its promulgation.

III. The Law was given in its several branches, Moral, Civil, and Ceremonial. First, in the order, as in worth, came the Moral Law, in the comprehensive rule of the Ten Commandments, with other precepts of essential duty connected with it; next, the digest of their Civil government; lastly, the complex code of their Priesthood, Ritual, and Worship.

Under this complete regimen of an inspired law, dictated in all its parts, they took possession of the promised land, through the overthrow of its inhabitants; whom their loathsome and obdurate wickedness, ripened to the full, had doomed, under a judicial sentence, to extirpation. On which side soever the Israelites looked, whether behind them or before, to Egypt or to the Wilderness, or to Canaan, they beheld in all that befell their enemies, and in all that was done for themselves, the manifestation of a supernatural power, authenticating by a proportionate evidence the obligations of the singular covenant under which they were placed. Such was their Law, and such the establishment of it.—But next of the peculiar Sanctions wherewith it was enforced.

IV. The sanctions of this covenant were Temporal. The blessings of Canaan, and the plagues of the present world, are the system of reward and punishment which the wisdom of God thought fit to bind upon it. No other sanctions, none acknowledged and expressed, are to be found associated with its enactments, to ratify them in the publication, or in the observance. Large and general declarations there are, interspersed throughout the books of the law, of the rewarding goodness and favour of God, and of the intensity of His displeasure upon disobedience; the force of which is to create indefinite hopes and fears, under an extent, which, as God had not limited, so neither could man presume to do so. But positive stipulations there are none, save the temporal. "The law of Moses whose endearment was *nothing but temporal goods* and *transient evils*, could never make the comers thereunto perfect;" says Bishop Taylor, in his sermon on the *Evangelical righteousness described*. Or, if we choose to take the judgment of one of the most exact and faithful explorers of scriptural theology, let it be that of the memorable Hales. "If we look into the Jews' commonwealth, and consider the letter of Moses' law, they may seem not only to have a direct promise of temporal felicity, but of no other save that. For in the law God gives to Moses the dispensation of no other but temporal blessings and cursings. In the xxvi. of Leviticus, and xxviii. of Deuteronomy, where God seems to strive with all possible efficacy to express Himself in both kinds, there is not a line concerning that which should betide them at their ends; all their weal, all their woe, seemed to expire with their lives[1]." To the accuracy of which representation nothing can be added.

In this quality of the sanctions of the Mosaic Law we mark a prominent example of that difference, which the whole tenour of Scripture commands us to confess, as subsisting between the Jewish and the Christian covenants; the Christian being founded on "the better promises;" and Moses, as the fact proves, having had no commandment to inscribe in his law the doctrine, or promise in it the reward, of eternal life, which it is the privilege of Christ openly to promise, as it is His gift to bestow: a subordination of inferiority in the Law to the Gospel, which is consistent with every other comparison we can make between them. But as a future eternal state is not made the sanction of the law of Moses, so neither is the doctrine of it made an explicit revelation either in the Law, or any other part of the Pentateuch. The text cannot be produced which simply declares it; and that none such exists, is evinced, or confirmed, by the discourse of our Saviour in His refutation of the Sadducees. For when, in proof of the resurrection of the dead, He referred those deniers of it to Moses, calling the Lord "the God of Abraham, the God of Isaac, and the God of Jacob," we must suppose that He selected this text as one of the most forcible and clearest of the book of the law, capable of imparting the knowledge of a resurrection and a future state. But since He deduced that knowledge from thence by an implication, is it not a sign that the doctrine was not to be found there expressed? His own just and emphatic reasoning establishes the truth in question by this medium; "God is not the God of the dead, but of the living." By the aid of His illuminating reason, we perceive the truth deduced. But who will say that the same truth could have

---

[1] Hales' Remains, p. 238. Augustine has occasionally expressed the same ideas.—See in particular Tractat. xxx. in Evangel. Joannis. Hieronymus Epist. 129. ad Dardanum. "In Evangelio promittuntur regna cœlorum, quæ Instrumentum Vetus omnino non nominat."

been inferred as a clear, or infallible consequence, without
His reason to derive it?   Suppose His medium of explication withdrawn, how few could have supplied it!   At
the most, since the doctrine was to be had only by being
so inferred, we must grant it was no article of the express
Mosaic revelation.   It lay indeed in its elements of proof;
but then it has been one office of Christ, and His revelation, to enable us to understand many things contained in
the first.   The Sadducee erred culpably by his *denial* of
the truth : yet there is a wide interval between his offence
in the denial, and the certainty of knowledge founded on
a direct revelation.   Within that interval the evidence of
the doctrine had its range ; till the fulness of truth came,
and turned the twilight of Jewish hope into the splendour
of the Christian.   Meanwhile, the hope which was thus
afforded, it was the depravity of some to cast away, and
the piety of others to cherish and embrace.   Such, I apprehend, is the true state of the evidence on this subject
in the Mosaic revelation.

But here a cloud of controversy has been raised.   The
absence of the doctrine of a Future Eternal State from the
sanctions of the Mosaic Law has given to the unbeliever a
topic of objection : to others, an occasion of scruple and
uneasiness.   As an argument of objection to the authority
of the Mosaic Law, it has been more than repelled by the
great Writer, whose name will always be remembered,
when the Divine Legation of Moses is called in question
on this ground.   But I am not certain that this eminent
person has directed the force of his mind with equal assi-
duity and patience on the other side, to satisfy, or remove,
the scruple existing there.

Since Prophecy is connected throughout with the course
of Revealed Religion, and the state of it contemporary with
the Law can never be understood, without a settled and
precise view of the Law itself, as to its character and stipulations, I am unwilling to pass this disturbed point without endeavouring to clear my way through the difficulties

which are thought to press upon it. The following considerations, therefore, are offered to the abatement of that scruple which the pure Temporal rewards and punishments of the Law have created in minds whose satisfaction deserves the most to be consulted.

Some of the uneasiness resulting to the piety of believers from this quality of the Mosaic sanctions, probably arises from a mistaken view either of the *principle* of moral obligation, or of the *moral value* of motives, seconding that obligation, as compared with the obligation itself. Now the religionist should consider that the obligation of man to obedience under the divine law, does not rest upon any specific pledge, or institution, of reward or punishment, at all. It rests upon this, the knowledge of the divine will imposed; consequent to which is the duty of obedience. The relation of man to God, as his Creator and Sovereign Lord, is the immediate reason and principle of duty; and the perception of this relation is the evidence of the duty. It is essentially a part of our reasonable nature in looking to God, to confess His title to our service; without staying to inquire "what profit is there that we should serve Him?" And although this sense of our reasonable nature is weak, and not to be intrusted with the whole interest of our duty, yet it is really a principle, and always to be acknowledged as such, in weighing the just claims of our Creator, and in cultivating our habits of duty. It is true the conviction of a rule of reward and punishment is necessary to the practical support of human obedience, as the rule itself is essential to the divine law, according to the decision of the Apostle, "He that cometh to God must believe that He is a rewarder of them that diligently seek Him." But this conviction of reward and punishment is not separable from our ideas of God, and all religion whatever; and still less is it separable from the act of God's own publication of His law. Consequently the publication of the divine law carries with it, under every form, an obligation complete. The duty is perfect, whenever the will is known. That the Jewish religion had this principle in its fullest extent, is certain. No law ever spoke more forcibly its authority. The very act of its publication was in miracle. The thunders and lightnings of Sinai were its ratification.

Now although we can never esteem too highly the great mercy of God revealed in the Christian Covenant, and the excellence of the reward therein proposed to our faith and duty, yet it is the piety and virtue of mind directed to Him as the object of homage and obedience, that gives to our action whatever degree of rectitude it can have. To know and to serve Him, that is religion, whether it be with a view to the present life, or to the next, and whatever inducements or encouragements He may choose to supply. The greatest rewards of endless felicity sought, or expected, in any other service than His, cannot consecrate that service, nor make it a part of essential religion. For this reason, an upright observer of the Mosaic Law, looking to God and His command, had more virtue than the votary of a false religion, who might seek a Pagan Elysium, or a Mahometan Paradise, for the retribution of his practice, or his worship: and for the same reason, a virtuous man, conforming to his conscience as to the will of God, has his virtue in that conformity, whether he know of any distinct reward or not.

It follows as a consequence from this principle of obligation, that neither the particular measure of the reward proposed, nor the indefiniteness of it, can affect the integrity of the obligation itself. When it was said to Abraham, " I am thy shield, and thy exceeding great reward," that general promise of the divine favour was the sufficient bond and motive of obligation. The duty was perfect, though the patriarch knew not the nature, or the extent, of the retribution assured to him. In like manner as the authority of a Parent and of his command is complete, whether the extent of his favour, or of his displeasure, be laid open or not, with the demand of obedience. In every original right of moral authority, the case must be the same. That is to say, the essence of the obligation, and

the virtue of compliance with it, are independent of the
kind, or the degree, of the retribution annexed.

Perhaps therefore we shall form more correct notions of
the ancient law of God, and of the dignity of the obedience
exacted to it, if we regard it less in its particular sanctions,
and more in its proper holiness and sanctity, as being the
clear revelation of the divine will, coming from God, and
directing men to Him; and on that account a holy rule of
obedience. That it offered a less excellent, and less ani-
mating motive, to obedience, than God was afterwards
pleased to reveal, can be no imputation upon it, or upon
Him; unless it becomes us to say on what terms we, or any
others, should serve Him, or that He shall always add to
His laws one and the same degree of explicit stipulation.

But though the precise sanction of the Law go no
further than to this scene of a present temporal retribution, this is not the whole of the case. There are, as I
have said, general promises and threatenings interspersed
through the volume of it. Whatever enlargement of men's
hopes and fears could be suggested by these indefinite discoveries of favour or punishment; whatever further ideas
could be suggested by the strong hopes and cries of nature, or the feebler voice of reason, concerning a future
state; whatever intimations of it might be conveyed by
particular prophecies, or the example and faith of saints:
—all these would remain collateral motives, not abrogated,
nor invalidated, by the Mosaic Law, but invested with
whatever evidence, or power of influence, they might possess, on their own footing, apart from the institution of
that law. For the Law in its sanction is only positive
that God will do so much, not exclusive, that He will do
nothing more.

In the end, I submit it to the Christian religionist,
whether he can take just offence at the omission of the
doctrine of an eternal reward in the Mosaic Code, when
he adverts to the important doctrine of his own faith, that

such a reward is not attainable by that Law. Neither by obedience to that Law, nor by any obedience, independent of the Christian Atonement, do we expect the gift of eternal life. It is among the first doctrines of Christianity that the Law in itself could not justify to immortality; far otherwise. The suppression, therefore, of the promise of eternal life coincides entirely with the declared inability of the law to confer it. Upon this ground, I put it to the judgment of the sober inquirer, whether the silence of the Law upon this article, an article far too momentous to have been excluded, except for a great reason, be not a clear and obvious intimation of its own insufficiency, and a mark, or designed evidence, for an evidence certainly it is, to instruct him, that for the life immortal he must look to the Gospel, whether for the doctrine, or for the gift; where he meets it both in the clear revelation, and in the *reason* of it also. But since the reason of it was wanting in the Law, the non-revelation of it there is abundantly consistent. In His own time, when God, by the work of Redemption, restored man to the confessed capacity of eternal life; when, by a plenary act of mercy, He reinstated him in the title of his original inheritance; then it was His gracious purposes were fully disclosed; and Christianity may, without the smallest derogation from the honour of the elder covenant, be admitted to contain the evidence, as it is confessed to convey the grant, of that mercy.

As to the labours of Philosophic inquiry, and the creeds of false Religion, they will confirm and complete this prerogative of the Gospel. For with respect to the first, the labours of Philosophic inquiry:

The patient investigators of truth, who in ancient times turned their researches, in the spirit of the best philosophy, to the question of a future immortal state, often to be honoured for their sincerity, and admired for their genius, have yet failed, we know how much, in making any clear discovery of the object of their inquiry. But their failure has proved, not so much their want of skill in the research, as the infelicity of their condition. For the immortal life which they sought to ascertain was a forfeited inheritance. The right and title to it were gone. It is not surprising, therefore, that they failed in adjusting the evidence of it.

As to systems of religion alien from Christianity, if any of them have taught the doctrine of eternal life, the reward of obedience, as a dogma of belief, that doctrine is not their boast, but their burden and difficulty, inasmuch as they could never defend it. They could neither justify it on independent grounds of deduction, nor produce their warrant and authority to teach it. In such precarious and unauthenticated principles, it may pass for a conjecture, a pious fraud, or a splendid phantom: it cannot wear the dignity of Truth.

The result should seem to be, that the Mosaic Religion yields to the Gospel, and to the Gospel alone, the glory of teaching the doctrine of "life and immortality." When this doctrine was brought to light, then the sublime prediction of later prophecy had its completion: "The Lord will destroy in this Mountain the face of the covering cast over all people, and *the Vail that is spread over all Nations.* He will swallow up Death in Victory, and the Lord God will *wipe away tears from off all faces*[g]." These were tears of Nature and her children, weeping in her ruins. But under that Vail the first Covenant by God's decree lay, except as Prophecy, and new discoveries of Revelation, turned partially aside some of its folds, and began to open a prospect of the approaching change, which in time rent the Vail asunder in the demonstrations of Christianity.

V. I return to the subject people placed under this Law, whose nature and sanctions we have so far considered.

Brought in safety and triumph through so many wonderful scenes, and wrapped from head to foot in their new Institutions, they were ultimately settled in the Land of

<hr>

[g] Isaiah xxv. 8.

Promise, and gifted with its abundance. There was no prophecy in being which pointed to any other territorial inheritance, or possession, still in reserve for them. With respect to any earthly donation, the promise had its completion in Canaan. The thing foretold had been, that "they should possess that land," and they possessed it; that "they should *be made a great nation*[b];" and they were established in the force, and regulated order, of a powerful people. What is more, their law had regard in some parts of its service to the same exclusive limits, being restricted in its capacity of a local observance, as in its One place of Sacrifice, and its frequent festival Assemblies embodying the whole nation. The temporal promise, therefore, was exhausted in Canaan; and the Law taking its sanctions from the temporal promise, and attaching its service to the seat of it, did not carry men's thoughts at the first beyond the range of the earthly inheritance.

The Law itself moreover, thus restricted in its views, bore some signs of a permanent duration. The excellence of it, as a religious and moral Institute; the majestic exhibition which it gave of the power and sovereignty of God, with the pledge of His protecting favour; the well-combined precepts of justice and mercy, and the discipline of public virtue, which it comprehended; the elaborate digest of its ritual and worship; the designation of its hereditary line of priesthood; above all, the mercies, and the terrors which had gone forth with its publication; these inherent circumstances argued no common, or momentary purpose, to belong to it, and looked like the presage of an enduring, if not an immutable character.

Upon this ground, it might be asked, what light or information, if any, did Prophecy supply, enabling them to judge of the completeness, or the perpetuity of their state, framed and ordered as it was. If it was designed only for a season, if it was a dispensation not final and complete, were any notices afforded or implied to that effect? There were

<hr>

[b] Genesis xii. 2.

such intimations afforded by Prophecy, and by a second
Evidence, which in sense and import, though not in form,
partakes of the nature of Prophecy, the delineation of
Types. Let me draw forth the joint information of direct
Prophecy, and Typical signs, bearing on this point, the
temporary and incomplete character of the existing dispensation.

First: The promise of the Universal blessing with which
this people began its existence, still waited its accomplishment. By that promise to Abraham, some order of things
different from the possession of Canaan, which could not
be the basis of an universal blessing; some institution different from their law, which did not admit of an universal
use, was necessarily implied. To the large scope of this suspended Prophecy, the capacity neither of their country,
nor their law, corresponded: yet it was a branch of the
Covenant made with Abraham: it was confirmed by being
often repeated; and God for ever reminded them of this
whole covenant, by taking to Himself the name of the God
of Abraham, Isaac, and Jacob, and making that name the
medium of His federal communication with them. The
promise itself was conspicuous in its kind: it had therefore
wherewith to command their attention, in turning their
thoughts to some object beyond what they saw. If deferred on the part of God, it could not be considered as
supplanted, or set aside: as the Apostle reasons—"that
the covenant which was confirmed before of God in Christ,
—the Law which was four hundred and thirty years after
cannot disannul, that it should make the promise of none
effect[1]." The lapse of time which had passed, four hundred
and thirty years, before their own peculiar inheritance, the
enjoyment of Canaan, was made good, might teach them
that none of the divine promises are lost simply because
they are delayed. And the permanent public evidence of
the covenant with Abraham was soon sealed up to them in
the Pentateuch, where it lay, without doubt to exercise the

[1] Gal. iii. 17.

H

hope and meditation of those to whom that first volume of Scripture was given.

In the next place, One branch of their law there was which did not seem to be founded upon an eternal reason, nor an adequate use, the Ceremonial. In proportion as men came to be instructed in the holy nature of God, by the guidance of that very revelation concerning His attributes, which they had in hand, the less could they think that such a law, taken by itself, was perfectly suited to the worship of Him. Its rites and its sacrifices seemed at least to want an explanation. They employed much of their time; might they not employ their thoughts also, in some question as to their use and fitness? "It is not possible that the blood of bulls and of goats," argues the Apostle, "should take away sins[k]." Why, then, such offerings ordained? For, as to the ritual atonement, the legal cleansing, to which they served, they were ends too small to account for the whole fabric of that kind of worship. The declared legal ends could not in reason be the sufficient.

Might we pronounce at once these rites and sacrifices to have been instrumental as Types, or Representative Signs, they receive the explanation which they want; they become the material and sensible symbols, predictions they might be called, of their counterpart in the second dispensation. The shadows of legal lustration and atonement will correspond with the sanctification and atonement of the Christian covenant. The analogy is a just one, and the capacity of the presumed Types to represent the greater subject will not be denied. And evidence of prediction might therefore be grounded upon them.

But then, the argument of Typical Prophecy has this previous question to be put, before the application of it can be made with any effect: Did the Types impart any, and what degree, of information, concerning the greater verities which they represented, at the time of their insti-

<hr>

[k] Heb. x. 4.

tution, or only at the time of their completion? Seen through Christianity, the shadow is understood by the substance; the Type thereby becomes a significant evidence now. But was it an evidence to the Israelite, who was busied with the ceremonies, and who lived amidst the shadows? This is the point; and, except by some solution of it, we know not how far we can make the Types a vehicle of information, or a prophecy of any thing, to the Israelite, in his own age, prior to the realities which superseded them; nor, without the same solution, can we judge either of the spirit of the law in which these prophetic signs were incorporated, or of the use of the other, the express prophecies. And since the language of some learned Divines has been so equivocal and involved, and that of others so remote from all sobriety, upon this material and most necessary subject, it is on that account the more pressing upon me to reduce it under some clear idea, before I can properly take from it any support, on the one side or the other, to my argument in the illustration of Prophecy.

I answer then to the question, that the Sense of the Types was a *latent* one. It was a Sense not disclosed to the Hebrew worshipper. This determination of the question is grounded on the clearest and strongest of reasons: the testimony of the Scripture itself. When those types are instituted, there is no discovery of their principle, nor hint of their interior signification, joined with them. There is no one corollary of the law deducing their sense, or pointing their reference. They are incorporated simply in the prescribed Levitical worship. To supply their interpretation for the primitive worshipper, by *assuming* that it was given to him, would be an arbitrary judgment of our own, not only not warranted by, but irreconcilable with, the Mosaic Scripture; whose silence, in such case, when so large a digest of the law is set down, is a complete negative testimony, repelling that assumption. I infer, therefore, that the sense of the Types was not explained, because the ex-

planation of it is not said, or implied, to have been given.
It is Christ who holds the key of the Types, not Moses:
and whatever access the Israelite had to the great signifi-
cations of his sacrificial and ritual worship, he obtained it
by the insinuation of prophecy, by imperfect and partial
arguments, which could not go so far as to reveal the truth.
But the law, as delivered, furnished no exposition of them.
It remains, that they were a covered mystery in their institution.

A second reason enforcing the same judgment of them
is this, that the sacrifices of the law are so palpable and so
explicit to their Christian sense, when they are interpreted
at all, that had the interpretation of them accompanied
their first ordinance, it is hard to say what room had been
left for any of the minor subsequent discoveries of prophecy
upon the same subject. The chief doctrine of the Gospel
would have been revealed, not shadowed in the law. For
the shadow, with its sense laid open, is really equivalent
to the express doctrine. And this is the virtue, and striking property of the Mosaic types, especially that principal
one, of Sacrifice, that they do reflect so clear and unequivocal an image of the Gospel system, when once they
are confronted with it. Their cryptic characters are illu-
minated, and their latent import is called forth: God's
first weaker ordinance becomes the expressive symbol of
His greater: the prophecy of the type is at once interpreted, and verified, in the fulfilment. If this view of
argument be applied to the Sacrifice of the Passover, there
is no one written prophecy in the whole of the Old Testament of a more distinct sense, or a more convincing evidence. But here man had the duty to wait for the divine
wisdom to disclose itself. That wisdom was fully developed,
when Christ came, and cast upon the types their proper
explication. For they are like things opaque in themselves,
which waited to shine by the reflexion. Then it was that
they offered their evidence in full force to the Jew. They
were an evidence indeed to all who would study the frame
of the Levitical worship, and compare it with the Christian

mysteries. But there was more than evidence offered to the Jew, when the coincidence of the two systems was disclosed. To him there was offered relief and liberty. For God now shewed, in the nobler substitution made by the Christian Faith, why it was that yoke of imperfect and unexplained rites had been imposed; and why it was no longer to remain. The darkest, and most questionable part of His former Economy, was *justified* by the dignity of the corresponding verities of the succeeding covenant; and Moses was seen to have ministered to the Redeemer by the shadows of the law, as well as by its confessed truths. If the ritual worship of offering, purification, and sacrifice, which formed so large a part of that older Economy, and seemed almost to stand in the way of its greater things, "justice, mercy, and faith," still asked for a meaning, the blessings of the real atonement and sanctification supplied the answer. The great extent, and consequent importance, which was conceded to that branch of the first dispensation, is not more than agrees with the magnitude and relative place assigned to the operation of these blessings in the second. And it may pass for one comprehensive evidence of the relative agreement of the dispensations, that when so much was to be taken away in the first, so much was to be added, and of that particular kind, in the second; the void being supplied by a strictly harmonizing, but a more excellent, appointment. For instance, the importunate and incessant demand of legal lustration and atonement run through the life of the Hebrew worshipper. Offence and pollution met him every where, and sent him to the appointed purifying, or expiatory means. What is all this but an apt adumbration of the moral offence contracted from the imperfection and sin of our daily life, implying a perpetual need of the gifts of the Christian pardon and purification; and plainly directing, if I mistake not, to a specific duty, in a perpetual recurrence to the source of those reliefs and mercies. If the Hebrew was for ever at his altar, the Christian must be no less so at the seat of the divine mercy. The altar is changed; but the duty

remains; wherein the greater and holier sacrifice has its
equal use.

If all this be so, there is no cause of objection in the
Mosaic ritual.   Its "dumb elements" are made animated
and eloquent when the Truth comes to act upon them with
its light.   They are like the Statue which had its chords
wrought within, but mute, till the morning sun struck upon
them.   They import not only the particular nature, but the
magnitude and value, of the things which they prefigured.
And if, after all, they are still an offence, they only bear
the reproach of Him to whom, as their prototype, they
direct us, who was Himself "a stone of stumbling and a
rock of offence," and most so in that particular character
wherein they represented Him.   In a word, none ought
to be dissatisfied with the form of the Mosaic worship,
who are not indifferent to the peculiar doctrines of the
Christian Redemption prefigured by it.

And here we cannot but remark, by the way, that the
error of the Jew who rejected the Christian Faith, and
would retain the Mosaic, is almost incredible.   There was
so clear, so excellent, and so desirable a substitution made
by Christ for the Ceremonial Law, and so high a confirmation of the Moral, that the disciple of Moses had
nothing to do in becoming a disciple of Christ, but to
change a shadow for the substance, keeping whatever was
most noble in his own Institution.   To believe in Moses,
and not accept the Christian Faith, on whatever account
the Jew might so do, was one degree of perversity of
mind: but to make the lowest part of the Mosaic law,
the ritual, which, in itself, was plainly the lowest, the reason for rejecting Christianity, as the Jew did, when the
whole scheme and nature of Christianity were laid before
him, is something more.   Hereby, however, is exhibited
that perversity and hardness of mind which became the
last and enduring reproach of that people.   For "the vail
was still upon their heart, when Moses was read"[1] in the

<hr>

[1] 2 Cor. iii. 15.

midst of light: apostasy from the spirit and love of the
Moral law being plainly the principle of their preposterous
infidelity and blindness[m]. This might lead to many reflections on the whole history of that people.

The conclusion from what has been said upon the nature
of the ritual Types, is this: They were a *concealed* prophetic
evidence, the force of which was made apparent by the
presence of the Gospel system. And further, they were
such an evidence as offered to the disciples of the religion
to which they were annexed, the most appropriate means
of conviction concerning the truth of the Gospel when it
came: being symbols of the subsequent dispensation, inserted into their Law, whereby God shewed to them that
His second covenant had always been in His view, and
that He had made the Law itself bear testimony to His
future purpose. If, therefore, they rested upon the high
origin, and the supposed unchangeable obligation, of their
whole Law, yet in the very heart of their mistake and misapprehension on that point, an evidence was provided to
allay that error.

It will be seen, that this conclusion, concerning the character and final use of the Types, takes from me the power
of applying them as an information of prophecy in the previous period of their first institution, or their subsequent
observance. It does so. Had the Scripture dropped any
notice of an earlier development of their sense, such notice
would have contributed to strengthen the ostensible case
of Prophecy, if I may so speak, by imparting to it so much
further illustration of its evidence. But by the silence of
Holy Writ, as well as by its direct information, all our reasoning upon it must be bounded. Within such measures,
therefore, I leave the prophetic significancy of Types.

But yet there is something more to be considered in this
ancient Ceremonial Law, under which God chose to keep

[m] See Isaiah i. 10, 11; Matth. xxiii. 23.

His people for so long a space of time. What shall we say? Did that Law, during the whole of its appointed reign, afford no help towards a perception of the principles of the Gospel? And whilst we take from it the benefit of a more direct light, shall we deny to it all use towards any notion whatever of the Christian system?

The explanation which I would offer on this point, concerning the Christian direction of the Ceremonial Law, is the following:—To the Jewish worshipper, his rites of offering, lustration, and sacrifice, presented perpetually the idea that some medium of purification and atonement was necessary to him, in his service, whether of practice, or worship. This was an idea obtruded upon him by the frequent and indispensable exaction of such rites. In the next place, I argue, that the insufficiency of those appointed means of approach to God, their insufficiency in respect of the soul and the conscience, would become more truly felt and understood, in proportion to the piety, seriousness, and probity of mind, of the individual worshipper; and that God designed to make them a vehicle of this instruction, concerning their own inutility and inefficacy to the great purposes of pardon and acceptance. The majesty of God could not be propitiated, the sanctity of His moral law could not be satisfied, by the appointments in being; they were too weak for those ends, being an institution "for the time present, in which were offered both gifts and sacrifices, that *could not make Him that did the service perfect as pertaining to the conscience*[a]." Their imperfection indeed is confessed; but what I think may be inferred is, that it could not be unknown to the Jewish disciple, if he were studious to consult his conscience, and explore the revealed character of God and His Law.

For the Moral Law prescribed great and substantial duties; duties of love to God and man: it was a rule of precept and discipline to the conscience; it fixed the essential principles of good and evil; and gave a strong commanding conviction of the demerit and penalties of sin.

[a] Hebrews ix. 9.

"By the law is the knowledge of sin." The law revealed, gave a peremptory and condemning knowledge of the transgression of it; and by this effect it created more terrors than the Ceremonial could relieve. For to the greater transgressions of the Moral Code the Ceremonial offered no visible relief whatever; it stood aloof from them; and this open chasm in its provisions, duly considered, might conspire with the sense of its general insufficiency, to set men upon some wish, or secret inquiry, after another more efficacious mode of atonement, than was to be had by the ordinances of the Levitical worship; or, if it could not prompt the idea of such an unseen atonement, might yet dispose to the acceptance of it. The action of the Moral and Ceremonial Law combined, I conclude therefore to have been such as would produce, in reasonable and serious minds, that temper which is in itself eminently Christian in its principle; viz., a sense of demerit in transgression; a willingness to accept a better atonement adequate to the needs of the conscience, if God should provide it, and a desire after inward purity, which bodily lustration might represent, but could not supply; in short, that temper which David has confessed and described, when he rejects his reliance upon the legal rites: "For Thou desirest no sacrifice, else would I give it Thee; but Thou delightest not in burnt-offerings.—Wash me throughly from my wickedness, and cleanse me from my sin. Lo, Thou requirest truth in the inward parts, and shalt make me to understand wisdom secretly[o]." In which state of mind, produced, as I understand it to have been, by the instruction of the law, there is such a preparation made for a Christian faith, although it is clear there was no distinct perception of the Christian *object* of faith, that we cannot reasonably doubt the penitent of the law would have been the devout disciple of the Gospel, had God been pleased to reveal to him the real Sacrifice of propitiation which the law did not provide, and thereby the pardon and acceptance which the penitent so earnestly desired.

[o] Psalm li. 16, 2, 6, &c.

If it shall still be thought that these suggestions and sentiments, the elements of a Christian spirit and temper, could not be communicated by the law, I would reply, that they are in some measure the natural effect and consequence, not of the law itself, but of the law joined with a personal sense of religion, and a reflecting mind, seeking the favour of God, and intent upon virtue and holiness, either for the attainment, or the recovery of them. Such impressions towards a Christian state of spirit might be feeble at the first institution of the law; but religion, established in its principle, is of an improving nature; progressively, it opens truth which might be at the first concealed or unnoticed, and directs the mind to juster notions in all the views we take concerning God, our duty, and our wants: and in that way I scruple not to attribute to the joint influence of the Moral and Ceremonial Law, some beginnings of a Christian piety in the devout Jewish believer, or penitent. What the law did not enable him to see, it disposed him to desire. It stirred some emotions of the humility of faith, though it could not satisfy them; and if these were but imperfect tendencies given by the law at the first, there is no objection in that circumstance: it was the work of subsequent prophecy to fix and strengthen the same impressions: which it did. For Prophecy spoke more and more to the disparagement of the legal and Levitical worship, at the same time that it pressed the Moral Law, and enlarged upon the promises and mercies of the Christian covenant[p].

Being constrained then, as I have been, to treat the Types of the Ceremonial Law, as no more than a concealed prophetic symbol of the Gospel, I would assign to them their office in a moral use, as preparations, from their first appointment, to the essential habits of Christian faith and virtue. They were not totally insignificant signs to the ancient worshipper; they contributed, by the sense which they gave of their weakness and imperfection,

[p] See Isaiah i. 11, 12; Micah vi. 6, 7; Isaiah liii.

to send him to seek some other atonement, or to meditate upon the promises of it which were occasionally given. As such, they were a yoke indeed, but a yoke fitted to bend his neck by a suitable disposition "to the law of Christ."

To the Gospel then, they were subservient, whether as a reserved evidence of its chief truths, or as the immediate instrument of a moral direction towards its habits. Nor can this latter use of them be invalidated by the small effect which, in the event, they seem to have produced. For, if "a stubborn people" resisted, or eluded, the right influence of their Typical Worship, it was not more than they did at the last, in rejecting the evidence inherent in the same worship. But a remnant believed in the one case; and it is reasonable to think that a like portion was instructed in the other.

If I have dwelt with some prolixity upon the elucidation of the state of Religion, as it was moulded by the Law, it has been to enable me, by that previous argument, to exhibit the use and import of Prophecy connected with it : whether we look for the prophetic sense in a multifarious ritual, framed to a general symbolical character, or in the more direct revelation of oracles delivered. And, having finished what it may be necessary to say of the Types of the Law, I go to the contemporary predictions which point to the same object, a future one, the Christian dispensation.

I. The prophecy of Balaam, coincident with the approach of the Israelites to Canaan, is such as was clearly intended, in one part of it, to carry their view to some more distant prospect. This professed diviner had been summoned by the king of Moab, to interrupt by his curse, by the spell of some malevolent or sinister prediction, their successful progress. His will to that effect was not wanting; but it was overruled. A word of real divination was put into his mouth; he was constrained to bless those whom he wished to curse; and to pass the word of prophecy for their present victory and triumphant establishment.

This was the question on which he had been consulted. But in the end of these predictions he is carried to a new line of prophecy, and introduces the vision of a Star and a Sceptre, a divine messenger, and a prince, whose advent however was still remote. " I shall see Him, but not now ; I shall behold Him, but not nigh ; there shall come a Star out of Jacob ; and a Sceptre shall rise out of Israel ; and shall smite the corners of Moab, and destroy all the children of Sheth[q]."

Every candid interpreter of prophecy will confess that this prediction could not be understood at the first, as afterwards when the accomplishment of it in the mission of Christ supplied its interpretation ; nor could it direct men's ideas either as to the character of the person whom it foretold, or the nature of his mission, so strongly when it stood by itself, as when supported by other predictions relating, or seeming to relate, to the same general subject. But yet it was a vivid prophecy, and adapted to keep men's minds and hopes intent, and prepare them for something beyond the law ; and that of no small importance ; since it was to be ushered in by a person of a remote advent, whose symbols, a Star and a Sceptre, imported most naturally the display of some new revelation, and a dominion combined with it. The historic facts related of the man, who was made to deliver this prophecy ; his solemn summons from the East ; his compact with the king of Moab ; his duplicity ; his reluctant submission to the word put into his mouth ; his strange rebuke ; all were of use to draw attention to his prediction, and signalize the memory of it.

Some, indeed, have sought the Star and the Sceptre of Balaam's prophecy, where they cannot well be found, in the reign of David ; for though a Sceptre might be there, the Star properly is not : and perhaps that vision of the prophet's mind carried far into futurity, " I shall see Him, but not now ; I shall behold Him, but not nigh," is expressive of something more than an ideal vision, the mirror of prophecy; perhaps it is nothing less than the mysterious foreboding of that real sight, which all shall have in beholding Him who is the chief object of pro- phecy, when " He cometh with clouds, and *every eye shall see Him;* and they also which pierced Him, and all kindreds of the earth shall wail because of Him[r]."

But whatever degree of completion this prophecy may be thought to have received in the reign of David, it is clearly no more than in those points of view wherein the kingdom of David is emblematic of the dominion of Christ. And if its sense could possibly be thought to reach no farther than to the scene of David's reign, even so it would have in part that effect which I ascribe to it, in raising the expectation of some considerable display of God's Provi- dence beyond the Law; and when one prophecy had brought men to the age of David, they would not be able to stop there; for there they would find other predictions opening the designs of God to a greater extent. This indeed is a principle of ancient prophecy, that it was con- stantly advancing in some or other of its prospects, till the point of rest was given to so many of them, in the advent and religion of Christ.

II. But let us turn from Balaam to Moses.

" The Lord thy God will raise up unto thee a Prophet from the midst of thee, of thy brethren, like unto me; unto Him ye shall hearken. According to all that thou desiredst of the Lord thy God in Horeb, in the day of the assembly, saying, Let me not hear again the voice of the Lord my God; neither let me see this great fire any more, that I die not.

" And the Lord said unto me: They have well spoken that which they have spoken.

" I will raise them up a Prophet from among their brethren like unto thee, and I will put My words in His mouth, and He shall speak unto them all that I shall command Him.

<hr>

[r] Revel. i. 7.

"And it shall come to pass, that whosoever will not hearken unto My words which He shall speak in My name, I will require it of him[s]."

Here is a Prophet announced like unto Moses, an inspired Teacher or Lawgiver, who might deserve to be compared, in the magnitude and clearness of his revelations, with the Prophet of the first covenant; and the obedience to him, which is exacted, imports that he was to be of not less dignity. That is, Moses is made to speak of Christ: the Legislator of the first covenant, to abate the exclusive pretensions of his own ministry, is directed to turn the eyes of his people to his successor, the Prophet of the second.

The scope of this prophecy is strongly decided by the origin and occasion of it. The Israelites could not endure the Voice and Fire of Mount Sinai. They asked an intermediate messenger between God and them, who should temper the awfulness of His voice, and impart to them His will in a milder way. In answer to this their prayer, God declares they had well spoken, and that He would accordingly raise up unto them a Prophet conformable to their desire. How aptly the prophecy, so modified, agrees with the compassionate mildness and condescension of the Christian revelation, both in the spirit of that revelation, and the mode of its delivery, any one must immediately see: or St. Paul may lead him to see it, in the contrast which he has drawn between the Law and the Gospel[t], in the principle of their terrific and attractive characters, opposed as they are the one to the other: or the Sermon on the Mount, which is Christ's promulgation of His Law, compared with the thunders of Sinai, may satisfy him in the justness of the prophecy. I ask no more, however, than that an inquirer should admit the prediction in question to bear this sense, *viz.* that the mission of the second prophet like unto Moses, was to be for a revelation of the divine Will; that will to be revealed by Him in a particular way, differing from the terrors of the Law given from Mount Sinai.

[s] Deuteronomy xviii. 15—18.   [t] Heb. xii. 18—24.

That the prediction was understood, in later times at least, in the sense here assigned to it, as relating to one distinguished Prophet, and not to a succession of inferior prophets, is pointedly shewn in the Gospel history, when, at the beginning of Christ's ministry, Philip, like a Jew acquainted with the ancient Scriptures, and expecting the prophet to come, concluded Christ to be the person described in the prediction. " We have found Him of whom Moses in the law did write[u]." The same is its most obvious and natural sense; and in that import I may consider it as having been understood, or as being open to be understood, from the first date of it.

The application made of it by St. Peter and St. Stephen[x], strictly determines its sense. This, however, is a determination made after "the Prophet of the Gospel" had appeared, which, as the proper event, clears the prediction; and so much now being seen, there ought to be no doubt as to its real sense, though some Commentators have looked for it another way. But our present inquiry is rather how the prophecy could be understood, when given, than since it has been accomplished.

To justify its application to Christ, the resemblance between Him and Moses has often been deduced at large, and drawn into a variety of particulars, among which several points have been taken, minute and precarious, having so little of dignity or clearness of representation in them, that it would be wise to discard them from the prophetic evidence. The great and essential characters of similitude between Christ and Moses are in the fulness and luminous intuition of their communications with God[y]; the magnitude of the revelations made, and the institution of a Religion founded upon those revelations. In these points, none of the other prophets were like to Moses; and in these, Moses is like to Christ, as the less to his greater. But there is also another resemblance, plainly included in the scope of the prediction, and resting

<hr>

[u] John i. 45.   [x] Acts iii. 22; vii. 37.
[y] See Numbers xii. 6, 7, 8; John i. 18.

in a quality which began with Moses.   For the greatest
part of former prophecy had been communicated in oracles
and visions from God to *Individuals*.   So it was in the
Patriarchal age;   and so before;   and when some of the
Patriarchs were inspired to prophesy, it was only upon the
occasion : they had no constant authorized office of that
nature.   " A prophet raised up from among his brethren,"
and set forth as the declared Interpreter of God's will, a
living Oracle of divine communication, was hitherto unknown till the mission of Moses; in which sense his own
prophetic office is to be distinguished, and in the same
sense his prediction of the Prophet, who should come after
him, is to be understood.

Let me combine then, and draw to a point, the intimations of Prophecy which now existed, implying some further change, or addition to be made, upon the Mosaic
Law; intimations either of an earlier date, or concurrent
with the Law, and offering themselves to view in a prominent relation with its history.   There were, 1. The original promise of a blessing to all the nations of the earth,
ratified to Abraham, and renewed again to the other Patriarchs.   2. The prediction of the distinguishing hopes
attached to the tribe of Judah.   3. The prophecy of Balaam.   4. That of Moses: the one an oracle put into the
mouth of an alien and enemy; the other delivered by the
prophet and messenger of the law itself.

Such were the communications extant, and serving to
direct the Israelite towards a new, or an enlarged economy
of God.   They plainly forbade him to rest his views altogether in Canaan, or his law.   They gave him reason to
look beyond both.   We refer the expectation which they
respectively raised to the universal grace and blessing;
the kingdom; the revelation; the Prophet, of the Gospel;
which satisfies the sense of them all.   But yet, if we will
place ourselves in the condition of the ancient Israelite,
and look at these prophecies with his eye, on his entrance
into Canaan, we shall confess that they could not convey

to him more than a very indistinct information concerning
the things in which they have had their completion. They
were "a light shining in a dark place." They were sufficient, however, to create hope and inquiry, and induce
men to watch and wait for any future discoveries which
God might be pleased to make, and by the scantiness of
their information might dispose attentive minds to profit
by some other more explicit revelations adding to their
sense and evidence.

The intent of Prophecy, therefore, at this period, with
respect to the Christian subject, we may conclude to have
been to promote the patient inquiries of faith, rather than
give to it any clear illumination. There broke forth from
the law some few rays of Gospel light. They were an
evidence, in their kind, of God's eternal purpose in the
mission of Christ into the world. The Types of the Law
were another, a suppressed evidence, in due time mani-
festing the same purpose. But it is withal exceedingly
plain, that God has chosen to make a great difference, in
every material respect, between the state of religion under
the Law and under the Gospel, excepting only in the authority of the Moral Rule, and the simple immutability of
His purpose concerning the Christian Covenant; for as to
the disclosure made by Prophecy concerning this Covenant
at the æra of the Law, the authentic page of Scripture
constrains us to acknowledge it was neither copious nor
distinct.

But yet this stock of Christian prophecy furnished to
the Israelite an adequate exercise of his faith. In the
Pentateuch he had before him, the original promise in
Paradise, the Patriarchal revelation, and some addition of
prophecy annexed to the Law. In his simpler resources
of Revealed Religion, a few predictions, like these, would
be of great moment. They would give him a considerable
object to his attention, and the duties of a religious principle to be exercised upon them, are not to be measured
by the degree of light which they afforded, so much as by

the integrity wherewith men were willing to attend to that light, whatever it might be.

Prophecy, however, had its subject at this period, whereon it enlarged in a more full and distinct revelation. But that subject was of another kind, the Temporal; of which I must speak by itself apart, and consider the greater clearness of evidence which is diffused over this second branch of the prophetic revelation accompanying the Law.

Note on page 90.

From this point of view, whilst we are examining the declared stipulations of the Mosaic Religion, perhaps we shall see into the import of that remarkable saying, which Moses has introduced upon one of his general enforcements of the Law, and whilst he is delivering at large what he had given him to say of its inducements and threatenings. "The *secret things*," he says, "belong unto the Lord our God; but *those things which are* revealed, belong unto us, and to our children for ever, *that we may do all the words of this law*[a]." Striking words in a *recital* of the legal rewards and punishments, and such as almost suggest the further retributions, which yet they withhold from open view. But *secret things* there were; and if we might conjecture of them at all, what so likely to be implied, as the other, and those the greater, requitals of the unrevealed world? The text has been accommodated to discourses upon such doctrines as that of the Trinity, or others generally of a mysterious nature, which, in some respects, will always be among the arcana of religion, the "*secret things of God*." But such an use of the text is only an *accommodation* of it—its proper force and spirit must be sought in the subject to which it is directed, *the constitution of the Law*.

<hr>

[a] Deut. xxix. 29.

A distinguished Commentator on the Laws of Moses, Michaelis, vindicates their *temporal* sanctions, on the ground of the Mosaic code being of the nature of a *Civil* System, to "the statutes" of which the rewards of a future eternal state would be incongruous and unsuitable. But this solution of the matter is inadmissible, inasmuch as the Law comprehends both a *moral* and a *civil* code, and prescribes to the *private* as well as the *public* duty. It was a Law of Religion, as well as of Government. The perfect love of God, which is one commandment of Moses; the Tenth commandment of the Decalogue, and many others, never can be reduced to "statutes of the land," to be administered and enforced on the rules of a civil government. It is only surprising that a person of so great learning and research should propose the solution, or entertain the hypothesis on which it is founded; which yet he does with great deliberation. But the divine Law has its true and proper vindication, on far other grounds than such a limited and incorrect view of its use. —*J. D. Michaelis, Mosaic Law*, art. xiv.

The same Commentator rests the defence of the occupation of Canaan, made by the Israelites, upon *an hereditary* title, derived to them, as he argues, from their ancestors, a Nomadic tribe of Palestine. He thinks, they had relinquished for a time the possession of that country, without surrendering, or forfeiting, their right to it; whilst the occupants, who were afterwards dispossessed, had not acquired in the interim, which was more than two hundred years, a perfect title by their more recent settlement. This claim of human right is to soften the supposed violence of the entry of the Israelites into the Promised Land: the supernatural grant, the declared gift of God, joined with His judicial expulsion or excision of the inhabitants, (which is the Mosaic account of the proceeding,) not appearing to the author to be a *sufficient* justification of what was done. —*Comment*. art. xxxi. Smith's translation. [Or see *Syntagm. Commentat*. tom. ii. p. 210]

Such expositions can scarcely be deemed Commentaries, when the comment has so little of consistency with the text; and I have cited this second instance of the vitiated latitudinarian Theology of this author, on a point connected with the Mosaic dispensation, to make it appear the more probable, that he has gone upon some wrong principle in the whole judgment he has

formed of that dispensation. A *mere civil law*, in the one case,
and a *human right*, in the other, agree sufficiently well together:
but how do they agree with the genuine character of God's
revelation, or the majesty of His gift ? The *gratuitous donation*
of Canaan is one of the essentials of the promise of it ; and so
it is perpetually represented to be ; a free gift, and nothing
else ; gratuitous as to the right, though not as to the condition ;
and both the letter and the spirit of the Mosaic history concur
in establishing the divine donation of Canaan, and excluding
the claim of right.

But what if a common human right could be proved ? Though
it might seem to conciliate the unbeliever, it will scarcely be
satisfactory to the Christian, inasmuch as it would impair or
confound in one chief point the harmony of the divine dispensations ; which have made the grant of Canaan under the Law,
and the promise of eternal life under the Gospel, equally a
favour and a gift. The Temporal promise, in this quality of
it, is of a kind with the Evangelical ; and all this is made so
plain in the text of Holy Writ, that it requires some learning
to miss it.

The extent of *right* which the Israelites really had in Canaan
was in a place of sepulture, the purchased burying-place of the
Patriarchs. To this spot of ground, Jacob was carried from
Egypt ; it was an asylum of their faith in God's promise, and
shewed their hope, but not their claim, to the rest of Canaan :
which indeed there is no proof that their ancestors occupied,
except in part.

But I fear the author's general ideas of the foundation of
this supposed right are as untenable as his theology. For, besides what may be justly urged against it on the common principle of all law, whether Civil, or that of Nations, viz. that the
free discontinuance of possession, in course of time, *impairs* the
dominion, and at last *forfeits* it ; leaving the *derelict property*
to any new occupant, unless the exposed right be guarded in a
far stricter manner than the Israelites in Egypt could guard
their territory in Canaan ; besides this, I say that the territorial right of a Nomadic tribe is of all others the most fugitive
and evanescent, inasmuch as it imprints upon the earth, the
subject of it, few or none of the improvements or modifications
of human labour. No labours of the plough, none of planting,

none of the operose building of houses or cities, attach to the pure pastoral state; and few of these could have taken place among the ancient Nomads of Palestine. But if a migratory tribe of herdsmen could acquire a lasting property on every spot where their tents have been pitched, or their herds have grazed, they might take much of the earth to themselves in a short time, against the plainest intentions of God, and the common justice of the world. The digging of wells is perhaps the greatest effort of the Nomadic life to an appropriation of the soil. Otherwise their right, without continued occupancy, is as perishable as the herbage which they consume. But how justly does Moses express to the Israelites their total want of pretension of right on these very accounts. "And it shall be, when the Lord thy God shall have brought thee into the land which He sware unto thy fathers, *to* Abraham, *to* Isaac, and *to* Jacob, to give thee *great and goodly cities, which thou buildedst not, and houses full of all good things, which thou filledst not, and wells digged, which thou diggedst not, vineyards and olive trees, which thou plantedst not;* when thou shalt have eaten and be full; then *beware lest thou forget the Lord thy God.*" Deuter. vi. 10, 11.—*He* it was who "*gave* them the lands of the Heathen, and *they took the labours of the people* in possession." Psalm cv. 43.

Lastly, the author insists on the general inconvenient consequences which would ensue to the world, if a title to enter a country were founded either upon a *prophecy*, or upon the *irreligion* and *wickedness* of its inhabitants; and he puts cases of imagined invasion and dispossession which might be justified among the Turks and Russians, and the Catholic and Protestant powers, upon the like pretences. [art. xxviii.] In all which he argues upon a double mistake. For, *first*, to the Israelites it was not *a simple prophecy*, but an *express command* to enter; [see Exodus, Deuter., Joshua;] and it was a part of their *imputed* sin that they were so unwilling to follow the leading of that command. But the sense and operation of such a *positive command*, can never be carried into *simple prophecies* of the event. *Secondly*, God did not constitute the *Israelites* judges of the Canaanites; he left it not to them to think what the wickedness of those nations deserved. It was His own judgment, His own sentence, passed upon them, of which the

Israelites were nothing but the instruments in part to execute it. The *divine command*, and the *divine judgment, fully revealed*, were in each case the authority. But if nations or men, *without* such a warrant, or special revelation, will act as if they had it, and break through the rules of justice, which are the known will of God, who can excuse them? His Word remains unimpeached, and their abuse of it would be not the least part of their crime.—I would be excused also from reckoning the Turkish and the Mosaic prophecies as of the same value even in this general argument about any kind of right grounded on a prediction. For a real Revelation has its proper authority, which an imposture has not. But it is not the *real prediction*, but the *direct command*, which puts an end to the question.

So fallacious is this whole hypothesis of the learned philosophic Commentator, whose various and extensive attainments of erudition are sufficiently known.

END OF PART I. DISCOURSE IV.

DISCOURSE IV.

PART II.

ON THE TEMPORAL PROPHECY CONCURRENT WITH THE PROMULGATION OF THE LAW.

----♦----

DEUT. xxviii. 15.

But it shall come to pass, if thou wilt not hearken unto the voice of the Lord thy God, to observe to do all His commandments and His statutes which I command thee this day; that all these curses shall come upon thee, and overtake thee.

THE people of Israel were no sooner incorporated into a nation by their legislator, and placed under the regimen of their law, than he was instructed to reveal to them a very different state of their national existence. His prophetic commission went to pronounce upon them, in the event of their disobedience, if that disobedience should pass to great corruption and impenitency, the dissolution of their polity, under a sentence of captivity, dispersion, and desolation, aggravated by circumstances of a rare, if not unexampled, atrocity of suffering. They were doomed to be made as great in their punishment, as they had been in their visible blessings. The avenging hand of God was to be upon them for evil; but instead of their being worn out and annihilated by the excess of their sufferings, they were to survive, "pining away" amidst the extremities of desolation and oppression, "to be a sign, a by-word, and an astonishment to the nations of the earth." "All these curses," saith the Prophet, "shall come upon thee,—and they shall be upon thee for a sign, and for a wonder, and *upon thy seed for ever*[a]." When broken to pieces, the very fragments of this people were to shew the stamp and dint of the singular character which had been impressed upon them, and by their imperishable hardness to remind the world by whose hands they had been made.

Such is the narrative of this monument of prophecy. There followed in later times other predictions of the like tenor, and directed to the same general event; for Prophecy gave the warning by reiterated alarms to this obdurate and insensible people. But none of the later predictions go beyond the Mosaic in describing the extent, the bitterness, and the long duration of the plagues appointed for the execution of the divine anger upon them. There is a vivid force, and an elaborate impression in the language of Moses, upon the doom of the Hebrew people thus foreshewn, which the other Prophets have not exceeded; and if they have added particulars concerning the approach of the punishment, and the nations by whose hands at several times the punishment was to be inflicted, they have left the oldest prophecy relating to it among the most conspicuous. It is a page of the Pentateuch to which we may turn, after we have read all that there is besides in the other prophetic books descriptive of the same event.

The prediction however, with all its force, was not absolute, or irrespective; it rested on a condition; the condition of a final impenitency and disobedience of the people to whom it was addressed. But yet the veracity of the prediction could not be uncertain; for if the punishment were inflicted, it was so bound to a particular kind and manner of suffering, that there could be no mistake in tracing the agreement between the fact and the prophecy. The general condition did not vacate the determinate character of the penal retribution foretold. But there is further a provision made to guard the prediction in this very point, as to the ambiguity which might be supposed to result from its conditional nature. Moses

* Deut. xxviii. 46.

does not leave it in doubt whether the sin would ensue, and the prediction take place. Read the xxxi[st] chapter of Deuteronomy: he there decides the alternative of their conduct, and the consequence of it. He foretells in terms, that they would so act as to bring the evil upon them. Among other words to the same effect, "I know that after my death ye will utterly corrupt yourselves, and turn aside from the way which I have commanded you; and evil will befall you in the latter days; because ye will do evil in the sight of the Lord, to provoke Him to anger through the work of your hands[b]." Nor is it without some evidence of the same foretoken of the evil, that in the joint description of the blessings and the curses portended to them, there is in each case, where that description occurs, a manifest superiority in the stress and copiousness given to the afflictive side of the prophecy, as if it were intended at once to awaken and to foretell. This statement will be justified by the xxvi[th] chapter of Leviticus, and the xxviii[th] of Deuteronomy, which are the principal documents of the whole subject.

The examination of this prophecy, concerning the extraordinary doom of the Hebrew people, as to the prescience and inspiration of it proved in its fulfilment, belongs to another place in my inquiry. I am now speaking of the structure of the Prophecies, and their use in relation to the seasons when they were delivered; and on this head I have some observations to make upon the temporal prophecy which is now before us.

I. First, it is a striking fact in the delivery of this prophecy, that it comes from the mouth of Moses, the legislator of the commonwealth whose dissolution he is directed to foreshew. It is concurrent with the foundation of that commonwealth, and delivered by its Founder: in which respect it offers a great instance of the wise design manifested in the order and communication of the Prophecies. For how unlike is it to the ordinary course of

<hr>

[b] Deut. xxxi. 29.

man's own spirit or wisdom to dwell upon the downfall of his own works, just at the moment when they come fresh from his hands. But how like is it to the wisdom of God to predict to the world, or to the nearer witnesses of His revelation, the fall of things which are appointed to a great change, at the season when appearances are most remote from it, and the march or state of events dictates other feelings and opposite anticipations. The approaching settlement of this chosen people, their first advance to Canaan, is the season when their ruin, and their expulsion from that land, are introduced to view. The prophetic tidings of their distant overthrow are made to sound in our ears as loud as the song of their present victory. A combination of things rarely made, and not conformable to the human feeling left to itself; but which is not without example in other conspicuous parts of Prophecy. For as Moses foretells the desolation of his people at the moment when he reared them into a community, so to Solomon were foreshewn the ruins of his Temple at the like season, when he beheld it completed in its magnificence, and bearing upon it the omens of hope and joy in the blessing of its first Inauguration. There is here, if I am not mistaken, an evidence of a divine wisdom of design, as well as a wisdom of prescience, manifested in the very order and time of such predictions. And among other proofs of fitness attaching to this Mosaic prophecy, I would remark the limitation which it gave, at the most critical time, to the temporary and partial purpose of the covenant of Canaan. It was made clear that the divine promises to all mankind could not be comprehended in that covenant, when the separated people, who had received the grant of Canaan annexed to it, were not permitted to expect a lasting possession of that inheritance.

II. Secondly, I observe that there is a perfect conformity between the Law, and the Prophecy, of Moses. The Law was founded on explicit temporal sanctions; his prophecy dilates explicitly upon the temporal subject, the scheme of earthly blessings and earthly evils. The prophecy, indeed, is no more than a full and graphic exemplification of the actual sanctions of the Law.

From this unquestionable state of the case, in the entire relation and coincidence between the Law, and the principal branch of prophecy contemporary with the Law, there are important conclusions which follow. *First,* The authority of the Mosaic Law has been proved to the letter, by the accomplishment of the corresponding predictions. God gave His first revealed law with such and such promises and threatenings annexed to it; He laid the scene of its sanctions in the present world. In the present world both have been exhibited in their turn, except that the curse has prevailed over the blessing, the excess of disobedience in the people placed under this rule giving the preponderance to the measure of the penal avenging retribution. "I will bring a sword upon you, that *shall avenge the quarrel of My covenant*[c]." But if that sword of God has avenged the quarrel of His covenant, it has manifested its truth. For hereby it is, by means of these particular sanctions and the prophecy joined with them, that the world has been made a spectator and the Jew at this day a witness, of the effectual authority of His Law. *Secondly,* By the visible fulfilment of the sentence of the first law, every other sanction which God has appointed to any part of His revealed word is established in its truth. He has made our eyes, or a known experience at least, in this point, to serve to the conviction of our faith. We have only to look at the Jew under the signs of his long and remarkable visitation, to judge of the veracity of other articles of revelation less subjected to the test and cognizance of a present experience. *Thirdly,* Hereby the atheist may learn to suspect that bold objection of his upon which he most relies. He would impute to Revealed Religion the choice of the sanctions of a future unseen reward and punishment, for the convenience of the uncertainty and

<hr>

[c] Levit. xxvi. 25.

disguise which seem to cover that distant scene. But the first Law meets him on his own terms: it stood upon a present retribution; the execution of its sentence is matter of history, and the argument resulting from it is to be answered, before the question is carried to another world.

III. In the next place, I would suggest to the attentive reader of Prophecy, the general adaptation, which may now be perceived, in the tenor of its predictions, at the æra of the Law, to the state of things then in being. In this period, as we saw before, Prophecy affords only a feeble light to the contemplation of the Gospel; and as we now see, it bears a luminous and decisive evidence to the specific genius and authority of the Mosaic Law: a statement this of its comparative use and clearness, which has not been taken from any previous hypothesis, but has been strictly deduced from the consideration of its own records.

Under this leading view of it, in its two branches, we shall be freed from the temptation or desire of straining single texts of prophecy from their proper scope, or assigning to them a higher sense or evidence than they will justly bear. The attempt to enlarge the interpretation of prophecy has kept pace in some degree with the like attempt made on the interpretation of the Mosaic Law. In a spirit of piety, but not of sound wisdom, men have wished to find the Gospel doctrines and sanctions in that law, as they have wished to find a Gospel sense in every prediction. But under the influence of this expectation it cannot but follow that we read the word of prophecy, and with it the rest of Scripture, with less sincerity of satisfaction than we might do, if we were prepared to receive its sense, rather than impose it. And a consequence is, that we shall ascribe the difficulty and want of satisfaction which will always be felt under this error, not to the principle by which we interpret, but to the Sacred Volume itself, which is subjected to our wrong conceptions of it. Whereas the most impartial and patient meditation upon the genuine sense of the inspired volume will give us far juster notions of its nature and use than any we can frame for it. Such meditation may discharge a prejudice; but it will requite us with truth perspicuous and consistent.

I shall conclude our view of Prophecy at the institution of the Law, with a few words of remark upon the occupation of Canaan which followed, and closed the economy of that period.

IV. The occupation of Canaan gave to the Israelites a domicile to their law, and an investiture of their covenant. It was the act of God establishing them in their relation to Him as His people. We do not find any further revelation attending this event. It was the stage of prophecy fulfilled, not the source of new prophecy given. The people were placed under their law, and prophecy remained silent for a season.

The glory of conducting them to their home of inheritance and rest was denied to Moses, and granted to Joshua. This was no more than had been foretold; and Moses[d] records the prediction which took from him the completion of his work, and the offence[e] which incurred that privation. Thrice has he repeated the recital of his offence and dishonour; though he inserts nothing of older date to foreshew his mission or his success. Such signs of truth are there in his publication of the documents of prophecy.

Joshua, at the close of his life, appealed to the people for their knowledge of prophecy fulfilled. They were possessed of the goodly cities and vineyards of Canaan; "they had rest from all their enemies; and they had seen all that the Lord their God had done unto the nations because of them[f]." But upon all this, he refers them to the divine promise, which had stipulated to them what they possessed and saw. "Behold, this day I am going the way of all the earth: and ye know in all your hearts

---

[d] Numbers xx 11, 12; xxvii. 12.   [e] Deut. xxxii. 51.

[f] Joshua xxiii. 1—3.

and in all your souls, that not one thing hath failed of all the good things which the Lord your God spake concerning you; all are come to pass unto you, and not one thing hath failed thereof." Such promises then had existed, and were known; otherwise it had been in vain for Joshua to appeal to all Israel " with their heads, their officers, and their judges," if they were ignorant of such things either foretold or done.

Prophecy, then, sealed the temporal covenant, on the part of God, by its predictions relating thereto fulfilled. It had been first the messenger of His purpose concerning the gift of Canaan; verified in due time, it became the witness of His providence; and of His particular revelation connected with that gift. But the prophetic promise had remained in suspense four hundred years: it had attended upon the migrations and pilgrimage of the Patriarchs; it had lingered through the unhopeful bondage of Egypt; it had passed through trials and delays; which ended in Canaan, in the demonstration of its truth.

From Canaan we look back upon much of former prophecy fulfilled. From the Gospel we attain to a similar retrospective view. A third point of rest and contemplation remains, which is yet afar off. But time has travelled to the former two; and that is an earnest, that the day will come, when the whole scheme of prophecy shall be viewed in its completion, and God's revelation shall be seen to have anticipated nothing which His Power and Providence shall not have made good.

END OF DISCOURSE IV. PART II.

DISCOURSE V.

Yea, and all the Prophets from Samuel and those that follow after, as many as have spoken, have likewise foretold of these days.

FROM Moses to Christ there is but one age of Prophecy. It comprehends the period reaching from the time of Samuel down to Malachi. It is preceded by the interval between Moses and Samuel, an interval without prophecy, and is followed by a similar interval, equally without prophecy, between Malachi and the advent of the Gospel. Of this age of Prophecy, and its inspired communications, and of the pause which precedes and follows it, I have now to speak.

I. The settlement in Canaan is succeeded by an intermission of Prophecy extending to the days of Samuel, a space of not less than four hundred years. Within this period no predictions are recorded; and it would appear that none were given. For that there was an intermission of the gift, and not merely a silence of the record, may be inferred by many arguments. 1. By that silence itself. 2. By the union of Samuel with Moses, when the ancient Prophets and servants of God come to be remembered together[a]. 3. By the implication of St. Paul, who reckons the government of the *Judges* to Samuel the *Prophet* as

---

[a] Jeremiah xv. 1. "Though Moses and Samuel stood before Me, yet My mind could not be toward this people." Compare Psalm xcix. 6.

distinguished from them[b]. 4. By the historic text, which informs us that "the word of the Lord was precious in those days; there was no open vision[c]." If we read of "Deborah, the Prophetess," within the period assigned, her history will direct us to think that her title to that name was her inspiration and call to government, or her gift of sacred Hymns, both of which are known, not her predictions, of which no notice is extant. From which reasons put together, I conclude a real cessation of Prophecy during that lapse of time.

It may be asked, is there any discernible reason for this long intermission? Has it any congruity with the circumstances and condition of the people to whom the prophetic oracles had been largely opened before, though now they were withholden? The reason, and the congruity, may I think be very clearly discerned.

For it will be seen that during the same space of time there is a kind of *rest* in the history of the Israelites, by the absence of any change permanently or deeply affecting their public condition. Their state is not a tranquil one; but, after the intervening interruptions, it returns still within the same limits. It is a succession of various fortune, afflictions and deliverances alternating, according to their public sin, or their repentance. The first generation of men, who had in their mind, and almost in their eyes, the mighty works which God had done for His people, are said to have lived under suitable impressions, in obedience to their law. The next ages degenerated: their offence of idolatry, or other sin, was visibly punished; the chastisement recalled to duty, or the divine mercy spared: and deliverers were at hand, raised up, and especially sent, to reinstate them in peace and safety.

These were vicissitudes which did not shake the frame

---

[b] Acts xiii. 20. "After that He gave unto them Judges about the space of four hundred and fifty years, *until Samuel* the Prophet." The context of Acts iii. 24. "For *Moses* truly said unto the Fathers,—Yea, and *all the prophets from Samuel*," &c.

[c] 1 Sam. iii. 1.

of their polity, their priesthood, or their law. They were
no more than exemplifications of the issue of obedience or
disobedience to a fixed duty. The wounds inflicted were
healed again, the blessings which were imparted only restored an interrupted security. There was no shock given
to their Institutions, nor any thing of lasting importance,
in respect of their Covenant, put upon a new footing.

Accordingly the pause of Prophecy, which holds on
through the space of these partial and temporary fluctua-
tions, seems to have been related to it. May we not say,
that no change occurred of magnitude enough to demand
the prophetic interposition? So much may be said with a
strong colour of reason, when we compare the failure of
prophecy, and the results of the history, together. And
yet if predictions had been indiscriminately given, or indiscriminately pretended, there was movement and variety
of fortune enough within the compass of this period to
have exercised the Prophet's tongue. But no commission
was given to speak; and the suspension of Prophecy, as
well as its renewal, may lead us to trace in it the directing
wisdom of Him who orders His works "in number and in
measure," and adapts and limits His word in the same
way. For what were the changes and calamities which
took place, whilst Prophecy thus remained silent? They
were the proper sentence of the Law put in force. The
Law, with its past comments, could perfectly explain them.
And since those mutations were not lasting or subversive,
it is consistent to suppose that men had the sufficient
information before them of the purposes of Providence,
without the further extraordinary aid of Prophecy to predict or interpret them.—So much concerning the *intermission of prophecy* subsequent to the Law; and the seeming reasons afforded to explain that intermission.

II. From the age of Samuel begins a different order of
things, and the disparity is striking. From that date the
commonwealth of Israel wears a far more disturbed appearance. It is pregnant with scenes of innovation; of extra-

ordinary transient success; of long confusion and overwhelming calamity; the priesthood transferred; the regal
government set up; the kingdom broken and divided; idolatry publicly established; thence a series of afflictions end-
ing in subjugation, captivity, and removal from their land:
in many cases the divine Covenant placed under such
dubious and questionable circumstances as to render the
word of prophecy highly expedient to the elucidation of
the passing events, and to the instruction of men's hopes
and inquiries concerning the future course and result of
the divine proceedings.

Corresponding to such a disturbed state of their history
is the revival, and afterwards the enlargement, of the prophetic revelation. Prophecy takes its station at the commencement of the whole. As Moses is the prophet of the
age of the Law, so is Samuel of the first age of the monarchy of Israel. But Prophecy does not stop with Samuel;
it is continuous and progressive; it proceeds without any
one material chasm or suspension of its revelations, through
the succeeding line of complex history, down to the days
of Malachi, the last of the prophetic order, when it came
to a close for a long season again, and interposed its other
great cessation prior to the Gospel advent.

This then is the reign of predictive revelation, and the
proper age of the Prophets. It is the middle period of the
first dispensation, standing equally removed, in time, and
in some of its characters, from the Law, and from the
Gospel, and the service of Prophecy during this period
forms a great connecting link of divine information between the two. It is moreover a period fully occupied by
Prophecy throughout; I mean to say, it had its succession
of inspired messengers following each other in order from
first to last; and it had its predictions embracing *every
remarkable change* affecting the chosen people, and included within the limits of the time in question; as well
as a continuation of predictive Prophecy carried forward,
and reaching to the Gospel age. Such is the continuity of
the prophetic scheme in this body of its predictions.

Meanwhile the matter of the enlarged communications so made equally demands our attention. Branching out in different directions, it enters into the Jewish, Christian, and Pagan subjects. The simple restricted Jewish subject comes first, as in the predictions of Samuel. The Jewish and Christian are next combined, as in the prophecies of David and Isaiah. Afterwards the Christian and Pagan are clearly and formally connected in the prophecies of Daniel. Whilst all these subjects, either apart or in-union, are filled up from time to time, with various accessions of prediction extending on every side the range of the revelation.

But in this train and series of prophetic disclosure one subject there is pre-eminent above the rest, the Christian. It is, of all others, the most frequently introduced, and the most copiously enlarged upon. It furnishes the proper topic of many great and perspicuous predictions; in others a transition is made to it, as though it were constantly in view. For to "Christ give all the Prophets witness." And whatever other matters they may treat of, to Him and His religion they direct our attention, some by express oracles, some by intelligible intimation, but all with a remarkable concurrence and agreement. The consummation of the designs and the promises of God in His particular covenant with the house of Israel is referred to the days of the Messiah. And the succession of the kingdoms of the earth is equally deduced to the Messiah's kingdom. So that nothing more certainly true can be said of Prophecy and of its scope than this: that in effect, as well as by the very form and structure of its records, the Redeemer and His everlasting kingdom are presented to the eye as the centre of Prophecy, and the end of the revelations of God.

Such being the enlarged scheme of Prophecy in its *one principal age*, I shall endeavour to explore it in part, according to the plan I have prescribed to myself, of investigating its structure and use in the several periods wherein it was dispensed. But here, more than in any other stage of my inquiry, I must confine myself to a restricted speculation. No attempt will be made to exhaust the subject even under the most general views of it; but only to treat of it in a few of its leading points, and by such inferences as may be obtained from them, to secure some determinate principles applicable to the whole argument concerning Prophecy in its *constitution* and *use.*

Some of the observations which I shall have to make will be simple and obvious; others of them may militate with particular notions of systematic opinion. The request I make in favour of them all is, that they may be laid together, and examined by these two tests; first, whether they do not truly express the state of Prophecy, such as it is found; and next, whether they do not assert and justify the objects and purposes which are assigned to it, so far as my investigation may go. No disputable conclusions can ever be of any avail in illustrating Prophecy in its character or its intent. Nor indeed is there any reason to have recourse to them. For though particular texts of it may be obscure, as many of them are confessed to be; yet the design and character of the whole, when impartially surveyed, is not so; and the fault must be in our own discussions, if, on those points, they end in obscure or inapplicable results.—Having said this, I proceed.

III. Of Prophecy in the age of Samuel.—That the first Prophet after Moses might appear with an authority, public and acknowledged, equal to his commission, which fell upon a season of great importance in the regulation of the religious and the civil state, we observe how he is invested with his office. A supernatural call and a prophetic vision were granted to him in the first rudiments of his life and ministry. For the public degeneracy having reached to the priesthood, Eli and his sons, in whose hands religion suffered contempt, were to be removed from their functions; and a train of exact prediction, first communicated to Eli by a man of God, and then to the child Samuel in a vision[d], foreshewed the judgment of God in the excision

<hr>

[d] 1 Sam. iii. 11.

of Eli and his house; the speedy fulfilment of which prophecy with other present signs of his mission, made "all Israel, from Dan to Beer-sheba, know that Samuel was established to be a Prophet of the Lord[e]." These immediate tokens corresponded with his office; for Samuel was a Prophet sent to govern and to judge, as well as to prophesy. He had, therefore, present credentials in predictions of an instant kind, to ensure the reception and acknowledgment of his inspired character; and so it is written that "the Lord was with him, and did let none of his words fall to the ground."

Thus initiated, he was called to regulate in the great change which straightway ensued in the appointment of a sovereign ruler over the people of Israel with the title and offices of king. The institution of the legal polity was an act of their own, adopted in conformity to the example of the nations around them, but opposed by the dissuasion and remonstrance of the Prophet, who had been raised up to control in some measure the aberrations of a people whom yet God punished by permitting them to follow their will. For their demand of a visible earthly Sovereign was in disparagement of their trust in the protection and government of that extraordinary Providence, which had distinguished them from the nations of the earth, and taken them by a privilege under an immediate Theocracy. Jehovah was their king. The majesty of His mysterious presence filled the throne of Israel. Their offence, therefore, and the reproof of it lay in this, as the oracle of God declared, "They have rejected Me, that I should not reign over them."

It were easy to vindicate the Prophet's reproof delivered on this occasion from the notable abuse to which it has been wrested, in defamation of the principles of monarchical government, as though the Scripture or the Prophet intended any such defamation[f]. The offence of the Israelites was a peculiar one in the instance: it sprung from

[e] 1 Sam. iii. 20.   [f] 1 Sam. viii. 10—18.

a condition in which no other people has been placed. When the Almighty shall again dictate a code of civil law and government for the use of any nation, and charge Himself with the superintendence and execution of it, it will then be time to think how far this passage of Scripture may have to do with the principles of any given polity. Meanwhile, however we think of it, let it be taken honestly and entire. Let men fortify their civil obedience by a stronger piety, by a sense of the impending power and presence of God, the principle from which the Israelites are censured for having swerved, and in that case their mistake, if any be made, will have some consistency, but no evil in it, unless it be in turning the edge of a cavil against its authors.

The sin of the Israelites was founded in a revolt from God, in the abdication of a perfect trust and reliance upon His providential government in that method in which, with respect to them, He had ordered it. But their fault, though uncommon in its form, is not at all so in its principle. Something to see, and nothing to believe, is the wish and the wrong propensity of more than the Israelites. And therefore, since the agency of the Providence of God is one chief object and principle of religion, whether that Providence act in the Theocracy of Israel, or by its more ordinary law, the doctrine of the prophet had its use, and has it still, in enforcing the habit and duty of faith in the one Invisible Governor of the world, though it can have none now in derogating from the just title and power of the earthly governors of it. I say, their just title and power; for it is not to be denied, that the reproof of the prophet is cast into such a form as to represent the abuses and excesses of a personal indulgence, to which the kingly power, and all other power, in human hands, is prone to seduce its possessors[g].

The prophet conceding a king, made choice by an inspired direction of the person; first of Saul: afterwards,

<hr>

[g] 1 Sam. viii. 10—18.

when he, for his transgression, was rejected, though not publicly disturbed or set aside, of David; Saul of the tribe of Benjamin; David of the tribe of Judah. But there was a great difference in the manner of the appointment and designation in the two cases. Saul was publicly nominated by Samuel, who continued to "judge Israel all the days of his life," in virtue of his Prophetic mission. Whereas David, though anointed by Samuel, to fix the divine choice resting upon him, did not attain to the throne of Israel, till long after the Prophet's death, a time remote from the prediction. The second appointment, therefore, was a signal prediction given by Samuel, and exhibited in the act of anointing; a prediction that the youngest of the seven sons of Jesse, a retired Bethlehemite, and he then living a shepherd, unknown and secluded in the privacy of his father's house, and depressed below the consideration and respect of his own brethren, was the heir of the kingdom of Israel.

By a series of events, following in the ordinary course of Providence, without any miracle interposed, this prediction was brought to pass. David was raised to his divinely appointed station, when his shepherd's staff became a sceptre, and his flock a great people; none contributing more to the preparation of this event than Saul himself, who in his jealousy sought to destroy the faithful friend he had called forth, but whose hostility placed him in the way to power by the necessities of a just self-defence; the decree of prophecy turning the counsels of Saul to counterwork their object.

I believe that no other single narrative of Scripture is so prolix and circuitous as that which describes the accomplishment of this particular prediction. The sequel of things described is protracted; often retrograde in the expectation, and apparently receding from the event; and it fills many chapters[h] before it is brought to a close. Upon which I would observe, that it offers, and seems to be designed to offer, an example, in the actual develop-

[h] From 1 Sam. xvi. to 2 Sam. v.

ment, of the progress of prophecy to its completion, whatever may be the mazes and flexures through which it has to work its way; and suggests to us, in other cases not so particularly narrated, how the divine prescience penetrates through the perplexity of human affairs, and its predictions, without a sensible miracle, pass to their near or their remote fulfilment. The complicated narrative is the exposition of the prophetic prescience. In that sense it ought to be read, and its import and reference, which otherwise might be overlooked, will be seen. Among other circumstances, advert to the visit of domestic kindness which David made to his elder brethren in the camp of Israel, when he was requited with their reproach, "With whom hast thou left those few sheep in the wilderness?" The circumstance is a casual and minute one. But it is interposed between the prediction and its fulfilment; and so interposed it serves to shew how wide was the interval of things from the one to the other. The same extended narrative has also a second reference, as a sign of the eminent importance which attaches to the throne and kingdom of David.

As the succession of David had been foretold, so the time and manner of the death of Saul, and of his sons, in battle, were exactly foreshewn[1]. And thus the whole of this public change, in each of its parts, was made a topic of prophecy. The event was considerable: the predictions of it exact and complete.

Upon the whole, the characteristic of Prophecy at this æra is exceedingly prominent and conspicuous. It was almost exclusively of a civil nature, being directed to the public state of the commonwealth of Israel: it watched over the change introduced by the establishment of the kingly government, and it appointed the sceptre to the person and tribe of David. The transference of the priesthood from Eli's house, the other chief subject of prophecy, is altogether of the like kind; for it made no change in the religion, but only in the public and ecclesiastical order

<hr>

[1] 1 Sam. xxviii. 19.

of it. The *civil* character of prophecy at this period is therefore the simple distinguishing note of it. In which light, though clearly adapted to its season, and applied to the state of things passing or emergent, it is something different from the prophecy of almost every other period.

Yet with all their adaptation to the circumstances of the time, it could not be said of these predictions that they were framed under favour of those circumstances, or after the bent and leading of them. For the prophet was subjected to this test; his adverse predictions concerning Eli and Saul, the priesthood and the throne, he delivered in the face of their power; his favourable prediction respecting David, he bequeathed to the hope of a distant and improbable fulfilment. His first prophecies challenged a jealous scrutiny; his last was placed beyond the command of his influence and direction. In each case the authority of the prophet was strictly tried.

But what prophecy had to foreshew of the first beginnings of the kingdom of Israel is but introductory to the enlarged revelations upon it which immediately ensued.

END OF DISCOURSE V. PART I.

DISCOURSE V.

PART II.

STATE OF PROPHECY IN THE REIGNS OF DAVID AND SOLOMON.

— ◆ —

ISAIAH ix. 7.

Of the increase of His government and peace there shall be no end, upon the throne of David and upon his kingdom, to order it, and to establish it with judgment and with justice, from henceforth even for ever; the zeal of the Lord of Hosts will do this.

IN the times which follow, the predictions of Prophecy begin to take a wider range, and present a greater variety of matter to be considered. To give perspicuity, therefore, to the observations which I have to make upon it in this its more extended state, I shall reduce them under distinct heads, and keep an arrangement of the whole corresponding with that of the history of the adopted people of God to whom prophecy was given. For as delivered to them, it took its stand upon their affairs, in their religion, their polity, or their public condition; and hence we find that the prophecies of the Christian or the Pagan subjects have their rise most commonly in the primary topics and occasions of that other history, and are introduced more or less in connexion with it. So that whether we look to the order of the prophetic oracles, or to the degrees and state of prophetic knowledge in its several periods, we are carried in each case into the annals of that favoured people, to whom, though not for themselves alone, the word of prophecy originally came. This formal notion of the prophetic subject, however, is taken only as an expedient of arrangement. Whilst the Scripture oracles are open to be examined in many other ways more freely, and it may be with equal advantage, I wish to render my own observations and the result of them, as clear and intelligible as I can, by borrowing for them the aid of some method and order.

The line of discourse thus premised, the chief points of it will be the more memorable events and seasons of Jewish history, which are briefly as follows:

I. The establishment of the kingdom of David.
II. The reign of Solomon, including the building of the Temple.
III. The division of the monarchy of Israel.
IV. The public establishment of Idolatry in Samaria.
V. The captivity of that kingdom.
VI. The captivity of Judah.
VII. The restoration of Judah, with the building of the second Temple, followed by the Cessation of prophecy.

Through these points I must endeavour to deduce some idea of the structure, adaptation, and progress of the entire prophetic revelation.

I. When prophecy had taken the crown of Israel from Saul, and placed it on the head of David, an Israelite of that day might have a question to ask. He might wish to know what prospects there were for him and his country hereafter: whether the translation of the kingdom from Saul to David, from the tribe of Benjamin to that of Judah, was straightway to be followed by other the like mutations and vicissitudes, without any permanence of a local or personal inheritance of succession. This was no vain inquiry, nor unworthy of the most sober and pious servant of God in that age. For the recent change, with the troubles and division of spirits which had preceded it, could not pass by without raising a thought what God would do with His people in this particular. God had strongly directed men's minds to that kind of consideration, by making the past change a subject of prophecy, and also by those long troubles and confusions which had entered with their possession of a king, as a consequence of it, if not a judicial visitation; it being clear to any attentive reader of this part of their history, that the Israelites were signally punished in the immediate effects of their choice; those wars of contention for the kingdom between the house of Saul and David, being some of the bitter fruits of their rejection of the sovereignty of God, as king over them.

Besides, an Israelite had a reason in his religion to inquire whether God would "give His people the blessing of peace." The repose and stability of their public government are benefits to all, and great in every country; but to a member of the commonwealth of Israel, in these temporal blessings, and others built upon them, the authentic signs of God's favour and the operation of His covenant were contained; and therefore he by his religion, as well as by other motives, had his eye turned to watch the order of Providence in such dispensations.

Now I say that the visible state of things could give that Israelite no answer; for the reign of David was neither tranquil nor secure, and in itself it promised nothing for the future. But Prophecy did give him the answer. Having foreshewn the exaltation of David, it went on to establish his house, and complete his greatness by a promise of the continuance of the kingdom in his family. The predictions to this effect are literal and clear; and they are such as make a great contrast with the ill-omened elevation of Saul, which had neither the preceding auspice of God's pleasure upon it, nor was followed by any promise of kingly succession after him. "I gave thee a king in Mine anger, and took him away in My wrath." This is the retrospect of later prophecy upon Saul. Far otherwise with David: "When thy days be fulfilled, and thou shalt sleep with thy fathers, I will set up thy seed after thee, which shall proceed out of thy bowels, and I will establish his kingdom. He shall build a house for My Name, and I will establish the throne of his kingdom for ever. I will be his Father, and he shall be My son. If he commit iniquity, I will chasten him with the rod of men, and with the stripes of the children of men. But My mercy shall not depart from him, as I took it away from Saul, whom I put away before thee. And thy house and thy kingdom shall be established for ever before thee. Thy throne shall be established for ever. According to all these words and this vision, so did Nathan speak unto David[a]."

Such were the hopes settled by Prophecy upon this king of Israel and his family. Of the Evangelical promises contained in all this, I shall speak presently; but now of the Temporal, the first in view, and the first to take effect. David's own life and reign, though they closed in victory and peace, had been full of agitation, warfare, and danger. The persecutions of Saul, the hazards of an asylum in banishment in an enemy's land, the insurrection of his subjects, and the treachery and rebellion of his children. reach far in the story of his life.

But as his throne was to be established, and his seed to inherit it, so he had the prediction of another kind of reign for his son, who should come after him; a reign of security and peace. "Behold a son shall be born unto thee, who shall be a man of rest; and I will give him rest from all his enemies round about; for his name shall be called Solomon," (a name, and therein, a promise, of peace,) "and I will give peace and quietness unto Israel in his days[b]."

Here then we have the engagement and stipulation of Prophecy at this period. A long stability, and an immediate peace, in his succession, with other blessings accumu-

---

[a] 2 Sam. vii. 12—17. The 89th Psalm dilates the same prediction.

[b] 1 Chron. xxii. 9.

lated upon his seed after him, are the promises made to this chosen king of Israel, and in him, to his people.

But this is only one part of the subject. In the person of David, Prophecy makes some of its greatest revelations. In him, as in Abraham, the temporal and the evangelical predictions are united. His reign is one cardinal point of their union, and of the entire scheme of Prophecy in its double character. He was made a Prophet himself, inspired to reveal many of the Christian promises, and there are no other such significant disclosures made of them since the days of Abraham and the Patriarchs, nor perhaps even then. For what have we in the Prophetic Psalms, (and those all, or most of them, ascribed to David,) but an assemblage of many of the most considerable attributes of the reign and religion of the Messiah foreshewn? There is a king set upon the holy hill of Sion; His law; the opposition made to Him by the kings of the earth; their rage defeated; His extraordinary sceptre of righteousness; His unchangeable priesthood; His divine Sonship; His exalted nature; His death and early resurrection outrunning the corruption of the grave; His dominion embracing both Israel and the Gentile world[c]. On which account this becomes one of the most distinguished periods of the prophetic revelation; and whoever would study that revelation, and see into the order and scope of it, in both its kinds, must take this æra of it for one of his principal points of view[d]. And as we have

[c] See Psalms ii. xvi. xlv. cx.   Also lxxxix., and others.

[d] Hence the joint reference which is made in the New Testament to *Abraham* and to *David*. St. Matthew begins with "the book of the generation of Jesus Christ, the son of *David*, the son of *Abraham*." The inspired hymn of Zacharias runs upon the same persons, in "blessing the Lord God of Israel, for He hath visited and redeemed His people, and hath raised up an horn of salvation for us in *the house* of His servant *David*—To perform the mercy promised to our Fathers, and to remember His holy covenant, the oath which He sware to our father *Abraham*[*].—In the Old: "*My Covenant will I not break, nor alter the thing that is gone out of My lips; I have sworn once by My holiness*, that I will not fail *David* [+]." It is the divine pledge, the oath "shewing the immutability of God's counsel;" as in the case of Abraham[‡].

[*] Luke ii. 68.   [+] Psalm lxxxix. 34.   [‡] Heb. vi. 17.

a great increase of the prophetic light breaking forth, and encompassing the family and kingdom of David, so subsequent prophecy reverts often to the same subjects, insomuch that there is no individual, king or other person, one only excepted, of whom more is said by the prophets, than of this king and his throne; "the throne of David," "the sure mercies of David," being recalled again and again, in the progress of their revelation; and the single person who is made still more the care and object of the divine oracles, is He who was both the Son of David and His Lord, and to whom the glory of David's kingdom, and of the prophecies relating to it, most eminently and perfectly belongs.

Upon this statement, some remarks come to be made concerning the frame and tenor of Prophecy so exhibited.

I. "Of the seed of David, according to the flesh," the Messiah was to be born into the world. This being the divine purpose, the first exaltation of the house of David is chosen, as we see, to be the time of originating some of the clearest and most illustrious prophecies concerning Him: as the heir of David's throne, the great King of Israel, the predestinated ruler of the people of God. Who can hesitate to say, that there is a congruity in this order of prophecy,—a congruity both as to its time of promulgation, and also as to the evidence, which it thereby affords in the most striking way, of the ultimate purpose of God in the selection and elevation of the house of David.

It is the same order as we saw observed in the Call of Abraham, and the Constitution of the Tribes. When God first separated the family in which the Messiah was to be born, the Seed of Blessing was revealed to the founder and Patriarch of that family. When that family began to divide and branch into Tribes, the tribe of Judah had the designation of prophecy fixed upon it in respect of the Messiah. When the kingdom of David appears, the reign and power of the Messiah are brought into view.

II. There is a further congruity in this frame of Prophecy. For the evangelical end is not only foreshewn with the temporal appointment, but it is stamped upon it. How is this done? In the house of David is founded a kingdom; but Christ has His kingdom, His protecting power and rule over the people of God, as truly as Solomon, and the other heirs of David, had theirs. The temporal kingdom bears some image of the other; they are two analogous subjects, and fit to be combined together, as prophecy has combined them; though the likeness would be more confessed, if the kings of the earth always answered to their high office, "if they would reign in righteousness, and princes rule in judgment," which is the model of the kingdom of Christ. But now that He has come into the world, and received His kingdom, and fulfilled the promises made to David, as well as the prophecies delivered by him, the relation between the two subjects is made so evident, that it is out of all reason not to admit that the relation was designed to be expressed in the prophecy, as it is illustrated in the fact.

III. This age of prophecy, in particular, brings the doctrine of " the double sense," as it has been called, before us. For Scripture Prophecy is so framed in some of its predictions, as to bear a sense directed to two objects; of which structure the predictions concerning the kingdom of David furnish a conspicuous example; and I should say, an unquestionable one, if the whole principle of that kind of interpretation had not been by some disputed and denied. But the principle has met with this ill acceptance, for no better reason, it should seem, than because it has been injudiciously applied, in cases where it had no proper place; or has been suspected, if not mistaken, in its constituent character, as to what it really is.

The double sense of prophecy, however, is of all things the most remote from fraud or equivocation, and has its ground of reason perfectly clear. For what is it? Not the convenient latitude of two unconnected senses, wide of each other, and giving room to a fallacious ambiguity; but the combination of two related, analogous and harmonizing, though disparate subjects, each clear and definite in itself; implying a twofold truth in the prescience, and creating an aggravated *difficulty*, and thereby an accumulated proof, in the completion. For a case in point; to justify the predictions concerning the kingdom of David in their double force, it must be shewn of them, that they hold in each of their relations, and in each were fulfilled. So that the double sense of prophecy in its true idea is a check upon the pretences of vague and unappropriated prediction, rather than a door to admit them.

But this is not all. For if the prediction distribute its sense into two remote branches or systems of the Divine Economy; if it shew not only what is to take place in distant times, but describe also different modes of God's appointment, though holding a certain and intelligible resemblance to each other; such prediction becomes not only more convincing in the argument, but more instructive in the doctrine, because it expresses the correspondence of God's dispensations in their points of agreement, as well as His foreknowledge.

Of the validity and rectitude of this interpretation by a double sense, there is a simple and decisive test, which will shew at once, when it may with safety, and should in reason, be admitted. The test is, that each of the subjects ascribed to the prophecy be such as may challenge the right of it, in its main import, and meet it in its obvious representation; other reasonable conditions being observed, as to the known general tendency of the whole volume of prophecy. When the divided application asserts itself in this manner, the principle is certain, the reason we have to follow is clear, and the prophecy is doubly authentic. But where it does not, the principle having no safe ground to rest upon, ought not to be entertained: least of all should it be applied to predictions of which the general import is doubtful, or of less note and prominence in itself. For the pursuit of a double mean-

ing under such circumstances must soon corrupt the
whole interpretation of prophecy, and engender infinite
conceits and trifling comments of a spurious unprofitable
ingenuity. Whereas, the wisdom of God has made prophecy, and all other Scripture, to minister to better and
nobler purposes of argument and information. Under this
conviction, I would understand the double sense to obtain only in some of the more distinguished monuments
of prophecy, where the force and clearness of the description, and the adequate magnitude of the subjects, concur
in giving simplicity to the combined view of them, and
render the divided application at once necessary, rational,
and perspicuous.

In vindicating this principle of interpretation, when so
restricted and governed, some examples may tend to confirm its use and fitness. Among the examples of Prophecy
which may be adduced as embracing a double subject, are
to be classed some of the predictions which foreshew the
restoration of Judah from captivity in Babylon[e]. It is
a subject akin to the Evangelical Restoration. Every
Christian understands the resemblance. There is nothing
dark or ambiguous in the combination of the two. The
prophecies which combine them are clear and consistent
in each sense; the images of description are perfectly just
and natural to both. But suppose it were pretended that
the resemblance of the subject, and the terms of the description, embraced equally some other unconnected events;
such as we might readily find in general history; as a great
sceptic[f] has asserted that the Prophecies belong as much
to things passing in modern Europe, as to those to which
Christians apply them: the pretence would be futile, and
incapable of affecting the certainty, or the application, of
the Prophecies; because there is abundant evidence of the
real direction of them to the course of God's dispensations; and a literal fortuitous coincidence between the
prophetic text and the events of a distant general history,
neither makes a claim for itself, nor affects the other, the

[e] See Jeremiah xxxi. Isaiah lii.

[f] Bolingbroke.

legitimate exposition of the same text, which rests on its proper grounds.

In like manner the prophecy of the judicial destruction of Jerusalem, with the dissolution of the Jewish Economy, symbolizes with that which relates to the final judgment, which will shut up the whole temporal Economy of God at the end of the world. In the New Testament they are united. In this, as in the other authentic instances of a double sense, particulars are found belonging exclusively to the one subject or the other: these particulars create a discrimination, but do not violate the general harmony of the things described; the chief propositions and images, and the substance of the prediction, are common to the two; and they are common by the nature of the subjects, which correspond so far in their main attributes as to give a plain ground of fitness and agreement to the prophecies which join them together in one comprehensive scheme of delineation.

Such are some of the examples of Prophecy in its two-fold sense. They are great in their kind, in each line of the parallel. The establishment of the kingdom of David; the restoration from the Captivity; the dissolution of the Jewish Polity, are among the most memorable events and objects of the first, the older dispensation. The corresponding events and objects are not less in their kind in the new[g]. The combinations which Prophecy has made of them may instruct us, not merely in the argument and doctrine of that kind of interpretation, but in other material inferences, which I must not now pursue. But so much may suffice to shew the principle of the double sense, its force and strict logical propriety.

IV. It has often been remarked that the prophecies of the Messiah belonging to this period partake principally

[g] Hence, by the like signatures, it becomes highly probable that the pro-fanation of the Temple by Antiochus, and the corresponding profanation of the Christian Church by the great Apostasy, the tyrannic corruption of Anti-christ, are rightly joined together as correlative terms of a joint prophecy.

of the *regal* character. We may extend the remark, by
saying of them that they partake mostly of the regal, and
the victorious or triumphal character, joined together. The
divine person predicted is shewn as a king; but "there is
the rod of His power sent forth;" and "He rules among
His enemies." That is to say, Prophecy has impressed
upon the Jewish subject, in the fortunes and successes of
the house of David, the corresponding anticipations of the
victories of Christ and His religion[h]. By which adaptation the Israelite was taught by what he saw passing before his eyes, in those times of triumph and exultation, to
transfer his ideas and feelings the more readily to the
second the more distant scene. His faith was assisted by
the materials of his present experience, which prophecy
moulded to the other object, that of Christ's kingdom.

V. It is observable also, that David himself, rather
than any other Prophet, is made the promulger of the
chief prophecies of Christ, communicated to this age. He
names Him as "his Lord[i]," and his predictions speak the
same homage and honour to His person, His law, and His
power. Whereby the royal Prophet effectualiy turns our
observation, much more our reverence, from himself to
his Greater. He is not the prophet of his own grandeur;
Samuel and Nathan conveyed to him the message of that;
but he is of the Messiah's; and he who had first received
the temporal promises, reveals and magnifies the Lord of
the future kingdom. May we not confess a significant
fitness in this method?

VI. Moreover an excellent provision was made to secure
the memory and impression of these great Christian pro-

---

[h] The *sufferings* of Christ have also a place, in the 22nd Psalm. But it
is remarkable that although some particulars of that Psalm are specially
pointed to our Saviour (as in ver. 18), the Psalm itself discloses no such personal appropriation of them. It begins and proceeds in the name of David.
Consequently the right prophetic sense of this Psalm could not be understood
till later times.   [i] Psalm cx.

phecies, and their use to the ends of a present faith and piety, from the time when they were delivered. For they were conveyed in the poetry of Hymns and Psalms, and so passed into the devotions, public and private, of the Church of Israel. Those Psalms were the greatest addition which had hitherto been made to the proper stock of the Mosaic revelation; and we see what kind of prophecy entered largely into their sense. By them, the devotions of the Israelite had imprinted upon them a Christian hope, and by them the faithful worshipper in the first temple offered praise to the Messiah in the sacred song of prophecy, as soon as there were any clear revelations made of the dignity of His person and His kingdom. For it is not to be forgotten that the prophetic Psalms are among the earliest discoveries made of the exalted nature and proper dignity of Christ. The promise of the blessing to come by the seed of Abraham shewed the magnitude of the benefit, but not the personal glory of the Benefactor. In the Psalms[k] His personal attributes and His divine Sonship invest the prophecy, and introduce the object of worship.

VII. Lastly, lest it should be surmised that the predictions of this age were framed, in the common strain of the diviner's art, to the flattery of kings, prognosticating the future greatness of their line, we observe that the same Prophet, who had the mission to reveal to David the establishment of his throne, was also the messenger of his shame and rebuke, and of the divine anger upon him for his most opprobrious personal transgression[l]. In each case it is Nathan who is the prophetic Seer. So also the glory of Solomon's reign, which bore so many prognostics of favour upon it, concludes with the opposite scene of his corruption and apostasy, and the consequent comminations of Prophecy[m]. It is true, the elaborate record which is made of these afflicting instances of man's frailty and transgression, has its first use to other ends, of a moral nature;

---

[k] See the whole of Psalms ii. xlv. cx.

[l] 2 Sam. vii. 12.—xii. 1.   [m] 1 Kings xi. 11.

but it has an oblique, and no less certain use, in excluding the imputation of deceit from the prophecies which are joined with it. The prophetic document is guarded with testimonials of its integrity, which denote it to be what it claims to be, the witness of Truth, not the interpreter of human vanity or folly.

Having so far explained the general state of Prophecy at this period, I must advert once more to the *Temporal* part of it, and shew how it was delivered and how fulfilled. For the temporal sense was the first to take place, and it is a true sense, intended by the Spirit of God, and witnessed in the completion; and we shall very imperfectly understand or estimate the Prophecies, unless we consent to follow them through the intentions of that Wisdom whose dictates they are.

Now Prophecy in this case is partly absolute, partly conditional. It is absolute, as to a difference which God would put between the house of Saul and that of David, by granting to the last a duration of power which to the other He had denied: "My mercy shall not depart from him as I took it away from Saul whom I put away before thee [n]." It is conditional, inasmuch as the actual duration of power is implicated in the piety and demeanour of the descendants of his family. More than once the condition is set by the side of the promise; "*If* thy children take heed to their way, to walk before Me in truth with all their heart, and with all their soul, there shall not fail thee a man on the throne of Israel [o]." Such was the moral compact on which Prophecy suspended its promise, that no unwarranted confidence in an immutable and irrespective decree might abuse to presumption God's stipulated favour. This is one view of the prediction.

But yet the terms of the Prophecy imply, indeed they express, an eternity of dominion to be enjoyed. "Thy house and thy kingdom shall be established for ever." In what sense could such words be taken? What is this "for ever?" To explain them, I shall not stand upon the right of blend-

[n] 2 Sam. vii. 15.   [o] 1 Kings ii. 4.—ix. 4.

ing the two subjects together, the temporal and the Gospel kingdom, for the sake of assuring to the prophecy a literal eternity, which can be had only in the Gospel kingdom; but taking a principle of Scripture language, I state that the phrase "for ever" is known to express a relative eternity, an unbroken perpetuity for a given time, holding on through a period or system of things, to which a reference is understood to be made. In fact no thrones upon earth shall or can last strictly for ever: they have their rise, and they have their end; and their eternity is no more than can be spanned by the small measures of time. There was, therefore, a relative term of continuance intended in that phrase, as descriptive of David's temporal kingdom. The measure might be either the whole duration of the Jewish polity, or the whole duration of the kingdom, if kings ceased to reign before the polity came to an end. It turned out that these two periods were not commensurate; for the polity survived the kingdom. But the one or the other must supply the understood limit of the earthly succession.

Such then was the sense of the temporal prediction; and the event sustained it. To the latest day of the kingdom, the heirs and descendants of David possessed it; they survived, and were kings in Jerusalem, without failure, or interruption of their line. Whereas in the opposed dynasty, which arose, and ruled the other branch of the kingdom after it was divided, the interruptions of it were as remarkable for their frequency and violence. In the kingdom of Samaria, deposal and usurpation were its habit. God took away the entire stock, first of Jeroboam's [p], and next of Baasha's house [q]. The usurpations of Zimri and Omri followed. Then Ahab's house was cut off [r]. Jehu succeeded; but God limited his succession to the fourth generation [s]; from which time to the end of the kingdom of Samaria there is nothing but a series of successful conspiracy and intrusion into the throne. The result is, that there is a series of descent unbroken in the one line,

[p] 1 Kings xv. 29.
[r] 2 Kings x. 10.

[q] 1 Kings xvi. 11.
[s] 2 Kings xv. 12.

and no continuity of it in the other. The family of David possessed his throne four hundred and fifty years, which indeed is not a great compass of time, but they possessed it till both king and people were carried into captivity; whilst the succession of the separated kingdom, with all its anomalies and changes, lasted but two hundred and fifty. And it is this contrast of things which placed before men's eyes, both the *sense*, and the *truth*, of the promise given in favour to David. But further; in the perpetuation of David's throne, the succession is by son after son; and when in some instances the reigning king was cut off, still his place is supplied by a son in the same line and order of descent. This is a fact strictly ascertained throughout the genealogy; and the evidence of it is obtruded upon us by the recurring phrase at the end of so many reigns,—"his son reigned in his stead." According to what had been foretold, "There shall not fail thee a man in My sight to sit on the throne of Israel [t]." Take then the entire circumstances of the two kingdoms. On the side of that of *Israel*, Three complete extirpations of the reigning families [u], each distinctly foretold; the deposition of the house of Jehu in the fourth generation, this also foretold ; with other confusions of the order of the kingdom. On the side of *Judah*, One family, through a longer period of time, One line, to the end of the kingdom [x]. There was therefore something stable and fixed in this comparative state of David's house, whilst it lay open to the inroad of the same causes of change; something which bespoke a protecting care. There was a security which even great transgression in its kings could not forfeit. Insurrection and conspiracy could not subvert it. Athaliah's sanguinary domestic treason could not defeat it. The confederacy of Syria and Ephraim, leagued to set up a new king in Jerusalem, could not disturb it. The great flood of the Assyrian invasion could not overwhelm it [y]. These are facts ; and they are

[t] 1 Kings viii. 25.   [u] Extirpations πανωλεθρίᾳ πανοικεί.   [x] 2 Kings xxi. 24.

[y] For these points, one by one, see the following passages: 1 Kings ix. 32; 2 Kings ix. 10 xxi. 24. xi. 3; Isaiah vii. 6; 2 Kings xix. 34.

facts in which the public annals of the two kingdoms could not be falsified. There was then a special Providence in the preservation of that one family and throne. It was upheld when ruin was around it. The fact of its preservation is a rock upon which Prophecy will rest.

Perhaps few persons read the history of these two kingdoms without some feeling of distaste and a painful repugnance : the general picture of it is so dark, so deeply charged with the crimes of bad princes, and an imitative people; their bold sin, public unthankfulness, apostasy, wars, tumults, and treasons. In the midst of this confused scene, it is some relief to watch the stability of prophecy, and perceive that the disorders and commotions, otherwise so distasteful, contribute to authenticate the veracity of one promise of God. There is a fixed point, a spot of light, for the mind to revert to. It is that of a prophecy always under trial, and always confirmed. Add to that prophecy its singular connexion with Christianity, and its confirmation touches upon our Christian belief. For Christ is " the root and offspring of David;" and the prophecies relating to both are in their evidence connected together.

To preserve the unity of the subject which we have in hand, it will be right to look forward here to the end of it. As this favoured kingdom rose upon the word of prophecy, its dissolution was marked in the same way. Jeremiah had one special mission to the house of the king of Judah. " Thus saith the Lord, Go down to the *house of the king* of Judah, and speak there this word : and say, Hear the word of the Lord, O king of Judah, that sittest upon *the throne of David.*" The burden of the prediction is the memorable text which follows; " O earth, earth, earth, hear the word of the Lord. Thus saith the Lord, *Write ye this man childless,* a man that shall not prosper in his days : for *no man of his seed* shall prosper, sitting *upon the throne of David, and ruling any more in Judah* [z]."

<hr>

[z] Jeremiah xxii. 29, 30.

The deep pathetic force of this chapter of prophecy cannot be unknown; but it must be read also in another view, as God's solemn revocation of the title to the earthly kingdom. It is His interdict laid upon the house of David; the withering of that sceptre which He had blessed. Why that invocation, "O earth, earth, earth, hear the word of the Lord;" but to attest the departure of the favour and prerogative of His promise? Nothing but His former word, sealing the promise, could have created the appeal, or given the earth an ear to listen to that invocation. But what is there for the world to listen to, if it be not these promulgations wherein God explains His righteous government over the kings and families of the earth, and proclaims the repeal of His most distinguished favour, when the transgression of man has wrought the defeasance of it?

From the time when prophecy passed this sentence of deprivation upon the person of Coniah, (or Jeconias,) there is an end of the power and lustre of the house of David; for as to the precarious and tumultuary reign of Zedekiah, who was set up for a few years by the king of Babylon, before the Captivity, or the transient delegated authority of Zerubbabel, after it, they make no exception of any moment to the perfect execution of that sentence. The people were restored, but not the kingdom. It fell, it lay prostrate, till Christ came, and repaired its ruins on a new foundation, in His greater kingdom[a]."

---

[a] Calvin, upon the text in Jeremiah, says, "Gratia Dei *abscondita erat et interrupta, non autem extincta ;* successu enim temporis rursus emersit, *partim* in *Zorobabele,* sed præcipue in Christo. *Fœdus ergo Dei nunquam excidit.*" Which comment of that great writer is a warning example, to shew how far the desire of accommodating Scripture to an hypothesis may wrest its interpretation. For the *temporal* dominion of David's house lasted *four hundred and fifty years ;* and it lay deprived, before the coming of Christ, for *a longer period,* even if the prosperous times of Zerubbabel be added to the former account. Consequently, we might as well say it was *not given,* as that it was *not taken away.* But the *conditional* tenor of it was made as clear as the most expressive language could make it. It runs thus: "There shall not fail thee a man to sit on the throne of Israel, *so that* thy children take heed to

The reign and success of the Maccabees, which intervened before the coming of Christ, make a bright epoch in the later history. But herein the removal of David's temporal throne was shewn the more, when the favour and glory of that prosperous time were given neither to his family, nor even to any family of the tribe of Judah. The reign of the Maccabees, and that of Herod, equally attest the continued cessation of the temporal promise in the house of David. But this long loss of God's favour was a preparative to make the restoration of it the more distinguished, when at last it appeared in the person of Christ. And perhaps we have ground to think that the intermediate deliverers were providentially chosen from the family of Aaron, for this reason among others; to exclude the idea, that in that momentary tide of success, the great promises of God given to Israel through the house of David, and in the tribe of Judah, were beginning to be revived. For the Maccabees, liberators of their country, and restorers of its public religion and worship, might have seemed to realize some of the chief prophetic hopes, had they been of the lineage to which those hopes were annexed; and there were no living inspired prophets to correct the mistake. But their family and tribe left the sense of the prophecies entire, and made it

their way that they walk before Me, as thou hast walked before Me." 1 Kings viii. 25. ii. 4. The event is consistent therewith; but the author was unwilling either to read the *condition*, or see the truth of the *fact*, however conspicuous.

The genealogy of Zerubbabel is not quite clear. The opinion which makes him by *birth* the grandson of Jeconias (Coniah) is adopted by a learned Prelate, the present Bishop of Winchester. "Zerubbabel, frequently called in Scripture Shashbazzar, was the *grandson of Jeconias*, and consequently descended from David." Elements of Christian Theology. But that opinion is scarcely to be reconciled with the rigorous denunciation of Jeremiah, "*Write this man childless.*" Under the conviction that this sentence was executed in the total excision of Coniah's offspring, and that he was *written childless* in the *genealogies* of Israel, if *childless* be the true sense of the word in the original, I was inclined to follow the idea of Grotius; viz., Zerubbabel the son of Salathiel; but Salathiel *hæres Assiris,* et *Jeconiæ* hæres *legitimus, non naturalis.*—Grot. in Luc. iii. 23. But see a further consideration of this point in a note at the end of the volume.

clear that the time was yet to come when God would visit "the throne and kingdom of David, to order it and establish it with judgment and with justice for ever."

Having thus shewn how Prophecy stood with respect to this kingdom at its beginning, and at its end; and also how it is connected with the kingdom of the Gospel, founded in the same line of promise; I return to the second head of my arrangement, the Reign of Solomon.

II. His reign, as had been foretold, was distinguished by its tranquillity and peace; as also by its wealth, its extent of power, and other attributes of a great and flourishing prosperity. For "he had dominion, and he had peace on all sides round about him. And Judah and Israel dwelt safely, every man under his vine and under his fig-tree, from Dan even to Beer-sheba, all the days of Solomon[b]." One of the monuments, and indeed the greatest, which rose out of his reign, was the Temple of Jerusalem. It had been a command and a prediction that he should build this edifice in his days the best suited to such a work[c]. "I will give peace and quietness unto Israel in his days; he shall build a house for My Name." Of the beauty and grandeur of this fabric we may judge something by the eulogy of its description, which has come down to us, and something more by the tears of those who in a later age beheld it unequally replaced by a second. Its visible splendour was such as became the majesty of religion. But it was its religion, and its ordinances of worship, and, above all, the prerogative of the divine approbation and blessing resting upon it, as "the place which God had chosen to put His Name there;" which were its greater boast and praise.

Among its other glories the rays of prophecy issue from this temple. Its dedication was a festival to all Israel; and in the rites of inaugural sacrifice and worship which hallowed it to its first use, a confession of antecedent pro-

[b] 1 Kings iv. 25.   [c] 1 Chron. xxii. 8, 9.

phecy takes the lead of Solomon's other acts of devotion, and is made the basis on which he rests his grateful exultation.

" Solomon stood before the altar of the Lord, in the presence of all the congregation of Israel, and spread forth his hands—towards heaven, and said, Lord God of Israel, there is no God like Thee in heaven above, or in earth beneath, who keepest covenant and mercy with Thy servants that walk before Thee with all their hearts: Thou which hast kept with Thy servant David my father, that which Thou hast promised him, and spakest with Thy mouth, and *hast fulfilled it with Thine hand*, as it is this day [d]."

This acknowledgment of predicted favour *fulfilled*, is followed by the prayer of hope claiming the accomplishment of other remaining predictions.

" Now therefore, O Lord God of Israel, keep with Thy servant David my father, that which Thou hast promised him, saying, There shall not fail thee a man in thy sight to sit upon the throne of Israel; yet so that thy children take heed to their way to walk in My law, as thou hast walked before Me. Now then, O Lord God of Israel, let Thy word be verified which Thou hast spoken unto Thy servant David."

On which be it observed, what a conspicuous place is assigned to Prophecy on this occasion. It is the prophetic revelation which breathes life into the Temple, and fills the mouth of its builder. And next, how such a mention of past and subsisting predictions, a mention made in the hearing of all Israel, certifies the fact that they were so fulfilled and so known. For how could this wise king have uttered a confession of prayer, to which, if unsupported by the case, his people might have given the ready contradiction? Or how could such a confession be ascribed to him if he uttered it not? It is one of the many *recognitions* of prophecy which are put forward in the front of the public transactions of their history, and establish its notoriety, and thereby its evidence. These predictions were not " uttered in a corner," nor were they kept out of mind.

<hr>

[d] 2 Chron. vi. 12, &c.

But the Temple itself was a Prophecy. So it was designed to be. The building of it was directed for this reason, that God had given " rest to His people," and henceforth would not suffer them to wander or be disturbed; so long as they enjoyed the privilege of being *His people* at all. "Moreover, *I will appoint a place for My people Israel;* and will plant them, that they may *dwell in a place of their own, and move no more* [e]." This promise of rest is connected with the Temple; for it was spoken when God confirmed and commanded the design of building it. A *fixed Sanctuary* of their Religion was the most appropriate token they could receive of the stability of their national fortunes; and to a people who had been pilgrims in Canaan, strangers in Egypt, wanderers in the Desert, and who even in Canaan again had sought a home for their religion in the removals of their migratory Ark, such a sign of final settlement and rest would be sensibly understood. "Whereas I have not dwelt in any house, since the time that I brought up the children of Israel out of Egypt, even to this day, *but have walked in a tent and in a tabernacle* [f]." As the seat of their Religion, and the habitation of the Divine Presence among them, this Fabric became the greatest glory of their land; and it was the one security which hitherto had been wanting to complete the repose and consolidation of their state. Men raise temples and other fabrics of costly labour upon the *presumption* of an assured continuance. But when a command of God is given for the work, the very fact of His command is a pledge of the stability of that system of things to which the work is directed. But here the pledge, virtually implied, was also explicitly given. "I will plant them, that they may dwell in a place of their own, and move no more." Such was the divine appointment and constitution in this matter.

It will be said that neither They, nor their Temple, had a lasting continuance: they were cast into captivity; it was burnt to the ground; and where then is this first prophecy respecting the destiny of their Temple? True; if

[e] 2 Samuel vii. 10.   [f] vii. 6.

their guilt deserved that doom, their Temple was not to be a spell to disarm the divine judgment. But this again is true, that their national estate was thenceforth attached to this Temple. It fell with them. When they returned and became a people again, it rose also. It was the place which the Almighty had "chosen to set His Name there," the record and instrument of His covenant with them, the acknowledged and authorized seat of their worship upon which their covenant stood. Excepting around this Temple, they had never been ab'e to settle themselves as a people, nor find a public home for their nation or their religion. It and they stood and fell together; and God has never transferred that seat by any *second* designation of a place substituted in the stead of it, for the exercise of their religion; nor can they pretend that He has done so. So that the long desolation of their Temple, and their lasting removal from the seat of it, are no inconsiderable proofs that their polity and peculiar law are come to an end in the purposes of Providence, and according to the intention of the Temple-appointment, as well as in the fact. The unrevoked destruction of that fane of their religion is one visible repeal of the religion itself, and a sign of the termination of their state as the peculiar people of God. He made it their "resting-place." If it exist no more, it is a proof that they have ceased to be His people.

Yet this Temple was reared with the sanctity of a blessing upon it, such as no other material and local edifice of religion in the world has ever received. Never was it said of any other seat of worship, "*Mine eyes shall be opened*, and *Mine ears attent* unto the prayer that is made *in this place*. For now have I chosen and sanctified this house, that My Name may be there for ever; and Mine eyes and Mine heart shall be there perpetually[g]." Thus spoke the mercy of God in answer to the prayers of its builder. What a felicity to the builder! what a sanction and privilege to his work! But as Moses, the Founder

g 1 Kings ix. 3; 2 Chron. vii. 15, 16.

of the commonwealth of Israel, was inspired to warn his people, in the height of their first union and growth into power, of their future afflictions and dispersion, so the Founder of this temple, the appointed abode of their religion, had foreshewn to him a view of its overthrow and destruction by the avenging hand of the Almighty, as one of the special acts of His judgment to be executed upon them. "Then will I cut off Israel out of the land which I have given them; and *this house*, which I have hallowed for My Name, *will I cast out of My sight*, and Israel shall be a proverb and a by-word among all people: *and at this house*, which is high, every one that passeth by it shall be *astonished*, and *shall hiss;* and they shall say, *Why hath the Lord done thus* unto this land, and *to this house*[h]?" Such was the oracular vision given to Solomon on his completion of this sacred edifice.

Except under the dictate of a constraining Inspiration, it is not easy to conceive how the master of such a work, at the time when he had brought it to perfection, and beheld it in its lustre, the labour of so much opulent magnificence and curious art, and designed to be "exceeding magnifical, of *fame*, and of *glory* throughout all countries[i]," should be occupied with the prospect of its utter ruin and dilapidation, and that too under the *opprobrium* of God's vindictive judgment upon it; nor to imagine how that strain of sinister prophecy, that foreboding of malediction, should be ascribed to him, if he had no such vision revealed. The contemplation of the hazards of vicissitude and decay which human greatness, with all its works, is heir to, is natural enough, we know, to great minds; but not natural at all seasons, nor particularly with a view to their own works and achievements. The builder seldom

[h] 1 Kings ix. 7, 8. In 2 Chron. vii. 20. "*This house* will I cast out of My sight, and will make *it* to be *a proverb*, and a *by-word* among all nations."

[i] 1 Chron. xxii. 5.

wishes to raise that kind of contemplation upon the forecast of his own ruins: the moralizing spirit seeks a subject elsewhere. Such restraints and humiliating checks of self-abasement, would be a great wisdom; but as I have remarked in the similar prediction of Moses, they are altogether unlike the bent of man's own feeling and wisdom. "Is not this *great Babylon* that I have built for the house of the kingdom, by the might of my power, and for the honour of my majesty [k]?" This was the arrogancy of an elated king: but the bias of nature, and the ordinary movement of human feeling, bears the same way. Men are kings of Babylon, according to the scale of their works; unless some "vision of God," some great light of religion, descend upon them. But Solomon's *calm* and *deliberate* anticipation of the *judicial* doom of his Temple is something more than a suppression of the vainglory of nature.

It were a mere want of reflection upon the history of the two cases, to think of setting this prophetic Vision of Solomon's on a level with the sentiment of the Roman conqueror of Carthage, when he beheld that city in flames, and straightway turning his thoughts upon his own country, broke out into the expression of feeling which is so well known [l]. But as I understand that this subject of comparison has been proposed by some persons as not so totally remote in its kind, let it be examined for a moment. —In the instance of the Roman chief, the sight of *one ruin, one* scene of *devastation,* in the fiery wreck of a city lately the seat of a great and flourishing empire, suggests the idea of *another ruin;* no uncommon train of thought. And, as Rome had before this scene a Carthaginian army at her gates, the possible *transition* of power was a trite topic to Scipio. But neither Rome, nor its empire, was *Scipio's work,* much less his present work, the new creation of his power; so that neither the *origin* of the sentiment, nor the *self-denial* of it, makes any approach in the two cases. Add to which, that if the Roman, with his enlarged

[k] Dan. iv. 30.

[l] Polyb. Histor. apud Appian. Bell. Pun., cap. 82.

mind, touched with a sense of the general instability of
human empire and greatness, spoke or reasoned ever so
well, he did it with a wisdom which the event has proved
to be very unlike to that which was imparted to Solomon.
For *Rome remains*, though Carthage is gone: the similar
fate of *deletion* has not come; and if it should yet come,
none would ascribe a true prescience of it to Scipio. But
where is the Temple? Long ago it has attested in its
ashes, and that twice, the prescience of Solomon's vision[m].
So I believe it will always be found on the examination,
that the Scripture Prophecies have their exclusive signatures, and whatever be the supposed *parallel*, it fails in
the trial.

With Solomon's distant foresight of the ruin of the
Temple must be joined what later Prophets foretold, when
that ruin was near at hand. Jeremiah had his mission on
this particular subject: he received not only a prophecy to
deliver, but a charge to deliver that prophecy in a singular
manner fitted to the occasion[n]. He was sent to stand *in*

---

[m] Burnt down, first by the Babylonians, next by the Romans, in each case,
on the *same day* of the *same month*, viz., the 10th day of the month Lous,
says Josephus de Bello Jud. VI. IV. 5. A striking *coincidence*, if it was correctly true, to create attention to the main substance of the prophecy.
Τοῦ δὲ ἄρα κατεψήφιστο μὲν τὸ πῦρ ὁ Θεὸς πάλαι· παρῆν δ' ἡ εἱμαρμένη χρόνων
περίοδος, ἡμέρᾳ δεκάτῃ Λώου μηνὸς, καθ' ἣν καὶ τὸ πρότερον ὑπὸ τοῦ τῶν Βαβυ-
λωνίων βασιλέως ἐνεπρήσθη. Conf. sect. 8.

[n] I must cite at large a portion of this prophecy, which *deserves to be
studied* in every line of it. "The word that came to Jeremiah from the
Lord, saying, *Stand in the gate* of the Lord's house, and proclaim there this
word, and say, Hear the word of the Lord, *all ye of Judah that enter in at
these gates, to worship the Lord.* Thus saith the Lord of hosts, the God of
Israel, Amend your ways and your doings, and I will cause you to dwell in
this place. *Trust ye not* in lying words, saying, *The temple of the Lord, The
temple of the Lord, The temple of the Lord, are these.* For if ye throughly
amend your ways and your doings; if ye throughly execute judgment between
a man and his neighbour; if ye oppress not the stranger, the fatherless, and
the widow, and shed not innocent blood in this place, neither walk after other
gods, to your hurt; Then will I cause you to dwell in this place, in the land
that I gave to your fathers, for ever and ever. Behold, ye trust in lying
words, that cannot profit. Will ye steal, murder, and commit adultery, and
swear falsely, and burn incense unto Baal, and walk after other gods, whom ye

the gate of the Temple, and there proclaim, in the concourse of public resort, *to the worshippers* who entered, *its approaching desolation.* The energy and pathos of the moral lesson which is incorporated with this prediction render it one of the most instructive parts of the book of prophecy. For when those worshippers looked to that place as their protecting sanctuary, whatever their life and practice; when they "came there, and stood before God," with the pollution of every broken commandment upon them; and confiding in the externals of religion and the privileges annexed to that seat of worship, cried, "The temple of the Lord, The temple of the Lord, The temple of the Lord;" then was the time that their false religion was exposed; then came the denunciation of prophecy levelled at the fortress of their trust, that Holy Place which their pollutions had desecrated from its service. "I will do unto this house, which is called by My name, wherein *ye trust,* and *unto the place which I gave to you and to your fathers,* as I have done to Shiloh[o]."

The approaching *destruction* of the temple was thus foretold by Jeremiah. But the subsequent *rebuilding* of it had been previously foreshewn by Isaiah, as a part of the restoration appointed to come by the hand of Cyrus.

know not; and *come and stand before Me in this house, which is called by My name,* and say, We are delivered to do all these abominations? *Is this house, which is called by My name, become a den of robbers* in your eyes? Behold, even I have seen it, saith the Lord. But go ye now unto My place which was in Shiloh, where I set My name at first, and *see what I did to it,* for the wickedness of My people Israel. And now, because ye have done all these works, saith the Lord, and I spake unto you, rising up early and speaking, but ye heard not; and I called you, but ye answered not; Therefore *will I do unto this house,* which is called *by My name, wherein ye trust,* and *unto the place* which I *gave to you,* and *to your fathers,* as *I have done to Shiloh.* And I will cast *you* out of My sight, as I have cast out all your brethren, even the whole seed of Ephraim. Therefore *pray not thou for this people,* neither lift up cry nor prayer for them, neither make intercession to Me; *for I will not hear thee.*"—Jerem. chap. vii. Compare chap. xxvi.

[o] For this prediction, Jeremiah was *questioned* and *arraigned* before the Priests, the Prophets, and all the Princes of the land[*]. The public *place* where it is said to have been uttered, (viz., the *Gate* of the *Temple,*) and the *commotion* which it excited, verify the fact that it was so spoken.

[*] Chap. xxvii.

"That saith of Cyrus, He is My shepherd, and shall perform all My pleasure, even saying to Jerusalem, Thou shalt be built, and *to the Temple, Thy foundation shall be laid*[p]." And as Jeremiah's clear and open prediction announced the ruin of the First Temple, so the prediction of Christ, spoken equally in sight of the place, announced in a similar manner the desolation of the Second. From all which particulars put together we deduce this fact, that *every part* of the *history* of the *Temple* was made a subject of prophecy. For it was God's own Institution, at its first Building. Hence the fitness why its fall should be solemnly and publicly foretold. Its Restoration was by His Command. Hence the equal fitness of the second prediction of its final ruin. And in neither case was the event foreshewn by *allusion*, or by *obscure, remote intimation*; but in each the prophecy was *open*, and delivered *within view of the devoted place*.

This combination leads me to point out a general congruity, which may be perceived in some other prophecies, and which I may express by saying,—that there was *no one* considerable Ordinance, or Appointment of God, under the First Dispensation, which was permitted to pass away, or be withdrawn, silently or by stealth; but prophecies the most definite and expressive always preceded the abolition or suspension of the ordinance in question. The chief of those ordinances may be thus enumerated: The gift of Canaan; the Mosaic covenant; the Mosaic worship; the Hebrew people itself, as the peculiar people of God; the temporal kingdom of David[q]; the Temple. Every one of these ordinances and appointments passed away; but the intelligent reader of prophecy will know that none of them was either abolished, or suspended, without the distinct

[p] Isaiah xliv. 28.

[q] Observe, *no such solemn personal mission* of a prophet, *nor equally formal and copious prophecy*, is seen to introduce the cessation of the kingly line in *Samaria*, as that of Jeremiah, with respect to the kingly line in *Jerusalem*. The reader will see that the difference corresponds with the special appointment and engaged promise of God which obtained in the one case, and not in the other. *Hoshea*, the last king of *Israel*, is set aside with a comparative obscurity and neglect.

information of prophecy previously given. The *temporary* loss of the Temple, and the *partial* loss of Canaan, under the captivity of Babylon, were foreshewn, and so also the *division* and *diminution* of the Temporal kingdom, as much as the *final* abolition of any of those appointments.

Whence I infer this *general Proposition*, That it was one office of Prophecy to give the adequate information concerning *the special institutions* of God's covenant; and those things which He had Himself ordained were not suffered to undergo any visible change, with a less comment upon them than that of His revealed prophetic word. Accordingly, a religious Israelite had in the prophecies a faithful account of God's government, as it respected His first dispensation, as well as the presages and hopes of a better. And no doubt his study of them, under the frequent shocks and vicissitudes of that Economy, was rewarded with many important observations, many supports to his faith and his knowledge, and thereby to his piety and virtue, which to us, in a cursory view of the prophecies as mere *predictions*, will pass unregarded or imperfectly valued :—a great reason for our looking into them with a more judicious attention.

I have thus considered the general state of Prophecy in the reigns of David and Solomon, as to the *Temporal Kingdom*, and *the Temple*, which had their origin in those reigns. I have also taken a view of the information given by later prophecy concerning the *removal* of the one, and the *destruction* of the other, and so far connected the prophetic notices relating severally to each of those important objects of the first covenant. I shall end my observations on this Age of Prophecy by adverting to an older prediction, which now claimed attention by its accomplishment seen in a conspicuous manner at this period.

" *Judah, thou art he whom thy brethren shall praise;* thy hand shall be in the neck of thine enemies : *thy father's children shall bow down before thee*[r]." It will be remembered that the whole scope of Jacob's prophecy was to the

<hr/>

[r] Genesis xlix. 8.

Tribes, not the individual persons of his children ; and I would ask what apparent clue he could have, except by revelation, to his foresight of the superiority and ascendency of the tribe of Judah ? As to his sons, the founders of the Tribes, they were on a level, excepting the Eldest, who might have the advantage by his right of Primogeniture; or Joseph, whose power in Egypt was his own, and might pass to the aggrandizement of his particular off-spring. But Judah was not the eldest, and in the partition of Canaan the Tribes took by lot. The prediction however did not go beyond the fact. A character of superiority attaches to this tribe whenever there is room for the comparison. In all great questions the men of Judah are the foremost and strongest. From the time of David's establishment on the throne, the greatness of the Tribe follows in some measure that of his family. " His father's children did then bow down before Judah." Let David himself connect the prophecy and the event : " Howbeit the Lord God of Israel chose me before all the house of my father, to be king over Israel for ever; for he *hath chosen Judah to be the ruler;* and of the house of Judah the house of my father; and among the sons of my father he liked to make me king over all Israel[s]."

Here was a completion of the prophecy, obvious and true to its unquestionable sense. An Israelite could not look at his country in the days of David and Solomon without reading there the words of Jacob fulfilled. And whatever other sense the prophecy may be thought to bear, it can bear none to exclude this. But after what has been said in defence and explanation of the *Twofold Sense* of *some* parts of prophecy, I think we shall be justified in adding the *Christian* to the *Temporal* accomplishment of this which is before us. There is at least a clear correspondence between the two. For in the Gospel age, the converts from among the remnant of the Twelve Tribes[t] *bowed down* to Christ and His religion : and " *the Lion of*

---

[s] 1 Chron. xxxviii. 4. So 1 Chron. v. 2. For *Judah* prevailed *above his brethren*, and of him was *the chief ruler*, but the *birthright* was *Joseph's*.

[t] St. James i. 1.

the tribe of Judah, the *root* of *David,*" is one of the Scripture characters of Christ[u]. Far greater will this second completion of it be made, when, according to other prophecies, the whole body of Israel shall be converted, and bow down before the same Lord.

But if a more jealous judgment must restrict the sense of this prophecy to the *temporal* pre-eminence of Judah, there is one view to be taken of it in which I think all judgments will agree. When we read in one and the same portion of the Patriarch's prediction, first, " Judah, thou art he whom thy brethren shall *praise; thy father's children shall bow down before thee:*" and next, " the sceptre shall *not depart from Judah,* nor a lawgiver from between his feet, *until Shiloh come,* and unto Him shall the gathering of the people be;" I argue that the accomplishment of the first, which was made so visible in David's reign, could not fail to draw attention to the second. When they saw the purposes of God unfold themselves in the tribe of Judah, with a singular pre-eminence of favour to that tribe, men must have been induced to think the more upon that other yet undisclosed object of the second prediction; they must have been drawn to consider for what end the tribe of Judah was to have its sceptre prolonged, and who " the Shiloh," the Sent of God, might be, to whose coming that great and favoured tribe was to be preserved in power. For the minds of men kindle into expectation on the sight of one part of a prophecy fulfilled: and such in the reign of David, and in the times following, we may conclude to have been the effect, with regard to this other prediction of the Patriarch's which waited yet for its elucidation and fulfilment; the effect I mean upon serious and considerate persons, who cared to attend to the prophecies, and direct their hopes by them. The contents of the prophetic Psalms would reinforce the same kind of observation.

<hr>

[u] Rev. v. 5.

DISCOURSE VI.

————◆————

PART I. *Temporal* Prophecy relating to the *Hebrew People,*
from the Time of *Solomon* to the *Restoration*
from Babylon.

II. *Christian* Prophecy ⎫
III. *Pagan* Prophecy ⎬ during the same Period.

IV. Last Age of Prophecy, from the *End* of the
Captivity to its *Cessation.*

————◆————

AMOS iii. 7.

*Surely, the Lord God will do nothing, but He revealeth
His secret unto His servants the prophets.*

THEY who have not turned their minds to consider the
actual contents of ancient Prophecy, may not be aware
how nearly it amounts to a complete history of the Hebrew
people, that people of God to whom it was given: a complete history, not indeed through the whole of their Annals,
but through that great period of them which includes the
most remarkable changes of their condition, and during
which the mission of Prophecy lasted: that period comprehending the time from the commencement of their
Monarchy to their resettlement after the Babylonian bondage and the restoration of their Temple. Within these
limits I believe it to be nearly the fact, that there is no
known event of any magnitude, affecting them as a people,

which had not its place in the antecedent warnings of prophecy; nothing befell them, which was not foretold; the apparent case of prophecy fully supporting this declaration of one of its messengers: " Surely, the Lord God will do nothing, but He revealeth His secret unto His servants the prophets." Through so full a probation did Prophecy pass in maintaining its cause with a people little disposed to a gratuitous conviction; and so great an insight did it afford into the Providential Government of God, to those among them who, with a more susceptible mind, sought that kind of instruction, and found it, as they might well do, in the explanations of their prophetic Oracles. In a certain sense, History has been justly called the interpreter of Prophecy; but to the Israelite, Prophecy was more the interpreter of History; for it gave him the intelligible notice of the approaching events, and it supplied him with the reasons of God's Providence in bringing those events to pass.

Prophecy did not inform the Israelite in so systematic a way of the changes destined to take place in other states and kingdoms. There is a plain reason why it should not; for in those alien affairs he was not equally concerned, and of the truth and prescience of the predictions of them he could not always be so good a judge. But it opened enough of the history of those kingdoms, which lay within his sphere of view, to instruct him in the *general* Providence and Government of God; whilst in his own particular dispensation it was more watchful and constant.

I have now to follow it in its progress; and the *completeness* of its revelation, in that sense in which I have described it as complete, will be one point among others which my investigation will go to establish. The *Division of the Kingdom* was the next Epoch in the arrangement to which I proposed to adhere, and I proceed to the prophecy connected with that Epoch.

I. With the peaceful and prosperous reign of Solomon ended the glory of the kingdom of Israel. There straightway ensued the great change, in the dismemberment of the kingdom, by the revolt of the Ten Tribes from Rehoboam, Solomon's son, and the establishment of a separate kingdom under Jeroboam : Judah, with Benjamin annexed, alone adhering to the house of David.

This was a convulsion in the whole body of Israel. Their monarchy, so lately compacted and settled, rent in pieces; their public union, under which they had originally been made subjects of the divine Covenant, broken; and a cause of discord, if not of a more active hostility, rooted between the members of the great Commonwealth, which God had planted in Canaan in a community of Country and Religion. It was a change which raised a question as to their covenanted relation; and this effect of it gives it its chief importance. For where did the promises of God, attached to that relation, rest? With Israel, or with Judah? or with both? or were they forfeited?

The shock was not permitted to take place without the prior information of prophecy to unravel the maze of things so disordered. The event itself had been foretold in Solomon's reign, by the prophet Ahijah, and other prophecy supplied discriminating marks of the purposes of Providence now in operation. For let us consider. There were the predictions of the ascendency of power to the Tribe of Judah, and the continuance of its Sceptre, that is, of its public existence and civil union, till the advent of the Messiah : there were the recent promises of an extraordinary favour to the house of David; there was the Temple at Jerusalem, that Temple so lately built with a critical coincidence of the opportunity, to predetermine the local seat of their religion, and thereby attach and appropriate the Covenant; lastly, there was the precise document of Ahijah's prophecy, which fully met the case, both in the particular form of the event, and in the reason of it. As to *the event*, that prophecy had limited the defection to the extent of the Ten Tribes, and had fixed the time of it, by throwing it beyond the life of Solomon, but bringing it within that of his son; and assigning the new kingdom to its master, who yet had to fly for his life into Egypt before he could aspire to the conquest which was promised to him. As to *the reason* of God's moral government in this proceeding, that was also explained: so much was to be taken away, because of the corruptions of Jerusalem, and the demerit of the degenerated family of David: so much was to remain, to make good the mercy and favour promised to that city and that family, and thereby carry on the ulterior scheme of the divine dispensation. " Howbeit, I will not take the whole kingdom out of his hand (Solomon's); but I will make him prince all the days of his life, for David My servant's sake, whom I chose, because he kept My commandments and My statutes. But I will take the kingdom out of his son's hand, and will give it unto thee, even Ten Tribes. And unto his son will I give one Tribe, that David My servant may have a light alway before Me in Jerusalem, the city which I have chosen Me to put My Name there[a]."

An event of such magnitude was preceded therefore, as we see, by an adequate information of prophecy. But for that information, the event might have seemed to be a catastrophe without hope; to break up the federal character of the chosen people; to interrupt, or confound, the transmission of the Covenant, under which they had been embodied. By the intimations previously given, all these points were adjusted; at least they were sufficiently cleared as to that which would be the first and principal object of a believer's attention, either then or now, the course of the divine Economy.

The particular prophecy of Ahijah is so exact in its terms, as to be a perfect history of the impending event. But there is one supposable way of attempting to invalidate that prophecy, which I may do well to consider. It may be said, that the *Partition* foretold was possible to be foreseen, inasmuch as the Ten Tribes had already shewn a disposition to act together (which is true) and oppose them-

---

selves in concert to the dominion of the tribe of Judah. Consequently under symptoms of commotion it might be expected that the confederacy in a revolt would be composed of those Tribes.

To this surmise I would reply, that the occasion and pretext of the revolt did not subsist till *after* the prophecy of it was delivered. It took its rise from Rehoboam's rigour of government; and the prophecy fell upon the prosperous reign of Solomon [b], who held all Israel together in peace; a peace undisturbed, till the prophetic warning had first been given. But suppose that this incident of the change, the Separation of the Ten Tribes, taken alone, was not a test of clear supernatural prescience in the days of Ahijah; how will the case stand? That disposition of the Tribes which united them together, and opposed them to Judah, was created and ripened, no doubt, by moral or occasional causes influencing the passions and conduct of human agents, although we have not those causes particularly explained. It illustrates, therefore, in a signal manner, the prescience of that older prophecy of Jacob, given so many hundred years before, which separated the Tribe of Judah to some destination *above* the rest, and *apart* from the rest; since nothing could prepare so well for the fulfilment of those restricted promises verging to the favour of that single Tribe, as this very disposition of union and of jealousy. What might be doubtful as a sign of divine foreknowledge in one age of prophecy, is a more pregnant proof of it in another. Let the arrangement of things, which issued in the division of the Kingdom, pass for an object of human calculation in the days of Solomon. What is it, when viewed from the death-bed of Jacob in Egypt?

The revolt, predicted by one Prophet, took place on the excitement of *human motives*. It was established and con-

---

[b] Jeroboam's flight into Egypt, (*a public fact;*) whom "Solomon sought to kill," because of this prophecy, shews that it was then published. **1 Kings** xi. 40.

firmed by *another*[c] *against* the current of *such motives.*
God forbade the attempt to subdue it. "Return every
man to his house, for this thing is from Me." Under this
command the extraordinary change was completed. The
agency of man had been prophetically foreshewn in the one
instance; it was authoritatively suspended in the other.

A ferocious and self-willed king, who would take no
counsel before the revolt, acquiesced, and all Judah with
him, in the dictate of a prophet, after it. Why did he and
his people so act, except upon a conviction which they
could not resist of that prophet's authority? Do princes
make a surrender of their kingdoms and their passions on
such easy terms, without knowing why they do it? The
time had been, when "the words of the men of Judah
were fiercer than the words of the men of Israel." But
now "an hundred and fourscore thousand chosen men,
which were warriors, and assembled to fight against the
house of Israel, to bring back the kingdom again to Rehoboam, the son of Solomon[d]," turned their steps in obedience to a prophet. Such men are not governed by mere
words. "When they hearkened, therefore, to the word of
the Lord, and returned to depart, according to the word of
the Lord;" I infer that they had reason to know whose
word it was which they obeyed.

I must advert once more to the *Moral History* of this
change, which the Scripture has very clearly expressed.
The judicial cause of the spoliation of the kingdom is declared to have been the idolatrous impieties introduced by
Solomon, and advanced by Rehoboam; whom therefore
God infatuated in his counsels to urge him to his punishment. Such was the will of God's providence, and the
reason of it. Whereas the proximate cause, by which the
human agency in the affair moved, was the violence and
rigour of Rehoboam, when he rejected the hoary wisdom
of the advisers of his father's throne, and thereby, in the

common course of human feeling, provoked his people to rebellion. But in the government of God, whence *events*, not the *sins* of men, spring; for those sins are of the *objects* of His government; Idolatry was the crime which led, in penal retribution, to the first defacing of the commonwealth of Israel; according to the sentence of the Law, which in its threats had said, " *I will break the pride of your power*[e]." And Ahijah's prophecy, when it promised to Jeroboam his kingdom, explained withal the *reason* of the gift, that it was not granted in favour to himself, but in *chastisement* to Jerusalem and her King.—Hereby this piece of history becomes a moral document definite and complete. For it presents an example, explained in all its parts, of *God's overruling power*, and *man's agency*, concurring to complete a *prophecy*; that *completion* a *moral end*, in conformity to a sentence of the *divine law*.

II. We have seen the *Establishment* of this new kingdom, and how prophecy directed it; we must look next to its singular and bold *Corruption*. Jeroboam, in his very acquisition, received a warning against the sin which had forfeited the spoil into his hands: but he was no sooner possessed of it than he outdid the offence which had incurred the prior forfeiture. He founded in Samaria a *system* of open Idolatry. To counteract the alienation of his people by any return of feeling to their worship at Jerusalem, he set up for their use a Priesthood, Ritual, and Altar, not of pure Religion, but of Idol Worship. The Golden Calves in Bethel and in Dan were the public monument of this impiety. "These are thy gods, O Israel," the creed of the new kingdom[f].

The Unity and the Spirituality of God being the first doctrines of their Law, and the confession and worship of Him, under that character, the first duties of their Religion, and all Idol-worship prohibited, whether as a *substitute* for, or an *addition* to, their proper religious service;

[e] Levit. xxvi. 19.   [f] 1 Kings xii. 28.

the sin of Jeroboam had this novelty and excess of enormity in it, that whereas the contaminations of Idolatry
before had been surreptitiously, or more openly, associated
with their better Institutions, it was now made the National
Religion, formally received and established. For the king's
apostasy met a ready participation among his people. He
incorporated them in allegiance to his throne under the
compact of this sin. Hence the reason of the title which
is affixed to his memory, to brand his crime, and the general contagion of it, the title of "Jeroboam, the son of
Nebat, *who made Israel to sin.*"

After what we have seen of Prophecy hitherto, we shall
scarcely expect it to remain silent in this crisis of wickedness, involving the whole kingdom of *Israel*, unless their
transgression was come to the height of cutting off from
them the access of such communications. But God's providence left them not to a state of dereliction. He continued to send His prophets to the divided members of
His people, to Israel, as well as to Judah, as if to demonstrate to them that His government was one of patience
and longsuffering; of which the continued mission of the
prophets, under such provocation of offence, was an exercise, and a sensible proof; nor was it the less so, when
those messengers could carry only rebuke and correption.
We know how prophecy dealt with this offence, which
may not improperly be called the original sin of the kingdom of Israel. The Idol Altar in Bethel, as soon as it was
reared, had its sentence of condemnation written upon it.
Whilst the king was in the act of hallowing it to its profane service, at its first festival, it fell by prophecy: its
polluter was foretold by name, and it was desecrated in
prediction with the ashes of its own priests. "Behold,
there came a man out of Judah by the word of the Lord
unto Bethel; and Jeroboam stood by the altar to burn
incense. And he cried against the altar in the word of
the Lord, and said, O Altar, Altar, thus saith the Lord,
Behold, a child shall be born unto the house of David,

Josiah by name, and upon thee shall he offer the priests of the high places that burn incense upon thee, and men's bones shall be burnt upon thee[g]." Every one will perceive that all this solemnity of prediction delivered by a prophet sent for the purpose out of the land of Judah, was not merely to certify the future fact, that the Altar should be so defiled, but to set a mark upon the sin which was established and propagated by that public scandal and seat of impiety. This was the immediate moral use of the prophecy delivered. The train of circumstances connected with the utterance of it had the like effect in giving force to this present object of its denunciation. The withering of the king's hand, when "he put it forth from the altar" against the prophet; the healing of it again upon the momentary pang of his humiliation; the signs given by the rending of the Altar, and the scattering of its ashes; the command laid upon the *messenger prophet* "to eat no bread, nor drink water" in that polluted place; his strange kind of death for prevarication of duty in this point; the dying request of the old *inhabitant prophet* of Bethel; these are the group of particulars gathered round the prediction. Do we ask what they all mean? They were instruments to heighten the prophetic warning, and enforce it upon men's senses and attention.

But what is more, they serve *now* to authenticate the prediction. Take the withering of the king's hand whilst he stood by the altar, in his high place, with his people around him, assembled for the establishment and celebration of their reprobated religion; a prophet from Judah being the accusing party on the other side. The king was no penitent; he had no more inclination to believe afterwards in judicial miracles wrought upon himself, or to uphold the credit of a Judah prophet, than the Altar had to scatter its ashes. I ask then, how this exhibition of a public miracle upon his person, done in the face of day, or how the story of it, could be shaped into a tolerable falsehood, if it was not a perfect truth?

[g] 1 Kings xiii.

Or take the dying request of the Bethel prophet: "He said to his sons, When I am dead, then bury me in the sepulchre wherein the man of God is laid; lay my bones beside his bones: for the saying which he cried against the altar in Bethel, and against all the houses of the high places which are in the cities of Samaria, shall surely come to pass." Such a command for the place of his burial was equivalent to an inscription placed over his grave, expressing the reason of his choice. Suppose the inscription to have been there; it would be an evidence, not that the prophecy was a true one, but that it was uttered. The public annals of Josiah's history, at the distance of three hundred and fifty years, will speak to its truth.

This interposition of prophecy was for a sufficient cause. It was a timely remonstrance with the separated part of God's people upon the crime which became the chief source and spring of their growing corruptions, and thereby the cause of their reprobation, miseries, and ruin. The remonstrance was planted upon the public ground and scene of their offence: a memorial of reproof, which might constantly meet the transgressor, whenever he came before the forbidden Altar.

But with what effect was this and other warning prophecy given? From Jeroboam, the *first* king of Israel, to Hoshea, the *last*, there is no one reign, no one king, excepted from the imputation of the general depravity. It is a line of unmitigated irreligion and wickedness[h]. King after king has his historic epitaph, annexed to his memory, that "he did evil in the sight of the Lord;" whilst his people followed his example. In that people a righteous few indeed there were. But a prophet's eye once explored in vain to find them: and it required a revelation of God to number the "Seven Thousand" in Israel. I need not

---

[h] Of Jehu, the single king "who destroyed Baal out of Israel," and so far "did well;" the other memorial follows: "but Jehu *took no heed* to walk in the law of the Lord God of Israel with all his heart: for *he departed not from the sins of Jeroboam*, which made Israel to sin." 2 Kings x. 31.

enlarge upon the service of prophecy during this period. It is clearly adapted to the state of reigning irreligion, in *commination* and *reproof*. The mission of the two great prophets, Elijah and Elisha, falls in the *earlier* time of this period, a mission directed chiefly to the house of Israel and her kings, and enforced by Miracles, to *convince* and *awaken* an apostate people. The duration of *Elisha's* ministry reaches nearly to that of *Jonah*; and from *Jonah* we enter into the series of the prophetic Canon. This is the *continuity* of Prophecy.—There is also another proof of that same continuity, *viz.*, the prophecy given to Jehu during the ministry of Elisha, "that his children should reign after him to the *fourth* generation," *expires* not till after the prophecies of *Amos* and *Hosea* have begun[i]: and these prophets, as will be shewn hereafter, begin to fore-shew the *deletion* of the *kingdom of Israel*. Consequently the series of prophecy is so far complete.

The result is, that the kingdom of Israel has its entire history written in the perpetuity of its wickedness, as re-corded in the ministry of its prophets; and the one general document which expresses what the state of that kingdom was from first to last, and for what object of merciful fore-warning its prophets were sent, is this: "*Jeroboam drave Israel* from following the Lord, and *made Israel sin a great sin*. For the children of Israel *walked in the sins of Jero-boam*, which he did; *they departed not from them: until* the Lord removed Israel out of His sight, *as He had said by all His servants the prophets*[k]."

III. It belongs to the outline of the structure of Pro-phecy which I am now giving, to remark, that the *dismem-berment* of the Hebrew nation became *one safeguard of the prophetic evidence*. The people of Samaria professed to hold the Law of Moses, and to receive the Pentateuch. The predictions contained in the Pentateuch were thereby placed under a jealous and divided care. The jealous feel-

---

[i] For this fact, compare 2 Kings xv. 8—12, with the date of time prefixed to the prophecies of Hosea and Amos.　　　[k] 2 Kings xviii. 21, &c.

ing would be addressed most of all to those predictions
which concerned the fortunes of the Tribe of Judah, partly
delivered in those books. If the Samaritans did not receive into their Canon some of the later predictions relating to the Tribe, or to the Family, of David, those predictions, and many others, were not on that account the less,
but rather the more submitted to their scrutiny, and might
have been discredited, either as to their promulgation, or
their fulfilment, if the eye of an enemy could have found
the means of inflicting any such discredit upon them. The
prophecy against the Altar in Bethel has all the benefit of
these invidious and hostile circumstances. That Altar was
set up in a spirit of schism to the Temple at Jerusalem.
A prophet of Judah was sent against it: a king of Judah
was proclaimed the person to pollute it. How desirable
would it have been to the separatists of Samaria, and how
easy, to have disproved, by a simple denial, the utterance
of a prophecy in their high place purporting to be for the
affront of their country, and the shame of their national
worship, if no such prophet were sent among them. This
guarantee of the evidence of Prophecy, in several of its
chief articles, was most perfect so long as the kingdom of
Samaria stood; it lost much of its force, when that kingdom was reduced; but there were relics of the Ten Tribes
left in Samaria and in Judæa, among whom the tradition
of history and of adverse public feeling continued: who,
therefore, were always some check upon the custody of
that evidence. And it will be borne in mind that much
of later prophecy continues to enlarge the distinction in
favour of the Tribe of Judah; a preference which must
therefore have kept alive that kind of inquisitive attention. The same spirit was animated again by the building
of the Second Temple, which became a known object of
jealousy to the Samaritan race[1].

IV. From the *Establishment* of the separate Kingdoms,

[1] Ezra, chap. iv.

I pass to their *Dissolution* and *Captivity*, and the State of
Prophecy connected therewith.

When these kingdoms stood up together, it was inde-
terminable by reason, for any thing that we can see, which
would be the more stable or prosperous of the two. That
of Samaria seemed to have the advantage, her greater
territory and numbers considered. Perhaps the spirit of
defection, in which her state was founded, portended ill to
her internal peace. That symptom excepted, it a doubtful
one, the problem of calculation apparently was either inde-
terminable, or the data of it inclined to the preponderance
and superior stability of the new kingdom.

Prophecy however supplied other data. What we have
already seen of the promises on the side of the Tribe of
Judah and the Family of David, might be taken by a plain
inference to negative the hopes of the other Tribes, and
other families. For those promises made to the first, being
matter of favour and distinction, virtually cut off other
Tribes and Thrones by a speedier termination of their
power.

But the question was not left to depend upon such an
inference. It was decided more positively, by direct prophecy. Of the Four Greater, and the Twelve Less, Prophets, whose books we possess, the most ancient are Jonah,
Hosea, Amos, Isaiah. The Chronology of the age of Joel
cannot be well ascertained; but no difficulty results from
thence to the point in hand. For whatever be his age,
his prophecy implies the protection and preservation of
Judah and Jerusalem : and the prophecy of Jonah relates
to a foreign subject, the city of Nineveh. Taking then
the other three prophets of the highest antiquity, *Hosea,
Amos,* and *Isaiah,* who are at the same time more copious
and articulate in their predictions, consider the information
they supplied concerning the relative destiny of the two
kingdoms. It is a striking fact, that the First Chapter of
Hosea, probably the *most ancient* of the three, is directly
to the point. It bears upon the difference to be made
between the House of Israel and the House of Judah.

Observe the text; "I will no more have mercy upon the House of Israel; but *I will utterly take them away.*   But I will have mercy upon the house of Judah, and *will save them by the Lord their God.*"   The whole book of this prophet inculcates the speedier dispersion and desolation of the house of Israel.   Both Israel and Judah indeed are threatened : but the burden of his prophecy is upon Ephraim, Bethel, and Samaria.

Take the other eldest prophets, *Amos* and *Isaiah.*   The words of *Amos* are those " which he saw concerning *Israel,*" and the main drift of his prophecy bears upon the desolation and captivity of Samaria.   Consult *Isaiah,* and you find him prophesying thus : " Because Syria, *Ephraim* (Israel), and the son of Remaliah, have taken evil counsel against thee, saying, *Let us go up against Judah and vex it,* and let us make a breach therein for us, and set a king in the midst of it, even the son of Tabeal ; thus saith the Lord God, It shall not stand, neither shall it come to pass.   For the head of Syria is Damascus, and the head of Damascus is Rezin : *and within threescore and five years shall Ephraim be broken, that it be not a people*[m]."

These texts which I have cited are decisive in expressing the *earlier downfall of Israel;* but they are only some of the first, with many following them, to the same effect.

Israel was to be broken within *threescore and five years;* and the *Assyrian* power, " the rod of the divine anger," was foreshewn by Hosea's prediction to be the instrument of the divine judgment so proclaimed[n].   The Assyrian conquest fell upon that kingdom, in three repeated invasions, which ended in its desolation and captivity in the fullest extent ; whilst the inhabitants of the land, the flower and strength of it, were swept away, transplanted among strangers in the cities of the Medes[o], and lost in the obscure

[m] Isaiah vii. 6, 7, 8.   [n] Hosea xi. 5.

[o] According to the original prediction of Abijah, and given at the beginning of the kingdom, "The Lord shall *root up* Israel out of this land ; and shall *scatter them beyond the river.*"   1 Kings xv. 15.

settlements of an irreclaimable exile. From that day Israel *has ceased from being a people.*

The question naturally strikes us here, Why did Israel fall, and Judah not follow in the overthrow? The Assyrian power was in the career of its victories, and meant to have overwhelmed Judah also. The attempt was made; the assailant army was on its approach, and had advanced within sight of the walls of Jerusalem. But Prophecy cast its shield in the way, and cut off the assault in the preparations of it. We have seen what was said by Hosea *long before,* in the difference of God's mercy to Israel and to Judah. But in the last moment of danger, Isaiah was sent with the message of deliverance. "Thus saith the Lord concerning the king of Assyria, He shall not come into this city, nor shoot an arrow there, nor come before it with shields, nor cast a bank against it, for I will defend this city to save it for Mine own sake, and for My servant David's sake[p]." By a miracle this prophecy was accomplished.

But both the prophecy and miracle require some further attention. Read the history of the Assyrian invasion, and you will see it was not an aggression of common warfare, in the mere lust of conquest. The Invader made it his boast, that he would confound the God who was known and worshipped at Jerusalem with the defeated idols and divinities of Polytheism, whose local tutelary name had been no defence against the power of his arms. His defiance is that of Infidelity and Irreligion, more than the vaunt of ordinary aggression. He sent to reproach and *blaspheme the Holy One of Israel*[q]. The vindication of God's own name, and the truth of His Revealed Religion, were in question. It was a case something similar to that of Egypt; and the prophet Isaiah has plainly suggested the comparison of the two[r]. Hence the evident *fitness* of the *miraculous interposition.*

<hr>

[p] Isaiah xxxvii. 33, 35.

[q] See Isaiah xxxvii. 23; 2 Chron. xxxii. 17.　　　　[r] Isaiah x. 26.

This *unequal* distribution of fortune between the two kingdoms is a fact in their history which Scepticism itself must admit.   It forms a broad indisputable record, which it would be idle to go about to prove; but it is no more than the previous state of prophecy required.   For prophecy had pledged its word for the preservation of Judah beyond the fall of Samaria, and specifically from the Assyrians[s].   Yet greater kingdoms than either of these had fallen under the Assyrian arms; and these two countries lay together, *equally exposed.* There was scarcely a natural line of separation between them; but it seems there was a wall of fire in the warrant of prophecy.   Admit the prophecy, and the moral reasons joined with it, those reasons regarding both the promises of God's covenant with Judah, and the singular Impiety of the Invader; admit this, and there is an adequate account of the miracle, and the miracle will answer for the event.   Otherwise the event itself would offer some difficulty to the historian, who should have to give an account of it in the ordinary way. It is true, there are great anomalies and inconsistencies in the comparative fate of kingdoms placed under *equal* circumstances of exposure and assault, and the difference is the greatest when it occurs under a general system of conquest, such as that of the Assyrian power.   In some such idea of the anomaly of events, stretched to the utmost, Unbelief must take refuge, if it decline the adequate explanation which assigns a *final* cause for the *known state of the fact,* and renders the whole history of the phænomenon consistent.

With respect to the preparation made by prophecy to foreshew this difference, which God intended to make between the two branches of His ancient people, in the earlier ruin and rejection of the one, and the preservation of the other, we should understand the case better, if we separated from the rest what prophecy there really was in hand at the time when the event was approaching, and

considered so much of it apart. For it happens, through
the mixt light, and various subjects, of the whole body of
the prophetic revelation, that we distinguish less clearly in
what line single portions of it were directed, or how they
operated to guide men's observation to the progressive
order of God's providence. But it is easy to correct our
inquiry by giving to it *the right point of view.* In this
way, with respect to the subject before us, *The different
condition of the two kingdoms,* if any person would read
the books of Hosea and Amos, and some few of the earlier
portions of Isaiah, I believe the whole impression of his
mind would be, that the general disclosure of prophecy
was altogether in the direction of the eventual state of
things, and such as rendered the intentions of God's providence sufficiently intelligible to any attentive inquirer.
Such a separation and adjustment of the prophetic evidence, bringing it more nearly into the form and order in
which it was delivered, would be seen at once to define its
application, and improve its force.

The prediction of Isaiah had fixed the *overthrow of the
kingdom of Samaria* to come within the precise term of
Sixty-five years. But there was more than this foreshewn.
It was not to be simply a subjugation, a loss of public freedom and safety, but the very body of the state was to be
dissolved—"they were to cease from being a people;" and
the prophecy of Amos is the solemn dirge of that kingdom's fate. "Hear ye this word which I take up against
you, *even a lamentation, O house of Israel. The virgin of
Israel is fallen, she shall no more rise : she is forsaken upon
her land : there is none to raise her up*[t]." The ruin so
foretold came by the Assyrian conquest. Samaria was
taken, and the land dispeopled of her inhabitants; the
mass of population composing the Ten Tribes being subjected to the rigour of that law of conquest often exercised
by the ancient Asiatic armies, in a loss of their country,
and a removal into a foreign region, where they were cast

[t] Amos v. 1.

out to waste and languish in the transplanted settlement of an inhospitable home among aliens and enemies; whilst barbaric colonies from the East, Cuthites and Babylonians, took possession of their lands and cities, and sunk their distinctive lineage, and thereby defeated the hope of any national revival in Canaan from their surviving stock. This is the æra of the dissolution of the kingdom and people of Israel. Not that their race was forthwith obliterated in their exile, or that the last scattering and remnant of them left behind in Samaria perished. But according to the terms of the prophecy, " they ceased from being a people." Their national state was broken up, and has not been restored. The sentence of civil desolation passed upon them has not been recalled. With it they lost their prophets, their covenant, and their last hopes under that Temporal Covenant, as a part of the people of God. If this extinction of *Ten Tribes* in Israel was a great and memorable event, the previous annunciation of it was proportionably clear. The prophecy is commensurate with the object.

V. I must next advert to the subsequent Captivity of Judah, and shew in this other line of the history what was the prophetic information imparted.

The kingdom of Judah, which prophecies and miracles had combined to protect, was to suffer in her turn. In a later age she too was visited with the calamities of desolation and captivity. Her king deposed; her Temple burnt to the ground; her inhabitants carried to Babylon. The preparations made by prophecy for this event are of the following kind. They begin at a distance from the event; they are clear and literal; they are copious, and delivered by several Prophets in succession; they comprehend a view of the moral reasons of the calamity; of its duration; of its issue; and of every material point connected with it, upon which a serious observer of the course of things under God's dispensation could be intent, and desire to be informed.

Take them at their origin, they open in the reign of

Hezekiah; and they open at once with a full disclosure of the subject in question; the occasion of the disclosure being as follows. It was in the reign of this virtuous and religious prince that Jerusalem was saved from the Assyrians. Babylon was then a subordinate kingdom, and its king in friendship with Hezekiah. Hezekiah having been sick nigh unto death, the king of Babylon sent messengers to congratulate him, by letters and a present, on his recovery from his sickness. In such a season of the expansion of joy, and of honour and entertainment to his guests, in the elevation of his heart, not free from some stain of pride, he made a display to them of his palace, his arms, and the treasures of wealth and decoration which he and his fathers had gathered for the splendour of his kingdom[u]. It is an impressive, and almost a fearful, circumstance, in the history of prophecy, that this season of exultation was chosen as the time of revealing to this virtuous king the future captivity and degradation of his children, and the spoliation of his house, and the evil appointed to come by no other power than Babylon, whose king was then his friend, and whose messengers had been exchanging with him the offices of kindness and congratulation. " Hear the word of the Lord," said the prophet Isaiah: " Behold the days come that all that is in thine house, and that which thy fathers have laid up in store, even to this day, shall be carried to Babylon, nothing shall be left. And of thy sons which shall issue from thee, which thou shalt beget, shall they take away, and they shall be eunuchs in the palace of the king of Babylon[x]."

Thus the Assyrian Deliverance, and the Babylonian captivity, were both predicted by one and the same Prophet; both foreshewn to one and the same king. They make consecutive subjects in the page of prophecy. It is not clear which was delivered first; for every purpose of substantial consideration they must be taken as coming together. The prediction of the Deliverance was of an event at hand, but against all imminent appearances; the

<hr>

[u] Compare Isaiah xxxix. 2; 2 Chron. xxxii. 27   [x] Isaiah xxxix. 6.

prediction of the Captivity was of an event remote, and beset by the uncertainties of time and the improbabilities of a present experience; for why should Babylon, a weaker and a friendly state, do that which the Assyrian, in the fulness of his power, was unable, or not permitted, to do?

The span of *prescience*, however, embraced in this example of prophecy, is not the whole of what is to be observed in its structure. It is the combination of things so dissimilar, in the same train and season of prediction, which calls for some part of our attention. The *contemporary* exhibition of the *near* and the *distant* event is sufficiently illustrative of the divine foreknowledge. But the force and severity of the prophetic Ethics, in connecting the view of the blessing and the evil together, exhibit another object equally striking. In the midst of Hezekiah's public and private joy the veil is drawn aside, and the opposite scene disclosed. The import of that disclosure is to chasten the exultation of man, and teach him, by the most affecting discipline, the principle of humility and self-recollection, under a sense of the unseen extent and variety of God's providence oper. ting in the dispensation of joy and evil, deliverances and afflictions. And he who is no believer in the inspiration of these prophecies, (if, after studying them, any remain such,) would yet scarcely be able to resist the impression they carry with them, combined and contrasted, as they are, to a great effect of ethical wisdom.

When the event arrived which began to be disclosed in this prophecy, and Judah was laid desolate, it was the *greatest shock of change* which had hitherto befallen the adopted people of God. The extinction of the kingdom of Samaria must be set aside in the comparison; because, whilst Judah remained, there was still a chosen people, a continuance of the covenant, a perpetuity of the dispensation. But when Jerusalem was taken and laid waste, the Temple thrown down, Judæa depopulated, and her inhabitants buried in the heathen city of Babylon, there seemed to be an end of all—Where were God's promises? where the hopes of His people?

I answer, they were safe in the custody of Prophecy. There existed predictions which covered every question, and cleared up every perplexity, which attached to this new and anomalous crisis of their condition.

To speak of them in a general way, the predictions on this particular subject of the Babylonian Captivity are the most extensive and the most elaborate, not of all the Prophecies, but of all those which come under the same head of the temporal condition of the Jewish people. Read the Greater Prophets, and read the Less, antecedent to the Captivity; it is the Babylonian subject that engages them most, the Christian only excepted. The magnitude of the event was therefore matched by a correspondent prophetic information. To speak of the same predictions more definitely, they decide those material points of the subject to which I have already adverted: *viz.*, the *moral reasons* of the calamity, the *time of its continuance, the issue* of it, the *course of means* by which that issue should take effect. They state the moral reasons of it to have been the visitation of a judgment, for a degree of sin and corruption, not otherwise to be purged away[y]; and they define it to be not for a punishment of final excision, but a discipline of repentance and humiliation[z]. They limit the period of its continuance to Seventy Years; they make the issue of it a complete public deliverance. They announce the name of the Deliverer who was to arise, Cyrus. They describe his previous conquest of Babylon, and the use he would make of that conquest to the emancipation of God's people. They add the most vivid picture of the ruin and subsequent desolation of Babylon, to enforce this truth, that the victorious power and greatness of that domineering state were only instrumental to the special purposes of the divine judgments; which purposes satisfied, the scene would change.

In a word, there is nothing wanting in Prophecy to the

[y] Ezek. xxiv.					[z] Jer. xxx. 1. 20. xxix. 13; Isaiah xl. 22.

entire order of the events, or the interpretation of them; and the most material parts of it are delivered with the perspicuity of a narrative, in which the particulars of time, persons, and place, are given under the most exact designation. For the evidence of this statement, I refer to the prophecies of Isaiah, Jeremiah, and Ezekiel, relating to the subject[a]; whilst I cite the two following texts from among all the rest. "Thus saith the Lord, that *after seventy years* be accomplished at Babylon, I will visit you, and perform My good word towards you, *in causing you to return to this place.* For I know the thoughts that I think towards you, saith the Lord; thoughts of peace, and not of evil, to give you an expected end[b]." Isaiah, speaking of Cyrus by name, assigns to him this office: "I have raised him up in righteousness, and *I will direct all his ways; he shall build My city; and he shall let go My captives,* not for price nor reward, saith the Lord of Hosts[c]."

Upon this event of the Restoration of Judah, and the prophecy of it, the following remarks are suggested. First, as to the Restoration itself, so predetermined by prophecy; I would observe that such a conclusion of a national calamity of that kind, so rudely inflicted at the first, and after so long a continuance, is not one of the ordinary occurrences of history. Of conquered and enslaved *nations,* transplanted from their home, how few are restored into a public community again; how few replaced in their own land. The frequent exiles and restorations of the small states of Greece were of another kind and scale. They were the violent transpositions of Civil War, or the removals of a migratory Adventure. Yet this Restoration of a people, in the case before us, so little to be hoped in the ordinary course of things, was foretold as plainly and constantly as the Captivity itself which it was to reverse. It forms a subject of prediction to each of the Three Greater Prophets, Isaiah, Jeremiah, and Ezekiel[d]. Consequently the fulfilment of it became an eminent demonstra-

<hr>

[a] Isaiah xiii. 19. xiv. 3. xxi. 10. xliv. xlv., &c.; Jer. xxv. 1., &c. Ezek. ii. xii. xxiii., &c.   [b] Jer. xxix. 10.   [c] xliv. 28.   [d] Ezek. xx.

tion of Prophecy, and thereby a support and revival of Religion. "When the Lord turned again the captivity of Zion, then were we *like unto them that dream.*" We need not wonder that those exiles, who "had wept by the waters of Babylon," could scarcely believe their deliverance, when it "filled their mouth with laughter, and their tongue with joy." It *was* beyond the probability of human calculation. But their *dream* of *joy* had been one of the past *visions of Prophecy.* And as God has made the known visible history of this people, in its uncontested facts, something different from that of all other nations on the face of the earth, so the two events of their deliverance from Egypt, and from Babylon, are monuments of His providence, on which His finger has pointed to the world, in two distant ages, this singularity of their character, and of His own work in the government of them. "Hath God *assayed to go* and *take Him a nation, from the midst of another nation,*" in this manner, once and again, in any other instance? or has the bare fact elsewhere been seen?

Secondly. The promise of restoration was a provision of God's mercy to His faithful servants, whilst it was yet only in prospect. The piety of Daniel was instructed and supported by it[e]. We cannot doubt that other good and pious men found in it the like resources of hope and consolation.

Thirdly. The distinctness of the prediction as to the temporary duration of the captivity, kept this and other parts of prophecy clear in their related sense. Otherwise there might have been a collision between the older and the recent predictions; the older given by Moses, the recent delivered by all the prophets of this æra. The overthrow of their state by the Babylonian conquest might have been taken to comprehend the whole of their ruin foretold by Moses. Many points are common in the two cases. But when their speedy restoration was foreshewn, the doubt was removed; and it was made clear that the wide dispersion and desolation which Moses had foretold could not be exhausted in the temporary bondage in

[e] Dan. ix. 2.

Babylon. Whatever their present visitation might have seemed to be, and however hopeless taken by itself, their emergent destiny was placed clearly in view. And herein we may observe an analogy in this instance of prophecy, and a former. The Bondage in Egypt, and the Captivity in Babylon, appeared to *extinguish* the people, and cut off their very tenure of the favour and promises of God. But in each case the equivocal circumstances of a present condition were counterchecked by limitations of time predicted. Four hundred and thirty years in the one case, Seventy in the other, defined the period of their Sufferings and their Hopes, and rendered the scheme of Providence clear.

VI. Before I leave this period of the *temporal* Prophecy, embracing the Captivity of the two Kingdoms, let me state in one brief and summary view the chief points which fall within it. If we take our station in the age of *Isaiah*, and look through his prophecies alone, we shall have the following draught of events, representing the respective fortunes of the two kingdoms, and reaching through a space of more than Two Hundred Years.

First, The prophetic scheme will present to us Samaria to be overthrown; but Judah to be preserved. Then, Judah and Jerusalem, though rescued from the Assyrians, to fall into the hands of the Babylonians[f]; a smaller and a friendly power at the date of the prediction. The catastrophe to be hopeless to Samaria; so that "Ephraim should be broken from being a people." The captivity not to be hopeless to Judah, but a restoration to ensue. The person appointed to be the restorer of Judah (Cyrus), to rise in a country which was *then* not thought of among the greater subsisting kingdoms of the East (Persia). The medium of their restoration, his capture of Babylon; which capture was to be effected by a singular form of art

---

[f] The *Chaldæans* are commonly named by the Prophets. I use the word Babylonians to describe the inhabitants of Babylon, whether the *natives*, or the *successful occupant* people, which last are the Chaldæans.

in drying the River, and obtaining access to the Gates[g]; the Medes and Persians to be the powers engaged in the siege; and all these characteristic points significantly expressed in the prediction. Lastly, the city of Jerusalem, and the Temple, to be rebuilt.

I am not canvassing now the *Evidence*, but the *Contents* of Prophecy; and such is a part of the extended range which is exhibited in the revelation of this single prophet. But upon the Evidence I shall make one concluding remark. For here I would put the question to any person acquainted with the history of those times and countries, as preserved in independent heathen writers; and enough is preserved for the purpose of the inquiry; whether there existed in the age of the prophet Isaiah the most remote preparations discernible by human foresight for the conclusion of this order of things, which is so described by him. In particular, whether the *Medo-Persian* victories by Cyrus, or by any person either of *Median* or *Persian* race, as the means of releasing *Judah* from *Babylon*, could have been foreseen, when the *Median* power, as we know, much more the *Persian*[h], had no existence: when there was neither *Captivity in Babylon* nor *victories of Babylon* to produce it: when, in fact, the elder *Assyrian* power was yet in vigour, the subversion of which was only the opening to the *possibility* of the several distant changes and events foretold. One prediction of this prophet penetrates through another; and each stage of the anticipated course of things leads to more remote positions of prophecy. There is a depth and a combination of prescience in the prolonged succession of his predictions, which oblige us to ask, whence it came, whence it could come, if not from

[g] Isaiah xxi. 2.

[h] The *latest* age of Isaiah may *possibly* reach the *first rudiments* of the *Median* kingdom, when Deioces was *beginning* to reduce it into order. Prior to which, the *Medes* and *Babylonians* were subjects of the *Assyrian* empire. —Isaiah's *prophesying* continued into *Hezekiah's* reign. Hezekiah *died* 698 B.C.; Deioces began to reign 700 B.C.

the revelation of Him " who calleth the things that are not as though they were?"

In order to evade this conclusion, nothing is left but to deny that Isaiah, or any person of his age, wrote the book ascribed to him; which is to affirm that the Jewish people knew nothing of the Book which they placed at the head of their Prophetic Canon; and, to say nothing of what they might think of its inspired authority, did not even know the age when it was written, or its author. An assertion without evidence, and against it. " Ye are My witnesses," saith God by this prophet, when he delivers to them these his comprehensive predictions. Let them be witnesses only of the date of the prophecies. The prophecies themselves will bear witness to their own inspiration, when compared with their counterpart in the volume of history. " Thus saith the Lord, the King of Israel, *Who, as I, shall call,* and *shall declare it,* and *set it in order for Me,* since I appointed the ancient people? *and the things that are coming and shall come? Let them shew unto them.* Have not I told thee from that time, and have declared it? *Ye are My witnesses.* Is there a God besides Me? Yea, there is no God, I know not any[1]." An appeal fitly made by the medium of the Prophet who has supplied materials for the fullest confirmation of that appeal.

[1] Isaiah xliv. 7, 8.

END OF PART I. DISCOURSE VI.

DISCOURSE VI.

PART II.

On the Christian Prophecy within that Period.

WHILST Prophecy enlarged its communications to the kingdoms of Israel and Judah, upon the affairs of their own Church and country, it extended also its discoveries concerning the new kingdom and dispensation of God, to be founded by the advent of the Messiah. The Temporal and the Christian predictions had their greatest increase together. But there is this difference in the order of the two, that for some time after the large revelations made in the reigns of David and Solomon upon the Christian subject, there is a pause of that kind of prophecy; whilst the other, directed to the state of the two kingdoms, their corruptions and their fortunes, continues without intermission; and in particular the missions of the two great Prophets, *Elijah* and *Elisha*, ministers of the Temporal Prophecy, are past, *before* the Gospel subject appears again in view; unless some few of the *Psalms* of an unknown date, and of a prophetic spirit, may be ascribed to this intermediate time.

There is no important object which I am aware of in fixing *the precise time* when the predictions of an Evangelical character commenced again; though perhaps there is a real satisfaction in watching the dawn and the progress of this light which God was pleased to dispense by Prophecy, before He gave it in the fulness of His Illumination. But this satisfaction is to be sought rather in the discoveri-

and doctrine of the prophet, than in the exact chronology
of his predictions: and the chronology is of moment, on
this head of Christian prophecy, only as it leads to the
more just observation of the general successive order of
the prophetic oracles.

Separating what is reasonably certain from what is
doubtful in this point, we shall have the following data[a]:
1. The book of *Jonah* is the most ancient in the Prophetic
Canon. 2. *Hosea, Amos, Micah,* of the Minor Prophets,
and *Isaiah,* of the Greater, will come in the following age.
In this series I shall trace the *revival* of Christian Prophecy.

The book of *Jonah* contains no prediction of a direct
Christian import. But in *Hosea,* and *Amos,* very expressive intimations of the establishment of the Gospel, or its
doctrines, are introduced; and it is *probable* that the last
chapter of Amos is precisely the beginning of the Evangelical prophecy contained in the Prophetic Canon. Let
me state how this renewal of the Christian promises begins.

1. The book of Amos is full of the warnings of punishment and destruction, partly to the Pagan enemies of God,
but much more to His own people, and most of all to the
House of *Israel.* In fact, the first inroad of ruin and desolation in the removal of *Israel* is the leading subject of the
book. We are accustomed to speak tritely of the past ruin
of the kingdoms of Israel and Judah. But this is our mistake. These instances of ruin were not only the great visitations of God, but they were the changes of His *own work,*
in the rejection of His people whom He had raised up to
be the subjects of His Covenant. Prophets and devout men
of that day must have seen these mutations with another
eye; they must have thought of their approach with another feeling. And we must look into the record of the

* "*Jonah,* the son of Amittai." B. C. *circ.* 825—800. See 2 Kings xiv.
25.—*Hosea,* in the days of *Uzziah, Jotham, Ahaz,* and *Hezekiah,* kings of
Judah.—*Amos, Isaiah,* and *Micah,* come within the same reigns, B. C. *circ.*
790—700.

administration of God in that age, in order to perceive the force and pertinence of some of the prophetic discoveries which were granted to it. For when religion had only imperfect hopes and unexplained informations of the greatest mysteries of Faith by which it is our privilege to live, the very least discoveries opposed to the darkness and confusions of the passing scene would be dear and precious to the observant mind, by opening prospects of hope which the present state of the Temporal covenant rendered most needful. Let us consider then, that in one of the earliest prophetic books which describe the desolation and rejection, either of the whole, or of the greater portion, of God's ancient people, the prediction ends with the contrary prospect of some state of Restitution promised : and he who should read there the promise, " In that day (of desolation) will *I raise up* the tabernacle of David that is *fallen*, and I will raise up *his ruins*, and I will *build it* as in the days of old[b]," would have an object of faith, and a direction of his mind to the mercy and favour of God, in which he would find consolation, though he might derive from it only a very indistinct knowledge. This prophecy, whatever obscurity might be in it, was opposed to the impending evil. It told of the rebuilding of the ruins of David, when the approach of those ruins began to appear; and, as the Evangelical promises had been given in that king of Israel, it was equivalent to a revival of all the hopes which those Evangelical promises had already consigned.

II. In the same order of consolatory and Evangelical prophecy must be placed that great oracle in Hosea; " I will *ransom* them from *the power of the grave;* I will *redeem* them from *death.* O *Death,* I will be *thy plague,* O *Grave,* I will be *thy destruction*[c]." It is in vain to attempt to confine this text to the subject of a *temporal* deliverance. Interpreters[d] who do so, forget that

---

[b] Amos ix. 11.   [c] Hosea xiii. 14.

[d] " St. Paul *naturally applies* to the resurrection what *the prophet* says of future *national happiness*."—NEWCOME'S *Minor Prophets, in loco.*

men of a serious mind were panting after some hope of a future eternal state; and when a Prophet spoke in such a strain of God's "ransoming from the grave, and redeeming from death," and of the plague being *retorted* upon *Death*, and destruction upon the *Grave*, if he did not intend by such promises to support and encourage the belief of the resurrection and a state of immortality, he spoke a hazardous, I might almost say a fallacious, language, little suited to the agonies of human nature, and the needs of religion. And what if the subject of the prophet be a *temporal* deliverance? the very *conditions* of the subject, even in the *temporal sense* of it, demand the *greater Truth* to be included in it. For what does the Prophet profess to promise? A restoration "to national happiness:" so it is said, and perhaps truly. But how does he express that promise? In the images of the resurrection and an immortal state. Consequently, there is *implied* in the delineation of the lower subject the truth of the greater. For when God declares "I will ransom them from the power of the Grave; I will redeem them from Death;" and not merely this, which might be limited to a deliverance from *approaching* death; but when His promise goes to a triumph *over the actual power of Death and the Grave;* and the state of men is considered in their inquiries on this greatest of all questions; it is not in our choice whether we will restrain the emphasis and sublimity of the prophet to the temporal blessing. It is impossible that any reasonable devout Israelite could so restrain it; his mind could not so far revolt from his ear. It is incredible to think that the divine oracle could mean so little when it expressed so much: could express the *destruction* of *death*, and intend only *a life in Canaan :* when the force and propriety of the promise, even as it regarded a temporal state, must yet stand upon the previous concession of the higher Truth[e]. For a fallacy *in rerum*

---

[e] St. Paul's citation of this text, or his reference to it, is in another form. "O Death, *where* is thy sting? O Grave, *where* is thy victory?" 1 Cor. xv. 55. The sense comes to the same. A *reversal* of the *victory* of the *grave*, that is, a *resurrection*, is expressed in both.

natura, or an equivocal assumption, would be a strange vehicle of the divine promise. When therefore it is said, that " St. Paul *naturally* applies to the resurrection what the prophet *says of future national happiness,*" I should hope that this comment might pass for a disparagement of the prophet's text, and that we should rather say that many good men, before the Apostle, justly applied to the resurrection what the prophet spoke of it, and directed them so to apply.—But this text of Hosea will give us only a part of the Evangelical doctrine. It promises a redemption from death—"a ransom from the power of the grave." How that ransom and redemption were to be obtained, by what victory, by what Mediator, is not at all expressed. For those points we must go to other prophecy.

As to *Micah*, the next of the Minor Prophets, his, like *Isaiah's*, are among the most illustrious of the Christian predictions. But they are direct and explicit, and carry us at once into the history of the Gospel. And the reason why I have selected these two passages of *Amos* and *Hosea*, and insisted upon them in the very summary statement to which I must confine myself on the head of the Evangelical Prophecy, is, that they are among the *earliest*, and it is probable that they are *strictly* the *first*, of their kind, contained in the Prophetic Canon. Whether other persons may attach any importance to such observation upon the progress of Prophecy, is more than I will venture to say. But I find it satisfactory to my own mind to observe the first rise of the Gospel revelation in the volume of the Prophets, and watch the earliest rays of that morning light, which soon begins to illuminate the same volume with greater strength and splendour.

For from these beginnings the Christian subject takes possession of the Prophetic books, and is scarcely absent from any of them. But the very copiousness of these prophecies will render it the less possible for me to enter into an examination of their structure, and the less necessary, whilst they explain themselves so readily in their whole import and character. For what less have we in the single book of Isaiah, than the *scheme* of the Gospel, and the *establishment* of it, unfolded?   The mission of Christ into the world; His original Divine Nature; His supernatural Birth in His Incarnation; His work of Mercy, and His kingdom of Righteousness; His Humiliation, Sufferings, and Death; the Sacrifice of Atonement for Sin made by His Death; the effusion of the gifts and grace of the Holy Spirit; the enlarged Propagation of His Religion; the Persecutions of it; the Moral characters of it: the blindness and incredulity of the Jewish People in the rejection of it; the adoption of the Gentile world into the Church and People of God; the peace of the Righteous in death, and the triumph and victory of God's mercy in behalf of man over death [f]: these are things which are either so clearly revealed, or so significantly implied, in the various predictions of Isaiah, that I shall consider myself justified in expressing the *structure* of his Evangelical prophecy as that of a *complete delineation of the Gospel subject*, both in its doctrines, and its history.   Some of his prophetic texts have indeed been assailed by a Socinian criticism.   But their just interpretation has been vindicated; and the vindication was easy; for the *Divinity* of the Holy Person, whose advent is foretold, and the *Grace* of His *Atonement*, will remain luminous *doctrines* of *Prophecy*, as they are *doctrines* of the *Religion* which has fulfilled that Prophecy, so long as the *vicarious Sufferings* of the Messiah shall be expressed as they are now expressed by this prophet [g], or the glory of His Nature and Office shall be described in a strain like this: "Unto us a Child is born, unto us a Son is given, and the Government shall be upon His shoulder, and His name shall be called *Wonderful, Counsellor, the mighty God, the Father of the everlasting Age, the Prince of Peace* [h]."

Instead of following, in detail, through the prophetic

[f] Isaiah vii. 14. ix. 6. xl. 1, 12. xlii. 1, 4. xlix. 5, 7. lii. liii. liv. lvii.
[g] Isaiah liii. 5, 6.   [h] Isaiah xi. 6.

volume its accumulated predictions which relate to the Gospel, I shall take the question *on the other side,* and examine whether there are *any* of the Prophets who have not spoken either directly, or by clear intimation, to some point of the Gospel subject.

Three of the Minor Prophets there are, whose prophecies may be thought to come under this idea of bearing *no distinct reference* to *Christ,* or His *Religion; Jonah, Nahum,* and *Habakkuk :* whilst in all the rest of the Prophets the point is clear, and that reference will be generally confessed. These Three then must be examined by themselves. Interpreters who give the rein to a mystical principle, might profess, perhaps, to elicit a Christian prophecy from the text even of these three Prophets, where a more just and discriminating observation will acknowledge such prophecy to be wanting. *Jonah* and *Nahum* have the subject of their prediction in *Nineveh :* Habakkuk, of his, in the invasion of the *Chaldæans.* And no further matter of predictive revelation seems to be introduced by any of them.

I. But this being the case, it is to be observed that *Jonah* is in his own person a *Type,* a *prophetic Sign,* of Christ. The miracle of his deliverance from his three days of *death* in the body of the whale is the expressive image of the resurrection of Christ. Our Saviour has fixed the truth and certainty of this Type[1]; the correspondence of the miracle has fixed it ; and so it must remain in its proper acceptation, with that kind of evidence which belongs to all the genuine Types of the Old Testament ; *viz.,* that of a concealed prophecy which the completion explains. It would be beyond all reason to think that the *Israelite,* in *his* day, could discover in the singular fate and deliverance of Jonah any thing of the presignified death and resurrection of Christ. It would be equally short of reason in *us,* not to perceive *now,* that this first miracle, exhibited in the person of the prophet, is the previous adumbration of the fact of the other miracle, in the person of Christ, and thereby a confirmatory evidence of its designed and predestined appointment. Jonah therefore, as I may say, *compensates* for the absence of any direct Christian prediction in what he delivers, by the typical prophecy embodied in his personal history. And as he is the *first* and *oldest* of the prophets, hence we perceive that the *first image*, or *introductory representation*, which meets us in the opening of the prophetic Canon, when we explore it in its Christian sense, is that of the great fact of Christ's Resurrection.

2. Further, the whole import of Jonah's *mission* partakes of the Christian character. For when we see that he is sent to carry the tidings of the divine judgment, but to exemplify the grant of the divine mercy, to a great Heathen city; that is, to be a preacher of repentance; and that the repentance of the Ninevites through his mission brings them to know "a gracious God, and merciful, slow to anger, and of great kindness, and repenting Him of the evil[k];"—without staying to discuss whether all this be a *formal Type* of the *genius* of the Christian religion, it is plainly a *real example* of some of its chief properties, in the manifested efficacy of repentance, the grant of pardon, and the communication of God's mercy to the Heathen world. Consequently we have in the book of Jonah a *second* point of connexion with the Gospel. But in this second article the Evangelical sense was clear. It needed not a future time to interpret it. The *preservation* of the Ninevites wrote the ample comment upon it.

3. There is probably a *third* intimation of a Christian truth, conveyed by this prophet, in his Prayer. His prayer is so strongly expressive of hope in death, and that hope was so highly established by the event of his deliverance, that I think no devout reader of it could fail to infer from it some confirmation to his faith, in those times, when the hope of immortality had to seek its support from

<hr>

[k] Jonah iv. 2.

feebler notices and arguments than we are indulged with. Let others read, and judge for themselves, whether the faith of Jonah, in the spirit of his prayer, might not be auxiliary to infuse that Christian doctrine, the belief of the Resurrection.

II. The Book of *Nahum* will be best understood, by being read as a continuation, or supplement to the book of *Jonah*. The prophecy of both is directed against Nineveh. But that of Jonah was followed by the preservation of that city; that of Nahum, which is more detailed in its circumstances, indicating the actual doom, was followed by its capture and destruction. They form connected parts of one moral history; the remission of God's judgment being illustrated in the one, the execution of it in the other. The attentive reader will perceive them to be contrasted in some of their contents, as well as in their general object; the repentance of the Ninevites, and their wickedness; the clemency, and the just severity, of the divine government; being combined together in the mixed delineation of the two books[1]. But of pure Christian prophecy, either direct or typical, *perhaps* the book of Nahum must be set down as affording no instance.

III. The Book of *Habakkuk* remains, in which although we cannot safely plead for any Gospel prediction, yet there are one or two passages in it which cannot be excluded from some relation to the Gospel. 1. That distinguished Christian principle, that "*the just* shall live by *faith*," finds a place in this prophet. I call it the Christian principle, as expressing the habit of faith in God, or His revealed word, without annexing to it a knowledge of particular Christian truths, which there is no ground to think that the Prophet had in view. It is that virtue of hope and reliance which moulds itself to the divine promises and revelations, whatever they are; that virtue which has been the strength of good men in every age, and is made most

---

[1] Compare Nahum i. 2. with Jonah iv. 2. Nahum iii. 1. with Jonah iii. 8.

eminent in the Christian system; in which general idea St. Paul enforces the text here cited, and the principle of it[m]. This text then is a vein of Christian doctrine, which if we might otherwise have overlooked, we can no longer do so when the Apostle has taught us to extract from it its proper ore.

2. The context introductory to this principle of "the life by faith," may not improperly be considered as of the like Christian character. In that context is expressed the patient "watching" of Habakkuk for a further opening of divine truth; and the promise made to him, "that the vision shall have its appointed time, and at the end shall speak," "and shall not lie, and though it tarry it shall come[n]." What is this but descriptive of a state of mind which cannot be cast off even under the Gospel revelation, but which must have been far more familiar to believers of an earlier time, who had to wait for the advent of that revelation, and in a dark and disturbed world could less discern how the *great vision of God* was to reach its appointed end? The sustained patience of the understanding, under an imperfect knowledge, is still a duty to inquisitive minds: before the Gospel light broke forth, this duty was a more difficult one. But to "*live* by faith," to live by that degree of knowledge which is imparted, is the *end* of it, be it more or less. This is the doctrine of the Prophet; and so much of a Christian principle and sentiment may be traced in what he has written; whilst the conclusion of his book rises into a higher strain of the exercise of that habit and duty which he had previously commended. For it contains a confession of his own faith, and that faith separated from all earthly and temporal

---

[m] Rom. i. 17; Heb. x. 38.

[n] "I will stand upon my watch, and set me upon the tower, and will *watch to see* what He will say unto me, and what I shall *answer* when I am re-*proved* ('*argued with*,' *questioned* for my faith): and the Lord answered me, and said, Write the vision, and make it plain upon tables, that he may run that readeth it. For the *vision* is yet for an *appointed time*, but at the end *it shall speak*, and *not lie*; though it tarry, *wait for it*, because it *will surely come*, it will not tarry." Habak. ii. 1, 2, 3.

hopes[o]. As such it is of a pure evangelical character. The conclusion of Habakkuk is in fact a beginning of Christ's proper doctrine, and whoever will read it, and then pass to the beatitudes of the Sermon on the Mount, will see in both the sanctions of Canaan recede, and the vision of the better kingdom opened.

The brief investigation which has thus been made into those parts of the Prophetic Volume which seem to contain the least of Christian prediction in them, will conduce to shew, how really small a proportion of that Volume there is which can be said to be devoid of a Christian sense. Thence I may be permitted to infer with the greater confidence, how general, how universal a testimony the Prophets conspire in bearing to Christ and His religion. "To Him give all the prophets witness;" a proposition which has now been supported and evinced in its substantial truth.—It is possible that some of the topics and articles which I have touched upon, in the consideration of this particular point, may have seemed less attractive, or even less important, than a hasty inquirer might wish. But all our speculations are important as they illustrate, or confirm, material truth; and if what has been said may conduce to explain the structure of Prophecy, and elucidate its connexion with the Gospel, that is enough.

I resume the *general state* of Christian Prophecy, prior to the restoration from the captivity; and upon this whole period of it I offer the following remarks.

I. The fullest, and the most expressive discoveries of the Gospel, prior to that æra, commence with Isaiah and

---

[o] Chap. iii. 17, 18. "Although the fig-tree shall not blossom, neither shall fruit be in the vines; the labour of the olive shall fail, and the fields shall yield no meat; the flock shall be cut off from the fold, and there shall be no herd in the stalls: yet I will rejoice in the Lord, I will joy in the God of my salvation."

Micah, and end with Daniel; but those discoveries were made concurrent with the decline and fall of the Temporal Kingdom, and the greatest disorders and interruptions of the Temporal Covenant. That is, when the first dispensation began to be shaken, the objects and promises of the second began to be substituted in its place. A new kingdom, a new covenant, are set forth to view; and the blessings and mercies which are most peculiar to the expected dispensation are set in a clearer light than ever before. For example, the pardon of sin by the death of the Messiah, and the atoning virtue of His sacrifice, are first unfolded in the prophecies of the 53d chapter of Isaiah, and the 9th of Daniel. In the Patriarchal Revelation this doctrine is not expressed; in the Prophetic Psalms, which yet are full of the Christian subject, it is not expressed. If a more accommodating interpretation may elicit some indirect disclosures of the same truth in those earlier times of prophecy, yet the article, the very doctrine, is not formally disclosed, as it is in Isaiah and Daniel. Within the same period of later revelation, there are innumerable other notices of the same kind, tending to describe the Gospel state, and to embody in a more distinct and luminous information the advent and history of the Messiah, and the nature of the mercy and redemption to be communicated by Him. I have said once before, that the Gospel promises could never appear to be out of season, whenever it should please the goodness of God to impart them. But the fact is, that He has imparted them in prophecy, in their utmost strength and clearness, at the season when His earlier dispensation received its rudest shock from the sin of His people: when He was proceeding to cast one part of Israel out of His sight, and the remaining part had least of safety and peace. Without pretending to any minuteness of the chronological comparison of history and prophecy, which my object does not require, this is unquestionably true, that the evangelical prophecies of Isaiah come in when the kingdom of Israel was approaching to its ruin. The first overthrow of God's ancient people was therefore accompanied with this contemporary revelation of the Gospel. As the proof of His ulterior purpose, the design which had been present to Him under every state of His first people, whether they rose or fell, this discovery of the Gospel, so renewed and so enlarged as it was at this season, is worthy of notice. It is the index of His unchanged Counsel and Providence. But it is also the instance of His great Mercy. For how can we think that such scenes of ruin and confusion, such times of perplexity and dismay, were not afflicting to the minds of the good and faithful servants of God, few as they might be, who, if not involved in the actual suffering, could not escape the doubt and disquietude of feeling attached to the mysterious course of Providence which was before them. What if the Prophets forespoke the evil before it came, and justified the ways of God, and explained that all which they suffered was for sin?   Could that administer to good men, who had the least share in the general guilt, any consolation or relief?   Was the cloud less heavy, because the public visitation was just? The later Psalms[p] perfectly express this kind of perplexity in the agitations and importunate inquiries of an afflicted faith.   " Lord, *where* are Thy old lovingkindnesses, which Thou swarest unto David in Thy truth?   O think upon Thy congregation, whom Thou hast purchased and redeemed of old.   Think upon the tribe of Thine inheritance ; and Mount Sion wherein Thou hast dwelt.   Look upon the Covenant: for all the earth is full of darkness, and cruel habitations."   In a word, " all the foundations of the earth, in such times, were out of course."

In the face of these troubles, the Evangelical prophecy was interposed.   It opened new resources of hope to the faithful servant of God.   When the first covenant was in its wane, the light of prophecy was augmented.   And it was augmented in all those respects in which the faith of religious minds required the greatest support, *viz.*, in the promise of a better covenant; in discoveries of God's unchangeable purpose of mercy; and the prospects of a future state of life and immortality;—a *conformity* of prophecy to the exigencies of religion, which speaks for itself in its wise and merciful adaptation.   Prophecy began at the first to remedy the dark and desolate state of Nature.   It now furnished the like remedy to the dark and desolate state of the existing Dispensation of Revealed Religion.

II. But within this same period the Prophets also bring the idea of religion nearer to the Gospel in a great and material point, by explaining the inferior value of the Ceremonial Law, and giving notice of its future abrogation. "*Wherewith* shall I come before the Lord, and bow myself before the most High God?" *Not* with *burnt-offerings* and *sacrifices*, answers the prophet Micah[q]. "But He hath shewed thee, O man, what is good; and what doth the Lord require of thee, but to *do justly*, and to *love mercy*, and to *walk humbly* with thy God."   And Hosea[r]—"I desire *mercy* and not *sacrifice*, and the *knowledge of God more* than *burnt-offerings*." It might be thought that such declarations were intended only against the vice and superstition of that false service which finds it easier to sacrifice than to obey, and thereby to correct the undue preference which men of their own will might give to the Ceremonial Law.   But the Prophets do more than this; they insist on the real inferiority of the ritual worship; they mark the essential difference which the several parts of His law had in the sight of God[s].   This is the proper force of that memorable passage in Jeremiah: "For I *spake not* unto your fathers, *nor commanded* them in the day that I brought them out of the land of Egypt, concerning *burnt-offerings*, or *sacrifices*.   But *this thing commanded I them*, saying, *Obey* My voice, and I will be your God, and ye shall be My people[t]." However both might be commanded,

[q] Micah vi. 6, 8.
[s] See 1 Sam. xv. 22.

[r] Hosea vi. 6.
[t] Chap. vii. 22.

the virtue of practical obedience was always first in the estimation and judgment of God, and in the intent of His law. And it is to be observed that the exaltation of moral duty here enforced by the prophet, is a sequel to his prediction of the fall of the Temple.

This exposition of the principle of religion, brought in by the prophets, was an approach to the Economy of the Gospel, which sets the Ritual Law wholly aside, and establishes the Moral for ever. In this light it was a preparation made for the future change. But it must be considered in another light also, as a most opportune instruction, introduced when the observance of the Ritual Law was rendered difficult or impracticable. For what could the real worshippers of God, devout and virtuous men, do, when they were beset by intestine trouble and foreign invasion, when their heathen enemies were beginning to make spoil of their land, and access to their Temple was denied them, and the Temple itself about to be destroyed; or when bad princes and a corrupted priesthood suspended, as often they did, the public Institutions of their Religion? In this anarchy of the Temple-service, how desirable was it to such men to know that the personal religion which God still left to them, was that which He most esteemed, and had always preferred. How instructive to find His prophetic law taking them up in the difficulties of their present situation.

But if these men were few, still to others the same kind of instruction could not be without its immediate force and use. For what little of religion they had, being more in rites, than in practice, their eyes might be opened to their mistake, when God took away their ceremonies, and that with some scorn, and yet their repentance, whenever it came, would not want the opportunity, or the invitation, of an acceptable worship. The spirit of the Prophets, whilst it spoke to their reproof, invited them to those duties of justice, mercy, and humble piety, which remained the most in their power. And thus, in the decline of the Temple-service, amidst the public judgments of God upon their land, the principles of essential religion were invigorated; those principles were taught with more clearness to console the devout, and direct the penitent; and the individual had his hopes secured, when the public ordinances of His Law were impeded, or wholly taken away; an adaptation of the prophetic doctrine which we may the rather admit to have been designed, since it holds in the fact, and is in the obvious tendency of it so like to a gracious and wise provision.

All this prophecy, whether of promise, or of doctrine, being consigned to one united record, the volume of the Prophets was added to that of the Law, and became the depositary of the best hopes of the people of God; a fund of instruction and consolation, open to all, but, no doubt, most resorted to by those who were of a temper to make the best use of every part of His revelation.—The same record which, to one age, was a *preparative* to the Gospel, became, as we shall find, to another, an *evidence* of its truth.

DISCOURSE VI.

STATE OF PROPHECY FROM THE REIGN OF SOLOMON
TO THE RESTORATION FROM THE BABYLONIAN
CAPTIVITY.

PART III.

On the Pagan Prophecy within that Period, and its Moral Use.

UPON the whole of that branch of Prophecy which relates to anything in the condition of Pagan States and Kingdoms, I shall speak very concisely; perhaps with more conciseness than the great extent of the subject may appear to admit. But it happens that many of the most eminent of the Scripture prophecies in this class, as those concerning Tyre, Babylon, and Egypt, and some others, by the ancient splendour of the states to which they refer, by the curiosity which watches the fate of great kingdoms, and by the collateral attractions of Pagan history and literature, have had, to a certain degree, the preference in the general attention, and have been advantageously set forth in those popular works upon prophecy which are the most commonly read: for which reason, in my survey of the structure of Prophecy, I may in this branch of it rely the more freely upon the stock of a received and known information. Another reason for some brevity in this line of my discourse is, that I shall have occasion to revert to some of the same subjects of Prophecy, in examining its *Inspiration*; and whilst they are brought forward in that second point of view, its *form* and *character* will partly be illustrated at the same time. On these accounts I shall confine and abridge my present remarks; the object of them being to shew, in one general view, the *moral use* of the whole of this branch of ancient Prophecy.

1. When prophecy began its communication to Abraham, he had discovered to him the remote judgment of God upon Egypt[a] and the Amorites[b], and the nearer judgment upon Sodom and Gomorrah. These were nations placed within his view, or connected with the future state of his family, the Hebrew people. The revelation, thus opened to Abraham, continued in its after-age to hold the same order: for the Temporal Prophecy continued to embrace the condition of the Hebrew Church and Nation, and the condition of other states and kingdoms, so far as the people of Israel were either affected by those other kingdoms, or were so placed as to see and understand the tenour of God's providence in their history. "Shall I hide from Abraham that thing which I do?" is the introduction of the prophecy which revealed to Abraham the doom of Sodom and Gomorrah. "Surely the Lord God will *do nothing*, but *He revealeth His secret* to His servants the prophets[c];" this is the range of prophecy concerning His *own people.* "I have ordained thee *a prophet unto the nations*[d];" this is the mission of Jeremiah at the time when prophecy took its largest scope among the kingdoms of the earth, and God's Government and Providence were to be most conspicuously displayed in their rise and fall, their conquests and desolations. In the Mosaic æra the like union of the Pagan subject with the others may be observed[e]; and throughout the one principal age of Pro-

---

[a] Genesis xv. 14. [b] Ver. 16.

[c] Amos iii. 7. [d] Jerem. i. 5.

[e] See particularly the predictions of Balaam, which give an instance of this union. They include the *Amalekite,* the *Kenite,* and the *Assyrian;* *i. e.* some of the less and the greater states; and also some of the nearer and more distant events. Moreover, if the whole chain of Balaam's prophecy be examined, it will seem to comprehend, 1st, the *condition of the Hebrew people;* their safety; their victories; their lonely and insulated character. 2dly, *The*

phecy, from Samuel to Malachi, the connexion is constantly maintained, including some prediction of the affairs of those states which gave to the Israelite a ground either of public interest and concern, or of clear observation. There is then a general consistency in the prophetic system, in this article of it; and the analogy begins in the revelation to Abraham, to whom indeed was exemplified the entire scheme of prophecy, though in its simplest form, in all its parts, Christian, Jewish, and Pagan.

2. The use of this prophecy concerning Heathen nations was in part the same as that of all other temporal prophecy; *viz.*, to demonstrate the Providence of God. For His ordination of things, although it might have been explained by His revealed word after the event, was yet more forcibly exhibited to men by the disclosure made before the event took place. His prescience, His counsel and positive appointment, were thereby manifested together. "Who shall *declare it*, and *set it in order* for Me[1]," is His double claim, expressed in the promulgation of prophecy, and attested in its completion. But had His prophets confined their revelation to the affairs of the Hebrew People, the proof of His providence would have been imperfect; His overruling sovereignty in the sphere of other kingdoms might have remained in question: and since His moral government in those kingdoms was of the ordinary and less sensible kind, administered by the agency of second causes, and with a rare interposition of miracle, it became so much the more useful to demonstrate, by the

<hr>

rise and dominion of the Gospel; if "the Star and the Sceptre" be admitted to be the signs of the advent and religion of Christ, which is their most legitimate interpretation. 3dly, the *visitation* of some of the *heathen* enemies of Israel. Thus it will comprehend the *Hebrew*, the *Christian*, and the *Pagan* subjects; and according to this view the constrained predictions of this perverse prophet will bear the greater testimony to the directing power of God, who put into his mouth every parable of prediction with a sense and import the most opposite to his will, and to the will of those heathen enemies who sought to suborn his prophecy, and try for "*divination and enchantment*" against Israel.   [1] Isaiah xliv. 7.

medium of prophecy, His equal direction in those other systems of human affairs, and by the unrestricted range of His revelation to shew the universality of His Providence. The state of religion in the world rendered this exercise of prophecy infinitely expedient. For one of the most prevalent notions of false religion was in the belief of local and tutelary divinities. Polytheism divided the world, and its own creed, in severalty; it set up its deities over particular regions or kingdoms, within which it circumscribed their power. Under such ideas, the God of Israel might have appeared the deity of one place or people. But all this error of belief was effectually refuted to the Israelite by the prophetic cognizance which he had imparted to him. In his prophecies he read the general disposal of the kingdoms of the earth, their changes and fortunes the subject of God's prescience, the appointment of His sovereign will.

3. A further reason, which gave to this one kind of prophecy a fitness, as a moral instrument of Truth, was in the universal reverence paid to oracles, or systems of divination[g]. The desire to see into futurity, which is a passion so natural to man, and so powerful, was soon abused by the craft of policy, or religious imposture; or, without such management, degenerated of itself into the superstitions of augury, necromancy, and other forms of credulous delusion. To the Israelite all these modes of *exploring* futurity were forbidden, as the devices of heathenism[h]. But the prohibition was made most rational, and the

---

[g] This general disposition of belief in systems of divination is expressed by Cicero, in the opening of his Treatise De Divinatione : " *Vetus opinio* est, jam usque ab *heroicis* ducta *temporibus,* eaque et *populi Romani* et *omnium gentium* firmata consensu, versari quamdam inter homines *divinationem,* quam Græci μαντικὴν appellant, *i. e.,* præsensionem et scientiam rerum futurarum. Magnifica quidem res, et salutaris, *si modo est ulla :* quæque proxima ad Deorum vim naturæ mortali possit accedere."—" *Gentem* quidem *nullam* video, neque *tam humanam* atque *doctam,* neque tam *immanem* tamque *barbaram,* quæ non significari futura, et a quibusdam intelligi prædicique posse sentiat."

[h] Deut. xviii. 14; Levit. xix. 31, &c.

argument of it enforced, by the genuine gift of prophecy, which shewed the omniscience of God in that quarter where the arts and oracles of superstition had their reign; in the affairs of those countries wherein they were practised. "*Those nations* which thou shalt possess, *hearkened unto observers of times*, and *unto diviners;* but as for thee, the Lord thy God hath not suffered thee so to do." This was the practice of the ancient Canaanite. The Egyptian, and the cultivated Chaldæan, in a later age, infused more of the mystery of pretended science into the same kind of superstition. But the inspired prophets of Israel furnished the antidote, and the refutation, of all this science, when they could contrast with its vanity the truth of their own predictions in one and the same subject. "Thus saith the Lord, that *frustrateth* the *tokens* of the *liars*, and *maketh diviners mad*, that turneth wise men backward, and maketh their *knowledge* foolish: that *confirmeth* the *word* of His servant, and performeth the *counsel* of His *messengers*[i]." By this test God vindicated His own foreknowledge, and put the pretences of human skill, and of idol oracles, to confusion. Nor were the Israelites free from the contagion of credulity in these heathen arts[k]. They were "*replenished* from the *East*, and became *soothsayers* like the Philistines." It was their inveterate fault to be for ever adopting the practices of false religion under all the light of their own: but to this their propensity the instruments of their own religion were opposed; and prophecy in particular maintained the contest with their spirit of defection.

Herein is evinced the entire *futility* of those insinuations of Collins, "that the Jews had an *order and succession* of *prophets* in *analogy* to the heathen *diviners;*— and that not only the *business* of the *diviners* among the *heathen*, and of the prophets among the Jews, was *much the*

[i] Isaiah xliv. 25.

[k] Isaiah viii. 19; Jerem. xxix. 8; Micah v. 12. "I will cut off *witchcrafts* out of thine hand, and thou shalt have no more *soothsayers*."

same, but also that the *prophets* were raised up in *Israel,* to *supply* the place of those *diviners*[l]." In which statement, (omitting some of the grosser phrase of it,) he objects to Revealed Religion a fact which resists the perversion he would put upon it. It is true that Diviners and Prophets *had* both the same office, to foretell the future. Prophets *were* sent to supply the place of Diviners. Real prophecy, real miracles, real revelation, *are* given to fill the place which their counterfeits attempt to fill. Truth supplies the place of falsehood by refuting and excluding it. What is there in this but what is reasonable, and even necessary? For Revealed religion does not differ, and *cannot* differ, from the inventions of craft and superstition, by the total absence of the like professed media of belief which they employ, but by the reality of those media in its own case, and the substantial evidence with which it invests them. It cannot differ from them by having no miracles, no prophecy, no communicated doctrine, but by having those things real and true. The question therefore is not whether Prophets and Diviners had the same business, to foretell the future, but which foretold it with truth; which performed the office in a manner worthy of the prescience of God, and to the service of religion. To which question, after a comparison made between the two, the answer cannot be difficult, or uncertain.

The sentiment of Origen, on this head, has therefore great truth and reason in it. He says of prophecy, that it had one use in being a kind of *compensation*[m] for the prohibited rites of augury, soothsaying, and other received modes of the prognostic art; and that, whilst heathens had these rites in repute among them, if the Israelite had been indulged with no discoveries of the future, and especially on *subjects* affecting *his present interest* and *experience,* despising his own religion for its defect in this par-

---

[l] Grounds and Reasons, p. 28. Scheme of Literal Prophecy, p. 259.
[m] Παραμυθία.

ticular, he would have revolted to the oracles or arts of heathenism, or set up for himself something like them[n]. A representation perfectly natural and consistent, and arguing the great reasonableness of making prophecy an instrument of Revealed Religion, which was thereby enabled to demonstrate the prescience and providence of God, and to expose and condemn the fallacies of human craft, otherwise too successfully making a prey of the world. For it is to be remembered, that Prophecy, and all the other evidence of Revealed Religion, was directed to the refutation of false systems, as well as the establishment of the true. The One God, and His *exclusive* truth, were the object of that evidence. — There is also good sense in the further observation of Origen, that by the gratification and conviction afforded by prophecy to the Israelites in some of its meaner occasional subjects, it gained, or might reasonably demand, their confidence and regard to its greater predictions, whether of a temporal, or a Christian kind, to which they might have been less disposed to pay a voluntary attention.

Origen's general doctrine on this subject is adopted by Spencer; in whose hands however it has passed into a license of representation, not to be reconciled either with truth, or with the dignity of God's appointment, when he describes the various gifts of prophecy, as so many concessions in *imitation* of heathen practices, and in lieu of them[o]. There is an original and independent reason of prophecy; that reason is, to authenticate, and unfold, the Revelation of God. Collaterally prophecy is opposed to the oracles of falsehood. But had there been no false oracles in the world, Prophecy, which had its beginning in Paradise, and was anterior to their existence, would have had its office in the scheme of Revealed Religion. Consequently it is a derogation from its origin and cha-

---

[n] Contra Celsum, p. 28.

[o] De Legib. Hebr. lib. iii. cap. ii. sect. 3. Diss. I. Deum Oracula et Prophetiam *seculi moribus* et *Hebræorum imbecillitati concessisse*, &c.

racter to view it so widely and so liberally as Spencer has done, in the secondary sense of an expedient, and an accidental provision. But this is a kind of fault from which the theory of his celebrated work, replete, as it is, with erudition and research, cannot, in some other parts of it, be wholly excused.—It would be nearer the truth to say, that Prophecy, as it respected the arts and devices of heathenism, was framed to their condemnation and exclusion.

To resume the point in hand;—When Ahaziah's messengers, going to consult the god of Ekron, received the reproof from Elijah, "Is it not *because* there is *not a God in Israel*, that *ye go to inquire* of Baal-zebub, *the god of Ekron?*" the reproof was valid, (as Origen justly argues,) because in Israel they *had* prophets of their own : and the prophecy which Elijah delivered on the occasion, was equally to the shame of Ahaziah, and of his oracle of Ekron[p].—When Daniel recalled and interpreted the vision of the king's dream, which the astrologers and the soothsayers of Chaldæa could not recall, the omniscience of God in "revealing the deep and secret things," the *inspiration* of *Daniel*, and the *ignorance* of the *Chaldæan sages*[q] with all their natural and mystical science, were equally illustrated. — Again : when Isaiah[r], foreshewing the destruction of Babylon, challenged and exposed the skill of those same sages, its inhabitants; the conclusion was evident. The prophet in Israel was the effectual witness of God and His Revealed Religion; and this testimony was the most convincing, when it struck upon those subjects or cases wherein the heathen art was sure to be consulted and appealed to; which of course was generally in the concerns of those heathen kingdoms.

4. It is a material fact to be observed, that the information of Prophecy on the subject of heathen states and kingdoms, becomes most copious and explicit in the age

<hr>

[p] 2 Kings i. 3.　　　[q] Dan. ii.　　　[r] Chap. xliv. 25. xlvii. 11.

when those states and kingdoms seemed to triumph the
most, in trampling upon, and overwhelming, the adopted
people of God. The most disastrous times of that people
are the most largely furnished with the evidence of prophecy concerning their spoilers and invaders. The success of the Pagan was in some measure the triumph of
Paganism. For we know how much of the honour of
their victories they were accustomed to ascribe to their
divinities: and the victor's triumphal return was commonly to the celebration of his idol's worship, or to some
new improvement of it; whilst the religion of the conquered sunk in the disgrace of their defeat. Accordingly
the memorials of these times of reproach and distress in
Israel shew how much the faith of men, and the credit
of religion, were assailed by the boasts of their alien conquerors. The cry of the oppressed Israelite was, " Wherefore should the heathen say, Where is now their God[s]?
Remember this, that the *enemy* hath *reproached*, O Lord,
and that the foolish people have *blasphemed Thy Name*.
The ways of Zion do mourn : her adversaries are the chief
—her enemies prosper." But the prophetic information
was one relief provided under these perplexing and questionable circumstances of heathen triumph. For all those
kingdoms of the East, which for a time filled the world
with commotion, had their rise and their victories, their
changes and downfall, delineated in the page of prophecy.
The controlling Providence of God was thereby explained,
when it was most liable to be called in question: His
people were most directed when their sufferings and their
fears were at the greatest height; His supreme moral government was elucidated equally in their own predicted
afflictions, and the appointed and foretold victories of their
present conquerors, or their expected deliverer. The predictions of Jeremiah, which immediately precede the Captivity, and those of Daniel, which are concurrent with it,
were the witness of God, previously set up in the heart of

 Psalms lxxix. lxxx. &c. Lament. &c.

the heathen world, and formed the most appropriate bulwark adapted to the necessities of Religion, as it then had to contend with its heaviest storm under its first dispensation.

5. Another fact to be remarked is, that the evidence of Prophecy gained a greater compass and clearness when the interposition of Miracles was withdrawn. For general miracles, either of destruction, or deliverance, miracles affecting the entire state of the Jewish people, were no longer wrought. The days of Moses and Joshua were past; but the days of Isaiah, Jeremiah, Ezekiel, and Daniel, that is, of the enlarged prophetic revelation, intervene; and theirs was a time when not only more of prophecy was given, but more of it was accomplished. It was in a constant course of fulfilment. It furnished therefore to religion a reinforcement of evidence.

6. I know not with what feeling others may read the afflictions, overthrow, slaughter, and dispersion of God's ancient people, His only Church in the world, delivered into the hand of barbarous enemies, with the utter extirpation of the one part of it, and the suppression and bondage of the other; or how they may reflect upon the apparent severity of His judgment upon His own adopted people, the dishonour of His name among heathens, or the afflicted condition of His upright and virtuous servants, whose faith and integrity were cast upon these times of perturbation, and tried in the furnace; but I think the impression made upon serious minds in a review of this scene of things will be of no ordinary sort, nor exempted from some degree of pain and amazement. When *Christian* Churches suffer in their temporal safety, or are shaken in their peace, the case is different. For Christianity stands upon other promises revealed. The captivity, devastation, and public orphanhood of the Jewish Church was a far more perplexing phenomenon—the trials, joined

with it, of the constancy and faith of good men, more severe.

One book of Scripture there is, in which God has pleased to preserve the memorial of this great struggle of religion, both in its public and its private state; wherein every feeling, and every reflection, adapted to such a scene, are recorded and expressed to the life. It is the short volume of "the Lamentations" of that Prophet who lived in the midst of it; a book which is the perfect moral history of those times, and of religion, in its public and its interior personal trials; a book of a more profound and exquisite feeling than can be equalled in any of the most boasted of uninspired writings, and of the most exact delineation on the whole question of the dark and fearful visitation of God, under which His Church and People were cast.

But after taking a full view of this troublous state of things, turn to the Prophets: see what they had already disclosed, and were continuing to disclose, both concerning the Pagan kingdoms, and in their renewed and enlarged promises of the Gospel dispensation. All that revelation which shewed God's controlling power over those kingdoms, proving them to be the regulated instruments of His Providence, and marking the appointed periods, the particular rise and fall, of many of them; all that other revelation which discovered the prospect of the Gospel, and opened more largely its doctrines and mercies; were fitted, in union, to support the cause of Religion, and to administer consolation and instruction to the minds of men who were willing to seek it. It is plain, that the prophetic revelation, at this great æra of it, corresponded to the difficulties, perhaps I might say, the decays, of the Jewish Covenant. When the apparent visible ruins of the elder dispensation were most likely to perplex and alarm, Paganism could not triumph, the Gospel could not be despaired of. In the very heart of the Captivity, in the abyss

of the Babylonian bondage, Daniel *weighed* and *numbered*
the *kingdoms of the earth.* There also he measured the
years to the death of the *Messiah,* and marked the place
of order, assigned, in the succession of the empires of the
world, to the establishment of *His kingdom.*—Great and
instructive revelations; fitted alike to uphold the Jewish
Religion, and to sustain the expectation, and complete
the prophetic evidence, of the Christian.

DISCOURSE VI.

PART IV.

AFTER some observations upon that part of Prophecy which was seen in its fulfilment, at the expiration of the Captivity, I shall proceed to consider what was further given, from that time till the mission of the Prophets ceased.

First, of what was fulfilled. When Cyrus became master of Babylon, the prophecies of Isaiah were shewn or communicated to him, wherein was described his victory, and the use he was appointed to make of it in the restoration of the Hebrew people[a]. " In the first year of Cyrus, king of Persia, (that the word of the Lord by the prophet *Jeremiah* might be fulfilled,) the *Lord stirred up the spirit of Cyrus*, king of Persia, that he made a *proclamation* throughout all his kingdom, and also in *writing*, saying, Thus saith Cyrus king of Persia, The Lord God hath given me all the kingdoms of the earth, and *He hath charged* me to *build Him an house at Jerusalem*, which is in Judah. Who is there among you of all His people? his God be with him, and let him go up to Jerusalem," &c. The word by the prophet *Jeremiah*, here referred to by Ezra, is the term of *Seventy* years. The *charge* which Cyrus himself confesses to have received is the prediction of *Isaiah*. Some prophecies there are, which, under given cir-

---

[a] Ezra i. 1, 2.

cumstances, tend to work their own accomplishment. The prediction in question concerning Cyrus may be reckoned partly of this kind, if we look at it from the time when he was master of Babylon, and beginning to apply his policy to the affairs of his kingdom. From that time, the conformity of his action to the prophecy may be thought to have been a natural, or very reasonable compliance with the dictate and impulse of such a prediction, which spoke to the honour of his victory, and dignified his liberation of the Hebrew people, a humane and generous act, in itself not unsuited to his natural character, with the sanction of a divine command. But yet there was a supernatural direction upon him, which prompted his mind and incited his doings; God so furthering the fulfilment of His word, wherein He had said, "He is My shepherd, and shall *fulfil all My pleasure*[b]." Accordingly the Restoration was instant. It was one of the immediate acts of Cyrus, and put in force in the *first year*[c] of his conquest; as though his conquest had been given to him, which indeed was the fact[d], only that he might fulfil the prophecy, when God "opened before him the two-leaved gates of brass," and he through those gates let go the captive people, redeemed into freedom; and that "not for price or reward;" unless he had a sense of that which is the greatest of all rewards, in being a willing instrument to execute the good pleasure of God. The solemn proclamation of Cyrus, his Edict, setting forth the prophecy, was a public recognition of it to his empire. As such, it would draw notice to the particular prediction, and might probably spread something of the knowledge and honour of the true God, where it

[b] Isaiah xliv. 27.

[c] "In the *first* year of Cyrus," Ezra i. 1. viz., reckoning from the *Initia Cyri Babylonica*, the commencement of his enlarged Empire.

[d] "Thus saith the Lord to His anointed, to Cyrus, whose right hand I have holden, to subdue nations before him; I will loose the loins of kings, to open before him the two-leaved gates.—For *Jacob My servant's sake*, and *Israel Mine* elect, I have even *called thee by thy name*: I have surnamed thee, though thou hast not known Me. I am the Lord, and there is none else.—*I girded thee*, though thou hast not known Me." Isaiah xlv. 1—5.

was conveyed. But one certain and important use of this *Edict* of Cyrus, *founded* upon the *prophecy*, was in securing the favour of succeeding kings of Persia[e] to the Hebrew people, for the safety of their affairs, and the complete restitution of their city and temple. It is well known what great reverence and honour was paid to the memory of the Founder of their empire, and to all his acts, by the Persian princes who came after him; in which hereditary reverence to Cyrus, "the appointed Shepherd" of God, that people had for some time their best security and protection, when miracles were withdrawn, and their reviving condition had to struggle its way through much trouble and danger. And thus this part of prophecy may be traced, in the disposition of things under God's ordinary providence, advancing to its fulfilment: that fulfilment taking its rise from the original act of Cyrus, who left to his successors a reason and an example for promoting the same purpose of the divine command. Hence Prophecy may be truly said to have governed the kings of Persia towards the re-settlement of the Hebrew people[f].

But having stated that the prediction in this one instance might tend to work its own accomplishment, I limit that statement simply to the use which Cyrus made, and was raised up to make, of his victory. It is only in that branch of it that such an influence to the effect could be derived from the prediction. Prophecy in Judæa could not raise up such a person, or such a conqueror; or bring the Medes and Persians before Babylon, or open the gates of that city, or dry up the Euphrates;—prophecy could not raise the Chaldeans into power, or give them the previous possession of Babylon, or the hand to provide materials for the completion of the last link in this extended

---

[e] See Ezra v. 13, 17. vi. 1, 2, 14. ix. 9.

[f] It is significantly said by Ezra, "The Elders of the Jews builded, and they prospered through the prophesying of Haggai the prophet, and Zechariah the son of Iddo: and they builded, and finished it, according to the *Commandment* of the *God of Israel*, and *according* to the *decree* of *Cyrus* and *Darius*, and *Artaxerxes* king of Persia." Chap. vi. 14.

chain of events. Herein, therefore, is to be confessed the clear and commanding evidence of the inspiration manifested in these prophecies of Isaiah; the extent and the complexity of them overwhelming the idea that the last issue of such an order of things could be the result of a fortuitous combination of circumstances, or of the will of men *following* the prediction, and thereby making it complete itself.

Seventy years was the term predicted for the duration of the Captivity. From the first deportation to Babylon to the first return, the period is that term of Seventy Years[g]. Had the career of Cyrus brought him to the capture of Babylon in a later year, or had he not granted the Jews an instant liberation, the prophecy could not have had so exact and precise a completion.

But Chronology has furnished to interpreters a *second equal* period of Seventy Years, to be computed from the *Destruction* of the *Temple* to its *complete* Rebuilding: the destruction of it having been subsequent to the commencement of the *Captivity* by eighteen years, and the completion of it having been delayed and obstructed after the *Return* by the like number of years: viz., from the first year of Cyrus to the sixth of Darius. This equality of time, between the whole duration of the Captivity and the desolation of the Temple, though not coincident the one with the other, is certainly a remarkable fact. But it does not appear that Prophecy any where *predicts* the *second period* relating to the Temple. The mention of that time in Zechariah[h] seems to be expressly *historic;* and Jere-

[g] Viz. from the 4th year of Jehoiakim, which coincides with the 1st of Nebuchadnezzar.

[h] Zech. i. 12. The observation is derived from Petavius (de Doctrina Temporum, lib. xii. cap. 25.), and is called *Pulcherrimum observatum,* by Vitringa, Prolegom. in Zachar. p. 17.

Est enim pulcherrimum Petavii aliorumque observatum, Periodum lxx. annorum, decretorum punitioni Judææ gentis, ad perfectum *implementum prophetiæ bis* representatum esse.

A *primo anno Nabuchodonosoris* (quem Scriptura copulat cum *quarto* Jehojachini) ad xxii. exeuntem Cyri, quo *captivitas* est *soluta,* anni sunt lxx.

miah's *prediction* is simply of the *Return:* "After seventy years I will *visit* you, and perform My good word towards you in causing you to *return* to this place." Consequently, although the observation of the double period is made much of by *Vitringa*, and some other commentators, I do not perceive that it can be properly drawn to the illustration of prophecy.

Another coincidence there is in this prophetic subject, less specious, but more exact to the letter of the prophecy. Isaiah's prediction concerning Cyrus had been, "saying to *Jerusalem*, Thou shalt be *built;* and to the *Temple*, Thy *foundation* shall be laid:" again, "He shall *build* My *city*, and let go My captives." And such was the literal fact, that during the reign of Cyrus the rebuilding of the *City* proceeded from the first return; but of the *Temple*, although Cyrus commanded the restoration of it, only the *foundation* was laid, the progress of that public work being impeded till the reign of Darius. An exactitude which holds in the event; and yet which I should propose as an evidence of prophecy only with some reserve, in the fear lest, by too minute a measure of its text, we should impair the proper splendour and magnitude of its comprehensive revelation.

But the great Providence of God in the Restoration of the house of Judah for the further purposes of His Economy, both Temporal and Evangelical, must not be overlooked in one conspicuous proof of it now given. It does not appear that *Heathen Colonies* had been planted in Judæa, to exclude the facility of a Return: no regular occupation of their land by the settlement of strangers filled the void, and interposed a barrier to their immediate resumption of their country, or to their growth and increase after they were restored. In *Samaria*, that positive

Adde Cyri viii. Cambysis et Magi viii. Darii ii. fiunt lxxxviii. Deductis annis xviii. restant lxx. ab *excidio* Urbis usque ad *annum* ii. *Darii*, quo vaticinatus est Zacharias.

exclusion was provided. The territory of Israel, when Israel was made captive, was filled in Canaan, by a heathen race; so much of the promised land was alienated by God from the original use to which He had assigned it; whilst in Judah the promises of prophecy, and the work of His providence, were still in force, and demanded the possession of the remaining part. I leave it to every one to reflect more deliberately upon this visible difference made in the two cases, and compare it with the tenor of foregoing prophecy in every age, from the death of Jacob in Egypt; the whole of that prophecy being full of preparations for this great result of a distinctive fortune to the tribe of Judah.—But some facts we have here above all controversy. One Tribe was spared, when the Ten fell. That same Tribe was restored, and re-established in its place; whilst the Ten saw their place no more: and heathen nations, as if under a sense of the respective destiny appointed to each, occupied the country of the one, and left room for the return and restoration of the other: a history full of the signs of a singular and discriminating Providence.

And so much having been said on the completion of antecedent prophecy, I go on to consider the further prophecy which was imparted after the Return from the Captivity, and the relation which it bore to the state of their public history and their religion.

II. The last period of the Annals of the Hebrew people, as subjects of their covenant and law, reaches from their return from Babylon to their final rejection and ruin, which coincide with the introduction of the Gospel. This concluding period of their history was not in its progress a time of security and peace; but neither was it marked by any great and lasting change in their public condition. Excepting their one serious, but short calamity, of a few years' continuance, under Antiochus Epiphanes, and that a calamity which had been formally predicted by Daniel[1],

[1] Dan. xi. 28—30. And *also Dan.* viii. 11—13.

their religion and their state remained essentially the same
as it was on their return, without any fatal disaster interposed by exterminating conquest, devastation, or captivity.
They were not the people they had been in the days of
Joshua, or David, "riding upon the high places of the
earth;" their Restoration to Canaan was not like their
first Settlement in it; they were a depressed and dependent people; but their internal polity, as to their Mosaic
Law, and the opportunities and exercise of their religion,
continued to the Gospel age, what they were when they
were replaced in Canaan, for their second and last probation under the moral government of God. And yet within
this time Jerusalem was *thrice* taken by a foreign enemy:
by Antiochus Epiphanes, by Pompey, and by Herod. But
in all these captures, there was no destruction of the city,
no subversion of the state; on the contrary, the conquerors
in these instances spared and preserved their city[k]. Their
persecution, and the suppression of their religion, under
the rage and impiety of *Antiochus*, who for three years set
up heathenism in their temple, form the single epoch of
any prominent change or concussion in their history; but
this epoch and its sufferings had been already described,
as I have said, by Daniel; and thus they had the notice
of it committed to prophecy before the commencement of
their restoration. On the other hand, it does not appear
that there is any formal or distinct prediction given of the
capture of Jerusalem by *Pompey* or by *Herod*; and since
no important effect followed from either of these aggres-
sions of conquest, the silence of prophecy respecting them
corresponds with their comparatively quiet and neutral
character. And here I may repeat the general summary
of the fortunes of the city of Jerusalem, as it is given by
Josephus. "Jerusalem," he says, "was taken *six times*, but
desolated *only twice*. Its several captures were by Sesac[l],

---

[k] Josephus says of them all, ἐλόντες ἐτήρησαν τὴν πόλιν, de Bello Jud. vi.
10. The remark is true upon the whole; but some qualification of it must
be admitted with respect to Antiochus Epiphanes, who in his ravages burnt
and destroyed certain parts of the city.   [l] 1 Kings xiv. 25.

the Babylonians, Antiochus, Pompey, Herod, Titus. Its desolation, by the Babylonians, and by the Romans under Titus[m]." Such is the historian's statement, and prophecy harmonizes with this distinctive history. For I would observe that prophecy is intent only on those *two greater judicial visitations* of the Hebrew people, in one of which, their *Captivity*, in the other, their *final Rejection*, were involved; the superior importance of these two visitations, in the scheme of the Divine Government, sufficiently indicating the reason why they are selected for the subjects of a copious prophetic revelation, the former of them in the Old Testament, the second in the New. Whereas the other instances of capture are either wholly neglected by the prophets, or slightly touched, if indeed touched at all; as in the case of Antiochus : for it is not his mere conquest of Jerusalem, but his profanation of the Sanctuary, his taking away of the daily Sacrifice, and the abomination of his Heathen Worship which that persecutor established, that are put forward, and make the prominent objects, in the predictive visions of Daniel. So just and perfect a correspondence is there in the structure of Prophecy, in all these points, with the essential history of the Hebrew people under the divine Government.

Such being the general state of that people from their Captivity to the Gospel æra, nothing of great importance befalling them which had not been already foretold, we find that prophecy soon ceased after their return from Babylon. It did not at once intermit its communications; but from Malachi, the last in the prophetic line, there is an interval and silence of it for four hundred years; Haggai, Zechariah, and Malachi, being the only prophets subsequent to the Captivity, and the mission of the two former falling in the first age, the mission of Malachi in the next age, after that epoch. It remains for me to state what was the nature and object of their prophecy, in that portion of it which closed the long series of God's ancient revelation.

<hr>

[m] De Bello Jud. vi. 10.

The predictions of these last prophets are confined almost entirely to two subjects[n], 1. The re-establishment of the Hebrew people and their Temple; 2. The annunciation of the Gospel.—I shall advert to each of these subjects of their prophecy, and endeavour to shew how the latter is introduced in connexion with the other; and also reply to the objections which have disturbed the *Christian* character of the prophecy of this period.

1. The first return of the Jewish people from Babylon was not to security and peace. Their establishment was opposed by the jealousy of the Samaritans, and the hatred of other surrounding enemies; the rebuilding of their temple, and their walls, was forcibly interrupted and delayed. The struggle affected their promised restoration as a Church and People; and the exercise of their religion was at stake in it. But prophecy was instructed to supply the encouragement which the conflict of their fortunes required. It did so by assurances of the repression of their enemies, and the complete re-establishment of their city, temple, and public peace. "Thus saith the Lord, I am returned to Jerusalem *with mercies;* My *house* shall be built in it, saith the Lord of hosts, and a line shall be stretched forth upon *Jerusalem. My cities through prosperity shall yet be spread abroad,* and the Lord shall yet comfort Zion, and shall yet choose Jerusalem[o]."—"For thus saith the Lord of hosts, *As I thought* to punish you when your fathers provoked Me to wrath, saith the Lord of hosts, and *I repented not; so again* have I thought *in these days to do well* unto Jerusalem, and to *the house of Judah:* fear ye not[p]." And such is the general scope of Haggai and Zechariah's predictions, as they relate to the affairs of the Jewish people.

II. But these prophets introduce also the Gospel sub-

<hr>

[n] I exclude here the concluding chapters of the book of Zechariah, viz., from the 9th chapter to the end, which cannot well be ascribed to Zechariah or his age, as Mede and others have, I think, convincingly shewn.

[o] Zech. i. 16, 17.   [p] viii. 14, 15.

ject; Zechariah especially, in mystic vision and by typical representation, which yet are sufficiently clear, as expressive of the kingdom and priesthood of *Christ*, the establishment of the *Christian Church*, and the concourse of nations resorting to that *future Temple*. For here, in this æra, we have a *second* application of the same *systematic* form of prophecy which was employed in the establishment of the Temporal kingdom. The nearer subject, in each instance, supplies the prophetic ground, and the prophetic images, for the future Christian subject. In the first instance, the kingdom of Christ is delineated in connexion with, and by analogy to, the actual kingdom which was seen before men's eyes rising to view; in the second instance, His *personal* priesthood, and His Church, are delineated in connexion with, and by an equal analogy to, the priesthood and temple of the Hebrew Church, at the time when that priesthood was reinstated in its functions, and that temple was rebuilt. As an example of this *symbolical* prediction, founded upon *the present scene* of things, consider the following oracle of Zechariah. The prophet had been commanded to take silver and gold, and make crowns, and set them, or set one of them, upon the head of Joshua, the son of Josedeck, the *high priest*, and then to deliver this prophecy: "Thus speaketh the Lord of hosts, saying, *Behold the Man*, whose name is the *Branch*, and He shall grow up out of this place, (or, there shall be a growth out of His place,) and He shall build the Temple of the Lord: Even *He shall build the Temple of the Lord*, and *He* shall *bear the glory*, and *shall sit and rule upon His throne*, and *He shall be a priest upon His throne*, and *the counsel of peace* shall be between them both." "And the crown shall be for *a memorial* in the Temple of the Lord. And they that *are afar off* shall *come and build* in the *Temple* of the Lord, and ye shall know that the Lord of hosts hath sent me unto you. And this shall come to pass, if ye will diligently obey the voice of the Lord your God[q]."

This oracle, I think, will justify and sustain the cha-

[q] Zech. vi. 10—15.

racter I have assigned to it.　Its mystic form, its sublime and emphatic spirit, its promise of glory, its union of the priesthood and the throne, its appointed memorial of the crown to be laid up in the Temple of the Lord, its assemblage of builders from afar, absolutely refuse to be confined to the literal idea of the present work of the Jewish restoration.　But since the form of the prophecy is assimilated to that primary idea of the Jewish restoration, in their national increase, their priesthood and their temple, the whole principle of the prophecy meets us in the face, first in its ground of analogy, and next in its proper extent, an extent wherein it leaves the inferior subject, from which it springs, far behind.　In truth, there is both reason, and sublimity, in prophecy; and we shall scarcely understand it, unless we are prepared to follow it in both.　Its sublimity is, that it often soars, as here, far above the scene from which it takes its rise.　Its reason is, that it still hovers over the scene of things from which it rose.　It takes the visible, or the temporal subject, as its point of departure (if I may borrow the phrase) for its enlarged revelation; and yet by that subject it governs its course. In this method of it, I believe that men of plain unsophisticated reason find it perfectly intelligible; and that it is only the false fastidiousness of an artificial learning which puts the scruple into our perceptions either of its consistency, or its sense.　But when we consider that this structure of prophecy, founded on a proximate visible subject, had the advantage, both in the *aptitude* of the representation, and in *the immediate pledge*, of the future truth; a sounder learning may dispose us to admit it, and that with confidence, whenever the prophetic text, or mystic vision, is impatient for the larger scope, and the conspicuous characters of the Symbols and the Fact, concur in identifying the relation.

The late learned Translator of the Minor Prophets[r] has therefore failed greatly, as I conceive, in doing justice to

[r] Archbishop Newcome.

this and other prophecies of Zechariah. His version and commentary will scarcely permit the Christian sense of them to be perceived; and in particular he has appropriated to Zerubbabel, or to Zerubbabel jointly with Joshua, the whole of that oracle which I have quoted as a clear and emphatic example of such a sense. With some modifications of the received version, and those modifications doubtful, he assigns the glory, promises, priesthood, and throne, and counsel of peace, described by the prophet, to those two Jewish chiefs. But this application, inadequate as it is to the spirit of the prophecy, to the symbolical form of it, to the large and exuberant phrase of it, is also inconsistent with the actual history of Zerubbabel. *He* did not "bear the glory;" he did not *sit* "and *rule* upon any *throne;* he wore no *crown.*" Zerubbabel and Joshua were some of the "chiefs of the fathers of Israel[s]," leaders, *with* the prophets, in the work of restoration, but holding *a delegated power under the kings of Persia.* How then could all that significant solemnity of a Typical Crown, and a promised Throne, ever fit Zerubbabel's person? And again, how unlike was it to the whole principle, and reasonable order, of a symbolical representation, to set a crown upon the head of *Joshua,* and deliver a prophecy over him, if a second person, a living *contemporary,* were the object of that representation. So also in Zechariah iii. 8, *Joshua, the high priest,* is *crowned,* and the typical promise of *the Branch* is renewed, which the same Prelate explains of *Zerubbabel,* as *heir* of *David.* Now had *Zerubbabel* been *crowned,* the Typical act might have presignified his power. But the imposition of a crown upon *Joshua* perfectly excludes *Zerubbabel.* Add to which that the title of "the Branch" had been already consecrated in prophecy to the Messiah. It is so given once by Isaiah[t], twice by Jeremiah[u]:—and the like designation in this later prophet Zechariah, reviving the memory of those ex-

* Ezra iv. 3.
[t] Isaiah iv. 2. In xi. 1, a *different,* though *equivalent* word, is employed.
[u] Jerem. xxiii. 5. xxxiii. 15.

isting prophecies, could only tend with them to one and
the same object. In a former Discourse I have shewn that
Zerubbabel could not be the *heir* of David, as heir to his
throne, because the temporal kingdom was *taken away;*
and from the time of its abrogation, Christ became the
only regal heir of David, as heir of the second and better
kingdom. And here I may introduce a prophecy of Ezekiel, which will establish and complete the whole history
of this abrogation of the temporal kingdom, since the want
of a clear perception of it is one of the reasons which
have obscured, or perverted, the interpretation of these
important oracles of Zechariah. " And thou wicked *profane prince of Israel*, whose day is come, when iniquity
shall have an end: Thus saith the Lord God, *Remove* the
diadem, and *take off the crown;* this *shall not be the same;*
exalt him that is low: abase him that is high. I will *overturn, overturn, overturn* it: and it shall *be no more*, until
he come whose right it is, and *I will give it him*[x]." The
prophecy of *Jeremiah* had denounced the end of the kingdom of the house of David in the person of *Coniah;* but
the *king of Babylon* set up *Zedekiah. Ezekiel's* prophecy
completes the doom, by this prediction against *Zedekiah,*
(" *I will overturn, overturn, overturn,*") and carries us forward through the long interregnum of continued subversion, to that time when " He shall come *whose right it is :*"
and He can be none other than the Messiah: in whom
alone it was ever restored.

Zerubbabel excluded, Christ is the object of Zechariah's
prophecy. *His* is the crown and the throne, and *His* also
the priesthood; for these He had. In Him, therefore,
the imposition of the crown upon *Joshua*, and all the correspondent prophecy, has its intelligible import: for He is
both *a king* and *a priest*, and *Joshua crowned* was capable
of being a *Type* and *Symbol* of Him; whereas neither
could *Joshua* be a proper *Type* of *Zerubbabel* at all, nor
could *Zerubbabel* answer to that particular representation

<hr>

[x] Ezek. xxv. 27.

of *a regal Type*, had it been exhibited in any other person. In a word, the Symbols, the prediction, the history, all concur in explicating and asserting the Christian sense of this Oracle. And a further observation to be made upon it is, that since the condition and character of Zerubbabel and of Joshua, as seen and known by their people, their brethren and countrymen, in their own day, were wholly incapable of bearing the dignity of the prophecy, it was an information from the time when it was given, directing men to some ulterior object. From the first it was necessarily significant of its more remote scope of application.

I have often considered that *one case* there is in the later history of the Hebrew people, which might possibly have subjected this very oracle of Zechariah's to a wrong idea of the person and state of things to which it referred. That case is the reign of the *Maccabees*. They were *priests*, and became *princes*, and might seem to verify the remarkable promise, " He shall be a priest upon His throne ;" or, according to another version, " There shall be a priest upon the throne." To such a misapprehension the prophecy, in this one clause of it, might seem to have been liable. But its characteristic signature of " *The Man*, whose name is the *Branch*" had been already set apart to a *prince* of the *house* of *David*, and thereby became a security to its right application. For Jeremiah had not simply foretold of a person to come under this title, but had connected His birth with the house of David; and had surnamed Him " the Lord our righteousness," a second exclusive signature, to which the Maccabees could prefer no claim.

Mark then the connexion of the whole prophecy, and the state of its evidence. Jeremiah speaks thus: " In those days and at that time will I cause the Branch of righteousness to grow up unto David, and He shall execute judgment and righteousness in the land. In those days shall Judah be saved, and Jerusalem shall dwell safely; and this is the name wherewith He shall be called, The Lord our Righteousness, or, the name where-

with the Lord shall name Him, our Righteousness[7]."
Hence it appears, that *Zechariah's* prophecy is a *revival*
of Jeremiah's; he introduces it as of a person already
known: "Behold the Man, whose name is the Branch."
The one had been among the last predictions in the commencement of the Captivity, the other is among the earliest after it; and Jeremiah's was delivered, *apparently* at
the time when he pronounced the sentence of deprivation
upon the temporal kingdom, but *certainly* in *connexion*
with *that sentence*[z]. Consequently the whole idea of the
original and the revived prophecy tended to the house of
David, but "*in those days,*" that *other system* of things,
which had been so often promised, as the intended dispensation of God. And I must add, that the Asmonean
family, although they were brave deliverers of their Church
and Country, had not much of the praise of "righteousness and judgment," or of sanctity and peace, in their
character; their glory was in their exploits, not in their
humanity, moderation, or spirit of justice; and as they
were excluded at once, by their race and lineage, from the
title to any of the greater prophecies, so their personal
qualities ill corresponded to the holy and righteous Branch
which was the subject of those reiterated predictions now
in question[a].—And as to Zerubbabel, he is excluded for
the reasons already given.

The entire harmony of prophecy, in this period of it,
will be further illustrated, by considering the predictions
which accompanied the building of the First Temple, and
comparing them with those of the Second. In the instance of the First there clearly is not the same combina-

---

[7] Jer. xxiii. 5.   [z] See Jer. xxii. xxiii.

[a] The Maccabees seem to have been well aware, that they were only inferior ministers of Providence, notwithstanding their princely and sacerdotal
office combined, as we may judge from the following eulogy of their Annals,
respecting one of their Chiefs   Καὶ ὅτι εὐδόκησαν οἱ Ἰουδαῖοι, καὶ οἱ ἱερεῖς τοῦ
εἶναι Σιμῶνα ἡγούμενον καὶ ἀρχιερέα εἰς τὸν αἰῶνα, ἕως τοῦ ἀναστῆναι προφήτην
πιστόν.   1 Macc. xiv. 15. "That Simon should be commander and priest *for
ever, till a Faithful Prophet* arose."

tion of the Mystical sense with the Temporal. The prediction joined with the building of Solomon's Temple is of a simpler kind; perhaps it relates purely and solely to the proper Temple itself. But the Second Temple rises with a different structure of prophecy upon it. Haggai, Zechariah, and Malachi, have each delivered some symbolical prediction, connected with it, or with its Priesthood and Worship. Why this difference in the two cases? I think the answer is clear; it is a difference obviously related to the nearer connexion which the Second Temple has with the Gospel. When God gave them their First Temple, it was doomed to fall, and rise again, *under* and *during* their first economy. The elder prophecy, therefore, was directed to the proper history of the First Temple. But when He gave them their Second Temple, Christianity was then nearer in view; through that second edifice lay the Gospel prospect. Its restoration, therefore, was marked by a kind of prophecy which had its vision towards the Gospel. And a great confirmation is derived to all this view of the structure of prophecy, from the following fact, when it is deliberately weighed and examined. In the days of David and Solomon, when the *temporal kingdom* was set up, the *Christian kingdom* was *copiously* and *eminently* foretold *at the same time;* but it cannot be said that *the Temple*, set up in those same days, had an equal illustration of *Christian Prophecy* cast upon it. The Temporal Kingdom, which was then beginning its course, was not to be restored, after it should once be taken away. But the Temple was destined to fall, and be restored. Hence it should appear, that the *first* institution of the *Kingdom*, and the *second* building of the *Temple*, were equally the seasons, wherein the Christian prophecy, connected with each of those ordinances, might be formed with the most clear and significant adaptation. And such is the actual case; such the date of the respective predictions, joined with, and grounded upon, the Jewish kingdom and Temple. Proceeding from these two *distant points* in the first Economy, prophecy, in each, directs our view to that æra which unites together the Temple and the Kingdom, and completes the divine promises and predictions, ingrafted upon both, in the Church and kingdom of Christ.

III. To proceed. The same origin and ground of the Christian prophecy may be discerned in *Haggai*, as in *Zechariah*. "For thus saith the Lord of hosts, *Yet once*, it is a little while, and I will shake the heavens and the earth, and the sea, and the dry land. And I shall shake all nations, and *the desire of all nations* shall *come*, and I will fill *this house with glory*, saith the Lord of hosts. The silver is Mine, and the gold is Mine, saith the Lord of hosts. The glory of this *latter* house shall *be greater* than the glory of the *former*, and in this house will I *give peace*, saith the Lord of hosts[b]." The shaking of the whole system of the world is the apt image of the introduction of a new economy of God; "the *desire* of all nations" is the Redeemer of the world: the *greater glory* promised to the Second Temple was exhibited in the advent and personal ministry of Christ, who came to that Temple: and by Him God gave *peace* there, when He sealed by His doctrine, and by His death, a *covenant of peace*, in the completion of the Temple Sacrifices and Worship. Such is the old, and apparently the just and consistent interpretation, of this prophecy. But this interpretation has been contested; and although I have endeavoured to demonstrate the structure and intent of Prophecy, in its several ages, as much as possible, from confessed and general premises, without passing through controverted questions; yet, in this last æra of it, it seems that the interpreter who would not sacrifice its *Christian sense*, must make some effort to defend it, and for that purpose must carry himself something like the Israelite of this same age, who had to build with one hand, and bear *a guarded side* on the other. For it is too plain how much the concluding period of the prophetic revelation is degraded and

<hr>

[b] Haggai ii. 6.

impoverished, if one or two of the latest books of it must be given up without a sign of the Gospel upon them.

The objections made to the *Christian* reference of Haggai's prophecy are two. The *First* is, that the text is incorrectly rendered, "the desire of all nations shall come." The *Second*, that *Christ* did not come to *Haggai's* temple; and therefore it could not derive *its greater glory* from His presence[c]. These objections I shall examine.

1. It is argued, that the text which is rendered "the *desire* of all nations," ought to have been translated "the *desirable things* of all nations:" by which the prophet would describe simply the contributions made to the re-building of the Temple, in gold and silver, and other such costly materials of extrinsic splendour[d]. But if this proposed version were adopted, still it would not render the phrase inapplicable to a *single person:* for the collective sense of plurals is often only an augmentation of their idea; and there is no doubt that the *desiderabilia* or *desiderata*, "of all nations," might, like the plurals τὰ κειμηλία, or *thesauri*, be a proper description of some one distinguished blessing. treasure, or object of desire.—The Septuagint translate the text, καὶ ἥξει τὰ ἐκλεκτὰ πάντων τῶν ἐθνῶν, and this translation is pressed as an authority to exclude the idea of an individual. This version certainly does exclude the idea of an individual, if its sense be "the precious or choice things, *taken from* all nations;"

---

[c] These objections, brought forward again, and urged with much zeal, by Dr. Heberden, are published at large by archbishop Newcome, with his version of Haggai. The Prelate does not agree with Dr. Heberden in his critical and historical interpretation, yet he has given to it his praise, and something of a sanction, by speaking of it as "a *valuable* communication, which will give the reader *great assistance* in *determining* the sense of the prophecy now under discussion."

[d] The Hebrew text joins a *plural* verb (*shall come*) with a *singular* noun, expressing what is *desirable* or what is *desired*. Hence it is alleged, that the verb shews that the text ought to be amended, by giving to the *noun* a *plural* form; and the ancient versions favour this emendation. But the criticism is equivocal: for there is the equal right on the other side to make the emendation by changing the *number* of the *verb*, to meet the *singular* form of the noun.

but not, if the Translators, simply following a plural term in the Hebrew, left room for the more general notion, "the precious or choice things *of* all nations," which might be some one eminent treasure, "the desired of the world." The same Interpreters translate another eminent prophecy concerning Christ in this very plural form : ἕως ἂν ἔλθῃ τὰ ἀποκείμενα αὐτῷ: where the phrase τὰ ἀποκείμενα, in grammatical form, and partly also in sense, is equivalent to that of τὰ ἐκλεκτά : and yet, without inquiring whether their version be a correct one, it is not supposed that the Translators had any other idea of the prophecy than as being capable of being applied to the Messiah.

So much premised ; whilst I should admit that the original text, in *this one clause* of Haggai's prophecy, both as to its grammatical form, and the genuine idea of it, requires some deliberation of a sober criticism, yet the version of it which is meant to be destructive of the Christian sense is only precarious, and the contrary interpretation, or such an interpretation as leaves room at least for the Christian sense, is very capable of being defended. Perhaps no just and satisfactory decision will ever be made upon the simple document of the text itself ; — but the context, the spirit of the rest of the prophecy, and the analogy of other contemporary prophecy ; that is, the collateral and subsidiary arguments ; must fill the void which literal criticism and philology leave to disputation. But all these second arguments go to the favour of the more enlarged, the Christian scope of prophecy.

2. But it is contended that Christ did not come to the *Second* Temple, but to a Third, built by Herod ; consequently that the promise of a greater glory, to be manifested in Haggai's Temple, could not be accomplished by the presence and ministry of Christ, but must be sought in the *splendour* and *wealth* of the Second Temple ; a sense which some of the later Jews have put upon the prophecy, in their endeavour to refute the evidence implied in it, that the Messiah either has come, or was to come, within the duration of Haggai's Temple.—It is impossible not to

say that there is a great deficiency of theological and reasonable judgment in the misapplication of the historic learning which has supplied this objection. If the Temple were to be considered as a subject of *architecture*, it might be disputed with some reason whether the substitution of Herod's fabric did not make the later Temple a *Third*, rather than leave it the Second. But in the history of the Divine Dispensation, and in the history of the Jewish people, there can be only two temples, the first, Solomon's, the second, the restored temple, of which Haggai prophesied, and to which Christ came; the moral, and the public relation, which the Temple bore to their religion, their covenant, or their civil state, admitting no further multiplication of its species. For the mere material fabric, though not wholly unimportant, can never pretend to enter into this relation. And it can the less enter into it, inasmuch as Herod's work, whether of enlargement, or of rebuilding, never broke the continuity of the moral subject, but was so conducted as not to interrupt the course of the Temple worship. In the eye of history, therefore, and in the estimate of religion, there were two Temples and no more.

This point being so clear on the principles of reason, I further add that the historic phrase of Josephus, from whose narrative of Herod's work the objection of *a third* temple is derived, is a direct *confirmation* of the statement which I have made. For after all that he had previously written of the extent and splendour of Herod's new edifice, how does that writer sum up the history of the Temple, when he comes to its destruction by Titus? "Twice," he says, "the Temple was burnt, on one and the same day in the revolution of time; and from its *first building*, its founding by Solomon, to its present destruction, in the second year of Vespasian, there is a period of 1130 years, seven months, fifteen days; but from *its later building*, which Haggai[e] *directed* in the second year of *Cyrus*, to

[e] ἐποιήσατο. De Bello Jud. vi. iv. 4.

its present capture by Vespasian, a period of 639 years and forty-five days." So that in his review of the Temple and its fate, he glances over all the enlargement and reconstruction of it from its foundations by Herod, and rests his eye upon a first and a second Temple. as the only objects worthy of an historian's recollection. Whereas, therefore, it is urged by the Author[f], who has endeavoured to give the utmost force to the alleged objection, "that *if* there be any difference between *rebuilding* or *repairing, if Haggai's* temple differed from *Solomon's,* and was a *second* Temple, then *Herod's* was not the same with *Haggai's,* but was truly a *third;*" I reply, first, that a *judicial desolation* of the Temple, which reduced it to ashes, and *extinguished* its service for *Fifty* years, creates a chasm in the line of its history, and a real distinction between Solomon's building and Haggai's, which the quiet and peaceful renovation of the later change does not introduce between Haggai's and Herod's:—and, secondly, that the Jewish historian, who describes at large, and with some pomp, what Herod did in his new work, still finds it consistent with historical truth to make Haggai's temple, and that which was destroyed by Titus, one and the same[g]; and, by the same reason, we shall be justified in taking the restored temple of Haggai to be that which had the privilege and glory of the advent of Christ.

In this instance again, the *collateral* arguments, and the internal reason of the case, support the Christian sense of the prophecy, and no other. First, it is improbable to think that the later Temple, either by the occasional gifts of its proselytes and worshippers, or the successive contri-

---

[f] Dr. Heberden.

[g] I do not enter into the question of Herod's renovation of the temple, what it was. whether it embraced a reconstruction of the whole, or only an enlargement of it. Josephus must be considered a competent witness in the case. And he clearly describes a complete *rebuilding* from the *foundation,* of *the Temple* properly so called. But most of his Commentators still argue that it was the Second Edifice perpetuated in a gradual renovation.—*See Antiq. Jud.* xv. xi. 3. and Interpp. in loc.

butions of heathen princes, or the promiscuous devotion of surrounding countries, or even by the greater efforts of Herod, was ever brought, in any age of it, to the splendour and real magnificence of the original temple of Solomon, in which the public and tributary wealth of the whole monarchy of Israel, in its height of prosperity and power, were appropriated, under the direction of a great and lofty-minded king, to the simultaneous completion of the work. —Next, it is still more unreasonable to think, that prophecy should direct men to any such quality whatever in the second temple, as constituting "its greater glory," when the visible glory of the divine Presence, the symbol of God's inhabitation, was withdrawn from its sanctuary; a loss for which nothing of material and earthly splendour could be any compensation: least of all could that compensation be had in Herod's work, the gift of no piety, but the ostentation of a vainglorious, sanguinary, and irreligious ruler, who reared many other sumptuous fabrics, castles and palaces, in the same spirit as he built the temple at Jerusalem, to be monuments of his pride, or instruments of his ambition; in all which there was nothing that Prophecy could regard, or be thought to hold forth to the Israelite, as his consolation, or as the glory of the temple of God. But Herod's pomp was not ordained to last; it came in the close of the duration allotted to that seat of worship, and only prepared it to be a more striking pile of ruin, with little of "*peace within its walls,*" if we regard it only in its material fabric.

Where then shall we look for the completion of all that sublime prophecy, which hung over the Temple, when it rose the second time from its foundations, and uttered such promises as these: "*According* to *the word* that I *covenanted* with you when ye came out of Egypt, so *My Spirit remaineth* among you. Yet *once,* it is a little while —and I will *shake all nations,* and the *desire* [or, the treasure] of all nations shall *come,* and I will *fill this house with glory* — and the *glory* of this *latter* house shall be *greater* than of the *former*—and in this house will I give *peace,* saith the Lord of Hosts;" where, I say, shall we look to find this august prophecy satisfied, except in the Saviour of the world, who by His presentation, and by His divine teaching, by His personal ministry, and the mystery of His sacrifice, gave to the second Temple the witness of "God's Spirit remaining with His people" according to the original design of their covenant, and manifested there such *a glory,* and such *a gift of peace,* as prophecy might acknowledge for the just and sufficient completion of its promises? Whilst "the new heavens and the new earth," the renovated moral universe of God, received Him as the Being, by whom, and for whom, their change and concussion had been made.

IV. The same prophet Haggai has a *second* prediction, which directs us equally to the Messiah. It is addressed to *Zerubbabel;* but, whatever be its import, it seems to be connected with the former by the introductory mention of the like concussion "of the heavens and the earth." " Speak to Zerubbabel, governor of Judah, saying, I will *shake the heavens and the earth.* And I will *overthrow* the *throne* of *kingdoms,* and I will *destroy the strength of the kingdoms of the heathen,* and I will *overthrow* the chariots and those that ride in them, and the horses and their riders shall come down, *every one by the sword of his brother.* In *that day,* saith the Lord of Hosts, will I take thee, O Zerubbabel My servant, the son of Shealtiel, saith the Lord, and will make *thee* as *a signet :* for I have *chosen thee,* saith the Lord of Hosts[h]." There is an apparent *connexion* in the subject of the two prophecies, expressed by the commotion and shaking of the world; and there is a *proximity* of time in their communication : for the second prophetic word came to Haggai *three days* after the former[i]. These are presumptions that they had a general agreement in their scope and object, but presumptions only : the proper evidence of that *agreement,* if it exist, will be in

<hr>

[h] Haggai ii. 21, 23.   [i] See chap. ii. 1, and 20.

the internal sense, and completion, of the second prophecy, which must be examined.

"In that day," in that season of commotion in the heavens and the earth, and of the kingdoms of the world, God promises to make *Zerubbabel* a "*signet;*" for he was *chosen* to be some instrument of His will. The question is, how is this prediction to be applied? Is it merely a personal promise, to be *completed* in Zerubbabel himself? or is it a symbolical promise, annexed to his person, but directed to *a greater* than Zerubbabel?

The second of these two interpretations, I propose to shew to be the only true one; the only one valid in the completion, and consistent with the text of the prophecy. And as I hope this will be the last occasion of any controversial argument, necessary to the elucidation which I wish to give of this concluding period of prophecy, I entreat my readers' patience, whilst I exercise my own, in canvassing the contrary opinion, which stands in my way, and is supported by *Grotius*, and by the recent authority of the *Translator of the Minor Prophets*, archbishop Newcome, as well as others before him, but which I consider to be wholly remote from the design of one of the most emphatic oracles of the last age of the prophetic revelation.

This contrary opinion I shall give in the representation made of it by that Translator. "Some think that Zerubbabel is put for his people and his posterity," (says that Prelate). "But it may well be said, that the *commotions* foretold began in the *rebellion* of *Babylon* which Darius besieged and took, and exercised great cruelties upon its inhabitants." Herod. iii. 20.—"Prideaux places this event in the 5th year of Darius; others, with more probability in his 8th year: compare Zech. ii. 9. Vitringa calls this event *secundum gradum interitus Babylonis.*" The same author includes, in the shaking of the kingdoms, which is described in the text, "the calamity of *Babylon*, the *Macedonian* conquests in Persia, and the wars which the *successors* of Alexander waged against each other." Of any reference of the prophecy to the Messiah, or His history, he does not entertain even the mention.

This interpretation, which in the end makes Zerubbabel the object of the prophecy, is untenable for two reasons: it neither holds true in the history, nor will it reach any one article of the prophetic text. First, it is plainly futile to make the insurrection and *rebellion* of *Babylon*, and its *re-subjugation* by Darius, any part of the matter of the prophecy; since in that scene of Babylon there were no "*new heavens* and *new earth*, no *overthrowing* of the *throne of kingdoms*, no *destroying* the *strength of the kingdoms* among the nations." The throne of the Persian kingdom stood; and none of the thrones of the kingdoms among the nations, with which Zerubbabel or his people had any thing to do, were overthrown, or destroyed. The *second* stage of the *ruin* of Babylon will never correspond with that large and general concussion of things, which is the previous ground of the prophecy. Grotius, to find a basis for his interpretation, includes the *revolt in Egypt*[k], as a part of the prophetic matter. But that revolt belongs to the *last year* of the reign of *Darius*, a time to which it is not certain whether Zerubbabel survived: and if he did survive, the revolt itself was suppressed and subdued, and only reduced *a vassal kingdom* to a stricter *coercion* and *subjection ;* and therefore it could never represent the prophetic idea "of the subversion of kingdoms." Think of that wide field of thrones and powers overturned, and you will see that a provincial rebellion can furnish nothing to occupy it. As to the later commotions of the world, the *subversion* of the Persian Empire by *Alexander*, and the wars of his *Successors*, they are more like to *the possible subject* of the prophecy : but with these commotions what had Zerubbabel personally to do? They entered not into the world till two hundred years after the prophecy, and almost as long a time after his death. But suppose there had been subversions of the thrones of kingdoms *contemporary* with *Zerubbabel*, which there were not: for in his

* Herodot. lib. vii. 1.

days the Persian empire, and other great kingdoms, as related to Judæa, remained rather in a stationary order; but suppose there had been such events passing, why, in respect of them should Zerubbabel be a "signet," the chosen of God, when he individually had in them no other part, either of fear or deliverance, than the rest of his people? and since these commotions did not break upon Judæa, the *whole people* of God would be more *the signet*, the peculiar care, of the protecting Providence, than any single person living in the heart of that people. I conclude, therefore, that Zerubbabel, as to his own history, is not, and cannot be, the object of the prophecy, which speaks of a far greater system of things than came within the compass of his time and condition.

This inadequate interpretation set aside, the other, which refers the scope of the prophecy to *the Messiah* and His kingdom, will appear to be the true. The just and regular evolution of the prophetic text will demonstrate its interpretation. First, "the shaking of the heavens and the earth" will be the sign of the introduction of the *new dispensation* of God. The "*overthrow* of the thrones and kingdoms of the world" will be the image of that general contrast, which prophecy so often makes, between the *fall* of those earthly kingdoms, and the *stability* of that *which cannot be shaken*; whilst the *subversion* of *some of the greater kingdoms*, which *actually* fell prior to the age of the Gospel, as the Persian, Macedonian, Syrian, and Egyptian, may be more distinctly included, (all of them subjects of other prophecy, particularly in Daniel, and so pointed out to the notice of the Israelite). Lastly, the *suppression* of *wars*, and the *destruction* of the implements of war, will denote the discomfiture of human power, opposed, whether knowing or unknowingly, to the purposes of God; and that there was such a pause and *suppression of war* at the first æra of the Gospel, in that region of the world where the Gospel had to run its course, is sufficiently known. The discomfiture specified to be wrought

"by *a brother's sword*" in all this earthly tumult, may be
either the common *mutual destruction* which the kingdoms
of the world generally make of each other : or it may describe more definitely the *Civil Wars* of the *East*, among
the Successors of Alexander, and the *Civil Wars* of *Rome*,
which wasted the world, both preceding the Gospel; together with the *Intestine Wars* among the Jews themselves, at the time of their final destruction, a phenomenon connected with the establishment of Christianity. The
general view, however, of these convulsions, and changes
of the kingdoms of the earth, is unquestionably clear in
the ground of the prophecy, whether we may choose to
take up the more definite references of it, which I have
mentioned, or not. So far the line of interpretation is
certain. But, in all this, why is Zerubbabel so distinguished in the prophecy, when it looks so far beyond
him? Why is he characterized as the signet of God? He
is so distinguished as being the *Representative* of Christ;
and his *fitness* to be that *Representative* is most evident.
Of his line and seed was Christ born into the world. When
God, therefore, restored His people, and reinstated them
in their covenant, and their land again, by this prophecy
He designated Zerubbabel, and set His choice upon him,
as the signet of His hand and purpose, in whom *some*
work of His providence and mercy should be accomplished; but the time and period of that future work was
to be measured by the circle of "the new heavens and the
new earth," and therefore it was to be in the ulterior system of God, after the great *change* of things in the *new,
the Christian* dispensation.

Consider, then, the whole case. In Zerubbabel the
genealogy of the Messiah, after the restoration from Babylon, begins. Zerubbabel is the head of that genealogy :
in him it has its double concourse[1] : both the lines of the
descent of the Messiah *meeting* in his person.

This headship of Zerubbabel is the *index* of the sense
and import of the prophecy. For the restoration of the

[1] See Matt. i. 12; Luke iii. 27.

Hebrew people, when they resumed the tenure of their covenant again, was an epoch when any special mark of prediction relating to the Messiah would come in season; and such prediction was the more opportune, when we consider the state of doubt and ambiguity which might now seem to attach to the former promises of God, given to the family of David, when that family had been set aside from the throne, and the whole body of it had been disturbed, in its civil order and hereditary privileges, by the troubles of the Captivity. The short, but emphatic prophecy, delivered to Zerubbabel, clears this disorder or ambiguity, and directs us again into the line of the divine promises.

How had the Captivity begun? It began with the rejection of Coniah and his seed; and Jeremiah's great prophecy to the *particular heir* of the throne and house of David had been, "As I live, saith the Lord, though Coniah the son of Jehoiakim king of Judah were the *signet* upon my right-hand, yet would I *pluck thee thence*[m]." The like image of "the signet" upon God's right-hand, in this prophecy of Jeremiah, could not escape the notice of Grotius. But it is rather surprising that this very image did not lead him into the connexion and joint moral import of the two prophecies of Jeremiah and Haggai. The Captivity begins with that sentence of rejection upon Coniah and his seed; the Restoration equally begins with the contrary promise to Zerubbabel; the parity of the image, the relation of the two seasons, and the doubtful condition of the house of David, all tending to shew the mutual aspect of the two prophecies. To Zerubbabel however *no throne* is promised, and *none was given*. Yet he is *chosen*, and has the divine adoption, or acknowledgment, set upon him. Whence I infer, that that *adoption*, or *acknowledgment* of him, in relation to "the sure" and yet remaining "mercies of David," the *promises* of the *Christian* Covenant, is the specific point of the prophecy of Haggai.

<hr>

[m] Jeremiah xxii. 24.

It is not to be maintained that all this force and connexion of the prophecy could be understood from the first
utterance of it; but they may be understood now; as they
might also have been in the first age of the Gospel. It is
one of those prophecies which time and the event would
set in their proper light. But yet, from the first, it was a
direction to the Israelite to expect in Zerubbabel, or in
his seed, a work of God connected with the renovation of
the heavens and the earth, and the succession of kingdoms;
a work which the Israelite assuredly never could see in
Zerubbabel's line, till he came to the advent of Christ.
Meanwhile this long repose and obscurity of Zerubbabel's
family, and of the whole house of David, during so many
generations prior to the Gospel, was one of the preparations made whereby to manifest more distinctly the proper
glory of it, in the birth of the Messiah.

In this view is presented one instance more of that
order and analogy which Prophecy has been seen to hold
in the designation which it made of Christ. In the
Call of Abraham, in the Partition of the Tribes, in the
Foundation of the Temporal Kingdom, in the Restoration
from the Captivity, there will be one and the same signature, set upon the persons, family, or tribe, wherein His
advent was to be expected; each more memorable season
of the first dispensation having inserted in it some distinctive notice, relating personally to Him, as well as the general promises of God's purposed work, which He alone has
fulfilled. The analogy confirms the single instance here
in question; and that instance, in its turn, tends to support and complete the analogy.

V. Perhaps I may now shake off the dust of a controversial discussion which I have not been able to avoid with
respect to the prophecies of Haggai and Zechariah, and
close my survey of later Prophecy with the Predictions of
Malachi, which have had their interpretation less disputed.

The last of the Prophets lived, and gave his oracles, after the Temple was rebuilt[n]. His moral admonitions shew that the service of the Altar and the Temple, with its offerings and sacrifices, was established, and in use; for it is a profane and insincere spirit in that service, a religion without purity, which he labours to reform; and both the *people* and the *priesthood*, have their share in the imputed contamination of their restored worship.

The *Christian* predictions of Malachi are singularly framed, in many points of them, upon this *existing state of religion*. "I have no pleasure in you, saith the Lord of hosts, neither will *I accept an offering* at your hands." Such is the reproof: but what the prophecy joined with it? "From the *rising of the sun* even unto the *going down* of the same, My name shall be great among *the Gentiles*, and *in every place incense* shall be *offered* unto My name, and a *pure offering;* for My name shall be great among *the heathen*, saith the Lord of hosts[o]." The concourse of worshippers to the restored Temple leads the prophet to predict the greater assembly of the Gentile world, when the knowledge and worship of God should have the circuit of the sun, and every place, as much as Jerusalem, should be fit to be a temple or an altar to His service: whilst the formality and hypocrisy of the Jewish worshipper prompt the prediction of the purer worship, and holier offering, of the Christian Church.

Again: "And now, *O ye priests*, this commandment is for you." After the prophet has delivered at large his reproof of them in their *public, sacerdotal* duties; "Ye are departed out of the way; ye have caused many *to stumble at the law; ye have corrupted the covenant of Levi*, saith the Lord of hosts:" the prediction follows: "Behold, I will send My messenger, and He shall *prepare the way before Me:* and the Lord, whom ye seek, shall suddenly *come*

---

[n] Chap. i. 10. iii. 10.   [o] Chap. i. 11.

to *His Temple*, even the *messenger of the covenant*, whom ye delight in: behold, He shall come, saith the Lord of hosts. But who may abide the day of His coming? and who shall stand when He appeareth? for He is like a refiner's fire, and like fullers' sope: and He shall sit as a refiner and purifier of silver : *and He shall purify the sons of Levi* as gold and silver, that they *may offer* unto the Lord *an offering in righteousness*. Then shall the *offering* of Judah and Jerusalem *be pleasant unto the Lord*, as in the days of old, and as in former years." The Covenant, the Temple, the Levitic Priesthood, the Offering, are all combined in this prediction ; but the force of the prophetic representation does not consist in the mere analogy of *the Jewish images*, but in the *action* and *import* of the *existing scene*, which gave life to that form of representation. The Temple was again in use : the prophecy is, "*the Lord* whom they seek shall suddenly *come to that Temple*." A prevaricating priesthood "was *corrupting the covenant*, and making men *stumble* at the *law :*" it is foretold, that the Lord will send His messenger " to *prepare His way* before Him." That priesthood had debased *religion* by *ignorance* and *personal corruption :* the prophecy is, that the messenger of the new covenant "will *sit* in judgment as a *refiner*," and discerner of spirits, and *purify* His *priesthood*, and *hallow* the *offering* by the *graces* and *sanctity* of His *apostles* and *evangelists*. So that this great predictive revelation of the Gospel is at once a *prophecy*, and a *moral parable*, putting to shame the priesthood of those days of Malachi, in the reversed exhibition of the holiness and spiritual illumination of the new Covenant and its purified ministers.

It is one predominant and general characteristic, therefore, of this last age of Prophecy, that its predictions of the Gospel are *modelled* upon the history of the Temple, the Priesthood, and Public Worship. In the auspicious *re-establishment* of the Temple and Priesthood ; in the profaneness and *irreligion* which soon entered with this renovated state of public Order; prophecy equally set forth the Gospel promises. What was fair and glorious, in this scene of Jewish history, was made a pledge of the glory to come. What was base and degenerate, had its opposed counterpart exhibited in the sanctities of the new Covenant. In a word, the Second Temple is covered with Christianity.

And now, when Prophecy was about to be withdrawn from the ancient Church of God, its last light was mingled with the rising beams of "the Sun of Righteousness." In one view it combined a retrospect to the Law with the clearest specific signs of the Gospel advent. *"Remember ye the law of Moses* My servant, which I commanded him in Horeb, for all Israel, with the statutes and judgments. *Behold,* I *will send* you *Elijah* the *prophet,* before the *great and dreadful day of the Lord*[p]." Prophecy had been the oracle of Judaism, and of Christianity, to uphold the authority of the one, and reveal the promise of the other. And now its latest admonitions were like those of a faithful departing minister, embracing and summing up his duties. Resigning its charge to the *personal Precursor* of Christ, it expired with the Gospel upon its tongue.

I have now traced the outline of Ancient Prophecy in its several ages: and a brief statement may suffice, to recapitulate what has been said in the survey which has been taken of the Structure and Use.

I. It has been shewn that the character of Prophecy is not simple and uniform, nor its light equable. It was dispensed in various degrees of revelation; and that revelation adapted, by the wisdom of God, to purposes which we must explore, by studying its records, and considering its capacity of application.

[p] Malachi iv. 2.

II. The *principal age* of Prophecy is from *Samuel* to *Malachi*. From the *Fall* to the *Flood*, and thence to the Call of *Abraham*, its communications are *few*. In the Patriarchal Age, they are *enlarged*. During the Bondage in Egypt, they are *discontinued*, but *renewed* with the Law. A *pause* of them, during *four hundred* years, follows the Law; and a *pause* of the like *duration* precedes the Gospel.

III. The *subjects* of Prophecy varied. Whilst it was all directed to one general design, in the evidence and support of religion, there was a diversity in the administration of the Spirit, in respect of that design. In Paradise, it gave the first hope of a Redeemer. After the Deluge, it established the peace of the Natural world. In Abraham, it founded the double covenant of Canaan and the Gospel. In the age of the Law, it spoke of the Second Prophet, and foreshadowed, in Types, the *Christian* doctrine, but foretold most largely the future fate of the selected People, who were placed under that preparatory dispensation. In the time of David, it revealed the *Gospel Kingdom*, with the promise of the Temporal. In the days of the later Prophets, it presignified the changes of the Mosaic Covenant, embraced the history of the chief Pagan kingdoms, and completed the annunciation of the Messiah and His work of Redemption. After the Captivity, it gave a last and more urgent information of the approaching Advent of the Gospel.

Thus ancient Prophecy ended as it had begun. The first discovery of it in Paradise, and the conclusion of it in the book of Malachi, are directed to one point. In its course it had multiplied its disclosures, and furnished various succours to religion, and created an authentic record of God's Providence and Moral Government to be committed to the world. But its *earliest*, and its *latest* use, was in the preparatory revelation of Christianity. It remains, as the general inference to be deduced from the whole, that the Holy Jesus, and His religion, are the one principal object of Prophecy, the beginning and end of the elder revelation of God.

St. Paul has intimated the varied form, and different degrees of light, under which prophecy was successively dispensed, when he says of it, that " God in sundry *partitions* of His Truth, and in divers manners, spake in time past unto the Fathers by the Prophets⁹." And if the inquiry, which has been so far pursued through these Discourses, might pass for a *Comment* upon this text of the Apostle, by elucidating, in any degree, "the manifold wisdomʳ" of the divine design which is embodied in the Volume of Prophecy, perhaps they may be thought to have their sufficient use.

⁹ Πολυμερῶς καὶ πολυτρόπως.   Heb. i. 1.
ʳ Ἡ πολυποίκιλος σοφία.   Ephes. iii. 10.

END OF DISCOURSE VI.

DISCOURSE VII.

OF THE DIVINE FOREKNOWLEDGE, AND ITS UNION WITH THE LIBERTY OF HUMAN ACTION.

ISAIAH xlvi. 10.

*Declaring the end from the beginning, and from ancient times
the things that are not done,* saying, *My counsel shall
stand, and I will fulfil all My pleasure.*

IN the first ages of Christianity, when its apologists
and teachers applied the argument from Prophecy to
demonstrate its truth, a discussion was soon introduced as
to the *reconcilableness* of the *Divine Foreknowledge* with
the *Liberty of human Action.* For some of the things foretold in Prophecy, being, in their obvious and formal character, of *the nature of sins,* and others, the effect and
consequence of them, it came in the way to examine
whether the agents could be left free, when their actions
were thus ascertained and foreknown. The question was
not wholly a new one. It had been discussed, though with
some difference in its form, in the schools of Philosophy,
where the debate commonly had been, whether the foreknowledge of future events, if such foreknowledge any
where existed, did not infer a fatal necessity of things.
From this previous entertainment of the question, it passed
into the Church, and the defences of religion; and there
it has been pursued into a more subtle and elaborate investigation than it had undergone before. For it has been
the fortune of Revealed Religion to attract all the objections which the stock of controversial philosophy could

supply, to render the reception of its truth jealous and reluctant; and even the very force and importunate authority of its evidence seems to have provoked the suspicion and scepticism of Natural Reason, and to have operated in many instances to a more pertinacious discussion of difficult points, which had any connexion with it; whilst men, whether with a good, or an ill faith, have scrupulously measured every sacrifice of doubt, and disputed every concession of belief, which the system of Religion, and its evidence, have demanded of them.

The ancient *Fathers* of the Church met this question, concerning the union of the Divine Prescience with human Freedom, wisely, and most reasonably. They stood upon the proofs of God's Prescience, which authentic and unambiguous prophecies supplied; they maintained the Liberty of human action, without which they saw there could be no religion: and, whatever solutions, or qualifications they attempted to give of the apparent difficulty subsisting in their view of the case, they sought no relief of it whatever, by going to invalidate the one principle, or the other, the prerogative of the divine Foreknowledge, or the responsible Freedom of man's moral agency. *Justin Martyr, Origen, Eusebius*, all concur in this judgment, and even *Augustine*, when he argues most coolly, does not dissent from them. " Wherefore we are by no means obliged, either retaining the prescience of God, to deny the liberty of the will, or, retaining the liberty of the will, to deny to God, which piety forbids, the prescience of things future[a]."

---

[a] "Quocirca nullo modo cogimur, aut retenta *præscientia* Dei, tollere *voluntatis arbitrium*, aut *retento* voluntatis *arbitrio*, Deum, quod nefas est, negare, *præscium futurorum*."—De Civitate Dei, lib. v. cap. 9, 10. I refer to this Treatise of *Augustine*, which I think may be considered as the most temperate, exact, and judicious, of all his works: the least infected either with the violence of acrimonious controversy, or the license of a popular and fanciful abuse of argument. As such it probably contains the *truest* expression of his *opinions*—and those *opinions* such as will be *most satisfactory* to others. For a monument of Christian learning and reasoning, it is clearly among the

Such is the conclusion to which Augustine brings his inquiry on the question proposed, " An voluntatibus hominum aliqua dominetur necessitas?" And the rest of the Fathers whom I have named, with others, are not less explicit in urging and maintaining the same conclusion.

In the doctrine, however, thus asserted, the *freedom* of man's *moral agency* is not to be taken for the *integrity* of his nature, or the absence of all *innate corruption* of his *will*. In such a sense, the Scripture, the Creed of the Christian Church, the sober Experience of the world, would disclaim and refute it. But such is not the necessary, and cannot be the true idea, of human liberty, in any general consideration of it. Moral agency may *consist* with great irregularity and disorder in the constitution of man's nature. Consequently, it is not in question, whether he is wholly free and perfect in the balance of his faculties and desires, his understanding and will; but whether he have so much freedom and power of rational election left to him, as to be a subject of probation, and, within the limits of that probation, to be responsible for his action : it being clear that his responsibility, and his moral power, must be commensurate the one with the other. His duty may be difficult in any degree, and the wrong bias and propensity may be ever so strong, short of an absolute and inevitable determination to evil. Yet the principle of moral agency will remain; and this is the state of that principle which alone it is of any serious importance to vindicate in the question at issue; and such a view of it, in a greater or less latitude, the Scripture every where confirms, the Creed of the ancient Church embraced, and Experience, as well as the best Philosophy, will sanction. The nature which is "far gone from original righteous-

most valuable remains of the Primitive Church.—*Justin Martyr's* doctrine may be seen in his Second Apology, p. 80, 81. ed. Par. 1636. *Origen's—* Contra Celsum, p. 73, 74; and more largely Philocal. cap. xxiii. xxv. *Eusebius's*, Præparat. Evang. lib. vi. cap. vi. with his extract from Origen, cap. xi.

ness," may yet, in all its disorder, which some men magnify so much, and others as unreasonably deny, retain the elements of its probationary character, the faculty to know, and the freedom to choose, in good and evil, though each greatly impaired; and in this condition, however fallen from integrity and rectitude, the essence of freedom, though not the strength and perfection of it, will have its place[b].

Resuming, then, the combined doctrine of the *divine Prescience* and *human Liberty*, I must observe, that the difficulty which we may experience in reconciling the one of these principles with the other, cannot justify us in rejecting either. *Each* of them is *established* upon a *competent evidence.* There are proofs, in Prophecy, of God's foreknowledge of men's actions. The liberty of those actions is proved by many media: by our personal consciousness; by the conditions of Revealed Religion; by all laws, human and divine; by the common sense of mankind, whose judgment and language are framed, not merely on the admission of this principle, but on rules of taking an account of it. It is further proved by the strictest reasoning of the best philosophers, who have asserted it, and by the concessions of others, who have denied it; for the reasoner, who denies human liberty, never fails in his life, to deal with others as though they possessed it, and proves himself to be so far free as the greatest inconsistency can shew him to be. In a word, Religion, Laws, Internal Consciousness, Society, all verify this doctrine. Consequently, although it may not be impossible to impugn it by some of our purblind speculative objections, yet the denial of it can never be made without a great and

---

[b] If I might transfer, with some variation, the words of the poet, I might say of this moral constitution of man's nature,

> . . . . "His form had not yet lost
> All her original brightness, nor appear'd
> Less than *God's image* ruin'd."

manifest difficulty, and that a difficulty pressing upon us
in the strongest relations of our whole nature and being.
But such *a difficulty* must be reckoned as *equivalent* to a
practical refutation of the system which includes it. Each,
therefore, being supposed as distinctly proved, God's prescience, and man's freedom; if their union and consistency
pass our *comprehension*, that will be no ground why we
should reject the first things proved by reasons which we
do comprehend. That would be for our ignorance to refute
our knowledge.

For where does the difficulty in this second case originate? Where is it situated? It originates in a province of
thought, wherein our notions confessedly are inadequate
and imperfect; in our estimate of the Divine Nature and
the infinite Perfections of God. Without insisting upon
what might be very justly said, that in many of our speculations concerning the Deity, and the extent and capacity,
if I may so speak, of His perfections, it is even reasonable
to *expect* great, and perhaps overpowering, difficulties; I
ask, whether the sense of such difficulties, when perceived,
can be allowed to be a sufficient answer to other conclusions presented to us in direct and convincing evidence;
or whether it be not wiser to think that the infinity of the
Divine Being, and the vastness of His Attributes, are the
true reason of the intricacy under which we view many
questions relating to Him, and to the exercise whether of
His knowledge, or His power. It *contradicts many axioms*
of our most certain knowledge, to deny man to be a free
agent. But it *contradicts no* such *axiom*, to admit that of
free and *undetermined* actions an Infinite Being may have
an *infallible foresight. How* this can be, is a hard and
mysterious point: it may be an absolutely insolvable
enigma to our understanding. But it is only an *enigma.*
The *contradiction* in it has not yet been shewn. And to
use the strict philosophic distinction of Clarke, applied by
him in another case, "*Absurdities, contradictions, disagree-
ments of ideas,* are things just as different from *difficult*

consequences of *demonstrative truths*, which *cannot* be perfectly *cleared*, as light is from darkness[c]."

In order to diminish the difficulty, however, in our present case, and reduce it within its proper bounds, there are many accurate distinctions which have been urged, to *separate* between the *divine foreknowledge*, and the *necessity* of the things foreknown. "He who *predicts*," says Origen, "is not the *cause* of a *future fact*: but the *future fact*, which would have been, though it had not been predicted, gave the occasion to the foreknower to foretell it[d]." Causation clearly is not included in knowledge: and "*foreknowledge* doth no more *necessitate* events to come to pass than *afterknowledge*[e]." The proper agent is the cause of his action; and neither the infallibility of God's prescience, nor the positiveness of the futurition foreseen, can affect the production of the action. When the ancient sceptic argued, that from the veracity of prophecy it would follow that the crimes foretold by it must come to pass, Origen justly replied, "*Infallibly* they would, but not by any *necessity*[f]." In fact, the free and voluntary production of such actions by the agents themselves, is understood, in the hypothesis, to be a part of the *object* of God's foreknowledge. His foreknowledge, therefore, cannot destroy that quality of them which is itself, by that hypothesis, one of the things foreknown.

Certainty and *Necessity*, not only are possible to be distinguished, the first as belonging to knowledge, the other to the nature of things, but as not implying either of them the other. For of necessary things there is often an un-

<hr>

[c] Third Defence of the Immateriality, &c. p. 303.

[d] Contra Celsum, p. 73.—So the author of the Quæst. et Respons. ad Orthodoxos, p. 425. Opp. Justini. καὶ οὐκ ἔστιν ἡ πρόγνωσις αἰτία τοῦ μέλλοντος ἔσεσθαι, ἀλλὰ τὸ μέλλον ἔσεσθαι αἴτιον τῆς προγνώσεως.

[e] Bramhall, p. 744.

[f] Εἰ γὰρ τὸ, Πάντως, ἀκούει ἀντὶ τοῦ, Κατηναγκασμένως, οὐ δώσομεν αὐτῷ· δυνατὸν γὰρ ἦν καὶ μὴ γενέσθαι. Εἰ δὲ τὸ, Πάντως, λέγει ἀντὶ τοῦ, Ἔσται, ὅπερ οὐ κωλύεται εἶναι ἀληθὲς, κἂν δυνατὸν ᾖ τὸ μὴ γενέσθαι, οὐδὲν λυπεῖ τὸν λόγον. Contra Celsum, p. 71.

certain knowledge, owing to the ignorance of the mind judging of them; and *thence*, as Limborch has acutely observed, there may equally be, by the perfection of the judging mind, a certainty of knowledge, where the things themselves foreknown are contingent, and undetermined[e].

Or again, if certainty be considered as expressive of the *truth of things*, it expresses merely the truth, not the manner, of their causation, or their being : which causation and being may be either necessary, or free. And these clear distinctions in the subject, although they may not completely satisfy the mind, or enable us to comprehend the union of the divine foreknowledge with man's freedom, yet go a certain way in abating the perplexity of the speculation, by shewing that consistency may well be believed, where contradiction is not obviously expressed, or implied.

My proper business, in this branch of my inquiry, is with the *prescience* and *inspir tion* of Prophecy : and the supernatural origin of scripture prophecy may be proved, whether we are able to reconcile it with the freedom of human actions, or no. It may be thought, therefore, that I might have proceeded to examine the evidence of the prophetic inspiration, without adverting to this other, an abstract inquiry. But there is too much at stake in the great question of man's moral agency, to permit it to be slighted in any serious argument of Religion ; and the result of the Prophetic evidence, in demonstrating ever so clearly a divine inspiration, I should consider to be of small use to religion, if that same evidence could be thought, as has been contended, to disprove the possibility of human freedom. The best arguments of Religion would then only destroy its proper subject. Hence it is of the

---

[e] Theologiæ Christianæ lib. ii. cap. viii. sect. xix. tit. discrimen inter *certitudinem* et *necessitatem ;* et *incertitudinem* et *contingentiam.* Where Limborch has stated concisely and perspicuously most of the chief points of the question.

first importance to uphold the entire doctrine of the Divine Prescience, and of man's moral probationary freedom, in those very instances of his action which have been most definitely foreknown and foretold.

Divines, as well as Metaphysical reasoners, there have been, who have disjoined these principles. *Hobbes* and *Bayle* have argued from the admission of the Divine Prescience against the possibility of human freedom. *Collins* has repeated their doctrine. The older writers of the Socinian School have chosen rather to deny the possibility of an absolute divine Prescience in things contingent, as the actions of free agents; whilst some of the later writers of that School have adopted the other hypothesis of a Necessity in the system of the world. Some few of our own Church have gone to the same side with the older Socinian writers, in denying the divine Prescience of free undetermined actions. In which number I must place a very candid and dispassionate inquirer, Dr. Pearson, who has lately preceded me in the office of this Lecture, and has devoted the first of his Discourses to the maintenance of his opinion.

That speculatists, such as Bayle and Collins, should entertain and press any unfavourable consequence, which can be represented as following from Prophecy, or any other part of the evidence of Revelation, is not inconsistent with the disposition which they have shewn towards Revealed Religion, in the general tenour of their opinions. For nothing so disturbs the foundation of religion, and the practical use of it, taken as a system addressed to man, as the disbelief of his free responsible character. Whether it be assumed to be a direct act of the Supreme Being, or any concatenation of objects and causes, extrinsic to man, which subjects him to one determinate and necessary inevitable course of action; his proper agency, and his probation, are equally destroyed. Thence, by any opinions, to undermine the belief of his freedom, is, in the result, to overthrow all Religion, Natural and Revealed, and do away with Virtue, as well as Faith. When, therefore, we observe that Bayle and Collins are apparently willing to admit the evidence of prophecy, as a proof of Revelation, so that they may carry it at the same time to the denial of human freedom, it creates some just suspicion as to the fairness and probity of their speculations. For although they loved not Revealed Religion, yet the Cause of Virtue, which they generally professed to regard, required a different treatment at their hands: and the coolness with which they consented, in theory, to disbelieve human liberty, or leave it in doubt, upon any supposed proof whatever, is one of the most remarkable, and not the least instructive points, in the history of their sceptical opinions.

The Philosophy which makes God to be the sole Agent, and efficient Cause of all things done in the world, has sometimes been disguised in the pretensions of a more exalted piety. But under whatever specious form it is proposed, it is refuted by the existence of *Moral Evil.* Other efficient causes of action there are, or *Sin* had not existed. Other efficient causes of action there are, or how could God judge the world? The inferior agents, deriving their being, and their *power of action*, from God, have that power, therefore, with the capacity of a determination of its exercise in themselves. The prevalence of Evil, and the positive doctrines of Religion, equally attest this inferior and subordinate, but responsible and free agency. Whatever colour of piety, therefore, there may seem to have been infused by some men into this ideal system, which would refer all things that are done to the sole power of one supreme efficient Agent, as their direct determining cause; it is unsound in its principle, and, in effect, makes God to be the Author of Moral Evil, which is one of the greatest contradictions that can enter any moral system. And although this philosophical scheme of Malebranche has had to reckon among its disciples, persons of an ingenuous and unquestionable piety, it can scarcely be thought on that account the less an aberration of reason, or less injurious to religion. The essential character of Scriptural Theology is necessarily subverted by it; for that Theology imputes to men their actions, as being the cause of them, which imputation must all be resolved, in such a theory, into a mere empty unintelligible figure.

There is "a Meditation" or Essay, of Lord Bacon, in which even that eminent writer *seems* to have made some approach to this theory, which ascribes to the Deity an universal causation of actions. He states it to be one source of heresy and religious error, to attribute a wider extent "to the divine *knowledge* than the divine *power*, or rather a wider extent to the divine *power*, simply *knowing*, (for knowledge is power,) than to the same *power*, *moving* and *acting*; as though God *foreknew* some things *inactively* (*otiose*), which He does not *predestinate* and *preordain*." But if this kind of opinion be a source of heresy, Bacon thereby intimates that he would consider the divine knowledge, and the divine agency, as inseparable[h] in the production of the things foreknown. But in this one instance we may say that the great Philosopher has been mistaken in his argument. The *knowledge* and *the active power* of God may be of equal extent, both infinite, and reaching to all things; and yet His power may be exerted, not in the causation of some actions, but in the moral government of them. Evil actions, which He does not produce, are yet under His *power*, in His control and appointment of their effects, whether in respect of the doer of them, or of others. The whole world therefore will be the subject of

[h] Tertius gradus est eorum qui arctant et restringunt opinionem priorem tantum ad actiones humanas quæ participant ex peccato, quas volunt *substantive*, absque nexu aliquo causarum, ex interna voluntate et arbitrio humano pendere, statuuntque *latiores terminos scientiæ* Dei quam *potestatis;* vel potius ejus partis potestatis Dei, (nam et ipsa scientia potestas est,) qua scit, quam ejus qua movet et agit; ut præsciat quædam *otiose*, quæ non prædestinet et præordinet. Sed quicquid a Deo non pendet, ut *auctore* et *principio*, per nexus et gradus subordinatos, id *loco Dei* erit et *novum principium*, et *deaster quidam*.

Et tamen admodum recte dicitur, quod Deus non sit auctor mali, *non quia non auctor, sed quia non mali*.—Meditationes Sacræ de Hæresibus, p. 717.

His power, and under His administration, as well as under
His knowledge—but without transferring to Him the origin
of actions, which, if evil, would convey to Him the origin
of their evil. And in this instance I should suppose that
Bacon had unawares carried a principle of his Natural
Philosophy into Religion. In *physical nature* it is per
fectly true that the Divine Agency is the one sole efficient
and adequate cause. In the Moral System, in the sphere
of intelligent beings, Revelation and Reason teach another
order. The *incongruity*, which Bacon suggests would follow from the admission of man to be a *principle* of His
actions, is beside the question. He says it would make
man an independent creature, a *little divinity*. There is
no independence in man, and none can be supposed. He
is a subordinate and dependent being, from first to last.
But if by a delegated power of moral agency he becomes
deaster quidam, it is only as his Supreme Creator has made
him so. And perhaps the authentic order of his creation,
which was "in the image of his Maker," may render that
title and character of him not so invidious, as it is here
intended to be. But in that communicated character of
man the first Giver of it has the proper glory, and the re-
ceiver has only, in the remains of it which are left to him,
a responsibility, which ought in reason to make him fearful and humble.

The distinction, to which Bacon here objects, between
the *knowledge* and the *preordination* of God, is asserted in
the whole scheme of the prophetic volume. The Prophets
describe the events of things to be altogether in the hand
of God; to be the work of His Providence, and according
to the rule of His predetermination and positive appointment. But the same Prophets make the evil actions of
men their own. The evil action they represent as the object of God's Foreknowledge; the effect of it, as the act of
His Providence. The sins foretold are not the less with
censure and blame imputed to men, but the consequences
attendant upon those sins are ascribed to God. This is a

difference which is maintained universally in the Predictions and the Ethics of Prophecy combined together; and there is no part of Holy Writ more opposed to the doctrine of Predestination, as a positive appointing cause of those actions of men *for* which the divine judgments are inflicted, than the book of the Prophets. At the same time no part of it is more explicit in vindicating the universal prescience of God as to those actions, and asserting His previous providential appointment of every consequence following from them, and every judgment inflicted upon them.

This distinction, so intelligible, and so important, is in perfect conformity with that great text of the New Testament which has cost Christianity so many painful disputes: " Whom He did *foreknow,* them He did *predestinate*[i];" a separation here expressed in the exercise of the divine attributes, which, if candidly considered, and strictly kept in view, might have prevented many rash decisions, which now remain upon record, to admonish and instruct by their inconsistency with, and opposition to, Scripture. The same distinction stands in equal conformity with that other memorable text: "Of a truth against Thy Holy Child Jesus—both Herod, and Pontius Pilate, with the Gentiles, and the people of Israel, were gathered together, for to *do* whatsoever Thy *hand* and *Thy* counsel *appointed* to *be done*[k]." The deed, we see, is imputed to the human agents. The effect of it, and the effect alone, to the hand and counsel of God. He, ordaining an effect from an evil act foreseen, appoints the suffering by His predestination, and permits the act foreknown to the doer's will.

The calm and temperate tone of Dr. Pearson's recent discussion of this question, and the sincerity and fairness with which he has stated his opinions, are entitled to re-

---

[i] Rom. viii. 29.

[k] Acts iv. 27, 28. γενέσθαι, [to *take place*]. It is not said " whatsoever Thy *counsel appointed them to* DO."

spect from those who may be very far from assenting to
what he has advanced in support of them. He contends,
without reserve, that the free actions of men are not within the Divine Prescience; resting his doctrine partly on
the *assumption*, that there are no strict and absolute predictions, in Scripture, of those actions in which men are
represented as free and responsible; and partly on *the abstract reason*, that such actions are in their nature impossible to be certainly foreknown[l].

The *assumption*, which the author here goes upon, is
certainly erroneous: inasmuch as there are prophecies in
Scripture definitely predicting judicial visitations for voluntary sin, and prophecies including equally the particular sin, and its punishment. The instance which he
has selected " of the punishments which were prophetically
denounced by Moses against the Israelites," instead of
being the uncertain and indeterminate prediction which
he states it to be, is a conspicuous example of a prophecy
absolute as to the *event*. " The Lord said unto Moses,
Behold, thou shalt sleep with thy fathers, and this people *will rise up*, and go a whoring after the gods of the
strangers of the land, whither they go to be among them,
and *will forsake* Me, and *break My covenant* which I have
made with them. Then My anger *shall be kindled* against
them," &c [m] Which declaration of their *foreknown sin*
Moses repeats in the same chapter[n]. In this instance,
therefore, the Divine Prescience comprehended their sin
and their punishment. But their sin was optional and
free. It was in breach of a condition which they had the
power to keep. The other examples, often cited, of the
predictions concerning the cruelty of *Hazael*, the treachery
of *Judas*, the denial of *Peter*, are only some among many
of the same class; *viz.*, definite prophecies of the yet undetermined actions of men. The prophecy of Jonah concerning the destruction of *Nineveh* is improperly and injudiciously put in comparison with that concerning the

[l] Warburton, Lect. i. p. 29, &c. &c.

[m] Deut. xxxi. 16.   [n] Deut. v. 31.

fate of the Israelites.   For Jonah did not foretell the *per-severing sin*, and the *impenitence* of Nineveh; but only its *destruction*.   Now the general conditional tenor of the Divine judgments may often, or always, be supposed to leave the hope of a possibility of their recall[o].   But where the obduracy of the sin is included in the matter of the prediction, as it is with regard to the Israelites, that point, upon which the recall of them might be expected, is already foreclosed in the prophecy.

As to the *abstract reason*, "that free actions are impossible, in their nature, to be foreknown," I have already considered it in the former part of this Discourse; and I have only to add, that the author seems, in advancing this objection, to have overlooked, or very slightly considered, the distinction which Origen, Clarke[p], and others[q], had so clearly shewn to exist between *certainty*, and *necessity* of things.

Upon each ground of Dr. Pearson's argument, I must be permitted to say, that I think he has scarcely exercised so much care and deliberation in forming his opinions, as the very questionable and startling nature of them required.   Many of his positions concerning the Divine Foreknowledge are hazardous in the extreme, and some of them are more than hazardous.   He speaks of God as foreseeing the contingent *possibilities* of things, and being *provided* with *means* adapted to them; but not clearly and absolutely foreknowing what in all cases will actually take place in the moral world.   Hence, the Fall of Man, and the appointment of the scheme of Redemption, connected with that Fall, are placed among the uncertainties of the Divine Mind, as though God had not an eternal foreknowledge of one, the greatest and most wonderful of His own acts.   "Known unto God are all His works from the

---

[o] This is expressed by Jeremiah xviii. 8.

[p] Demonstrat. of Being and Attributes, vol. i. prop. x.

[q] As Limborch and Episcopius.   Limborch, quoted page 262 above.   Episcopius, *Instit. Theol.* lib. iv. sect. xvii.

beginning." This text, the author properly observes, relates to the works of God, not of man. But since the works of God, in His moral Economy, are in many instances adapted to the works of His creatures, how can His own works be foreknown to Him, if theirs are not? His declared preordination of His own works of Providence, in judgment and mercy, is one explicit and invincible proof of His perfect foreknowledge of theirs. Whereas, therefore, the candid author intends his opinions to be such only as can be reconciled with Scripture, I think it must be conceded that they are no less repugnant to that authority, than are any of those opinions of the Calvinistic doctrine, the avoidance of which has precipitated his theology into these exceptionable tenets: and it is to be regretted that he should have departed from the wariness and sobriety of Mr. Locke, whose sentiments on this subject he quotes, but only to differ from them. "I own freely," says that excellent philosopher[r], "the weakness of my understanding, that, though it be unquestionable, that there is omnipotence and omniscience in God, our Maker, and I cannot have a clearer perception of anything than that I am free; yet I cannot make freedom in man consistent with omnipotence and omniscience in God, *though I am as fully persuaded of both*, as of any truths I most firmly assent to."

One remark more I shall offer upon the abstract question under discussion. If we begin our speculation by saying, since God foresees the action and already beholds it, how can it be free, we attempt to look through the immensity of the Divine Mind, and place ourselves on a height far above the level of our faculties. But if we begin from below, by supposing our actions to be free, as we have the best reason to suppose them, then the creed of natural piety, and the conviction of the infinite and unlimited scope of the Divine Intelligence, will more readily help us into an apprehension of the article, and an acqui-

[r] Locke, vol. iii. p. 487.

escence in it.   And this is a mode of consideration which I suggest, partly after an idea of Origen, as deserving to be kept in view whilst we attempt to explore this question.

Nor is erroneous opinion in such points as these a thing indifferent.   Derogatory notions concerning the attributes of the Supreme Being are unquestionably among the deteriorations of Religion.   Whilst it is acknowledged that we can have no sufficient, no adequate ideas, of the excellency and perfection of His nature, yet the mistakes of a false and an unworthy apprehension of Him it seems to be more within our power to avoid.   And if our opinions are cultivated, as they ought to be, for the purposes of faith, not to be mere matter of discourse; if a sense of the majesty of God and His perfections, is to be a bond and instrument of religion, none of these perfections can be impaired in our opinion of them, without detriment to our essential piety.   Whether it be His Justice, His Mercy, or His Omniscience, as the highest ideas of them will be the truest, because, though inadequate, they are the nearest to the truth which we can reach, so the same will be the best for ourselves, both because they are the truest, and also because they set Him before us as the object of the greatest adoration of which we are capable.

In this question, concerning the extent of God's omniscience, there is a peculiar honour belonging to Him involved.   For His foreknowledge of men's free actions is the highest instance of that omniscience, the highest, I mean, which is distinctly brought before our observation. To foreknow, to any extent, the events of Physical Nature, which follow from the arranged constitution and laws of that nature; or to foreknow the actions of men, if those actions are the result either of a system of external causes, or of innate principles exercising a constant and inevitable influence; this, in a manner, is only according to the scope of human knowledge and science; wherein the primary data of knowledge include the whole remote conclusions of it. But the prescience of the mysterious and voluntary action of free agents is of another order. It accords with the prerogative of God. It is "to understand the thoughts long before." If there be freedom in those thoughts, the foreknowledge of them is worthy of the Omniscient Mind. If they are a necessary and mechanical result of causes already in being, the foreknowledge of them is a less distinguishing attribute. In that case, it is but equivalent to a longer deduction.

Perhaps the *omniscience* of God, in this one exercise of it, may be estimated, in some measure, by His *omnipotence*, though both exceeding our comprehension. But one act of His *power* we believe to have been in the *creation* of the world from nothing. May not His omniscience be apprehended as acting in a like manner, in seeing "the things which are not, as though they were?" The power which *modifies* the things that *exist*, is, *in its kind*, like the knowledge which *surveys* the things that *exist*. But the *creative* power is like the knowledge which *anticipates* the existence of things and their causes. If the first be a mystery, it is on that account the fitter to illustrate the other.

There seems, therefore, to be both philosophic truth, and rational piety, in conceiving the whole order of things to be ever present to the omniscience of God. Such is the mode of viewing this subject, in which many wise and excellent men have chosen to rest. But whether this be only an expedient of a rational imagination, or a more strict and accurate truth, I leave it as it is expressed in the noble words of *Dr. Henry More*, (who however inclines, with some reserve, to the opinion that prescience and contingency are inconsistent,) or the more severe and wary representation of another excellent writer, *Archbishop Bramhall*. It may be conceived, that " the evolution of ages from everlasting to everlasting," says the former, " is so collectedly and presentifically represented to God at once, as if all things which ever were, are, or shall be, were at this very instant, and so always, really present, and existent before Him: which is no wonder, the animadversion and intellectual comprehension of God being absolutely infinite according to the truth of His *ideas*." The latter: "Concerning the prescience of contingent things; in my poor judgment, the readiest way to reconcile contingence and liberty with the decrees and prescience of God, and most remote from the altercations of these times, is to subject future contingents to the aspect of God, according to that presentiality which they have in eternity[t]."

[s] Divine Dialogues, p. 60.   [t] Works, p. 709.

DISCOURSE VIII.

1. *Criterion of it.*
2. *Proof of it in the Predictions concerning the Gospel.*

ISAIAH lx. 3.

*And the Gentiles shall come to Thy light, and kings to the
brightness of Thy rising.*

IN considering the Inspiration of Prophecy, as demonstrated in its Fulfilment, my intention is, first, to propose a *criterion* of Prophetic Inspiration, as clear and definite as the nature of the subject will admit, under which
the Scripture Prophecies may be severally examined; and
then to select particular instances of them, upon which to
institute an examination, according to the Criterion so
proposed. Examples of Prophecy, considered apart, and
under a distinct view, will give perspicuity to the argument to be deduced from them, and shew the grounds of
reason upon which the inspired Prescience of the Prophetic Volume is asserted.

To guard, however, against an erroneous estimate of
such detached inquiry, let me repeat again the observation which I have made in the beginning of these Discourses, that it is not the accomplishment of one *portion*
of Prophecy, nor of the entire *series* of it, which consti-
tutes the proof of our Religion. Separate prophecies are
only parts of one head of evidence, and the whole of pro-

phecy is but one kind of evidence concurrent with others. The sufficiency therefore of single points of the argument must not supersede the more comprehensive inference; and the supposed insufficiency of them, if there be any, must be corrected and supplied by the weight of reason in reserve. As to *negative* evidence, evidence tending to disprove the Christian Revelation, I venture to say there is none.

It is the more necessary to keep in mind that this is the true state of the question, inasmuch as we may observe persons who are continually arguing, or rather speaking and writing, in such a way as is utterly inconsistent with it. If they find obscure prophecies, which they think have little force in them as proofs of inspiration, or proofs of anything else, they are for prompting the inference that Revealed Religion is but a precarious cause. And perhaps there are others who, although far from having any doubt of its truth, are yet not without some uneasiness and disappointment in missing a more complete satisfaction in particular points of its various proof. But the evidences of Christianity are, in this respect, like those of Natural Religion. The fabric of the world is full of the marks of the Creator's agency, wisdom, and goodness. From a blade of grass up to a planet, or a sun, there is every where some element of evidence, some ground whereon to rest a rational belief. A single living creature, or the limb of a living creature, may convince. But if scepticism fall upon weak parts of this great natural argument; if it quarrel with some phenomena of it, ill understood, or, it may be, positively obscure; we must refer the inquirer for satisfaction to the structure of the world at large, we must carry him from one class of being to another, from the earth to the skies, and annihilate his doubts by the copiousness and ubiquity of the demonstration. So it is with the evidences of Revealed Religion. The *system* of them embraces the proper reason of our Faith, and gives the last reply to the demands of unbelief.

These considerations premised, I pass to the subject in hand : And, first, I shall endeavour to fix something of a *Criterion* of Prophecy, by ascertaining, or describing, the conditions which are necessary to assure us that we have in any instance an inspired prediction.

To constitute an *original* and *direct* proof of prophetic inspiration, it is necessarily required that the event foretold be such as man could not foresee at the time when the prediction of it was delivered : that it should have been therefore remote from the subsisting state of things, so as to exclude the supposition of the event having been virtually contained in that previous state of things, or the prediction of it having been suggested by Experience, Probability, or other ordinary means of rational foresight. In a word, the prophecy must have been independent of the calculations of human knowledge; and further, it must be seen to have been so.

Contiguity of *time*, between the prophecy and the event, does not disqualify the proof, so much as *proximity* of *relation* between the present and the future, if any such can be reasonably supposed in the given prophecy. It is the obscurity consisting in the *real*, or the *moral* remoteness of the event predicted, which takes it out of the grasp of human knowledge. If, however, the facts foretold be distant in time, as well as in the natural sequel of things; if they stand aloof from the prophecy by years and ages interposed, as well as by that chasm of darkness which intercepts the range of man's prospective view, when he attempts to penetrate the unlimited uncertainties of the future; then we have an aggravation of the disproof which takes the prediction from him, and imposes upon us the necessity of ascribing it to another origin.

Under these general ideas, I may describe the *conditions* which would confer this cogency of evidence on single examples of prophecy, in the following manner. First, the *known promulgation* of the prophecy prior to the event.

Secondly, the *clear* and *palpable fulfilment* of it. Lastly, the *nature of the event* itself, if, when the prediction of it was given, it lay *remote* from human view, and was such as could not be foreseen by any supposable *effort of reason*, or be *deduced* upon principles of *calculation* derived from *probability* or *experience*. These conditions will constitute a test, or standard of prophetic inspiration, in the rigorous estimate of its evidence. Where they clearly obtain, there we have an adequate proof of an inspired prescience. If they attach to many separate cases of prophecy, we shall have, in the whole combined together, a multiplied evidence, higher in proportion to the certainty there may be that each case is invested with the qualifications required.

I offer the criterion now stated as a standard of the *original* proof of a prophetic inspiration; a standard of such proof as independently, and by its own force, without the aid of any collateral presumptions, may command our assent. Nothing is assumed in behalf of the prophecies which answer to it. They are simply taken as so many documents contained in a Book which we call the Scripture. Their date of publication, their completion, the contingent nature of their subject-matter, will all be open to be scrutinized. The result of that scrutiny will determine the character to be assigned to them. Prophecies in Scripture there are, which do not come up in their evidence, at least in the present state of it, to this standard. Upon these we cannot insist, in the first instance, nor offer them as direct and integral proofs, although they have their use, even as evidence, when taken jointly with others, upon which they lean in part for their support. The higher test alone is the decisive one.

Now it may be affirmed, that both in the Old Testament and in the New, there are examples of Prophecy corresponding with the conditions which have been laid down: and my endeavour will be to shew, in cases selected from each, the conformity of the prediction with the conditions, and thereby demonstrate the prophetic Inspiration.

The first instance of Prophecy which I shall examine is that which relates to the *Establishment of the Christian Religion.* There was a time when Christianity was not in the world, but only foretold : a time when it had no being, but in prophecy. The point which I wish to establish is this, that the whole prediction of the future establishment of the religion of the Gospel was an inspired prediction, a prediction answerable to the highest test of a supernatural prescience.

In order to the proof of this point, I must assume your knowledge of the public history of the world, as connected with the propagation of the Christian Religion ; and some acquaintance with the general nature and doctrines of that religion, as well as with the chief records of Prophecy, which it would be impossible, in the progress of a discourse, to quote at large. My object will be to place your knowledge of the event in question, and of the prophecy of it, so together, as to shew the force of the argument which results from the comparison of the two, in demonstrating the inspired prescience of the prophecy.

First, then, be it observed, that the professed and extensive propagation of any religion, merely as a religion, a code of faith and moral duty, is not an ordinary occurrence in the history of the world. I confess that I know only one clear and prominent example of it; that example is the case of the Gospel itself in its first propagation, with, perhaps, *some* of the missions which have sprung from it. The propagation of Heathenism, ancient or modern, bears no resemblance to that of Christianity. Heathenism, in any of its creeds, has spread from country to country as a component part of the popular opinion ; it has travelled with migration, or conquest : it has passed in the train of things, and by the usual channels of communication. But the enterprise of a regular and systematic conversion of any great part of the world, undertaken and achieved as a distinct and direct work, is a phenomenon unknown in the diffusion of any of the forms of Heathenism or Idolatry, new or old. The genius of Paganism, jealous enough of its otiose dominion to resist encroachment, has wanted the charity, or the zeal, to go forth to attempt instruction and conversion. Distant lands have been none of the province of its labours.

The spread of Mahometanism, which may seem on the first view to have been something like to that of Christianity, was essentially unlike it, not merely in the means, but quite as much in the object. Because, Conquest, not Religious Faith, was the manifest object of Mahometanism when it began to be an active power. But if you deny that the religion was merely a pretext for the conquest, it cannot be denied that the two went together.—Whereas in the case of the Gospel, Religious Faith, Religious Doctrine was the single object either professed or followed, and the diffusion of that faith was made the exclusive and independent work. When, therefore, the Founder of Christianity said to the first Messengers of His Religion, " Go, teach all nations," we have reason to believe it was strictly the first instance of such a commission having been given, or undertaken, in the world; for Judaism had no such warrant for the communication of *its* truth; and hitherto the second instance has not been subsequently witnessed.

So much, then, as to the establishment of Christianity, in this one peculiarity of it, in being a new Religion taught and propagated, as a business of set design, and introduced upon the existing institutions of mankind, with an authority of its own, demanding and obtaining acceptance.

Secondly, Consider what this Religion is in itself, and whether it be not as singular in its *genius* and *doctrines*, as in the method of its propagation. No man, no reasonable man at least, will pretend to confound the Christian

Religion with any other. Be it from God, or from man, it is essentially unlike every other; it has a character perfectly its own, and it will remain for ever a witness of *something* without precedent or parallel. This distinctive character of it lies in the following properties of it united together; its spirit of benevolence, meekness, and peace; its general purity and elevation of doctrine; its uncontaminated Theology; the simplicity of its institutions; its doctrine of Redemption and Atonement; its promise of spiritual aid and illumination; its proposed reward of eternal life. By these marks of originality, or of distinction, taken collectively, I appeal to your judgment whether it does not stand alone, discriminated from all that has been taught as a system of religion, before it and beside it.

In the *third* place, Look to the seat and source from which this Religion sprung. It sprung from Judæa; it had its origin from a place and people the most unlikely, in all human reason, to have given such a gift to the world. Insulated by their civil institutions, by their prejudices, and by the disadvantageous feeling of contempt with which other nations were accustomed to regard them, they were the last people to be expected to be the founders of a dominant religion spreading to the East and the West, the North and the South. Their law was a barrier between them and other nations. It cut them off from the habits of communication and influence. They had no lead in arts; none in an enlarged distant commerce; none in policy; to make way for their doctrine. They were not the people to attempt a wide conversion; nor to succeed, if they attempted it.

But this is not the whole of the impediment which stood between the establishment of the Gospel and the capacity of this people, from among whom it rose, for such a work. The spirit of their own religion was in some great points exceedingly unlike the new religion which took its rise among them. They had a religion highly ceremonial, local, and restrictive. So it was designed to be, and such it was. Their institute of positive ordinances gave them a remarkable system of Church-polity and worship; and nothing in it is more to be observed than its prevailing dissimilarity with the simple and liberal religion of the Gospel; a religion which puts a disparagement upon forms and ordinances, to exalt the worship of God "in spirit and in truth;" which spreads its arms to all mankind; and is, in its nature, as applicable to every clime and country, as it is declared to be universal in its destination. It was once the question of prejudice, " Can any good thing come out of Nazareth?" With more justice and reason, humanly speaking, might it have been asked, " Can any good thing like the religion of the Gospel come from Nazareth?" But the fact refuted the calculation, reasonable as it might be.

Infidelity has often taken pains to expose the character of the Jewish people, and with no small exaggeration to decry them for their narrowness and poverty of mind; their bigotry; their want of literature and cultivation. Take these reproaches in what measure you will, they tend only to shew the extraordinary and improbable nature of that change which was effected by this despised and disqualified people when they became the teachers of an enlarged and comprehensive religion, and freed the world, so far as they did, from the dominion of idolatry and superstition, which philosophy and other human learning had ineffectually attempted to do. It is admitted that they had a peculiarity in their institutions, and in their manners resulting from those institutions. But this peculiarity, aggravated as it was in its worse sense by their own mistake and the perversion of their law, placed them the more in opposition to that new and better religion, which, through them, by their untoward means and inadequate instrumentality, was communicated to the world.

One advantage of ability indeed there may be *supposed* on the side of Judaism for the enterprise of a general instruction of mankind; that advantage was in the essential Truth of Judaism itself. If this resource be granted to

have existed, it is so much conceded to the reality of
Revelation. If denied, then the future success and triumphant establishment of a new religion coming from the
professors of Judaism, will be left an event which had nothing to redeem it from pure and absolute improbability.

Consider the *difference* in aptitude and qualification, for
spreading any system of doctrine, between Jewish and
some other teachers. Had it been foretold, for instance,
that a novel and prevalent religion should one day appear,
and take a lasting possession of a considerable part of the
civilized world, emanating from *Athens,* or from *Rome :*
the popular philosophy and literature of the one, which
had a certain freedom of access to the world at large, or
the growing empire of the other, might have furnished
some pledge for the accomplishment of the prediction.
But *Jewish* doctrine could look to no such auxiliaries in
civil or intellectual empire, to favour its introduction, or
recommend its pretensions. Prophecy, therefore, we may
say, when it predicted the reception of a Law of Religion,
which was to have Jews for its teachers, and Kings and
Nations for its converts, had nothing to build upon, nothing either in present appearances, or the ordinary calculation of things.

One circumstance there was, their wide national *dispersion,* which, although a badge of their slavery, might have
promised the Jewish people some *dubious opportunity* of
erecting, or attempting to erect, a prevalent and general
religion, if they had agreed together to improve the use of
their extended communication under such a dispersion.
But this condition of their national fortunes did not take
place till after the prophecies were promulgated which
foretold the conversion of the world by their means. The
prediction was contemporary with their earlier confined
state in Judæa. It was delivered when Judaism itself
was stationary and quiescent, and not rich in proselytes;
whereas it appears that a considerable proselytism did
actually accompany it in its dispersed fortunes. But in
that earlier state of things, there was nothing in reference

to the future predicted event, but disability and disqualification; unless we choose to admit the *truth* of Judaism
itself, and so diminish the improbability of the introduction of Christianity by conceding the reality of the prior
Revelation.

Let me now combine together the chief points which
compose the history of the establishment of Christianity,
as a known unquestionable event. *First*, we have its
direct and systematic propagation. *Secondly*, its internal
distinguishing character, as proposing such and such doctrines. *Lastly*, its origin in Judæa, from a secluded
people, whom their own institutions, and the prejudice
of the world, laid under a disqualification for the work
in question.

This is the case of the Gospel; a case not to be denied
or contested. And I think we shall not exceed the lowest
statement of the truth in affirming that the direct establishment of such a religion, coming from such a people, was
not merely a very memorable event, but something more;
a novel and unprecedented thing, which has produced
the greatest *moral* change, known in the public history of
man, but such as was indicated by no probability, nor
could be suggested by prior experience. If so, the positive
and unhesitating prediction of it, a prediction recorded in
prophecy for many ages before it took place, confidently
announcing it, and fully anticipating its introduction, and
its reception, was a prediction of supernatural prescience.

We are born in the *midst* of this Religion, and therefore it requires some effort of thought, though not a great
one, to carry us to that point of view from whence we may
contemplate the extent and magnitude of the work of
change by which it first made its way, and still holds it
on. But all reflection will serve to heighten your ideas
of the phenomenon. Had you seen the finger of an unknown power at first, eighteen hundred years ago, strike

the rock, and bring forth water in the desert, you would more readily have owned the wonder, as every impartial and disengaged spectator must have owned it. But whilst you look at it only in its existing course, you may forget whence it came, or cease to be affected by its presence. Trace it to its source; Judæa was the rock from which it broke, and the world around it was, and still is, the wilderness through which it flows. Now, without inquiring whose hand it was which *could* produce this effect, (which is another topic,) I argue only that the propagation and institution of Christianity, an event so extraordinary in its kind, and so improbable in the circumstances of its origin, is sufficient to authenticate the inspiration of the prophecy by which it was foretold.

As to the documents of Prophecy which announce and describe the Gospel; they occupy the prophetic volume from Genesis to Malachi. But it is not necessary to ask the benefit of all this range of Prophecy, in order to shew that the establishment of such a Religion, as the Christian is, was foretold. The predictions of Isaiah, Daniel, Zechariah, and Malachi; or those of Isaiah alone; or even so much of them as is contained in the last fourteen chapters of the book of this single prophet, would suffice for the purpose of our inquiry.

In some measure to open this proof, take the following characteristic predictions of Isaiah; " It shall come to pass in the last days, that the *mountain* of the *Lord's house* shall be *established* in the top of the mountains, and shall be *exalted above* the hills; and all *nations shall flow* unto it. And *many people* shall go and say, Come ye, and let us go up to the mountain of the Lord, to the house of the God of Jacob; and He will teach us of His ways, and we will walk in His paths: for out of *Zion* shall go forth *the law*, and the *word of the Lord* from Jerusalem. And He shall *judge among the nations*, and shall *rebuke many people*[a]:" i. e. *instruct* them by reclaiming from error.

<hr>

[a] Isaiah ii. 2—4.

" Behold My servant, whom I uphold ; Mine elect, in whom My soul delighteth ; I have put My spirit upon Him : *He shall bring forth judgment to the Gentiles.* He shall not cry, nor lift up, nor cause His voice to be heard in the street. A bruised reed shall He not break, and the smoking flax shall He not quench : He shall bring forth judgment unto truth. He *shall not* fail, nor be *discouraged, till* He have *set judgment in the earth :* and the *Isles* shall wait for *His law.*"

" I the Lord have called Thee in righteousness, and will hold Thine hand, and will keep Thee, and give Thee for a *covenant of the people, for a light of the Gentiles ;* to *open* the *blind eyes,* to *bring out the prisoners* from *the prison,* and them that sit in *darkness* out of the prison house[b]."

" Arise, shine ; for Thy light is come, and the glory of the Lord is risen upon Thee. For, behold, the darkness shall cover the earth, and gross darkness the people : but the Lord shall arise upon Thee, and His glory shall be seen upon Thee. And the *Gentiles* shall come to Thy light, and *kings* to the brightness of Thy rising[c]."

In all these prophecies the conversion of the Gentiles to a religion proceeding from Judæa is unequivocally foretold. For that such expressions as, a *law, judgment, covenant, light,* in the prophetic volume, are descriptive of some *doctrine,* or *revelation* of a *religious nature,* is no more to be doubted than that the phrases of Euclid relate to the subject of Geometry. " The *law going forth* from *Zion,* and the *word* of the Lord from *Jerusalem,*" is therefore a definite and unambiguous description of a religious doctrine thence communicated to the world. And " the influx of all nations into the *mountain of the Lord's house* in Zion," is no less definite in describing the conversion of the Gentiles to a Faith or Worship of the true God, originating in that mountain, as the place

[b] Isaiah xlii. 1. 7.   [c] Isaiah lx. 1—3.

where it should be first instituted or taught. Consequently, these predictions which I have quoted, as well as others of the like tenor, are prophecies of the Gospel: for besides giving some of the appropriate lineaments of the Gospel doctrine, they state the extent and certainty of its propagation among the Gentiles: and this its propagation in the Gentile world they foretell in as strong and positive a way, as if it had then been an ordinary thing for any set of men to make it their object and business to spread religious opinion of any kind, or for Jews to instruct and convert the other nations of the earth, and that by a religion above the standard of their own.

But in the midst of this assemblage of prophetic matter which relates to this future order of things, there is delineated the character, or history of a person, of whom it is clear that He is eminently connected with the introduction of the foretold dispensation, and who appears, indeed, by the text of the prophecy, to be the Minister, or appointed Messenger, by whom it should be ushered into the world[d]. For the office and agency of this person are joined in the prophecy with the foundation of the predicted religion[e]. Thereby the unity of the subject is ascertained. Moreover, His personal history is sufficiently discriminated. His state of humiliation, His sufferings, His judicial condemnation, His death, His subsequent power and prevailing success in the work which He had undertaken, are among the things described; and they are described in one continued draught of prediction, and with a perfect sequel and connexion, incorporating them into a common subject. Add therefore these limitations of peculiarity to the idea of the distant event, limitations which confessedly existed in the person of the Founder of Christianity, and you will advance one step further into the extent and combination of the prophetic prescience. For the Christian history is, in these points, notorious

---

[d] Isaiah lii. 13. liii.　　　　　　　　　　[e] See chapters lii. liii. liv.

and indubitable. The Founder of Christianity *was* an afflicted, suffering, condemned, slain, victorious Person. His sufferings and violent death are attested by Pagan evidence; but supposing they had not been so attested, they could not by any possibility have been *feigned;* for the pretended scene of them was a public, and therefore it must have been a real one. As to His prevailing power and success in the accomplishment of His proposed work, the effectual establishment of Christianity is the visible proof of that. Consequently, the prophetic and the historic subjects coincide in these particulars; particulars discriminating in the prophecy, public and palpable in the fact. The result is, that we have the prediction of a dominant Religion, originating from Judæa, embracing the Gentile nations, and either formally introduced by a person of such and such a history, *viz.*, a suffering, condemned, and slain person, or at least having such a person eminently and conspicuously joined with it, and bearing a principal part in its promulgation. But, since the complex fact, thus foretold, is such as was in its whole kind improbable, and, so circumstantiated, by any human foresight utterly undiscernible; and since the event has undeniably answered to the prediction, it remains that the prediction of it, a prediction far removed in time from the event, was an inspired prophecy.

But there is an accumulation of the evidence. For the same prediction describes the suffering Minister, or Promulger, of the future Religion, under the following qualities :—" bearing the sins of others ; healing by His stripes ; procuring peace to men by His chastisement; giving His soul an offering for sin; making intercession for the transgressors." That is to say, it asserts the virtue of an Atonement, and propitiatory Intercession, to belong to the person so described. Now that the Founder of Christianity has such a power of atonement and intercession for sin, appropriated to Him, is a fact the truth of which I cannot put in here, as of other facts of His life and history; because it is of a secret invisible nature; and the belief of it rests upon the previous belief of the general truth of Christianity. But one thing is certain, that this His atoning and interceding office forms a conspicuous tenet of Christianity. It is at least a matter of fact, that the doctrine of it enters into the Religion. There is therefore a concurrence of no small moment between the prediction and the event, in this particular. The prediction announces a singular and most critical fact. The religion recognises the doctrine of that fact, and is mainly grounded upon it. And this is all that the Religion historically *can* do; *viz.*, to teach and affirm it. But this is enough to fix the capital point of our present argument, which is the identity of the Christian Religion with the subject of the prophecy. And whilst the prediction itself, by this characteristic attribute of it, becomes more complete in its substantial resemblance, and more explicit in its reference; every man endowed with any reflection must see that it was no common work for a system of religion to take up this property, the notion of a personal Atonement and Mediatorship, and make it a distinctive and fundamental tenet of its faith. This the Gospel has done, and the principle belongs equally to the religion, and the prophecy of it. In like manner the direction of other texts of prophecy to Christianity is made out by further qualities, contained in the prediction, corresponding with other essential doctrines and precepts of the religion: the specific genius of the Religion being so defined, as to leave no reasonable doubt that the prophetic texts in question describe, not merely a new scheme of religion, but, more exactly, such a scheme of religion as we behold in the actual plan of Christianity. So far, therefore, as these several instances of correspondence and agreement are admitted, so far there is a reiterated confirmation both of the direction, and of the inspired prescience, of the prophecy.

But once more; for we have not exhausted our fund of evidence; select from the Prophetic Volume other predic-

tions, as of the *time* when this Personage should appear in
the world, who was to be the author of the foretold dispensation; the *place* of His birth; His tribe; His family;
and associating these particulars, with the rest, into one
mass of prophetic requisition, all attached to that change
and crisis of a system of religion so novel, and so improbable in itself; and you will approach more nearly to an estimate of that multiplied evidence of prophetic inspiration
which centres in the single point of the establishment of
Christianity.

These prophecies, it is true, lie dispersed in the prophetic books; consequently whether their reference be to
one and the same subject, is open to some dispute. *A
posteriori*, it is easy to shew that Christianity fulfils them;
but we admit that events may fit and agree to many descriptions which yet may be neither inspired, nor specifically directed to them. But the state of the evidence, in
this matter, is as follows: The prophecies, severally, speak
of some distinguished person or persons to whom such
and such appropriate marks should belong; as the Shiloh
coming at the departure or removal of the sceptre of
Judah; the Son of David, establishing an universal kingdom of Righteousness; the Messiah being cut off, at such
a period of the world; a ruler of Israel coming forth from
Bethlehem. Now the fact is, that these and other complicated attributes of description have been realized in
one single person, and in the institution of His religion;
whose advent, birth, death, and religious kingdom, all
correspond with their several mixt characters. But such
coincidence and concurrence of the postulata of the whole
range of the prophecy, in that one person, must I think
be held of itself sufficient to appropriate them to Him.
If several lines, separately taken, have an unascertained
bearing, and tend we know not whether to a common
centre, yet if when viewed from some one point their tendency to it is apparent, that point must be concluded
to be the true locus of their direction and concourse,
and the very fact of their capacity of meeting there

will be a proof of their having been so designed to meet. This is analogous to the case of some of these divided prophecies which we apply to the Gospel: and the application of them so made, is just and rational, on the most hard and unfavourable conditions. But this application is, at the same time, greatly strengthened by many internal indications of the prophetic text which plainly suggest, or imply, the joint and common bearing of the several members of the divided prediction. These various prophecies, therefore, confirm and enlarge the proof of an inspired prescience announcing the future establishment of the Gospel Religion.

For that an event, as that was, out of the course of experience, and warranted by no deductions of probability, should be not only announced, but delineated with a variety of circumstantial limitations attending it, limitations of personal character and individual history, in the Founder; with internal limitations, as to the nature and genius of the predicted Religion; and others external, as to the time and place; this is an aggregate of prediction, beyond which we cannot well ask any stronger marks of a prescience divinely communicated. The suffering founder of a triumphant religion; that religion, distinctive and peculiar; preached by Jews abroad to the world, and from Jews by the world received; I do not now argue that such a combination of things was a miracle; but that the confident and decisive prediction of it was a *prophecy;* and that, first, the prophecy, and then the religion, were from God.

It is hardly necessary for me to observe that in the case before us, there obtains the *known promulgation* of the prophecy prior to the event, which was one condition of the criterion proposed. The prophecies of Isaiah, which alone would embrace the greatest part of the subject, are among the more ancient of the Prophetic Canon; and the Translation of the Old Testament made into the Greek language, and thereby submitted to a general cognizance, long before the æra of the Gospel, will abundantly satisfy us in that respect.

The document of prediction was therefore extant, and in the hands of men, before there were any signs of the event. I say, before any *signs* of the event. For the more any person looks into the intermediate history of the *Jewish people*, as related to the rest of the world, in the course of time between the promulgation of the *Christian* prophecies and their accomplishment, the less probability will he see to expect from *them*, in their broken and humbled fortunes, the enterprise of an instruction and conversion of the other nations of the earth; the greater reason, therefore, to acknowledge the prescience which foresaw, and the power which wrought that extraordinary event.

The Jewish people did not make these prophecies work their own completion: they did not even further it. They neither understood the Gospel Religion, when it was offered to them, nor adopted it, nor promoted it. But they are in this, as in other instances of prophecy, unwilling witnesses to its truth, unwilling agents in its accomplishment. For so Prophecy had spoken, that the religion which was to come from Judæa, and the Teacher of it, should be rejected by the people from among whom it came; that a remnant of them should be saved, but the nation cast off; and from that remnant, in the general dissolution of the Jewish church and people, should spring the proper glory of Jerusalem, and that the nation rejecting this "word of God," and rejected by Him, should yet bear His name, by a chosen seed, and under the new institution of things, to the ends of the earth. These adverse particulars contribute to the complexity of the prediction. The entire and reconciled completion of them significantly attests its inspiration.

In conclusion, I observe that the actual state of Prophecy, on this head, has a singular agreement with the whole nature and design of Christianity. It is plain that nothing ever was so important to mankind as Christianity, if it be true; nothing so worthy to be foretold; nothing so *fit to be made the subject* of an early and continued course of prediction. Well; it *had* the foremost place in the prophetic revelations; it was the oldest subject, and the latest, and the most frequently revived. There is in this general congruity of Prophecy with the pre-eminent importance of the Gospel subject, a moral evidence in favour both of the Gospel and of the whole prophetic Revelation, which I leave to the reflection of every impartial mind to pursue to its just consequences; it being clear that no art of man could model prophecy into such proportions as that it should bear this just, and well-constituted relation, in its whole extended structure, to the moral dignity and magnitude of a future unseen dispensation of things. And this is a kind of evidence quite distinct from the fulfilment of the particular things foretold.

The accomplishment of the prophecies relative to Christianity, so far as they have been drawn into the present argument, being, as I conceive, unequivocal, and the proof of a divine prescience, grounded upon that accomplishment, strict and conclusive, two observations remain which I wish to offer, the one bearing upon the *kind* of prescience thus proved, the other upon the measure of accomplishment which the prophecies in question have received.

First, The Divine Prescience manifested in this instance is more in the revelation of God's own work and design, than of the actions of men. The institution of Christianity, the mission of its Founder, its first propagation, are to be ascribed solely, and its successful establishment principally, to Him. His previous revelation, therefore, of these things is expressive simply, or chiefly, of His own purpose. By prophecy He communicated His intended work. As to the ultimate reception of Christianity, we have no reason to think that the agency of man, or the concurrence of things dependent on human conduct, were excluded either in the divine foreknowledge, or in the event; but even in this case the interposition of God was pre-eminent, both an open and a secret act of His Spirit, and His power, being engaged in subduing the world to the reception of His Truth. The general prediction of Christianity is therefore to be considered as a prophecy of the greatest, and most enduring miracle, which has been exhibited in the moral government of God. The prophecy spoke for ages; the miracle, or the extraordinary fact, call it by either name, still subsists.

The second observation is upon the measure of accomplishment which the prophecies in question have received. The phenomenon of Christianity, it may be said, was clearly predicted, but the credit of Prophecy may seem to labour on the other side; for that its predictions speak of a wider range than the Religion has reached, and the doubt is not whether all that has been effected was foretold, but whether more was not foretold than has been effected.

The prophetic promises concerning the prevalence of Christianity unquestionably are large and comprehensive. They seem to embrace the whole earth. "*All nations shall flow unto it.*" "*The earth shall be filled* with the knowledge of the Lord as *the waters cover the sea.*" Such predictions as these, if pressed to the letter, open the prospect of an unlimited, universal reception of the Gospel; which hitherto it has not had. Its dominion, wide as it has been in ancient or in modern times, and in regions rude or civilized, has yet only shared the world with other powers of a gross Heathenism unenlightened, and Infidelity unreclaimed: whilst the march of its early propagation has been suspended in after ages, and stationary, if not contracted limits, have confined its pale. If, therefore, the letter of the prophecy express its true and proper sense, it is plain that prophecy, in this great subject of it, waits a more perfect, and a more extended accomplishment.

Meanwhile, even upon this admission, what has been

already fulfilled is no small warrant and security for a more adequate consummation. The first institution of Christianity was a far greater change than its extension would be; the difficulties and improbabilities infinitely exceeded, in the first instance, the force of any now existing. It conquered more than remains to oppose it. Truth, firmly established, and placed in commanding possession, has in its own nature a principle of strength, and thereby offers some promise of the probable enlargement of its reign. And in the next place, although we ought not to measure the credibility of a supposed divine promise by the actual appearance of things, because that appearance, adverse as it may be, is no criterion of the power which is understood to be engaged, yet the present state of the world, and a reasonable estimate of things as they lie before us, may afford a reply, and a sufficient one, to the precipitate inferences of doubt and objection. On this footing of argument, it may be alleged, that a wider diffusion of Christianity is at this day a probable prospect, and an object of reasonable calculation. The state of the world, in many of its relations, suggests the hope, as it offers the opportunity and the means, of such a diffusion. For the public confession and reception of the Christian Faith by the most improved and cultivated nations of the earth, nations now bearing a sway over the rest of their species, by their superiority in all the resources of moral and intellectual power, and by their possession of those great instruments of dominion, letters, science, institutions, and national character; instruments which prepare some men, in the common order of Providence, to be masters of others by an innocent and peaceful subjugation; this general condition of the world, I say, humanly speaking, affords a visible inducement to believe in great possible advances of Christianity beyond its present bounds; advances, to which a rational judgment would be loath to set any limits. And in this kind of consideration let no one imagine there is any thing of the presumptuous spirit of an attempted prophecy. The use of it is simply in shewing that a visible probability may be an answer to a precarious objection. But such probability can be no measure either of the sense, or the truth of prophecy, or of the power of God's providence engaged for the perfect fulfilment of it, in whatever sense that truth may have been delivered. Whether the sense of prophecy really be that the pale of the Christian Faith shall ever be as wide as the whole world, is a point which I do not discuss. Unquestionably a greater prevalence of it is foretold, both in the Old Testament and the New, than it has yet attained. But the conspicuous phenomenon, and the incontestable prophecy, were exhibited in its foundation and its triumphant settlement. And there the evidence of Christianity and of Prophecy is complete.

One point, however, is certain and equally important, *viz.*, that the Christian Church, when it comes to recognise more truly the obligation imposed upon it by the original command of its Founder, " Go teach all nations," a command, which, having never been recalled or abrogated, can never be obsolete, will awaken another energy of its apostolic office and character, than has been witnessed in many later ages, in this most noble work of Piety and Charity combined; and thereby begin to discharge an inalienable duty, in furthering the clear design of the Gospel, and perhaps also the consummation of Prophecy. Whether Belief shall be universal, we know not: but as to the duty of making an universal tender and communication of the Christian Faith, it is too clear to be denied, and too sacred to be innocently neglected.

Apart from the operation of this command, and a due obedience to it, the mere opportunities afforded by the state of the world, for the extension of Christianity, could not excite any very serious hope of such an effect, however they may favour the possibility of it.

END OF DISCOURSE VIII.

DISCOURSE IX.

ON THE INSPIRATION OF PROPHECY.

Proof of it in the Predictions concerning the Jewish People.

----◆----

Deut. xxviii. 59.

*Then the Lord will make thy plagues wonderful, and the
plagues of thy seed, even great plagues, and of long continuance, and sore sicknesses, and of long continuance.*

IT has been urged by the defenders of Revelation, and
not by others generally denied, that any one unquestionable miracle would to the eyewitnesses of that miracle
be sufficient to prove a revelation attested by it, a suitable
moral end of both being supposed. The miracle granted,
the inference from it could not be resisted. The acknowledgment of the supernatural agency must be followed by
an admission of the doctrine. It is but the connexion
which subsists between the lightning and the thunder;
when we see the flash, we know the thunder, which follows, comes from the same cloud.

But miracles being to the use of the present age an
evidence transmitted by testimony, it has been so ordered,
as to this ground of our faith, that the number and variety
of the original proofs by miracles, should come in compensation for the loss of force, which those proofs severally
might be thought to suffer by transmission. If we have
not the conviction which would result from seeing any[a]

----

[a] *Single* miracles are often said to have convinced eyewitnesses on the first
publication of the Gospel. John vi. 11. "Then those men, when they had
seen *the miracle* which Jesus did, said, This is of a truth that prophet that
should come into the world." So chap. ii. 11, &c.

The same Evangelist puts the miracles *collectively*, for the written evidence one miracle with our own eyes, we have the satisfaction which rests upon many competently authenticated and recorded. "We are encompassed by a cloud of witnesses," by whom, whatever is wanting in the intensity of the proof as addressed to the senses, is supplied in the extent and accumulation of the same proof addressed to our rational understanding.

Now the force which has been thus ascribed to single miracles, may be attributed also to single prophecies. It might be argued, if the defence of Revelation required such a mode of argument, that single prophecies, taken alone, are sufficient, under certain conditions, to prove a revelation; and that there are Scripture prophecies strictly satisfying such conditions. The conditions, which would confer this cogency of evidence on detached prophecies, are those which are included in the criterion which I have laid down, *viz.*, the known promulgation of the prophecy prior to the event; the clear fulfilment of it; the remoteness of the event itself from all human prescience; conditions which joined together form the true conclusive standard of a prophetic Inspiration. Tried by this standard, the evidence of any particular prophecy, in its original and perfect force, may be either permanent, or temporary. It is permanent, so long as it can be *shewn* to be conformable in each point to the test proposed. It declines, and loses something of its force, as an independent proof, when we want the materials of information necessary to evince that rigorous conformity of it.

One example of prophecy has been submitted to this test: and the next which I now take up to be examined in like manner, is that portion of the Prophetic Volume which relates to the degraded and exiled state of the Jewish people.

to the *future faith* of the world. "Many other signs truly did Jesus in the presence of His disciples, which are not written in this book; but *these are written*, that ye might believe that Jesus is the Christ, the Son of God" xx. 30, 31.

I. The publication of the prophecy in this instance
was long anterior to the event. The substance, and the
most characteristic circumstances of it, are contained in
the books of Moses, Leviticus, and Deuteronomy, from the
latter of which I shall hereafter quote a part of it. It is
referred to in the book of Nehemiah[b], as a prophecy which
had been delivered by Moses. The same prophetic subject is resumed in the books of Amos, Jeremiah, and
Ezekiel, as well as other books of the Old Testament. If,
with regard to some of these predictions, as those of Jeremiah and Ezekiel, which are among the latest of them,
scepticism should object that they might be grounded
upon the pregnant signs, or actual commencement, of
the desolation and dispersion which they profess to foreshew : no such surmise can be thrown in the way to invalidate the antiquity of the records of the prophecy included in the books of Moses. For besides other proofs
of the authentic æra of those books, and of the prophecies,
which they contain, ascribed to Moses, their antiquity, so
far as it is involved in the present question, is established
by an evidence obvious and conclusive. The division of
the monarchy of Israel, after the death of Solomon, placed
the books of Moses under the custody of an hostile and
acrimonious schism in religion between the two kingdoms
of Judah and Samaria; and Samaria, acknowledging the
Pentateuch as the basis of its religion, though with a very
corrupted and heretical faith, bore a second, and yet more
than independent testimony, to the antiquity and authenticity of the Mosaic records and prophecies; most certainly
to the authenticity of those portions of the Pentateuch
which are, in the very tenor of its text, explicitly ascribed
to Moses as their author. Such are all those connected
with the publication of the Law.

The *first* condition therefore is largely secured in our
inquiry.

<hr>

[b] Chap. i. 8.

II. The second qualification of the prophecy can as little be denied. The notorious facts of history open to all the world, bespeak the eminent and palpable accomplishment of the several heads of its prediction. Following the prophecy as it is set forth in the Pentateuch, we are carried through an extraordinary state of long and aggravated national calamity: turning to history, old and recent, we see its narrative holding an equal pace with every denunciation of the prophet. The comparison has often been made between this chapter of prophecy and the accomplishment of it. It formed a subject of illustration and argument in the apologies of the Fathers, and in their popular discourses: as may be seen in the writings of Justin, Tertullian, Chrysostom, and others; the forcible delineation of the prophecy, on the one hand, the strange and singular fate of the Jewish people, on the other, furnishing such images as arrested observation, and such media of conviction as every understanding might apply. Among other writers, Bishop Newton is one who has drawn out the comparison, and to his Dissertations I refer for the detail of the historic evidence, so far as the general notoriety of the principal points of it can leave the occasion for a more complete information.

III. But the considerable question in this case is not, whether the things foretold have been fulfilled, of which there can be no doubt, but whether the prediction of them did not exceed the powers of human foresight; and to that question, which brings us to the third condition of the criterion laid down, I shall direct my attention.

It is freely admitted that a general prophecy of the future ruin and desolation of any g ven people or kingdom, to take place at a distant period, is, if it should be fulfilled, no test of a prescience more than human; because the desolations of conquest, and other rude vicissitudes of kingdoms and communities, are among the ordinary materials of history. Something distinctive, something of a special characteristic kind, must be introduced in the prediction, to guard it against the suspicion of having been drawn from the usual beaten course of human affairs. Prophecy, in our present instance of it, furnishes more than one such distinctive and appropriate mark. It is part of the prediction in Deuteronomy : "The Lord shall *scatter thee among all people*, from *the one end* of the *earth* even unto *the other.*—And *among these nations* shalt thou find *no ease*, neither shall the *sole of thy foot have rest;* but the Lord shall give thee a trembling heart, and failing of eyes, and sorrow of mind."—"I will bring your land unto desolation, and your enemies which dwell therein shall be astonished at it; and I *will scatter you among* the heathen, and draw out a sword after you[d]." Add to which that in the prophecies of Amos, Jeremiah, and Ezekiel, the doom of *scattering*, or *removal* into the uttermost parts of the earth, is pronounced upon the Jewish race not less than six times, prophecy thereby denoting that dispersion was a special plague ordained for God's visitation upon this people. "I will cause them to be removed into all the kingdoms of the earth," was His sentence upon them[e].

On this point the argument takes its stand, and challenges our assent to the inspiration of the prophecy. *Dispersion* has been the fate of the Jewish people in a manner and degree in which it has befallen no other people. From the period of their first overthrow, or rather from the first mutation and decline of their commonwealth, it has pursued them to the present day. It has been the habit under which they have existed, in ten of their Tribes, or in all, for seventeen hundred years, or for twenty-five hundred.

The infliction of this national calamity began with the Assyrian conquest, when their Ten Tribes were swept into a captivity and exile in the East, from which, in any public strength, they never returned. The second infliction of it befell the surviving kingdom of Judah, in the Babylonian

<hr>

[c] Chap. xxviii. 64, 65.   [d] Levit. xxvi. 32, 33.   [e] Jerem. xv. 4.

conquest, when the main body of the population of Judæa was broken up, their king, their nobles, and other draughts of their fugitive inhabitants, were carried to bondage in Babylon, whilst a second part of them, the force of their military population, fled into Egypt[f], there to experience only a later capture, and a wider dispersion, in as many as survived the sword, through the provinces of the Babylonian empire. But when this Tribe, which was reserved for a destiny of its own, and that a destiny already foreshewn by prophecy, was, for the fulfilment of that intermediate prophecy, restored, and though not without a great loss and severance of its people left behind, replanted in its own land again, and had there passed through the period of its appointed and foretold continuance to the days of the Messiah and the Gospel, then the last catastrophe of its fate, dealt by the Roman arms, extended and aggravated the calamity of dispersion beyond the example of any former period of the like suffering, and the final scattering of this devoted people, which then ensued; when the sword and captivity divided between them their whole stock and race, has continued a lasting phenomenon even now fresh in the eyes of men, a phenomenon attesting, with an importunate energy, the prescience, and the veracity, of Prophecy.

Yet this tribe was once exempted, as we see, from the most natural consequence of a seventy years' captivity in a foreign land. Subjugation and captivity did not always lead to irrevocable dispersion. This broken Tribe could be preserved and restored, when prophecy had predicted to it the precise term of its bondage, and the subsequent repossession of its own land. During this its temporary bondage, it was sealed up, rather than dissipated; it had from prophecy a principle of vitality and preservation; for there remained predictions to be fulfilled in that Tribe, and by it, in its own proper place of abode, and in its public character. But in the fulness of time, the extreme measure of predicted punishment by dispersion overtook

<hr>

[f] Jerem. xliii.

this remaining member of the Hebrew people, as it had
the rest. The advent of the Messiah announced the departure of the sceptre from Judah, and released, if I may
so speak, the last obligations of prophecy, which stood
pledged for the continuance of that sceptre no longer.
Then it was that the threats of penal prediction took their
full effect, when the Almighty was seen accomplishing
His word, which had long been suspended over the last
remains of His people, and bidding all the plagues of
desolation to chase them from the land which He had
originally bestowed upon them, and, by His gift, made
their inheritance; their deprivation and expulsion from it
having from the first been made the declared token of
their rejection, as the grant of it was of their stipulated
adoption.

To revert then more closely to the prominent circumstance by which prophecy distinguishes the fate of the
Jewish people, their *dispersion*, their *removal* into distant
lands, it must be observed that this is one critical proof,
an index of the inspiration of the prophecy. The decay
and dilapidation of kingdoms take place in various ways;
nothing more frequent than violent subjugation by conquest; nothing uncommon in the silent and crumbling
decay of populous states by the lapse of time; and even
extirpation and exile are not unknown as the fortune of
smaller communities. But in the case of the Jewish people, there is a modification of their fate by a general and
distant dispersion, to which there are few other instances,
if any, to be compared at all, and in the permanence
and duration of that accident there is, I believe, no one
case parallel to it, or like it, whatever. It is not a bare
desolation of their land, nor desolation with the exhaus-
tion and disappearance of the people from their original home; but a driving of them to the four winds of
heaven, superadded to the local calamities of an exterminating vengeance, which makes the peculiarity of their
fate, and of the prediction of it. Other, and long settled
nations, may have been driven from their native country;

of which, however, in nations of the scale and strength of the Hebrew people, it will not be easy to name the second example; but such a devious dispersion, and such a perpetuity of it, are strictly unparalleled. For where is the other country in the world, and in what quarter of it, which lies so vacant, so thinly occupied, whilst its proper race are to be seen everywhere else: they, and it divided; a solitary soil, and a displaced, distracted population, abounding any where rather than in their own land? In that divided state they remain; present in all countries, and with a home in none; intermixed, and yet separated; and neither amalgamated nor lost; but like those mountain streams which are said to pass through lakes of another kind of water, and keep a native quality to repel commixture, they hold communication without union, and may be traced, as rivers without banks, in the midst of the alien element which surrounds them.

In searching for a case like to theirs, I cannot suppose that any person will seriously set up, for the parallel to this fate of the Jewish people, the equivocal history of an obscure wandering race, not unknown in our own country, who are permitted to hang upon the outskirts of society, and who keep up certain usages and habits of life, without settlement, or intermixture and incorporation with others. Of this wandering horde there is no evidence of their having ever existed as a collective independent people, and having lost that state; there is no evidence of their having existed in any form, and maintained their succession, for a length of time to be compared with the Jewish dispersion; and they escape now, in their insulated freedom, by connivance and toleration, in the open neglected frontier between society and solitude. Whereas the Jewish people have lived in the full communication of public intercourse; they have lived in the heart of cities, in the crowded seats of commerce, and in those relations and habitudes of life which most effectually obliterate original distinctions of lineage and country. And these their re-

lations of civil life, in which they are known at this day
almost to a proverb, connecting them with the business of
traffick in all its details, are none of a modern date. Such
has long been their mode; having no root of territorial
occupancy, they have been thrown upon it; and it is as
ancient with them, as the time of Chrysostom, who speaks
of them as conversant in the same medley of commerce,
and to be seen among the busiest traffickers in the market
of the world[g].

But if the two cases had a real resemblance, which they
have not, how could the evidence of Scripture prophecy be
impeached by that similarity? To foretell a future national
condition to a given people, so strangely rare in its kind,
so anomalous, so remote from the common, and indeed
the uncommon vicissitudes of nations, would still be a test
of supernatural prescience, even if a second instance like
it could be pretended. How rare it has been, needs no
other proof than this, that out of the storehouse of history, modern and ancient, amidst the manifold varieties of
fortune which have marked or ended the course of kingdoms and communities, an operose, and indeed a frivolous
ingenuity, is driven to seek, where it does, for the parallel required; among the desultory tribes of Gipsies or
Guebres.

Review the whole of this extraordinary case. From the
settlement of the Hebrew colony in Egypt by the Patriarch Jacob, to the final expulsion of the whole people from
their country by the Romans, is a period of nearly eighteen
hundred years. Within that compass of time twice have
they passed through public bondage threatening their extinction. But from their first bondage they emerged to
the conquest of Canaan; from their second to the repossession of Judæa. It was in their progress to their earlier

<hr>

[g] Chrysost. tom. i. p. 656. ed. Montfauc. μή γάρ μοι τοὺς πατριάρχας
τούτους εἴπῃς, τοὺς καπήλους, τοὺς ἐμπόρους, τοὺς τῆς πάσης παρανομίας
γέμοντας.

triumphant establishment, that the doom of their dispersion began to be foretold; prophecy so setting its seal upon them from the first, and in the beginnings of their history. Dispersion has been their fate; the reversed, but equally conspicuous, sequel of their public polity. It has been their fate in each branch of them; first of Israel, next of Judah; and this final and comprehensive dissipation of them has now lasted nearly eighteen hundred years, equalling the extreme period of their former national existence. In every stage of their course, these eighteen hundred years have borne witness to the Mosaic oracles.

The visible cause which has preserved the distinction of the Jewish race, under circumstances naturally tending to confound and destroy it, no doubt is their adherence to their peculiar law; an adherence to the name and memory of it; a traditionary nationality upon an antiquated obsolete principle. This has been the bond of their dislocated union among themselves, and the preservative of their separation from others. By their law, they were at first separated, but to nobler moral ends, from the rest of the world; by the same law, under their degradation, they are separated still. Does not this look like a Providential direction of things? But whatever it be, the evidence of prophecy has been authenticated by it.

Take the subject in another view. There are prophecies of the Old Testament describing the downfall of many different states and kingdoms. They do not make removal and dispersion the striking accident of calamity in the overthrow and dissolution of any other of these kingdoms. Tyre, and Nineveh, and Babylon, have not their end signalized in that way. Yet one instance there is in which that very form of national suffering is introduced, and singled out to be made the topic of prediction. It is a prophecy relating to Egypt, and delivered thus by Ezekiel[b]: "I will *scatter* the *Egyptians* among the nations, and will *disperse them through the countries.*" A hasty

<hr>

[b] xxix. 12.

judgment might seize upon this text, and say, here is the same thing over again. But observe the definite evidence of prophecy. In the next sentence it follows; "*At the end of forty years* will I *gather* the Egyptians from the people whither they were *scattered;* and I will bring again the captivity of Egypt; and will cause them to return into the land of Pathros, into the land of their habitation, and they shall there be a base kingdom." We see it is a scattering for *forty years,* and not *into all the kingdoms of the earth,* but into certain countries; which by the prophet Jeremiah are denoted to have been the countries of the *Babylonian empire,* not of any vast extent[i]. After this partial scattering, the Egyptians are to be restored, and be *a base kingdom in their own land.* The local limits of the dispersion, the period of it, the sequel of it, are therefore unlike in the two cases, and in the respective prophecies of them. That of the Jews is a lasting and total dispersion. For of this people, as "*their plagues*" were to be "*wonderful*" in other respects, so in this, that they should be "*of long continuance :*"—Their doom is denounced upon them, and *their seed.* "All these curses shall come upon thee, and shall pursue thee, and overtake thee, *till thou be destroyed;*—and they shall be upon thee for *a sign* and for *a wonder,* and *upon thy seed for ever*[k]."

To the texts of prophecy already cited, I add one more from the prophet Amos. He delivered his predictions, whilst the whole body of Israel was yet entire in Canaan and unremoved; but place his age where you will, it makes little difference as to the authority of the following singular prophecy. "Behold the eyes of the Lord are upon the sinful kingdom, and I will destroy it from off the face of the earth; saving that I *will not utterly destroy the house of Jacob,* saith the Lord. For lo I will command, and I *will sift* the house of Israel *among* all nations, like as corn *is sifted in a sieve, yet shall not the least grain fall upon the earth*[l]." This concise prophecy contains a draught of determinate history; the kingdom, the body politic, to be

[i] Jerem. xlvi. 13, 26.   [k] Deut. xxviii. 45, 46.   [l] Chap. ix. 8, 9.

destroyed from off the face of the earth; but the people, the stock, not to be destroyed. The people to be sifted through all nations; but the seed so sifted not to perish, nor its least grain to fall to the earth. It is a history made up of opposite particulars; destruction and preservation, scattering and perpetual custody, combined. It is the true outline of Jewish history. Is it of any other whatever? Place the prophecy in any imaginable age; after the fall of the kingdom of Israel, or after the Babylonian conquest; the phenomenon of its fulfilment remains; its constant, perpetual fulfilment.

Lastly, with the rest of their predicted condition, take one circumstance more into the account. It is foretold of them that they should become "an astonishment, a *proverb* and a *by-word*, among all the nations whither the Lord shall lead them:" words which imply, that this degraded people should pass into a mark and object of proverbial notice, approaching to scorn. Herein we have a further characteristic set upon their condition. A contingency dependent upon the precarious feeling and capricious judgment of men, is subjected to a specific prediction. And the event has justified the prophecy so understood. For is it not one of the most observable things, among all which this outcast people has been made to endure, that over and above spoliation of property, civil disfranchisement, severe, and sometimes insulting, persecutions of law, their cup of suffering has had that one last ingredient of bitterness so largely infused, and, with every other hardship, they have been marked out for the contempt and unkind feeling of the world? Deserved, or undeserved, scorn has been their portion. The proverb and the by-word have not left them. It seems to be the brand inflicted by the blasting voice of prophecy. At the same time, if it be urged that "the astonishment, the proverb, and the by-word" may be simply the badge of the atrocity of their sufferings, and the strangeness of their general fortunes: this may be granted, and the prophetic text will vary its sense, not its truth. Their fortunes, if not their persons, will carry the *proverb* and the *by-word*, and the subject is fitted to the prediction: for *their plagues*, from first to last, have been *wonderful*, and make them justly the *proverb* among the nations of the earth.

If then the foreknowledge of prophecy, in this example of it, has been shewn to be clear and determinate; if the prior publication of it is certain; if the form of it has been vindicated in its peculiarity, and proved to be such as could not be suggested by any thing observed elsewhere, at the time when it was delivered; if the accomplishment of it has been full and eminent; then the conditions of the highest standard of prophetic evidence will be substantiated in this instance, and we may conclude it to have been an inspired prophecy.

I close this subject with some observations upon collateral points connected with it.

1. What shall we say to the season and occasion wherein this subject of prophecy was introduced? It stands coeval with the publication of the Law, and the whole system of the Jewish Polity. Could any station be occupied by the prophecy so conspicuous, or so critical? Their legislator and founder is he who delivers it. These circumstances give prominence and force to the prediction itself. But there is also a great moral fitness discernible in the occasion. The charter of Canaan, and the predicted forfeiture of it, were thereby made to go together. Prophecy, as the instrument of God's moral Government with that separated people, disclosed to them at once the scheme of His Providence, with respect to that covenanted, but conditional, gift.

2. An obstinate and pertinacious attachment to the name and memory of their law, is the proximate visible cause, as I have said, which now cements and perpetuates their scattered race. But their rejection of Christianity when it was offered to them, is imputed in the Christian scriptures, to

their corruption and violation of the moral law, and their
culpable blindness as to the sense of the prophecies. This
immorality and culpable blindness, we may suppose to be
the hinderances which still keep them at a distance from
the Gospel. I say, we may *suppose* this; but no more;
because we have not the same authoritative information
whereby to interpret the whole case and conduct of the
Jews throughout, which we have with respect to their positive refusal of Christianity, when it was tendered to them
by the Messiah. Whatever be the explanation of their present unbelief, it must not be thought that a real attachment to God's *Moral Law*, as it is taught either in the Old
Testament, or any where else, ever kept either Jews, or
others, from the Christian Faith. This I remark, lest in
ascribing the permanence of their present condition to an
adherence to their law, I seem to impute a strange effect
to a virtuous principle. But men may place their religion
in names and formalities : and actual Judaism, the worship
of the Synagogue, may be something very different from
the spirit of the Mosaic Religion. " If they believe Moses
they will hear Christ." This is a doctrine which we believe presses upon them; and the inference from it is not
to their favour.

3. By this wide and lasting dispersion of the people of
Israel, one purpose of God's Providence has been promoted, and an evidence of Revealed Religion supplied,
which could not have been secured by the like condition
befalling any other nation. Had it been foretold of the
people of Babylon or Nineveh, Tyre or Egypt, that they
should be scattered over the face of the earth; it might
have so been : and that particular prophecy would have
been confirmed. But there is something more than this in
the case of the Jews. Their dispersion is like a dissemi-
nation of a general evidence of Revealed Religion. Wherever they have been seen, they have pressed upon men's
notice the authentic history of their covenant, their law,
and their prophets. They have been a living proof of one
half of Revealed Religion. So that in an eminent manner

the execution of the divine judgments upon them has been, in this instance, as in others, an *instruction*, as well as an extraordinary sight. "So shall it be a reproach and a taunt, *an instruction*, and an astonishment, unto the nations that are round about thee, when I shall execute judgments in thee in anger, and in fury, and in furious rebukes. I the Lord have spoken it[m]."

4. We have cause from the Scripture oracles to expect that this people will one day be restored, under the covenant of the Gospel, to a happier and more honourable state; and perhaps also to a public re-establishment in their own land. But this last event, their national restoration, is a point in which we wait for a clearer information of the prophetic sense. Meanwhile, so much is certain, that, till their conversion to the Christian Faith, Prophecy, like the cherubim with the flaming sword, guards the entrance of Canaan, and forbids them the approach.

5. Lastly; The prophecies which relate to the subversion of the Jewish state, and the introduction of Christianity, are raised in the evidence resulting from them, by their joint and coincident completion. Upon one æra and crisis of things there falls an aggregate of prophetic fulfilment. Either event, so modified as each was, would have been a memorable fact. Together, they are a rare and wonderful fabric of providence. Nor is prophecy without its indications that this coincidence should take place. For the two events are not only each foretold, but they are sometimes so brought together in the prediction, that their concurrence appears to be manifestly intended to be expressed; and if this interpretation which unites them is not imperative from the text, it is at least the most fair and direct. Such is the impression of the prophecies of Moses and Isaiah[n], as well as some others. But whether this concurrent accomplishment can be strictly deduced from the text of prophecy, or no; still it is, in the fact, such a mark of a special providence in the consummation

<hr>

[m] Ezek. v. 15.　　　　　[n] Deut. xxxii. 21; Isaiah lxv. 1—9.

of things so produced, and such a key to the exposition of
the Divine Economy, as well as to the solution of the mixt
oracles of prophecy, that we shall be warranted in laying
some stress upon it, on each of those accounts.

Something of this kind of remark is enforced by Tertullian in the following passage. Speaking of the Jews,
and their condition in his day, he says of their fugitive
anarchy, " Dispersi, palabundi, et cœli et soli sui extorres,
vagantur per orbem sine homine, sine Deo rege, quibus
nec advenarum jure terram patriam saltem vestigio salu-
tare conceditur." After which he subjoins: " *Cum hæc
illis sanctæ voces præminarentur, eædem semper omnes in-
gerebant fore*, uti, sub extremis curriculis sæculi, *ex omni
jam gente et populo et loco cultores* sibi allegeret Deus,
multo fideliores, *in quos gratiam transferret*. Hujus igitur
gratiæ disciplinæque arbiter et magister, illuminator atque
deductor generis humani, Filius Dei prænunciabatur°."

° Apol. cap. 21.

END OF DISCOURSE IX.

DISCOURSE X.

Proof of it in the Prediction of the great Apostasy.

Rev. xix. 10.

For the testimony of Jesus is the spirit of Prophecy.

THE instances of prophecy which have been stated in
the two preceding Discourses, and argued upon, as
satisfying the highest conditions of prophetic inspiration,
were taken from the Old Testament. The next case which
I shall adduce, will be taken from the New. " For the testimony of Jesus is the spirit of prophecy." The prophetic
spirit is an evidence of Christ, by its use, and by its donation. It is a testimony which He brought with Him, and
vested in His Apostles, as He had sent it forth by the
prophets before Him; a supernatural sign inherent in His
religion, as well as preceding and announcing Him. But
this prophetic spirit in the New Testament is eminently
" the testimony of Jesus" on another account, by its subjects of prediction. For it preserves a great unity and simplicity in the general aim of its revelation, which is directed almost wholly to the condition of the Christian
Church, its progress, persecutions, corruptions, and ultimate triumph. Such are, upon the whole, the scope and
tenor of the prophecies which accompanied the publication of Christianity. Their collective force, therefore, as
an evidence, is in bearing testimony to Jesus, in His re-

ligion. How far they support their pretensions to an inspired origin is the material question to be examined.

The case in which I shall consider the inspiration of Gospel prophecy, is that portion of it which describes the corruptions of some reigning power in the Christian Church; a chapter of prophecy which may be shewn, first, to agree in its character with the history of the Church and See of Rome; and next, by that medium of fulfilment, to evince its inspiration. And as the distinguished Prelate, the Founder of this Lecture, had it in view, as one object of his institution, to enforce a special reference to those parts of prophecy which will fall within my present Discourse, by bringing them under your notice I shall comply with that his particular design, and at the same time prosecute the inquiry into the use and inspiration of the Scripture oracles, which I have wished to follow in a settled course and order, and with a more extended view. As to this one subject of prophecy, on which his mind was intent, he has not only prescribed it to others, but he has cultivated it himself; and that with so much strength of reason, and eloquence of discussion, in one of those learned and argumentative discourses, which he delivered in this place, that the Author has in a manner surpassed the Founder, by anticipating, in this argument at least, with too much skill and success, the purpose of his institution[a].

I. The principal document of prophecy to be examined in the case before us is contained in the Apocalypse. But as this is a book of Scripture which unbelievers have set themselves, with more than a common confidence, to assail, and which has been discredited by the mistakes, or indiscretion, of some of its interpreters, who, in the real difficulty of the book, have further embarrassed its interpretation by the vagueness, and by the discordancy, of their opinions upon it, I shall premise, by way of introduction,

---

[a] In his Sermon on the Rise of Antichrist.

a few remarks upon the structure and general form of this part of Holy Writ, from which the chief premises of argument are to be drawn.

The Apocalypse consists of three parts: 1. The proœmium in which the Divine Author of the ensuing revelation is exhibited in the person of Christ. 2. The prophetic and didactic charge given to the Seven Churches of Asia. 3. The extended prophetic revelation, which occupies the book from the fourth chapter to the end, and embraces an ampler period and scene of things. This last comprehensive portion of it is the great field of Apocalyptic prophecy. It consists throughout of a series of visions, communicated under a scheme of symbolical imagery. Persons and actions are drawn in it under the substituted character of a figurative representation. Hence its mysteriousness and first difficulty. Hence also the main objection which has been turned to the prejudice and defamation of the book.

But on general grounds of presumption, there is no reason to think that the Apocalypse, from the nature of its style, is incapable of a rational and satisfactory, that is, a determinate interpretation. As all language abounds in metaphor and other materials of imagery, imagery itself may form the ground of a descriptive language. The forms of it may become intelligible terms; and the combination of them may be equivalent to a narrative of description. Nor is the Apocalypse all mystery and figure. There is an admixture in it of the civil and moral idiom, both in names and phraseology, limiting in some measure the subject of the symbolical representation; and in certain points the book furnishes a key to its own sense, by a positive interpretation given. With these data, the general ænigma of its figurative and symbolical style has been satisfactorily solved; the metaphor of it has been translated, upon principles neither arbitrary nor precarious; and thereby the objection made to it on account of its obscurity has been answered, so far as that obscurity arises from the scheme and structure of the visions under which its prophecies are conveyed. Those prophecies therefore come before us as a fair document of prediction, as much as others expressed in the more obvious and direct language of civil and historic description, modified, as the prophetic style usually is, by a tropical character.

Moreover, the entire subject of this book is strongly marked by a system of chronological order. Subsequent and coincident periods of time are noted; and the course and succession of events is made a part of the prophecy as well as the events themselves. The effect of this chronological structure is a guard upon the reference of the several prophecies, whereby one of them checks the appropriation of another, and reduces it within a certain position, both as to series of time, and dependence of history. Lastly, the business of the whole work is manifestly to pourtray the state of the Religion and Church of Christ. No man can read it without discovering that this is its aim. It does not deviate into things unconnected with this main design. But the preaching, or the resistance and persecutions, the decline, or the revival and triumph, of the Christian Faith, are distinguishable in every part of its visions, whilst other matters are admitted only in subordination to this master-subject of the whole.

With such internal reasons and principles, to guarantee the character of the Apocalypse, as a volume fit to be studied, because capable of being interpreted, it is scarcely necessary to resort to the authority and names of men, for a defence in its favour. But if such adventitious sanction were required, it might be had in the names of Newton and Clarke, the first of whom has commented, and the other argued upon it; the one the most profound, the other among the most severe and closest of reasoners. What then, if the infidel leader of the last age thought it worthy of the levity of his mind, to make a jest of their pains? How does that affect either them, or the book in question?   I shall think it an abuse of your attention to occupy it with any comparison of the masculine powers of mind, the integrity and severity of inquiry, and the unimpeachable love of truth, possessed, and shewn in their writings, by the two interpreters of the Apocalypse whom I have named, and by any, or all, of those who have said any thing against it.   Their deliberate testimony is an answer to a thousand vague cavils. With regard to Newton, I would add this remark, that the plan of the Apocalyptic volume was a study suited to the reach and habits of his mind.   There was a comprehensive system to be adjusted; though not indeed to be unfolded for the first time, for Mede had gone before, but that system gave scope to the exercise of his capacious understanding; and there was an extended induction of history to be made, and that also coincided with the course and spirit of his inquiries, and with his practice of trying speculation by its harmony with a series of facts.   And as his researches into the Chronology of ancient Kingdoms confirmed him in his belief of the authenticity of the account of things historically delivered in the Old Testament, his investigation of the history of the later Kingdoms served as much to convince him of the truth and prescience of the descriptive scheme of things prophetically delivered in the New. Such were his researches; and such the result of them.—With these preliminary remarks I take up the example of prophecy, which is in hand to be examined.

In the 17th chapter of the Apocalypse we have the predictive vision of some mystical power about to arise in the Christian world, a power called "Babylon, the great, the mother of harlots and abominations of the earth."   But that we may not look to the East, to the Euphrates, for the object so described, the vision becomes its own interpreter, and supplies the specific determination of the place and home of this power, by the mention of "the seven mountains" on which it should be seated; a sign sufficiently exclusive of the champaign site of Euphratean

Babylon, but the popular and the known appropriate attribute of the city of *Rome.*

Its place of abode thus ascertained, we find it characterized, as to its proper nature and genius, in many different ways. First, its external pomp and pageantry of show are put forward. For at the opening of the vision, the Woman who is the personated emblem of the state, or public entity, in question, meets our view in "an array of purple and scarlet, and a decking of gold, and precious stones, and pearls :"—such an external decoration being one of the easiest marks to see and understand. Thus habited in splendour, and seated on the same ground with the ancient mistress of the world, this power is next pourtrayed in her spirit of fury and persecution : "I saw the woman drunken with the blood of the saints, and with the blood of the martyrs of Jesus." Again, the system and combination, by which this Power should exercise her influence, is made a part of the prediction. It was not to be a State of simple monarchical rule, but of a sway embracing many kingdoms, yielding to her policy for a time, and allying themselves to her purposes, whilst they retained their local sovereignties within themselves. These vassal kingdoms moreover are defined to be some which had no being at the time when the prophecy was given, but were to spring up afterwards, and exist together, contemporary for a season with the domineering state seated at Rome. These several particulars are placed together in the explanatory words, which follow : "The ten horns, which thou sawest, are ten kings which have received no kingdom as yet, but receive power as kings one hour, (that is, for a season,) with the beast. These have one mind, and shall give their strength and power unto the beast." Which Beast, having "the ten horns," is introduced at the beginning, as the slave and creature of burden to the Woman who is the great ruling power, "the mother of abominations."

The Power so described in her place of abode, habit, and policy, was to be known for nothing so much as in being a source and fountain head of corruption, and that defined to be a religious corruption, propagated by her through the earth, but chiefly among her subject kingdoms. She bears in her hand "a golden cup full of abominations and filthiness of her fornication :" and "[b]the kings of the earth" are said to have "committed fornication with her, and the inhabitants of the earth to have been made drunk with the wine of her fornication;" and her judgment is for this crime, that "she corrupted the earth with her fornication[c]." This crime of fornication, so imputed, is a charge of the most definite kind; the idea of it, being determined by the idiom and usage of the Old Testament, wherein purity of religious faith and worship is designated under the emblem of chastity, or conjugal fidelity, in the Church of God; and apostasy, or corruption in religion, but especially idolatrous corruption, is branded as the gross pollution of virgin-modesty or plighted faith. It is the language both of the Law and the Prophets. To the other marks, therefore, by which we may know the state, or power, designed in this elaborate prophecy, add this, that there should be introduced by its means and influence some most single corruption and depravation of the Christian Faith, the same to be actively propagated among the kingdoms and inhabitants of the earth, so far as the harlot's cup could go round, so far as there was access to communication, and her arts of influence.

Lastly, to describe once more, and fix, beyond the liberty of a doubt, the place destined to give birth to this portentous power, the prophecy ends, and comes to a rest, upon the note of description which follows; "The woman which thou sawest is *that great city, which reigneth over the kings of the earth.*" When the Apocalypse was written, the vision could not have been made more determinate, had the name of Rome been put in lieu of this description.

Let us then unite together the several component parts

<hr>

[b] Chap. xviii. 3. [c] xix. 2.

of this vision, which have been mentioned, and see what they amount to in the general view, and how they are to be applied. There are, indeed, one or two minor texts of the prophecy which I have passed over; because their sense is dubious, and would demand a detailed examination; but they are clearly not of such a kind as to interfere with, or transfer, the representation of the prophetic subject contained in those parts of it which have been considered. The identity of the subject will remain undisturbed; and those minor articles would only add to its completeness if they were correctly explained. The sum of things, the general draught of the vision, which we have clear and unambiguous, is this: a domineering power to be established in the city of Rome; to corrupt the faith; to spread that corruption; to be distinguished by its display of gaudy splendour; to persecute the professors of Christian faith; to intoxicate itself in the blood of persecution; to be supported by subservient kings; to requite them for their homage with the larger draughts of her cup of abominations.

The complexity of the event thus delineated takes the prophecy of it out of the range of any vagueness of application. The circumstances, and formal characters of it are too many, and too peculiar, to leave it at large. One history in the Christian Church has fulfilled the prophecy, in all its points; that the history of the See of Rome. Gross and flagrant corruption of doctrine and worship; meretricious splendour; a sanguinary spirit of persecution; a system of domineering policy exercised over dependent kings, and infatuated nations; these are the qualities concentrated, by the prophecy, in that power which was to wear so deadly an aspect on the Christian Faith. They are also the qualities which any faithful and competent historian, taking a comprehensive view of his subject, and intending to give the general picture of the Church of Rome, through the long period of her power, reduced and condensed into a few points of description, would be obliged to select and insist upon; as the narrative of their effects does, in point of fact, comprise the mass and bulk of the ecclesiastical details of the Papacy, written in any manner whatever.

The attempt which the Romanists themselves, and some others, with an indulgence to their cause, have made, to shift the prophecy from them, and fasten it upon Pagan Rome, can be of no avail, upon the slightest investigation. First, the prophecy, with all its might, refuses and resists that application forced upon it. It is not the truth, to say that Pagan Rome *corrupted* the world with false doctrine. Her empire persecuted, but did not deprave, the Christian Faith. Nor were any violent efforts put in motion to obtrude her native heathenism upon the rest of the world: which, indeed, had its own multifarious heathenism, its depraved and idolatrous creed and worship, previously in use; so that a forced conformity to the religion of Pagan Rome, had such conformity been imposed, could only have been a change of error for error, and no shocking innovation of a fabricated impiety. But, perhaps, there never was a sovereign victorious state, which, in the plenitude of its power, produced less of impression, either by policy, or by the free influence of other causes, upon the religious opinions and institutions of other nations, than ancient Rome. Her instruments of empire, her civil character and genius, were of another kind. So that in no sense can there be ascribed to her the propagation of religious depravity.

Secondly, the import of the prophetic language strongly denotes a *Christian*, rather than a *Pagan*, state, to be the offending harlot; according to the authentic and most usual sense of the same language in the Old Testament, wherein the crime of spiritual whoredom, or fornication, attaches to the infidelity of the Jewish Church[d], far more

<hr>

[d] See Exod. xxxiv. 15; Levit. xvii. 7. xx. 5; Psalm lxxiii. 26; Jerem. iii. 1—10; Ezekiel xvi. xxiii.; Hosea i. 2. ii. 2. iv. 12, &c.   In which passages the *Hebrew* people are the object of the language.—The passage in Isaiah (xxiii. 16, 17.) wherein *Tyre* is personified as " an harlot," and said " to com-

than to the natural, or inherited irreligion, of heathens; who not having been brought into covenant with God, or to the pure knowledge of Him, were in a state of inevitable pollution, and had no chastity of religious faith to preserve, or to forfeit.

Thirdly, The chronological order of the prophetic vision, as it stands in the general plan of the book, is totally repugnant to the hypothesis of the Romanists. That order demands the subject of the vision to be placed in some æra much later than the age of St. John himself, or than many of the first visions which he has delineated. Whereas the power and persecutions of Heathen Rome were of an earlier origin; they preceded his communication of the Apocalypse.

Lastly, "The mother of abominations" is "seated on a scarlet-coloured *beast, having ten horns.*" Such was the divided state of the Western Empire, when, in the middle ages, the Papal dominion rose, and rode upon the back of the Civil Power, existing in the separate kingdoms into which that empire was disparted. But no rational account can be given of this symbol of the vision, if the harlot be ancient Pagan Rome; for her empire, if that be *the beast,* did not, in its Pagan form, admit of, or co-exist with, a civil sovereignty in such a diversity of kingdoms. In this point, as in the others, the application of the prophetic symbol recoils from the Heathen, upon the Christian, power.

mit *fornication* with all the kingdoms of the earth," refers solely to her traffic, her interchange of *commercial,* that perhaps a corrupting, luxury, but manifestly having nothing to de with *religious* infidelity.

This restriction of the phrase, in the matter of religion, to the Hebrew people, is not, however, without its exceptions. Once, in Exodus, the *Canaanite* is included in it, chap. xxxiv. 15. And in the prophet Nahum (iii. 4.) "the *whoredoms* of Nineveh" must be understood of some open and avowed propagation of idolatry by that city; of which the historical record is lost. If any flagrant guilt of the same kind could be justly imputed to Ancient *Rome,* so far, and in that one point, the Pagan and the Papal States *might* each fall under the terms of the prophecy; though there can be no comparison between the supposed Pagan, and the known Papal, enormity, in that offence. But other conditions of the prophecy decide the case between them.

The offending Church therefore vainly endeavours to remove the accusation of the prophecy from herself to fix it upon her Pagan ancestor; an ancestor who, with some features of resemblance to her, was still, it must be confessed, far from shewing so foul and hideous an air of moral and religious deformity. In the elder power, her civil tyranny, and her usurpations of conquest, her persecutions and stains of martyr blood, were not aggravated by the profligacy of false and antichristian doctrines systematised, and taught under the scourge of a sanguinary inquisition, and the sway of a domineering religious supremacy. If the kingdoms of the earth fell under her arms, they were not made drunk with the cup of her abominations. She did not wield an iron sceptre in one hand, and an intoxicating chalice in the other. The religious sorceress, the Circe of the Christian World, unhappily is of a later age; and though her wand was broken, as we have cause to rejoice it was, at the Reformation, and her arts and corruptions have long been fully disclosed; corruptions in which we ourselves had once our full share; yet some of the kingdoms which had drunk the deepest of her cup, have not yet recovered from the transformation she had made of them, but still retain something of the irrational unchristianized visage upon them, imperfectly discharged by the action of Reformed Truth, and by that improved religious knowledge, which has, however, greatly qualified and softened error, in places where it has not yet been able to establish the genuine purity, or assert the public dignity, of Truth. "For by thy sorceries," such is the complaint of outraged religion, "were all nations once deceived." And the delusion has been too strong, too deeply imbibed, to be quickly obliterated, except by great efforts, and a masculine spirit of reformation.

So far the character and lineaments of this Christian Apostate power have been traced in the Apocalyptic vision of St. John. To extend the prophetic subject, we must include in it the prophecy of St. Paul. This Apostle, in his Second Epistle to the Thessalonians, furnishes other points of description, whereby to designate the internal enemy of the Christian Church. He announces some great apostasy to take place, and "the man of sin, the son of perdition," who has his time in a future age "to be revealed, opposing and exalting himself above all that is called God, or that is worshipped, sitting in the temple of God, and shewing himself that he is God." His coming is to have these marks upon it; it is to be after "the working of Satan with all power, and signs, and lying wonders, and with all deceivableness of unrighteousness[e]."

The *identity* of the subject in this prophecy of St. Paul with that in the Apocalypse, is the main point to be established, in order to the validity of the argument to be deduced from them combined together. The text of neither supplies sufficient data, from the mere force of the terms, to prove that connexion. The "Man of Sin, the Son of Perdition," cannot be immediately assumed to be the same with the Harlot Mother, or to belong to one and the same period, or local seat, of corruption. Some data, however, there are, approximating the two prophecies. "The man of sin sits in the temple of God," and "the mother of fornications" is the *innate* corruptress of the Christian Church. There are "signs" and "lying wonders" in the one: there are successful "sorceries" in the other. "The mystery of iniquity" is St. Paul's great object[f]; St. John's iconism is, in its essential idea, of some "mystery;" some strange system of iniquity, differing from the common simple operation of human error, or wickedness, in its more natural form. Moreover the scale of St. Paul's prophecy seems to have something of the extent and magnitude of St. John's. For the apostasy which St. Paul describes is of such proportions, in the history of the Christian Church, as to make it a fit Chronological index of the remoteness of the day of the general resurrection. The two subjects, therefore, having so far an agreement, or a capacity of agreement, in their general form, may probably be coincident the one with the other.

It is the event, however, which I appeal to, as the medium of proof whereby to verify this agreement. The Hierarchy of Rome has in its day fulfilled every iota of St. Paul's prophetic description. The claims of infallibility which the Roman See has arrogated to itself; the demand of an implicit faith in its doctrines, those doctrines many of them the most contradictory to Christianity; the tyranny of its tribunals over the consciences of men; the blasphemous titles of address and impious homage which its Pontiff has heretofore extorted or accepted; the dominion over other Churches which it has assumed; assumed without justice, and exercised without reason or mercy; perfectly agreed with the pride of that rival enemy of God seated "in God's temple" figured out by the Apostle. For these inordinate pretensions are all of them, in the strictest sense, invasions of the honour and supreme rights of God, due to Him alone, or to the authority of His inspired word. Romish Infallibility disputing precedence with His authentic Truth; traditions disfiguring His attributes and His worship; a servility and prostration of the conscience to man, dethroning God from His dominion over the believer's understanding; these are the usurpations of the Roman Hierarchy, concentrated in its Head, which fall nothing short of the character of "that man of sin who opposeth and exalteth himself above all that is called God, or that is worshipped," either God, or Jesus Christ His Son; "so that he as God sitteth in the temple of God, making a show of himself that he is God;" a character which might have defied credibility, had it not been as truly verified, as accurately foretold.

Again, the multiplied delusions of the Romish system of debased Christianity, and its machinery of pious frauds, pretended prophecies, and miracles, have corresponded but too correctly with the second member of St. Paul's prophetic delineation. For such an usurpation of tyranny, and such a change of the Christian faith, could not be

supported and conducted, without the instruments of a
suitable policy. These instruments were taken from the
only forge which could supply them. "They were to be
after the working of Satan (who is the father of *falsehood*) with all power, and signs, and *lying wonders*, and
all *deceivableness* of unrighteousness." Nor is it easy to
see what other words could more faithfully describe the
practices and arts which have made the chief resources
of the Papal power. Its legends, its relics, its meritorious
pilgrimages, its indulgences, its dispensations, its liturgy
in an unknown tongue, its images, its spurious miracles,
its mediator-saints, its purgatory, and others its plausible,
or its revolting, superstitions, were set up as much against
the genius of the Gospel, which teaches the worship of
God, in *spirit* and in *truth*, in the faith of "*one Mediator*," as against the moral honesty and godly sincerity
which are the glory of the Christian ethics. And these
delusions have been the work of a See and Priesthood,
which, having made a kind of religion too corrupt to bear
the light of Scripture, and too incredible to be examined
by Reason, have, with sufficient consistency, prohibited,
or discouraged, the use of the one and the other, and
obtruded the phantom of their infallibility, in the very
height of its errors and abuses, as the substitute of compensation for both. This "mystery of iniquity" "in the
temple of God" had its reign. If Christian Faith was
well nigh extinguished by it, the truth of Christian Prophecy has thereby been the more illustrated [g].

[g] The *external* historic limitation, which St. Paul has joined with the subject of his prophecy, is not to be omitted. "And now *ye know* what with-
holdeth, that he might be revealed in his time. For the mystery of iniquity
doth already work, only he who now letteth will let, until he be taken out of
the way." An obstruction there was, hindering and retarding the revelation
of the iniquity. What that obstruction was, cannot be elicited from the words
of St. Paul, who has studiously left it under a dark and involved allusion understood by those to whom he writes. The explanation of it given by the
most learned of the Fathers, makes it to be the Civil Roman State; upon the
ruins of which rose the usurpation of Papal power. The explanation is con-
gruous to the text, and true in the history. And the judgment of these
learned Fathers in this point is of the greater weight, as it was *prior* to the

III. There is a second prophecy of St. Paul which seems to bear upon the same point in foretelling the corruptions of the Papal Church. It is as follows: " Now the Spirit speaketh expressly, that in the latter times some shall *depart from the faith*[h], giving heed to *seducing spirits*, and doctrines of devils; *speaking* lies in *hypocrisy*; having their *conscience seared* with a hot iron; *forbidding* to *marry*, and *commanding to abstain from meats*, which God hath created to be received with thanksgiving of them which believe and know the truth." The following of seducing spirits, in *forged visions* and *miracles*, and other *pious frauds;* the gross casuistry, an insult to Scripture morals; and an avowed practice, a *scared conscience*, governed by that immoral casuistic code; the compulsory *prohibition of marriage* to her clergy; a rigorous *ritual of fasts*, and an operose *distinction of meats*, enjoined to all her members; these are the reproaches deeply ingrained in the Roman See in her worst age, and truth forbids us to say that the pollution of them is even now purged away. But each mark of the fraudulent superstition is figured in the prophecy; and the mixt and motley garb was long worn in the eye of the world, without any sense of its shame, by the disfigured Apostate Church.

It is true that there is no other evidence in the terms of this prophecy, whereby to appropriate it to its subject, excepting the essential and internal characters of the apostasy foretold. But those characters are of themselves the conclusive indication. The mixture of *licentiousness* and *formality;* the licentiousness expressed in " *the speak-*

event, and must have been founded, either upon the probable sense of the text, or upon a received tradition of that knowledge of its sense, which the Thessalonians are said to have had. And indeed the expectation which prevailed in the ancient Church that the fall of the Roman Empire would be followed by the rise of Antichrist may well be thought to have had its origin in this very passage of St. Paul. It is enough, however, for my purpose, that this obscurer part of the prophecy is *not inconsistent* with that general interpretation of it which I have argued upon, and that it is a neutral, if not a favourable, element in the argument.

[h] ἀποστήσονται. 1 Tim. iv. 1, 2, 3.

ing of lies in hypocrisy," and in "*the seared conscience;*" the other, *the formality* in the prohibition of *marriage* and *meats;* the *subtilty* and *system* of *art* with which the fabric of imposture is sustained, denoted by "*the seducing spirits;*" the particular and positive signs contained in the institution of a *forced celibacy* and a *spurious Judaic ritual;* compose equally the specific form of the prophecy, and the actual lineaments of the depraved religion, into which the Roman Hierarchy perverted the Gospel. The prediction is of an apostasy from the faith to take place "in the latter times;" in the latter times it came: prominent in the fact, and palpable in its agreement with the letter of the prophecy. And as the inordinate ambition and spiritual pride of the apostasy is prefigured in the former prediction of St. Paul, its spirit of deceit and doctrinal immorality, together with its superstition, are delineated in this. These two predictions united find their joint completion in the one historical subject, and thereby the confirmation of their sense and the evidence of their truth.

To foretell that a religion, pure and excellent as that of the Gospel, would in some future time be depraved, was to foretell nothing improbable. For what is there so sacred in truth which the wickedness and the mistakes of men, or the love of novelty, or the spirit of enthusiasm, or unlearned rashness, or policy and interested designs, will not model anew, and distort from its original rectitude. Error and heresy are nearly coeval with Truth. They began to work as soon as Christianity was taught, and they may be expected to attend it to its latest day of trial. But in the predictions of the corrupted state of the Christian Faith which we are now considering, there are definite signs of a foreknowledge very different from the deductions of probability, calculated on the general principles of human weakness or human depravity. The prophetic criteria are precise; and they are such as must be thought to have militated with all rational probability, rather than to have been deduced from it. For that the doctrines of celibacy and of a ritual abstinence from meats, against the whole genius of the Gospel, by an authority claiming universal obedience, should be set up in the Christian Church; that "a man of sin" should exist, exalting himself in the temple of God, and openly challenging the rights of faith and honour due to God; that he should advance himself by signs and lying wonders, and turn his pretended miracles to the disproof and discredit of some of the chief doctrines, or precepts, of Christianity; and that this system of ambition and falsehood should succeed; that it should be established with the submission, and indeed with the deluded conviction, of men still holding the profession of Christianity, which is the prophecy of St. Paul[1], is a paradox of prediction which must be allowed to surpass the ordinary limits of human observation, and almost to exceed the power which man has to corrupt the best gifts of God. The natural incredibility of it is, not that such errors and abuses should be established in the world, but that they should be grafted on the Christian Faith, in opposition to, and in outrage of, its genius and its commands, and take a bold possession of the Christian Church. There, however, they have been grafted; and there they have had possession. And the strength of the improbable fact is the proof of the prophetic inspiration. Nor is it *strictly* necessary to this proof, that a formal connexion be shewn to exist in their very *terms* between these prophecies of St. Paul and the particular Apocalyptic vision of St. John. It is a strange event, that such flagrant perversions of Christianity should break forth, and grow into credit, and pass for a Christian, or a *Catholic* Faith at Rome, or any where else. The locality of the corruption is a circumstance indifferent to the prodigy of it. The fact that it has had its reign in a particular Church, to which the Apocalyptic vision is by more positive notes directed, is a coincidence not necessary to be demanded in the argument, though the event has been in that order.

<hr>

[1] 2 Thess. ii. 10, 11.

To conclude then—I shall revert to the substance of the prophecy in St. John. It supplied these circumstances of description: a tyrannical power, of a Christian race, to be seated at Rome; dressed in a robe of gaudy decoration; spreading its abuses and errors over the kingdoms of the earth, persecuting the Church of Christ, and deeply stained with its blood, especially the blood of its martyrs, its public witnesses and confessors; that same state holding a number of dependant kings under its yoke; and turning their strength and power, with their consent, to the furtherance of its designs. The complexity of things in this single piece of prophecy is sufficiently manifest. And since the complex whole has, point by point, been fulfilled; and that not in an obscure corner, but in the heart of Christendom, and in the most conspicuous station of the Christian world; the inference from that completion is not to be evaded.

For as to the publication of the prophetic documents, it is here, in each case, unquestionable. The Apocalypse was written before the end of the first century. The latest period of St. John's life so far certifies its antiquity. And although it was not for some time received into the general Canon of the New Testament, it was known, and published; and it was admitted into that Canon, before the dissolution of the Western Empire; and some centuries before the æra of the Papal dominion, which it describes. But our business is simply with its publication. The early publication of the Epistles of St. Paul is abundantly notorious. — The conditions therefore, which were originally proposed, are found to obtain in this branch of Scripture prophecy, conditions warranting a divine Inspiration.

One remark more I shall subjoin; it extends to the three cases of Prophecy which have been examined. Those have been, 1. the prophecy which predicts the establishment of the Gospel; 2. that which foreshews the rejected and outcast condition of the Jewish people; and 3. that which describes the great eclipse and corruption of Christianity under the dominion of the Church of Rome.

These are no prophecies of curiosity. The subjects themselves are of that kind in which the history of Revelation is deeply concerned. They comprise the cardinal points of the supposed dispensation of God; the Christian Church established; the Jewish cast into exile; the Christian corrupted.

These instances of prophecy have been selected because of the perspicuity of the proof by which they appear to be supported. For I believe it will be found, that these prophecies are among the most copious and prominent, and have the greatest stress laid upon them, in the whole volume of Scripture; and that the evidence of a clear completion falls at this day, and has always fallen, with the greatest force upon these particular instances. But whilst the simplicity of the argument to be framed upon them recommends them to our attention; it is also true, that they are the most important, in their subjects, that are brought forward in Holy Writ, or that can affect the visible history of Revelation. A coincidence this, between the intrinsic importance of the subjects, and the corresponding state of the evidence, which will convey to us, upon reflection, some idea of the wisdom shewn in the structure of Prophecy; a wisdom distinct from the foreknowledge manifested in these predictions, but, like that foreknowledge, leading us to a divine source. For this is now seen to be the provision made for the Prophetic Evidence, that so long as Christianity shall exist as a public Religion, or the Jew survive, or the history of the long dark age of the Christian Church shall be known, the prescience of prophecy will not want a clear and commanding proof.

Note on Page 325.—The *distribution* of the Prophetic subject, concerning the Rise of *Antichrist*, into its leading members, is made with great justness and decision of judgment. by *Tertullian;* who has, moreover, connected together the predictions of St. Paul with those of the Apocalypse, and reduced them into a scheme of combined and perspicuous interpretation. I shall extract from his Exposition a passage, which, to the learned reader who has considered the subject, will bespeak at once the exactness and comprehensive views of Tertullian's thoughts upon this great Gospel-Prophecy, and that too, *before* it had been *unfolded by the event.* "Jam enim arcanum iniquitatis agitatur; tantum qui nunc tenet, teneat; donec de medio fiat. Quis, nisi *Romanus Status?* cujus abscessio *in decem reges dispersa Antichristum superducet.* Et tunc *revelabitur iniquus,* quem Dominus Jesus interficiet spiritu oris sui, et evacuabit, apparentia adventus sui, &c."—*De Resurrect. Carn.* p. 397, ed. Lutet.

END OF DISCOURSE X.

DISCOURSE XI.

ON THE INSPIRATION OF PROPHECY.

*Proof of it in the Predictions concerning Pagan Kingdoms;
Nineveh, Babylon, Tyre, and Egypt.*

------◆------

ISAIAH xiii. 19, 20.

*And Babylon, the glory of kingdoms, the beauty of the
Chaldees' excellency, shall be as when God overthrew
Sodom and Gomorrah. It shall never be inhabited,
neither shall it be dwelt in from generation to generation: neither shall the Arabian pitch tent there; neither
shall the shepherds make their fold there.*

JUDÆA, though separated from the rest of the world,
by the enclosure of its peculiar law and religion, stood
full in the way of those states and kingdoms, which in
ancient times agitated the earth. It was from the East
that the flood of human affairs held its course. It was
there that the kingdoms of Nineveh and Babylon, Tyre
and Egypt, rose into power, and these are the Pagan states,
the earliest of which we have any authentic account, as
having been great enough materially to affect the condition
of neighbouring and distant countries. Judæa fell under
the influence which resulted from its contiguity to them
all. With respect to them, it held a station of exposure
and collision; and Prophecy, occupying that station, took
a range proportionably extended. Accordingly the prophecies of Scripture embrace something of the actions and

fortunes of each of these kingdoms; their conquests, their vicissitudes, their overthrow, or final degradation.

But the prophets of Israel and Judah direct also many of their predictions to the affairs of smaller states, of less note than those which I have now mentioned; states, of which we read little beyond the records of Holy Writ, and scarcely know in any other way than by their connexion with the people of Judæa. Of this kind are Moab, Edom, and Ammon: these have their place among the subjects of Scripture prophecy. But as to our information respecting them, they are little more than appendages of Jewish history.

It follows, that in examining the evidence of Inspiration attaching to these two branches of prophecy, we shall find a difference in our power of applying to them the conditions of the Test proposed. External and independent history will enable us to judge of the predictions which regard the greater empires; whilst the means will fail of exploring the truth of prophecy, in the instance of the smaller kingdoms, by the like evidence of extrinsic information. For these less considerable states have buried with them the documents which might have thrown light upon our inquiry. They were soon crumbled into oblivion; and the confirmations of prophecy have in some points perished with them. Whereas the others, the greater kingdoms, have left behind them their memorials, which serve to verify the oracles of Scripture. Prophecy has struck its root in the relics of their history; and the shadow of it overhangs and overspreads their ruins.

I do not intend to insist upon the prophecies concerning kingdoms of inferior note. They are less suited to the purpose of an inquiry into the first proofs of the prophetic Inspiration, and they address themselves less powerfully, than some others do, to our attention at the present day. But before I quit the mention of them, I would say a few words to obviate any suspicion which may be raised to their disparagement.

Be it considered, then, for the honour of the Scripture Oracles, that the divine prescience might be as truly manifested, and God's Providence as justly explained, by predictions on the smaller scale as on the greater; and, secondly, that these inferior subordinate states whose importance is now so lost to us, were seen in a very different light by the people of Judæa. To them they were jealous neighbours, or active enemies; and they were felt by them in the contentions, or other interests of vicinage, which is itself equivalent to a relation of importance.

The pertinence, therefore, and the use, of these minor predictions, as delivered to the Jewish Church, are not in the least impaired by the magnitude of some other subjects of prophecy. We have seen before [a] that one of its ends and purposes was in being the interpreter and expositor of God's providence to His ancient people, who might be competently taught by means, suited to them, which, in the lapse of time, may have lost something of their original force and clearness. And this change in the degree of evidence attending the several portions of prophecy, instead of arguing any defect in it, rather shews its integrity, by representing to us how truly and closely it was accommodated, in certain parts, to the known condition and circumstances of that people to whom it was immediately given; whilst others of its oracles have been of such a kind as to offer a conviction to every age. To the Israelite, assuredly, prophecy was not less important, or less capable of being scrutinized, when it spoke to him on things affecting his particular national concerns; but rather, that circumstance in it, which may seem a defect relatively to us, was, to him, an advantage, in the proximity of these its more confined and local subjects.

Having said so much on this head, I turn to the other

------

[a] Disc. VI. Part iii. p. 212.

class of predictions, those which carry us into the more considerable empires or communities of the ancient Eastern World.

First, I state that there are prophecies extant of the complete overthrow, or signal degradation of all the four kingdoms of Nineveh, Babylon, Tyre, and Egypt, which overthrow and degradation have come to pass. In this general view, the broad page of prophecy, and that of history, agree together.

But let it be supposed, that in these events, thus briefly described, there is nothing unusual, nothing so different from the common course of things, that any proof of a divine prescience can be grounded upon the prediction of them. Empires, it may be said, rise and fall; their mutability, and their decay, is a matter of experience; and human foresight confidently predicts the termination of their greatness. In this kind of remark there is some reason; but not so much as may at first appear. For it is to be remembered, that we are now living late in the world, and Experience has had a long study of human affairs. We have therefore principles whereupon to calculate, which in foregone times, two thousand five hundred years ago, were not established. In an earlier age, when the general march of things was more progressive, and the efforts of man, in policy, arts, and conquest, were expanding in their first circle, the notion of a great shock of ruin and decay befalling consolidated and settled kingdoms was more remote from view: and to most of the kingdoms which I have mentioned, for example, to Nineveh, Babylon, and Egypt, such a shock of decay could not be predicted upon the observation of a similar fate having befallen others like to them; because none like to them had existed, none equally furnished with the elements of a secure and permanent greatness. So far as these things have subsequently happened, prophecy has preceded the experience of them; and, in their great unfrequency, it has gone beyond the mark of our experience.

But prophecy speaks a language, with respect to these ancient flourishing kingdoms, which will oblige us at once to change our hypothesis of objection. For, in each case, it combines with the general event, particulars of distinction which cannot be mistaken for the anticipations of human foresight. Some of these particulars it will be necessary to quote.

I. The predictions of the prophet Nahum are confined exclusively to the destruction of the kingdom and city of Nineveh. 1. One of the things foretold by him is this: " For while *they be folded together as thorns,* and while they *are drunken as drunkards,* they shall be *devoured* as *stubble* fully dry." 2. Another: "The gates of the *rivers* shall be opened; and the *palace* shall be dissolved," or " molten." Each of these particulars of the prophecy is something distinctive; and each of them happens to be verified to us by the testimony of a distant and neutral witness, an heathen historian, who had it little in his thoughts when he was transmitting such incidents of his multifarious Compilation, that he was confirming the exactness of an ancient Jewish prophet. From Diodorus Siculus[b], who is the author here referred to, we learn that the Assyrian camp, in a state of drunkenness, during a general festival, was surprised and overwhelmed. The prophet's image, of their being "folded together" and entangled "as thorns," accurately expressing the embarrassment and inability of defence, in which they were involved; and the sudden mastery which was made of them, and pressed to a complete victory being equally described in the image of "a flame devouring the dry stubble," and enwrapping it in an instant conflagration.

From the same writer we derive this other critical circumstance; that during the siege of Nineveh, in the third year of it, an inundation of the river (which was the Tigris), caused by an excessive and continuous fall of rains, burst the walls, and laid them open, such was the magnitude of the city, to the extent of twenty stadia;

<hr>

[b] Lib. ii. p. 112. ed. Rhodom. quoted by Bishop Newton.

upon which the king, seeing no hope of safety in defence, raised a vast pile, on which he consumed himself in the flames of his wealth and his *palace*[c]. Here are two articles to be noted. "The gates of the rivers shall be opened;" so it was, when the flood opened those gates of ruin in the walls. And the palace was not to be simply taken, but "dissolved, or molten:"—an incident equally marked in the prophecy and in the fact.

But let us suspend our judgment of this prophecy, till we have compared it with a second, that which relates to the taking of Babylon. In the two predictions we shall observe a certain measure of agreement, checked and limited by a difference adequately expressed. In both, a state of revelry and intoxication is foretold. In both cases it occurred. Speaking of Babylon, Jeremiah says, "In their heat I will make their feasts; and I will make them drunken, that they may rejoice, and sleep a perpetual sleep, saith the Lord." (Chap. li. 39. 57.) So far the agreement.—But the same prophet fixes the instant of the surprise upon the actual capture of *Babylon*, which neither was foretold, nor happened, in the capture of Nineveh; for it was the *army* of Nineveh, in camp before its walls, that was so surprised, before the siege had commenced. "I have laid a snare for thee," is the definite prediction of Jeremiah, "and thou art also *taken*, O *Babylon*, and thou wast not aware: thou art found, and also caught." (Chap. l. 24.) Every one knows, from the narrative of the Greek historians, that the Persian army obtained possession of Babylon by a capture of surprise, that its people were taken as in a net, and that the one part of the city knew not of the entrance of the enemy, till the other part was in their power. Here then is one point of difference.—A second, and greater difference, will add to the contrast. Each of the cities stood on a great river, Nineveh on the Tigris, Babylon on the

<hr>

Euphrates. These rivers were to be instrumental to the taking of them both, but in a dissimilar, and even opposite, manner; by an inundation in the one case, and by drying up in the other. This last particular, as to Babylon, is elaborately insisted on, again and again, in the prophecy "That saith to the deep, *Be dry*, and I will *dry up* thy rivers [d]." "A *drought* is upon her waters, and they shall be *dried up* [e]." A repetition of phrase, which, by its pleonasm, serves to lay the emphasis of the prophecy in the right place, upon one distinctive note of the divine foreknowledge. For it is a matter of trite history, that Babylon was taken in a manner corresponding with this prediction concerning her great river, when Cyrus, by a vast enterprise of stratagem, drained off the waters of the Euphrates from their channel, and so reduced them as to open a passage on foot within its banks for the entrance of his army.

Let the two events then be compared together, and with the prophecies. And when we see prophecy furnishing such determinate marks of prescience; when it speaks in the one instance of "an overrunning flood." and of "the opening of the gates of the rivers [f];" and, in the other, bids the river be dry; when it appoints a mighty army, or a city, to be delivered to their victors in an hour of drunken revelry and intoxication, surrendering them to an easy capture; when it gathers into the exigency of its predictions these, and other circumstances, dependent on causes so arbitrary and uncertain as the accidents of nature, or the devices and actions of men; how shall we resist the inference that, in all this, so accurately foretold, so punctually fulfilled, it spoke under some supernatural direction?

The date of these prophecies, however, is one ingredient in their evidence. If they were delivered at all before the completion of the events foretold, they were inspired;

---

[d] Isaiah xliv. 27.　　　　　　　　　　　　　Jerem. l. 38.

[f] Nahum ii. 6, and i. 8; where the actual inundation of the *river*, and the *figurative* inundation of the *invading army*, are united in one image.

because those events are so circumstantiated, that they could no more have been humanly foreseen one year, than an hundred years, before they took place. How then stands the proof as to their date? If we admit the only positive testimony to be had in this point, that testimony the public judgment and decision of the Jewish Church and People, it will be abundantly decisive as to the age of Isaiah and Jeremiah, and the date of their prophecies. And indeed these two great prophets were too much connected with the civil history of their country, and their writings were too important in the Jewish Canon, to leave any the most captious doubt, whether their age is properly assigned to them, or the true date to their predictions[g]. The one will therefore come at a distance of not less than fifty years, and the other of two hundred, from the capture of Babylon, which, with such circumstances as have been mentioned, they foretell.

But as to the age of the prophet *Nahum*, it must be confessed that we do not possess equal data of information. His is the main prophecy which we have concerning the capture and destruction of Nineveh. The admission of his book into the prophetic Canon proves so much as this, that the Jewish Church esteemed it a real prophecy, that is, a document delivered before the event which it describes. But there are not the auxiliary notices of his personal history, or of a chronological date prefixed to his book, to satisfy us in the strict demands of our inquiry. The testimony of the Jewish Church, seconded as it is by Josephus[h], (who places the prophecy of Nahum 115 years prior to the capture of Nineveh,) must be allowed indeed to be a *fair* and *reasonable* warrant to the antiquity of Nahum's predictions; but yet the proof here is not so high and imperative as it might be; and as it actually is with regard to Isaiah and Jeremiah. If, therefore, we measure the

<hr>

[g] For instance, Isaiah was *publicly consulted* by Hezekiah. Jeremiah *publicly questioned* for some of his prophecies.

[h] Συνέβη δὲ πάντα τὰ προειρημένα περὶ Νινευῆς μετὰ ἔτη ἑκατὸν καί τεντε-καίδεκα. Antiq. Jud. ix. 11.

prophetic evidence, in the instance of Nahum, and as it relates to the capture of *Nineveh*, by the standard proposed, we must grant that it answers to that standard only with some qualification. The plenary evidence would be addressed to those who originally received the prophecy; who would know sufficiently well whether, when they received it, the great city in question had met its fate. — I reckon it no concession made to the detriment of Prophecy, to follow the true state of its genuine evidence.

But the inspiration of the prophecies concerning these great cities may be proved, or confirmed, by a second medium, in another point of their predictions. Zephaniah, as to Nineveh; Isaiah and Jeremiah, as to Babylon, foretell, not only the capture of the cities, and the overthrow of their grandeur and empire; but they pursue the subject with this addition, a memorable one, that the cities themselves should pass under an exterminating desolation, and be converted into a waste, a wilderness without inhabitants, a seat of perfect solitude. Zephaniah: " He will stretch out His hand against the North, and destroy Assyria; and will make Nineveh a desolation, and dry like a wilderness. And flocks shall lie down in the midst of her; all the beasts of the nations: both the pelican and the bittern shall lodge in the upper lintels of it; their voice shall sing in its windows; desolation shall be in its thresholds: — This is the rejoicing city that dwelt carelessly, that said in her heart, I, and none besides me: how is she become a desolation, a place for beasts to lie down in[i]!" Nahum speaks the same doom more concisely: " She is empty, and void, and waste[k]." What the two other prophets have said of Babylon's desolation is equally full and expressive.

Zephaniah is *stated* to have prophesied in the days of Josiah, king of Judah[l], the *last year* of whose reign falls

---

[i] Chap. ii. 13—15. [k] Chap. ii. 10.

[l] Chap. i. 1. "The word of the Lord which came unto Zephaniah, the son of Cushi, the son of Gedaliah, the son of Amariah, the son of Hizkiah, in

B. C. 608. But when was Nineveh taken? This is one of the unsettled points of ancient Chronology, and it will remain so; for the time is long past, when it might have been cleared and reduced to certainty. In the diversity of the accounts extant, we must approximate the truth, by taking what is most credible, and that is the relation of Herodotus[m], the author the nearest in age, and the best informed in the affairs of the East. *He* assigns the capture of Nineveh to Cyaxares, and he places it after the *expulsion of the Scythians from Asia*[n], which will be some years below the latest period of Zephaniah's prophesying. So far then as we can go, on probable grounds, the argument will be made good, that the desolation of Nineveh was predicted before its capture.—The case of Babylon is perfectly clear; its *capture* was long subsequent to the prophecy of its *desolation*.

The desolation foretold has ensued. Those two great flourishing cities, the ancient glory of the East, the abodes of empire and overflowing population, have vanished. It has become an object of research to the inquisitive traveller to ascertain the spot on which they stood. With some difficulty and suspense, he explores in heaps of otherwise unappropriated ruins the vestiges of their local memory. For what are they now? What have they long been? The haunts of beasts. Man has disappeared. "The pelican and the bittern lodge in the lintel" of their forsaken houses. Those creatures possess the waste, the characteristic inhabitants of an assured and unmolested solitude.

Once more; make the most large, and indeed unwarrantable, suppositions, as to the time of publication to be ascribed to the prophecies which speak of this final destiny of *Babylon*. Suppose them to have been published, and first known, after the taking of Babylon by Cyrus: that they were published after the catastrophe of this extreme

the days of Josiah, the son of Amon, king of Judah." A chronological notice, which has its force from the *testimony* of the *Jewish Church*.

[m] Lib. i. 106.   [n] B. C. 596.

devastation which they announce, is wholly impossible to be maintained, or believed, even on the most sceptical principles. Because the collection and promulgation of the Jewish Canon of Scripture, made in the age after the Return of the Jews from Babylon, was prior to the time when we know Babylon not to have been so desolated. In fact, it was the work of some centuries to break down this gigantic city into a heap of ruins. It follows, that the truth of the predictions of Isaiah and Jeremiah, in this point, is established, even upon the most extreme hypothesis. There is no date which can be assigned to them, ever so licentiously, which will not leave them in possession of a clear prophetic character in this one branch of their subject. The proof is absolute, and beyond the reach of objection.

And this I may remark, that as the æra of the conquest of Babylon by Cyrus, is the basis of Pagan Chronology[o], the point from which it begins to be clear and consistent; so the extraneous proof of the truth and prescience of prophecy takes its proportionate force and clearness from the same æra. The greater regularity and completeness of the Pagan narrative supplies a fuller comment upon the scheme of things delineated in the Scripture oracles.

With regard to Nineveh, it is granted that we cannot constitute so exact and decisive a confirmation of these oracles, out of the imperfect and ill-adjusted remains of Oriental history. And in this instance the sacred history itself, and the formal chronology of the prophecies, as to the time of their promulgation, are not so explicit as to answer every question which might be raised respecting them. But in this unequal measure of evidence, it is only a bold ignorance, or a very unthinking piety, that can presume any sort of objection.

For brevity's sake, I shall pass over any discussion of

---

[o] Primus hic Cyri annus non solum solutæ Captivitatis, sed etiam totius vetustioris *Chronologiæ basis* est; et res Ebraicas cum extraneis connectit. Marsham. Canon. Chron. Sæc. xviii. p. 630. ed. Francq.

the discriminating particulars which may be traced in the prophecy concerning Tyre. Those particulars include the subjugation of that city; her restoration to power after a servitude of seventy years; her later calamities of capture, burning, and demolition; her religious conversion; her last desolated state, like that of Nineveh and Babylon. For so it is foretold: "I will scrape the dust from her, and make her like the top of a rock; it shall be a place for the spreading of nets; thou shalt be built no more; though thou be sought for, thou shalt never be found again[p]." Time has wrought the perfect completion of this extremity of ruin: as the earlier and intermediate things foretold had their due fulfilment. In this instance, however, the anterior publication of the prophecy, as to a chief part of it, is indisputable. For even the age of Ezra, and the collection of the Sacred Canon, precede by a century the destruction of Tyre, made by Alexander; still more do they precede the subsequent conversion to Christianity, and the last stage of the ruin and solitude, foretold.

Will it be alleged, to invalidate the force of all these prophecies combined, that this catastrophe of three of the greatest and most flourishing capital cities of the ancient world, is possible to have been within the range of man's foresight, or was nothing more than what is conformable to experience? History refutes the allegation. It is not the common issue of things that great and flourishing capitals of empire are so swept away and obliterated. The merciless ravages of war and the progressive decays of time have rarely accomplished such absolute extermination. Certainly when the prophecies were uttered, such things had not been seen. It would be in vain to adduce, as a similar event, the fate of Troy, or other ill-established cities of an earlier foundation, in times when the habits of migration and settlement were yet at war with each other. For as to Troy, whatever that city might have

<hr>

been, it was as much like to Babylon, as a pile of sand to a rock. The ruin of Carthage is, perhaps, one of the best parallels that can be mentioned. But this case not only came later than the prophecies, and therefore could not have directed them; but it may reasonably be taken as included in the Scripture prediction of the doom of Tyre; for it is a part of that prediction that the people of Tyre "shall disperse themselves over the *isles*," the Mediterranean coasts, which they did; and "there also they should find no rest [q];" which very sentence robbed them of the hope of any secure asylum, or resting-place, to their fortunes, in their colony of Carthage.

To complete our view of the signs of inspiration contained in this aggregate of prophecy, it will be necessary to advert to what is foretold of *Egypt*, the oldest seat of policy, arts, and civil grandeur. Here again, however, I shall omit several discriminating circumstances which pervade the substance of the prophecy, and pass on to the issue of the whole. When Ezekiel had first foretold, as a thing imminent, that Egypt should be conquered and *wasted*, and visited with a captivity of her inhabitants, but had fixed this first stage of humiliation to a period of forty years; he subjoins this second prediction: "Yet thus saith the Lord God; At the end of forty years, I will bring again the captivity of Egypt; and will cause them to *return* into the land of Pathros, into the land of their habitation; and they shall be *a base kingdom*. It shall *be the basest of kingdoms*; neither shall it exalt itself any more above the nations; for I will diminish them that they shall no more rule over the nations; and there shall be no more a prince of the land of Egypt [r]." Here is a significant and appropriate language, descriptive of a condition distinguished from that which is denounced upon Nineveh and Babylon: the kingdom, the body of the nation is to remain, but in *baseness*, in *degradation*, without sway, as before, among the nations; without a sove-

[q] Isaiah xxiii. 6. 12. [r] Ezek. xxix. 13, 14, 15.

reign prince of its own; without dignity at home or abroad.

What is here foretold, Egypt has suffered. The prophecy has been fulfilled, whether we take it in a contracted, or a more enlarged view: whether we embrace, in that view, the period of two hundred years from the date of its prediction, or the period of two thousand. The conquest of Egypt by the Babylonians, was followed by the Persian; from that time Egypt was reduced, from the height of its power and greatness, to a debilitated condition, from which it has never subsequently emerged.

In regard to this prophecy, the former state of Egypt should be well considered. Originally it was the most prosperous, opulent, and powerful of kingdoms; till the growth of the Assyrian power divided with it its glory, and then together they were the two foremost nations of the ancient world. There is the accuracy of historical truth, as well as the beauty of a poetic, and the force of a moral representation, in the picture which Ezekiel has given of the Assyrian and the Egyptian grandeur, as of the fairest and "loftiest cedars in the garden of God[s]." Nebuchadnezzar's conquest made the first change upon Egypt, and with that change foretold the prophecy begins. Now it is the difference which is foreshewn in the respective fortunes of these two ruling kingdoms, that marks the definite prescience. A *debased* and *a diminished* state is foretold to Egypt; *a total destruction* had been foretold to the other. Correspondent with that distinction has been the event. Egypt survived with the form of a kingdom, but subjected, and sunk in its power. The Persian conquest reduced it again, to a lower humiliation, and to such a state as answered to, and sufficiently completed, the prediction. But the completion has been more ample: century after century has verified to the letter this peculiar prophecy upon Egypt. The doom of that kingdom has been *baseness* and *degradation*, not *destruction*. The

---

[s] Ezek. xxxi.—This admirable chapter is, in effect, one of the truest and noblest monuments of Oriental history.

body of it has lasted, diminished, but not annihilated;
many of its great cities have been dilapidated; still the
carcass of its ancient being remains, like one of those objects of its own native art, a withered figure, a mummy,
preserved in decay. In succession it has served every
conqueror; and it has besides been subjected to an anomalous bondage, almost peculiar to itself, in being ruled
by a dynasty of slaves; that the prophecy which con
demned it to be *the basest of kingdoms* might not want
this signal attestation. Babylonians, Persians, Greeks,
Romans, Saracens, Mamluks, Turks, are enumerated, as
having been its masters in turn. When once it had a
partial revival of its lustre, under the Ptolemies, they
were a foreign race; according to the prediction, "there
shall no more be a prince of the land of Egypt[1]." Settled
dynasty of its own, it has had none; a moral and national
degeneracy has defeated the benefit of all its gifts of nature; nor has it interposed one æra of enterprise, or independence, to break the long line of its unvaried, excep-
tionless degradation.

Prophecy, therefore, has not dispensed any uniform and
indiscriminate sentence of ruin and downfall of those re-
nowned Pagan kingdoms of the world which were selected
to be made the conspicuous monument of its truth. On
the contrary, it has limited and varied its predictions respecting them. The *overwhelming destruction*, foretold of
Nineveh and Babylon, is something different from the
prostrate degradation of Egypt. And each of these modes
of prophecy is distinguished from the singular sentence of
dispersion, to which the Jewish people was foredoomed. The
prophecies and their subjects could not be interchanged.
The prophecies are discriminated in their form, and, in
that form, appropriate to their subjects, and the truth of
them is extant in the present face of things. But such
predictions, although in some points of them the state of

their evidence may be unequal, are too vast, and too regular, in the whole compass of their scheme, to be mistaken for the essays of human judgment calculating upon the general instability of nations and empires; still less can they be referred to the fortuitous suggestions of a daring conjecture. What but a divine prescience will account for their proved veracity? " Quid enim potentius patrocinabitur testimonio earum, nisi dispunctio quotidiana seculi totius? Cum *dispositiones regnorum,* cum *casus urbium,* cum *exitus gentium,* cum *status temporum* ita omnibus respondent, quemadmodum *ante millia annorum prænunciabantur* [u]."

[u] Tertull. Apol. cap. xix. Fragm.

END OF DISCOURSE XI.

DISCOURSE XII.

ON THE INSPIRATION OF PROPHECY.

Proof of it in the Predictions concerning the Descendants of Ishmael, and the Succession of the Four Empires.

DANIEL ii. 21, 22.

And He changeth the times and the seasons: He removeth kings, and setteth up kings: He giveth wisdom unto the wise, and knowledge to them that know understanding: He revealeth the deep and secret things: He knoweth what is in the darkness, and the light dwelleth with Him.

THE conditions which have been laid down as being at once necessary, and sufficient, to establish the inspiration of any given prophecy, are the following:—That the prediction be known to have been promulgated before the event; that the event in question be such as could not have been foreseen, at the time when it was predicted, by any effort of human reason; and that the event and the prediction correspond together in a clear and adequate accomplishment. Forged prophecies, late in their coming forth, will be excluded, by the first condition; probable anticipations, by the second; and equivocal coincidences, by the last, from having any place in the argument.

Under such a view of single portions of prophecy, they are put strictly on their trial. Nothing is supposed of them, but that they are so many alleged predictions found in an ancient record. Afterwards, when we have examined into the time when they were delivered, and the nature of the things foretold, and have verified their completion, we shall know what to think of the pre-science which dictated them, and how far they are to be reckoned among the essential and original proofs of a prophetic inspiration.

But it should withal be borne in mind, that the principles here laid down admit of some latitude, within which there is room for a modified, but, at the same time, a real and effective evidence. This point is of so great importance to be clearly understood, that I shall crave your attention whilst I endeavour to place it in its true light.

The first condition is, "that the prediction be known to have been promulgated before the event." If the pretended prophecy be *known* to have been published *after* the event, there is an end at once of its credit and pretensions. But there is a wide difference between knowing that any given prophecy was so uttered after the thing described in it had come to pass, and not knowing upon the highest and most incontrovertible evidence that it was uttered before. *When* it was delivered, is a fact to be examined; and though matters of fact are in themselves the most absolute and determinate of things, who knows not how many shades of certainty, or uncertainty, may be blended with our information of them? Circumstances of vagueness, or obscurity, attending the first promulgation of some of the prophecies, must, therefore, be allowed to qualify our conviction of their true antiquity, so long as we are inquirers into that particular point. But the less certainty of the fact will never amount to a disproof of it. And when the real grounds of belief are on one side, they may be weak, or they may be strong, probable or decisive; only such as they are, our belief must be governed by them, if we profess to inquire at all.

So of the second condition proposed; that "the event be such as could not have been foreseen by any efforts of human reason;" it will be seen that some things are so clearly beyond the reach of all human foresight, that the predicting of them compels us at once to admit a divine communication; whilst, in others, the supernatural prescience even of a real prophecy may not be so manifest and unequivocal. For the intelligence and forecast derived from a well-studied experience, and the acuter efforts of a daring speculation, have enabled men at times to predict considerable things without the gift of any supernatural illumination. But though a sagacious wisdom may calculate upon the future, and a felicitous ingenuity usurp upon it, there are limits to the greatest essays of this kind, and the question to be answered is, how far it is credible that such particular prophecies as we have before us in Scripture, could have been foretold or foreseen by man; even if they are not such, which many of them are, as clearly to exceed the range of his sagacity, and leave far behind all the principles of his knowledge.

Again, "the correspondence between the event and the prophecy" may vary in fulness and precision. For either the prophecy may not have been couched in terms definite and perspicuous, or it may have been fulfilled less rigorously, or history may fail to supply from its mutilated pages the information necessary to illustrate the fulfilment. Under any of these circumstances, the prophecy will fall short of a direct and indisputable illustration of a divine prescience, and yet may retain force enough to engage our attention, and incline our belief, and contribute, in its degree, to the general proof of Revelation. For God may have so tempered the evidence which He designed to give us, as to spare it, in some points, and shed it more fully in others; and in the texture of prophecy, though there are some of its predictions which neither now, nor perhaps ever, could be said to furnish an explicit proof of their divine origin; yet, by their number, variety, and connexion, even these minor elements of the prophetic volume may serve to multiply the presumptions on its side, and corroborate our faith in that one system of Scripture in which they all inhere.

The statement, thus made, of the disparity of the prophetic evidence, which may be supposed, and which indeed exists, involves nothing illusory in the argument, or disadvantageous to Revelation. Disadvantageous to Revelation that statement cannot be; for this reason; if every separate part of the proof of religion were to be uniformly complete and decisive, there is no cause to think that so many various and connected attestations of it would have been given; the very appearance of which, a case not to be denied, leads us rather to expect that the parts of them would not be severally a perfect and final evidence.

With these reflections, which may have some bearing upon the sequel of my present discourse, I shall advert to two other examples of prediction; and these belonging, as the last which have been examined, to the *Pagan* branch of Prophecy. I concluded my foregoing discourse with some of the predictions which describe the state of Egypt. It is an adjoining country, that of Arabia; and there too Prophecy has pitched her tent, and given her oracle in the desert.

One of the oldest Scripture prophecies relates to the people of Arabia, the progeny of Ishmael, the son of Abraham and Hagar. It is the prediction delivered to Hagar, and comprises these things; "I will multiply thy seed exceedingly, that it shall not be numbered for multitude—And thou shalt bear a son, and shalt call his name Ishmael. And he will be a wild man; his hand will be against every man, and every man's hand will be against him; and he shall dwell in the presence of all his brethren." To which was afterwards added this circumstance, "Twelve princes shall he beget, and I will make him a great nation [a]."

The publication of this prophecy is *ascribed* to the time of Abraham; it is said to have been given before the birth

---

[a] Gen. xvi. 12; xvii. 20.

of Ishmael, who was to be the progenitor and founder of this future nation; of which nation we must in reason understand what is here foretold; "he shall be a wild man," and "his hand shall be against every man, and every man's hand against him;" since such a state of general hostility could hardly attach to an individual, except as the representative of his progeny or nation. But since the date of this remote prophecy rests upon the word of Moses in the Pentateuch, we cannot assume that this particular, respecting its time of publication, is true; and though the faith and veracity of the sacred historian have been often effectually vindicated, that is a previous, or collateral topic, from which our present examination shall borrow nothing. Suppose then that the public knowledge of the prophecy was only contemporary with the Pentateuch itself. The Pentateuch, containing the public code and solemn annals of the Jewish people, could not be put forth surreptitiously, nor in any other age than that which it bears upon the face of it; the age of Moses its author. At that time, if not before, the prophecy was extant.

At that time then we shall have a prediction delineating under a brief, but expressive, description, the genius and manners of a people who have always been reckoned a very singular race; and that description, in all its brevity, marking the very habits of life by which this race has been distinguished from the rest of the world. "He will be a wild man; and his hand will be against every man, and every man's hand against him. And he shall dwell in the presence of all his brethren." If we call for the report of the historians and travellers of every age, they will inform us that we have here the very character of the Arabian. They will tell us of his roving habits; of the desultory career of his rude freedom, which has neither been subdued by conquest, nor reclaimed by the milder restraints of settlement and civilisation. They will tell us also of the license of his predatory warfare, and the state of defiance and hostility which forms the international law between him and those around him. There appears therefore, in this instance to have been an exact and remarkable accomplishment of this aboriginal prophecy concerning the Arabian race.

Will it be said, however, that so soon as in the time of Moses, to which, for the sake of argument, I have consented to refer the publication of the prophecy, the Ishmaelite then was what he since has always been; and that the subsisting picture of his national manners was converted into the semblance of a prediction? History is too imperfect for us to sift the allegation. If we admit the prophecy to have been a real one, we may easily believe that the people who were the subject of it soon began to verify it. But, since apart from the prophecy we know nothing of them in this respect, let us consider what is probable. Now I think it will be granted, that the imperfect settlement of the world, and the general rude state of nations at that time, render it highly improbable that any such deep appropriate marks could have begun to distinguish the Arabian, as would arrest the attention of a common historian, and enable him to select, and seize so truly, the *one example* of those peculiar national habits which was ultimately to survive and exceed the rest. There were too many wild men then, to make one instance of it in a race a rare one. Too much of promiscuous rapine and violence, to give a single people the privilege of a reputation on such accounts.

But one certainty we have, that is the long-continued fulfilment of this prophecy. The Arabians have occupied one and the same country. They have roved, like the moving sands of their deserts; but their race has been rooted whilst the individual has wandered. That race has neither been dissipated by conquest, nor lost by migration, nor confounded with the blood of other countries. They have continued to dwell "in the presence of all their brethren," a distinct national family, wearing, upon the whole, the same features and aspect which prophecy first impressed upon them. The "wildness" which is incident only to a certain stage of man's social nature, has been permanent with them; and, although they have been compacted and embodied as a nation for more than three thousand years, they have resisted those changes of habit which it is the effect of civil union, so long continued, to induce. Plainly there is something unusual and remarkable in their case. And yet the account which could now be given of them, with all the advantage of knowing their whole past history, is no other than was given of them long ago, in the first rudiments of their national existence, if we take the prophecy at the lowest supposable date of it; and before they existed at all, if we rely upon the only direct testimony which we possess, and that an unimpeached one, as to the real time of its publication.

It adds something to the force of this prediction to consider the nature of its subject. It cannot be said that the manners and civil character of nations, if we look at them through any long period, are otherwise than fugitive and mutable in the extreme. In that extent they offer a far less tangible object to the calculations of human foresight than do the vicissitudes of national fortunes. Yet the prophecy in question is boldly expressive; and its merit, if I may use so unequal a phrase, is, that it has proved so just, not without some cause of observation that the people who are its subject should have persisted so long to verify it.— But thus the *Ishmaelite*, in his own country, and the *Jew*, in every country except his own, have each, through ages, exhibited, in the peculiarity of their condition, an object of some inquiry and attention, and thereby drawn men's notice, first to the records of prophecy, and thence to a visible confirmation of its truth and foreknowledge. And since these are kindred nations, derived from the same patriarchal Founder, though with a great dissimilarity in their most important relations to Revealed Religion, the early prophecy annexed to the alien Ishmaelite contributes to seal and corroborate the whole primitive history of that religion, and places the divided progeny of Abraham under a public cognizance of prophetic designation.—There is a ground and reason for the matter of this remark, which might bear to be opened more at large. But perhaps enough has been said to justify both the foreknowledge, and the moral object, of the prophecy under discussion.— (Gen. xxi. 13.)

II. The other, and the last, example of prophecy, which I propose to touch upon, is from the book of Daniel. It is that branch of his copious and extended predictions, in which he has described the *Succession* of the four great Empires of the ancient world.

The prophetic subject which I here adduce is delineated twice by the same prophet. This is done in two separate visions, visions in dream; which are first pourtrayed, and then interpreted and explained. A great Image, "whose brightness was excellent,—and the form whereof was terrible," composed in its several parts of four different Metals, is the machinery of the divine revelation, in the one vision; a file of four great Beasts, coming up from the Sea, diverse one from another, in the second.

The identity of the subject designed in the two visions is incontestable. For if the respective symbols themselves in their Fourfold partition, and in other points of analogy and agreement, did not fix their own coincidence; the literal interpretation annexed to the visions, and completing the revelation, shuts out all doubt on that head. The duplication of the vision is not unimportant. It adds to the steadiness and confidence of the prediction.

I shall take the first of the two, that which is pourtrayed in the Image composed of four metals; and its plan is opened in the following scheme of interpretation.

"This is the dream; and we will tell the interpretation thereof before the king;" the king of Babylon;

"Thou, O king, art a king of kings; for the God of heaven hath given thee a kingdom, power, and strength, and glory.

"And wheresoever the children of men dwell, the beasts of the field and the fowls of heaven, hath He given into

thine hand, and hath made thee ruler over them all.—
Thou art this head of gold.

"And after thee shall arise another kingdom inferior to
thee; and another third kingdom of brass, which shall
bear rule over all the earth.

"And the fourth kingdom shall be strong as iron; for-
asmuch as iron breaketh in pieces, and subdueth all things;
and as iron that breaketh all these, shall it break in pieces
and bruise[b]."

Here is presented a clear and unambiguous statement of
the rise of *four* kingdoms; the four not to be contemporary, but *successive;* to be *diverse* one from another, *not
originating* from the same power; to be kingdoms of *conquest* and *empire,* not confined to the sway of a domestic
sceptre, but bearing rule over the subject nations.—An extension of the *limits* of *dominion* is indicated in the *third*
kingdom.—A *superior force* in the fourth.

Four such ruling kingdoms did arise. The first, the
Babylonian, was in being when the prophecy was represented to have been given. It was followed by the Persian;
the Persian gave way to the Grecian; the Roman closed
the series.

It seems, therefore, on the first survey, that we have a
conspicuous and connected prophecy of the most comprehensive changes and revolutions which were wrought on
the face of the ancient world.—The subject is great and
complex; the plan of the prophecy is luminous; its sense
clear[c] in every article of it; and the corresponding history

---

[b] Dan. ii. 36—40.

[c] This assertion which I make of the internal certainty and clearness of
the prophetic sense, and of the completion of it in the four empires which
have been named, is not shaken by the fact that there has been some difference of opinion as to the third and fourth kingdoms intended. The opinion
which would make the reign of *Alexander's Successors* a kingdom *distinct*
from his, and thereby the *fourth,* can be reckoned nothing better than a mere
mistake, inconsistent with the principles of the vision, and with the plainest
ideas of the history of kingdoms. The dynasty, the name, the foundation
and title, were all *Grecian,* derived from the *first* conqueror to the whole
clan and body of his successors. The language of Appian, in the Proem to

confessed and notorious.   Nothing is wanting to vindicate the prophecy, but that we be assured of the time of its publication.

It has happened that this very point, the epoch of the publication of Daniel's prophecies, has been directly disputed.   Others of his predictions there are, though not more clear, yet more minute in their detail; and against those others, on account of their minuteness and exactitude in that detail, scepticism in old times employed its engines of opposition and objection to discredit their antiquity; since otherwise there was no way to the refutation of their evidence.   The objections of Porphyry are sufficiently known.   He contended, among his other allegations, that the prophecies of Daniel were not written and published at the epoch ascribed to them, *viz.*, during the Babylonian Empire; but in a later age, specifically, he said, about the age of Antiochus Epiphanes.

It may amount to a refutation of this hypothesis to reply, first, that the Jews who had their Canon of Scripture completed and closed long before the time of Antiochus Epiphanes must have been more competent judges of the genuine writings of their chief prophets and teachers, than a stranger, and he of a later age, could be; and, next, that it is infinitely improbable that a forgery, in the name of Daniel, could have been obtruded upon them for a book of his, produced to light three centuries after the life-time of the prophet, and by the bare fact of its late appearance contradicting the credit, and defeating the use, of its prophetic revelations, which must have been given for some other designed purpose than that of so long a suppression and concealment.   The very lateness of their appearance, considering that many of their most notable subjects of prediction would have

his History, when he speaks of the partition of this empire, is obviously the only correct and natural language that can be used upon the subject ;—ἧς γε, καὶ διαλυθείσης ἐς πολλὰς σατραπείας, ἐπιπλεῖστον ἐξέλαμπε τὰ μέρη.   The kingdoms of the succession were *members* of the *same empire*, not a new fabric.

already gone by, must have operated to their discredit, if not their instant rejection. Yet we have it on the authority of Josephus, that Daniel's prophecies were read publicly among the Jews in their worship, as well as their other received Scriptures, and he knows nothing of any doubts of their genuineness, or their authority, having disturbed their reception. On the contrary, he has given a more *copious* and *explicit* testimony to the authority of *this one Prophet*, than to any other whatever.

But although these considerations ought to be conclusive, we are not laid under the necessity of relying solely upon them. It may be shewn that the notion, thus offered, concerning the supposed *late publication* of these prophecies, will not solve the difficulty which is in the way; nor cut off their inspired predictive character. And if Porphyry, and Collins after him, have found nothing better to advance, I shall suppose the objections of minor name to be included in theirs.

The hypothesis will not solve the difficulty. For how will the case stand, supposing that hypothesis to be admitted? The prophecy, concerning the succession of the Four Empires, if delivered during, or about, the reign of Antiochus Epiphanes, will fall on the period of the third of those Empires, the Grecian or Macedonian. At that time, the Romans were only beginning to take an active part in the affairs of the East; for they had not so far extended their conquests. But let us make a liberal concession, and suppose that at that time the future, the approaching conquests, of the Romans, in the East, might have been foreseen. We must take notice that one especial object in the prediction is the *superior strength*, the *paramount solidity and force* of their empire, as compared with the others which had preceded it. Theirs was to be "the iron power, breaking down, and bruising all things." So it was foretold; so it was. The solid and well-cemented fabric of its military despotism, the overwhelming force, and the continued impression, of its reiterated wars and victories, held the

world in stronger chains, and subdued it to a more humbled subjection, than had been inflicted by the force of
any of the older masters and destroyers, to whom God
had permitted the usurpation of a wide-ruling conquest.
Those legions were truly "the breaking and bruising
engines," the massive iron hammers of the earth. This
character of difference between the Roman, and the preceding empires, is *prefigured* in the *symbol* of the prophecy, and *foreshewn* in the *express interpretation* of it.
But to a Jewish eye, or to any eye, placed in the same
position of view, in the age of Antiochus Epiphanes, it is
utterly impossible to admit that this superior strength of
the Roman power, to reduce and destroy, this heavier
arm of subjugation, could have revealed itself so plainly,
as to warrant the express and deliberate description of it.

Here is one barrier of the prophecy. But again, let us
advance a step further: suppose, improbable as it is, that
in the age of Antiochus the effect of the future Roman
victories over the earth could have been foreseen. We
shall yet have to inquire how it could be foreseen that
this Fourth, and yet unestablished, Empire, should be
the *last* in the line. The prophecy delineates *four*. So
many there were: and no more; for not a fifth empire of
general dominion, but a multitude of separate kingdoms
were erected on the ruins of the Fourth. How shall we
account for this striking coincidence between the history
of the civilised world, and the vision recorded by Daniel,
if he were no prophet, and that vision not inspired? If
the prediction was uttered in the midst of the vortex of
these changes and revolutions of empire and dominion,
when two of the kingdoms had passed away, a third was
declining, and a fourth coming on, how did the prophecy,
if it were a human device, happen so accurately to fix the
destined limit to these revolutions, and compute the true
number of them; and not rather be impelled to draw
from the flux of the past and yet changing scene, the
anticipation of further successive and continued changes
of the like kind? We must suppose this uninspired pro-

phet to have resisted the most natural impressions arising from what had already been seen to happen, and to have been endowed with an union of *boldness* and *forbearance* in his computation of future contingencies, which no reason, no knowledge of the workings of the human mind, can enable us to comprehend, or excuse us in believing.

What secondary moral causes may have operated in putting an end to the succession of extensive empires, immediately after the Roman, and cutting off the line of conquerors, from the civilised world, by a long pause and interval of discontinuance, is a question foreign to our present inquiry. By whatever means and instruments, so the event was ordered. This is a memorable fact. But it is a fact represented in prophecy before it came to pass. The great Image in its whole stature, and its four divisions, from head to foot, is the just emblem of the actual annals of the world. There is, therefore, in the prophecy which we have examined, something more than can be explained by the arbitrary supposition of its publication in the age of Antiochus Epiphanes. It contains a surplusage of evidence which leaves that hypothesis behind. It establishes its inspired authority, by the extent of its prescience.

But the argument admits of a material enlargement. In each of the visions of Daniel there is introduced a Fifth conspicuous object. "A stone cut out of a mountain without hands," is the new object, concluding the vision of the great Image. "One, like the Son of Man, coming in the clouds of heaven, and receiving a dominion, a glory, a kingdom that *all people*, nations, and languages should serve Him; His dominion is an *everlasting dominion*, which shall not pass away; and His kingdom that which shall not be destroyed;" this is the conspicuous object introduced upon the conclusion of the other vision, concerning the Four Beasts. These *two new prophetic emblems*, occupying a similar place in the order and sequel

of the two visions respectively, thereby denote some conjunction, or some agreement, if not an identity, in their
subject. The aptitude and justness with which they express, the first of them, the establishment of the Christian
Religion; the second, the extent, eternal duration, and
victory, of the Christian Kingdom, oblige us to own that
they are adequate prophecies of those events, which have
had their completion, in one and the same subject. For
the establishment of Christianity is a past fact: and its
mode of establishment justifies the emblem; that emblem
which describes it as "a stone cut out of a mountain without hands;" a rock quarried out of the mountain by other
means than the known methods and resources of human
power. As to the extent, eternal duration, and *victory* of
the Christian Kingdom, if it is not yet a past fact complete, it is in such a state of credibility, by its advances
to a completion, that, in reason, the truth of the prophecy
in that point is sufficiently sustained. Consequently, the
evidence of the inspiration of these connected prophetic
visions is augmented by all that accession.—The introduction of Christianity is foreshewn to be incident upon the
time of the fourth Empire. This alone would amount to
a decisive proof of the prophetic prescience.

Once more—The *termination* of the Fourth Empire, by
its subdivision into a multitude of separate kingdoms is a
further ingredient in the information of the prophecy, and
a new test of its prescience. Those separate kingdoms are
indicated to be *Ten.* The *definite* number may, or may
not be, a strict postulate of the prophecy: a *multifarious*
division unquestionably is denoted. That multifarious division took place, in the cluster of petty contemporary
kingdoms, which replaced the Roman Empire upon its dissolution.—In that cluster of kingdoms the Ten horns of
the Fourth Beast, diverse from all the rest, find their interpretation, and their correspondent realities.

So long therefore as the civil history of the ancient

world shall last, under the scheme of its four successive
Empires; so long as the introduction of Christianity, in
the place and order previously assigned to it, shall remain
upon record; and its visible reign exist; so long as the
conclusion of the Iron Empire of Rome shall be known
in the promiscuous partition made of it by the host of
Northern and Eastern Invaders; so long there will be a
just and rational proof of the inspiration of these illustrious prophecies of Daniel. If we try to refer such discoveries to any ingenuity of human reason, they have too
much extent and system for the substituted solution. In
that attempt of solution, we are cramped by improbabilities
on every side. One adequate origin of them there is, and
that alone can render them intelligible in their manifest
character, if we consent to read them as oracles of God,
communicated by Him to His prophets, and by them to
others, for the manifestation of His foreknowledge, and
overruling Providence in the kingdoms of the earth; and
next for the confirmation of the whole Truth of Revealed
Religion. In that light they fall into order. In that
same light too, their Origin and their Use, explain each
the other.

The survey which has now been taken of the state of
Prophecy, and of the evidence of its Inspiration, may
be reduced, in a summary, under the following general
observations.

1. There are prophecies in Scripture complete in their
evidence, and answering to the standard of an absolute
proof. Their publication, their fulfilment, their supernatural prescience, are all fully ascertained. They borrow
nothing of favour, or secondary support, from the other
evidences of Revealed Religion: they are themselves some
of the direct and independent attestations of it.

2. There are other prophecies which do not reach the
same conditions, for the purpose of inquiry at the present
day. For the light of Prophecy bears some respect to the
position of the inquirer. Many of its predictions are of

a kind and subject which would offer a more distinct information of its inspired character to one age, than to another. The subsisting condition of things, the field of contemporary circumstances, such as they were at the time when the prophecy was delivered, would remain more clearly in view, and thereby its inspired prescience be demonstrated, through a certain period of time; its promulgation, and its completion, would be more capable of being rigorously ascertained. These are inequalities of evidence, incident to particular predictions, from the nature of their subject, and the changes of historic information.

In one branch of the proof, that which relates to the *date* when the prophetic record was delivered, it is obvious that the ancient Jewish Church had the superior means of knowledge, with regard to some parts of Prophecy. The judgment and authority of that Church is a fair and reasonable testimony, worthy of our confidence, as to that one fact, *viz.*, the age of their prophets, and the date of their predictions. But the collection and publication of the whole Canon of the Old Testament, and the Version of it subsequently made into the Greek, a general language, become additional, and greater, securities to us, in this important branch of our information. Consequently, the recorded prophecies which have received their fulfilment at a time subsequent to the Collection of the Ancient Scriptures, or to the Translation of them, contain a more complete evidence, than those whose accomplishment was anterior to either of those public acts. It is this fact, the great notoriety of the existence and promulgation of the record, which confers so absolute a proof upon those prophecies which have been fulfilled in the Institution of Christianity, upon some of the predictions of Daniel, and upon the prophecies which describe the final condition of the Jewish people. — We have the like security in the known publication of the Apocalypse.

3. Nor is it any derogation from the perfect authority of Prophecy to admit, that some of its predictions may perhaps at no time have carried with them the clear and

convincing signs of their divine origin, which others have had. Reasonable inducements of belief there may be, short of commanding proofs. If the whole of the prophetic evidence were of this inferior kind, that would make a different case. Whereas the actual state of Prophecy is this, that its greater, and its less, arguments are combined together, and its presumptions concur with its more decisive proofs.

And thus God, who has never left His revelation without a witness of this kind, has so dispensed the word of Prophecy that every age has received from it its share of light, though not always the same. For if I might illustrate what has happened with respect to the evidence of different portions of prophecy, by an analogy taken from the natural system of the world, I should say that men's reasonable Faith, like the earth beneath their feet in its revolutions, has only come, from time to time, under a new meridian line, and another aspect of the heavens; where that faith has still found its group and constellation of prophecy ready to illuminate and direct it; whilst some of the lights which have shone upon it have held a more constant aspect on its course, and neither set nor vary, but remain uniform and unchangeable monuments of a divine guidance.

But all our previous conviction, of this rational kind, of the *truth* of Revealed Religion, is but introductory to its *use*. In its use the argument passes into Piety and Morals, and the duties of a personal Religion. It is in the exercise and cultivation of those duties that Christianity comes to be really understood. It is there that our speculations concerning it attain, not only to their proper end, but to a more direct and feeling perception, I might say, a consciousness, of its Truth.

END OF DISCOURSE XII.

NOTES.

———

Page 78.

I ADHERE to Bishop Sherlock's view of this prophecy, concerning *the sceptre of Judah*, which he has stated and defended in his discourse upon it; *viz.* that it was a *Tribal Sceptre*, a state of *civil union*, and *government* under its own hereditary laws, the continuance of which was promised to this Tribe;—notwithstanding the severe and elaborate censure which that opinion has undergone in the Divine Legation. (Book v. sect. 3.)

Bishop Horsley has made the following observation: "And in this very year the *sceptre of royal power departed from Judah; for* it was in this year that *Archelaus* the son of Herod the Great was deposed by the Roman Emperor, and banished to Lyons, and the Jews became wholly subject to the dominion of the Romans. *Thus* the prophecy of Jacob *was fulfilled* by the coincidence of the subversion of the *independent* government of the Jews, with the first advent or appearance of Shiloh, in the Temple." (Sermons, vol. i. p. 36.) Yet the same author, with no small inconsistency, gives a different idea in the same volume. "Their *temple* was demolished and burnt, and the *forms of the Mosaic worship* abolished. Then it was that the sceptre of *ecclesiastical sway* (for *that* is the sceptre meant in Jacob's famous prophecy) departed from Judah. The Jews were no longer the *depositaries* of the *laws* and *oracles* of God. They were no longer to take the lead in matters of religion and worship." *Ibid.* p. 100. I have not cited these different opinions for the sake of noticing the inconsistency of this learned writer, who excels always more in force of style, than severity of reason; but to remark, that although his two ideas of the *kingly* and the *ecclesiastical sway* cannot be reconciled with each other, the last of them may harmonize with the *civil* polity of Judah's sceptre, since the *civil existence* and the *public religion* of that tribe were linked together.

Page 95.

It has been an object, which I have kept constantly in view, whilst I was tracing the course of Prophecy, and explaining its order, to shew that the system of *Gospel Truth*, in all its parts, was unfolded by degrees in the Prophetic revelation. Nor have I barely stated this method of a *progressive revelation*: I have offered some proofs of it, by observing upon the topics which are introduced in the *later* periods of prophecy, as compared with the more ancient. The principle itself is simple, and there was no need to devise any reasonings to establish it. All that was required, was to explain it by its own evidence in the Contents of the Prophe ic Volume.

The same method which Prophecy has followed in the disclosure of other Gospel Truths, it has preserved in its communications respecting hat principal one, concerning a Future Eternal State. In the Psalms, in Isaiah, in Hosea, in Ezekiel, in Daniel, there are such distinct notices given of a Future State, as cannot be found in the earlier periods comprehended in the Pentateuch: *viz.*, either in the Antediluvian, the Patriarchal, or the Mosaic age. For example, there is no such significant and express declaration to be found in the Pentateuch, as this of Isaiah :—

" He will *destroy* on this mountain the *face of the covering cast over* all *people*, and the *vail* that is spread over all nations. He *will swallow up death in victory*, and the Lord God will *wipe away tears from off all faces*, and the rebuke of His people shall be taken away from off *all the earth*."

Nor as this other of Daniel : " And many of them that *sleep* in the dust of the earth *shall awake*, some to *everlasting life*, and some to *shame and everlasting contempt*." From the day when Daniel delivered this sentence of Prophecy, I consider that there was extant in the Jewish Church a more intelligible revelation of a Future Eternal State than had been given before. The Jewish believer, by it, had an *addition* made to his knowledge.

Hence, it will be seen, that I am far from concurring in that criticism and reasoning of Bishop Warburton, by which he has endeavoured, either to exclude the doctrine of a Future State from the Psalms and Prophetic Volume, as much as from the Pentateuch, or to dilute and neutralize the texts which seem to express it, either in man's hope, or in God's promise. His assertion, that the Jews got their notions of it from Pagan sources, and at a period later than the Captivity, is perfectly untenable. For why should devout men in the Church of Israel go to Pagans for the information, when they might have it from their own Prophets; as in the texts of Hosea, Isaiah, Ezekiel, Daniel? And if Pagans had any light from Reason or Nature, to promote their *hope* of a *Future State*, as no doubt they had, then the Jewish believer had the same collateral inducements to his persuasion in that doctrine. And as the general wish to reduce and neutralize the Prophetic Information on this head, is inconsistent with my ideas; so nothing appears to me more violent and unnatural than many of the expositions, in detail, of texts in the Psalms and the Prophets, which that Prelate has advanced as destructive of their enlarged sense. His remarks are exaggerated, and not very consistent with each other. It is an exaggeration to assert " that the doctrine of a Future State *never once appears* to have had any share in this *people's thoughts;* and never did indeed make any part of their opinions." (Vol. v. p. 176.) " That the doctrine came from a distant quarter; namely, *from their Pagan neighbours, patched up* out of some dark and scattered insinuations of their *own Prophets*." (p. 186, & 281.) And " that the Holy *Prophets* speak of *no other* than *Temporal* rewards and punishments." p. 159. On the other hand, he admits, and contends, that the later Prophets opened the *first dawning* " of the doctrine of a *Resurrection*, and consequently of a *future state of reward and punishment*." p. 297.

The spirit of his interpretation, in this line of his argument, may be judged of by the following example, among many others. In the Book of Proverbs it is said, " The wicked is driven away in his wickedness; BUT THE RIGHTEOUS HATH HOPE IN HIS DEATH." Upon which he says, " That is, the righteous hath hope that he shall be *delivered from* the most imminent dangers." But the phrase is, " *In* his Death," and such is the proper and unequivocal sense of the text. Under such a management of interpretation, I conceive that this eminent man does as great violence to the Scripture by a curtailment of its sense, as others have done by their additions. Many other examples of equal unfairness, and devoted partiality to an hypothesis, occur in his criticism.

On the memorable and disputed text in the Book of Job, I cannot now enter into an exact disquisition. But that I may disguise no part of my notions on this important subject, I shall simply state what is the interpretation I assign to it, as the most probable. I understand Job to express his persuasion of a proper Resurrection; not of the Temporal Restoration of his Fortunes. The Redeemer whom he speaks of, I understand to be God, as his Vindicator and Deliverer:—A Deliverer from his Enemies, his Afflictions, and the Grave: not as a *Redeemer* of himself, or the world, from *Sin*. In this sense I apply the text as an instance of the declared Faith and Hope of one Saint of God: consequently, an encouragement to the Faith of others. And I have said already, that under the Mosaic Law which contained no distinct and open promise of Immortality, Individuals, according to their piety, or their illumination, drew from God's general promises higher prospects than others. In such a way as this, Job's knowledge, or assured belief of a Resurrection, I maintain.

To conclude this course of remark, let me observe once more that, the *Fact*, not the *Theory*, which I have deduced from Scripture, is this. The several Truths of the Christian System are brought forth in various degrees by Prophecy; and when other doctrines of the Gospel, as those which relate to the *Divine Nature* of the Redeemer, His *Incarnation*, His *Atonement*, and His *Grace*, are propounded by the Prophets, at the same time the prospects of *Eternal Life* are more largely opened. The Gospel Doctrine grows up together in its fulness. This state of the case I offer as the matter of Fact. The result which I draw from it is, That the Prophets bear witness of Christ and Eternal Life together: and that the whole structure of their Prophecy is such as shews that the gift of Immortality is restored to Man by the Redeemer.

As a *corollary* to this statement, I will add that the account thus given of the ancient dispensation of Religion, vindicates, and coincides with, the Article of our Church, which asserts that "the Old Testament is *not contrary* to the New: for both in the Old and New Testament, Everlasting Life *is offered to mankind* by Christ. And that they are not to be heard, which feign that the old Fathers did look only for transitory promises." Article VII.

Had there not existed some kind of *difference* between the Old and New Testaments, there had been little occasion for an Article to disavow their contrariety. The difference is in the less perspicuous and direct, and also in the tardier, communication, in the Old, of Truths which are the first Axioms of the New. The Article justly condemns those "who feign that the old Fathers did *look only* for transitory promises." But had our Church asserted a distinct *Revelation* of *Eternal Life*, to have been given from the first, or to be contained in the *Pentateuch;* it might have been not so easy a task to defend that assertion. Her article is now in perfect unison with the Truth; which is more than can be said of some of the comments occasionally made upon it.

The following *Cursory Observations* may perhaps tend to *illustrate* the *history* of this subject; the proper truth of it being, as I hope, already settled.

1. Origen mentions a circumstance which may deserve to be noticed. He says, that there were persons in his time, who referred our Saviour's words concerning the Scripture: "'*In them* ye think ye have *Eternal Life;*' not to the Books of Canonical Scripture, but to the Apocryphal Books, in which were given *clearer* accounts of *the Future Blessed State*[a]." Whether those Apocryphal Books were merely those which we now possess under that name, (see 2 Maccab. vi. vii.,) or included others, is immaterial. I allude to this circumstance of the greater clearness, real or supposed, in those *Apocryphal* Books, only to observe, that uninspired assertions, or human declarations, of the belief in an Eternal State, are something exceedingly short of God's own Revelation of it. Suppose a Pagan, or a Jew, to *believe* ever so *strongly* in the Article, still it was Divine Revelation that gave it its sure basis. Consequently, it matters less what men *thought;* but much more what God had *declared*, on this subject.

The *Hope*, not the *Knowledge*, of Immortality is, in fact, both

* Comment. in Matth. p. 498. vol. i. ed. Col. ἐπὶ τοὺς ἀποκρύφους καταφεύξεται, ἔνθα δοκεῖ σαφέστερον τὰ περὶ τῆς μακαρίας γεγράφθαι ζωῆς.

natural and *reasonable,* to Man. But we perceive that God, since the Fall, had left Nature and Reason under a great struggle of uncertainty and darkness in this hope; and that it has been the prerogative of His Revelation to give an *authentic Faith* which they could never bestow.

2. *Josephus* does not scruple to attribute the open Promise of a Future Life to the Law of Moses[b]. This pretence of the Historian's is not surprizing; it is the proof of his partiality to his Law, in wishing to give it every doctrine which he thought would redound to its honour. But the sincerity of a Christian's examination of that Law must not be ruled by an assertion of its national Historian. His assertion will not put into the Pentateuch more than its Inspired Author left there. It is clear that he had a prejudice of piety and veneration, which inclined him to ascribe to the Original Law one of the noblest understood truths of his own age. And perhaps some persons will even now take the word of the human Historian, and reckon his affirmation one of the proofs that the Pentateuch contains what he assigns to it. But the Scripture itself is the higher authority.

3. The *Samaritans*, as it appears from the account of them, fully stated by Origen, were, down to his day, *Deniers* of a *Resurrection*, and of the *Soul's Immortality*[c]. It can never be said that the *Pentateuch justified*, or *encouraged*, such gross unbelief. But the intelligent observer of things will see, that this their unbelief might meet with a less palpable contradiction. if they took, as the tradition is, the Pentateuch alone for their rule, without the larger informations of the Psalms and later Prophecy. Perhaps their *Schism*, which broke them off from the foundation of the Church of Israel, lost to them the benefit

---

[b] Contra Apion. lib. ii. cap. 30. Τοῦ μὲν νομοθέτου προφητεύσαντος, τοῦ δὲ Θεοῦ τὴν πίστιν ἰσχυρὰν παρεσχηκότος, ὅτι τοῖς τοὺς νόμους διαφυλάξασι, κἂν εἰ δέοι θνήσκειν ὑπὲρ αὐτῶν προθύμως ἀποθανοῦσιν, ἔδωκεν ὁ Θεὸς γενέσθαι τε πάλιν, καὶ βίον ἀμείνω λαβεῖν ἐκ περιτροπῆς.

[c] Οἱ Σαδδουκαῖοι μέντοι λέγοντες μὴ εἶναι ἀνάστασιν .... παντελῶς ἀνῄρουν τὴν τῆς ψυχῆς οὐ μόνον ἀθανασίαν, ἀλλὰ καὶ ἐπιδιαμονὴν, οἰόμενοι μηδαμοῦ ἐν τοῖς Μωσέως γράμμασι σημαίνεσθαι τὴν τῆς ψυχῆς μετὰ ταῦτα ζωήν. Τὸ δὲ αὐτὸ τοῖς Σαδδουκαίοις δόγμα περὶ τῆς τῶν ἀνθρώπων ψυχῆς φρονοῦσι μέχρι τοῦ δεῖρο Σαμαρεῖς, καὶ οἰκοδομοῦντες ἐξ αὐτῶν εἶναι νομομαθεῖς, καὶ ἕως θανάτου ἀγωνιζόμενοι περὶ τοῦ Μωσέως νόμου καὶ τῆς περιτομῆς.—Comment. in Matth. p. 486.

of that other Scripture. And thus their Schism had its fruit in the depravation of their faith into that debased doctrine, which is commonly known as the Sadducean Heresy. But this Heresy of the *Sadducee* is said to have taken its rise, or its avowed and public prevalence, from *Samaria;* and from this very principle of rejecting the Authority of the *Prophets*[d].

In this shape of the Samaritan Heresy, one may remark a resemblance to the practice of some recent Sects, who insist upon the *Gospels*, to the exclusion, or the disparagement, of the *Apostolic Epistles;* and would limit their faith by other measures than the whole Canon of Inspiration. Meanwhile enough is found in the Pentateuch, and in the Gospels, respectively, to refute the partial creed both of the Ancient and the Modern Depravers of Revealed Truth.

This subject of the Samaritan Schism has also a connexion, which I shall here advert to, with the question concerning the age of the Book of Job. It does not appear, so far as I know, that the Samaritan Canon embraced that Book : and this absence of it from their Canon forms perhaps the only direct presumption, that occurs, against its high Antiquity; or its credit, as the work of Moses.

4. The obscurity, of a partial information, and an indefinite promise, under which I have represented the doctrine of a future life to be left in the Pentateuch, was a state of things which gave rise to the exercise of the desires and patient hope of piety, in the Individual; and the greater piety, we may justly think, grew into the greater strength of belief. Instead of disputing against this apparent state of the case, I see many reasons for acquiescing in such an order of Divine Revelation, and recognise in it one of the many proofs that the *Gospel* is, what it professes to be, the *perfect oracle* of Divine Truth, and the Saviour Himself, and none before Him, the *light of the world.* "Christo enim servabatur, omnia retro occulta *nudare,* dubitata *dirigere,* prælibata *supplere,* prædicata *repræsentare*[e]."

<hr>

[d] " "Taceo Judaismi hæreticos. Dositheum inquam *Samaritanum,* qui primus ausus est *Prophetas,* quasi non in Spiritu Sancto locutos, *repudiare.* Taceo *Sadducæos,* qui ex *hujus erroris radice surgentes,* ausi sunt ad hanc hæresim etiam resurrectionem carnis negare." *Tertullian.* de Præscript. Hæretic. p. 219. Conf. Pearson. Vindic. Ignat. p. 301. apud Patr. Apostol. Cotelerii.

[e] *Tertullian. de Resurrect. Carnis.* Sub init. p. 379. ed. Lutet.

Page 115.

It appears that Dardanus, a contemporary of Jerom, had the
same idea which Michaelis has here adopted, that the land of
Canaan was a possession restored, not a free gift bestowed.
See Jerom's Epistle to him, p. 606. tom. iii.

Page 154.

There is a second opinion, which I have to suggest, as to the
interpretation of that part of Jeremiah's Prophecy, which is
thought to relate to Coniah's *offspring*.

I believe that the original word (עֲרִירִי), which, in our Eng-
lish version, is rendered, *childless*, will admit of the more general sense of *destitute*, or *deprived:* and in this text may be
understood to express simply Coniah's failure of *kingly succession.* It is true that the term in the other texts, wherein it
occurs, (which are only three, and those in the Pentateuch,)
appears to describe a privation of *posterity*, either in the want
of children, or by their death and excision. See Genesis xv. 2;
Levit. xx. 20, 21. But the etymology of the word favours the
larger sense of *privation*, or *destitution*, of any kind: and it is
possible that even in those other texts in the Pentateuch, the
precise notion of orphanhood of *children* may be derived partly
from the context, giving a modification of the use of the word.
The radical notion of the word is that of *nudus.* It is possible,
therefore, that it might bear a double sense, as *orbus* does;
which is sometimes *bereaved of children;* sometimes simply
destitute. The *Hellenistic* versions give some sanction to this
opinion. *Symmachus* here renders the word κένον; although in
Levit. xx. 20, 21, he had rendered it ἄτεκνος. The *Septuagint*
and *Theodotion* render it ἐκκήρυκτον, (*proclaimed as dethroned*,)
and yet they too employed the more definite term ἄτεκνος in *Leviticus.* Had the Greek translators resorted to these versions,
κένον and ἐκκήρυκτον, without any apparent reason for them in
the original word, such as we ourselves could perceive, I should
say that they did so, in order to adapt their translation to the
genealogy of Coniah's family, which mentions his *descendants.*
But the word itself seems to justify a more enlarged and indefinite signification than that of *childless.*

The sense then would be, " Write this man *deprived*, or *desolate*, (an *heirless king*,) *despoiled in his throne;* a man that shall

not prosper in his days; for *no man of his seed shall prosper*, sitting upon the *throne* of David and *ruling any more in Israel.*"

This view of the passage, as derived from its phrase, is that which I now adopt. Yet I propose it with some diffidence, inasmuch as I do not see it formally offered by other interpreters; although several of them have put the question "how could Coniah be *orbatus liberis*," when we read the *continuation* of his genealogy distinctly recorded (*Matth.* i.). A further reason which qualifies my reliance upon the opinion which I have suggested, is, that it includes a change of our Authorized Version. That Version, for its great fidelity and skill, ranks in the first place of authority in all disputable points.

Grotius, who was convinced that the word signifies precisely *decessurum nullo filio relicto*, was led, by a just consequence, to think that the genealogy embraced the *adopted heirs* of Coniah's family, not his *natural offspring;* those adopted heirs being still of the family of David. He shewed a righ᷾ sense, in maintaining the perfect and literal completion of Jeremiah's prophecy; and under the same conviction, in my own mind, that the prophecy is one which was absolute and peremptory, as to the event which it declared, I was inclined at first to follow the opinion of Grotius respecting the genealogy. My more mature thoughts, however, are in favour of the second interpretation which I have now stated. That interpretation preserves the sense of the Prophecy in its fullest terms, and requires no conjectural suppositions to be made in the order of the genealogy. It exhibits the whole prediction as bearing upon that event which is its proper object; the *deposal* of Coniah and his line, and the abrogation of the Temporal Kingdom in the house of David. And as the Promises granted to David had been, not simply that he should never want a son, but that "he should never want a son to sit on his throne," so the Repeal of those promises is made more conformable to the first scope o᷾ them, if it pronounce the excision of *kingly heirs*, rather than of *offspring*.

And in harmony with this view, the observant reader will perceive, that the Evangelical prophecies of Jeremiah, opposed to these which are Temporal ones, introduce specifically a "future king upon the throne of David," as the contemporary supplement to this *Deposal of Coniah and his line.*—See especially Jerem. xxxiii. 21.

Dathe, in his Version, has rendered the clause in question thus: "Literis hoc mandato, Virum istum *infelicissimum* futurum esse:" a translation which is intended, I presume, to hinder the collision of the prophetic text with the genealogy. *Buddeus* (Hist. Vet. Test. tom. ii. p. 461.) in like manner, *destructum, infelicem, et miserum.* I am not aware how these vague translations can be justified.

Michaelis[1], after some doubt and hesitation, settles upon the notion of *exul*, or *extorris ex patria*, as the most probable sense of the original noun, in all the Four passages in which it occurs; and expresses a wish that he had so translated it in his German Version. But this sense is introduced without any leading authority, either in the Etymology, or the Ancient Versions, to sanction it; on which account it is unsatisfactory.

Thus far I had made up my opinion respecting the sense of this prophecy, and stated it, in a preceding edition. Subsequently I have observed that the very same view and interpretation are proposed by Bishop Kidder, in his Demonstration of the Messias, part ii. p. 121. It is highly satisfactory to me to have the countenance of so able and judicious a writer in the interpretation which I would assign to this important text of prophecy; and I feel less scruple, therefore, in relying upon the version of it here advanced, which I was not aware had so considerable a name to support it.

It should be noticed also, that the word in question is found in Irenæus, (Advers. Hæres. 3. 30. as cited by Bp. Kidder,) rendered by *abdicatum hominem*: whilst *abdicatus* is the Latin word used by Jerom (in loc.) to express ἐκκήρυκτος of the Septuagint and Theodotion, and plainly denotes *regal deprivation*. Jerom includes in his commentary (in loc.) a plain reference to this sense of the prophecy. "Sed fuit in captivitate et Salathiel et Zorobabel, et *usque ad Christum nullus regiam obtinuit potestatem;—nullus* deinceps de *stirpe David* in terra Judæa tenuit principatum."

He also gives the history of the Hellenistic versions more completely, thus: "Aquilæ prima editio, *sterilem;* secunda, ἀναύξητον, *non crescentem;* Symmachus, *vacuum;* LXX et Theodotio, *abominabilem* et *abdicatum* interpretati sunt."

<hr>

[1] Supplem. ad Lex. Hebr. No. 1984.

Surenhusius's mode of reconciliation applied to this history is very unsatisfactory, p. 131. Theol. Hebr.

Page 176.

A *tradition* is preserved by Josephus, which, if the substance of it be true, serves to shew the *confessed notoriety* of the facts of the miracle wrought upon Jeroboam and his Altar, and also the *importance* felt to be attached to the miracle, in *Samaria*. He relates, that the *Bethel* Prophet, of whose deceitful mind we have proof sufficient in the Scripture History, instructed the Idolatrous king, how to relieve himself from the apparent miracle, by explaining the case in a natural way. The explanation offered was this: " That the king's hand was seized with a *torpor* of paralysis, from the *pressure* of the victims which he had to offer, and, after a *pause* of the service, was restored again: and that the *Altar* also, *being new, burst under its load*." According to this narrative, the palpable *facts*, the *withering* and *restoration* of Jeroboam's hand, and the *rending* of the Altar, were granted by the Samaritan unbelievers: and this their admission includes all that can be wanted to authenticate the miracle by their adverse testimony. For as to their explanation of it, it is obvious that such expedients of unbelief can never fail. It is no less obvious that the *accidental coincidence* of the facts with the message and purpose of the Judah prophet, would itself be hardly less than a miracle.

The tradition, if it be authentic, presents what is perhaps one of the oldest essays of Infidelity, transmitted to us, in *explaining* a Scripture Miracle, and it seems to afford no bad measure of their usual *success.*—Joseph. Antiq. lib. viii. cap. 8, 9. To the *Judah* prophet Josephus gives the name of Jadon.

Page 197.

The same principle, by which I apply Hosea's prophecy to the doctrine of a Future State, " in the *destruction* of Death," will explicate the Vision of Ezekiel, in the Resurrection of the Dry Bones, to the sense of a proper Resurrection. In each case the *Temporal* state of the House of Israel appears to be the proper subject, and in each case the Temporal Promise is conveyed in the envelope of the real and greater consummation of the things expressed or figured. The anxious hope and inquiries of men, in those subjects, created the pledge, that God did not exhibit an illusion to their mind, in the form either of the Prophecy or the Vision. I would not contend that every envelope of a prophecy must have declared a literal truth: for some of the modes of representation chosen might be such as *affected no important truth;* but in the question concerning Death and the Resurrection, a Vision must be understood to intend a real information to the craving hope of the human soul.

Bishop Warburton has endeavoured to deprive this Vision of Ezekiel of its higher application. But I see a great superiority of discernment in the reasoning of *Tertullian* on this head; who has maintained and enforced the same principle which I rest upon; *viz.,* "that the *veracity* of the prophecy implies the *higher truth*, though the *proper subject* of it may be the temporal state of Israel." That acute and eloquent Father has thus expressed himself: "Denique, hoc ipso quod recidivatus Judaici status de recorporatione et redanimatione ossium *figuratur,* id quoque *eventurum ossibus probatur.* Non enim possit de ossibus *figura componi,* si non *idipsum* et ossibus *eventurum esset.* Nam etsi figmentum veritatis in imagine est, imago ipsa in veritate est sui. Necesse est esse prius sibi, quo alii configuretur. De vacuo similitudo non competit; de nullo parabola non convenit. Ita *oportebit ossium* quoque credi reviscerationem et respirationem, qualis dicitur, *de qua possit exprimi* Judaicorum rerum reformatio qualis affingitur," &c. The whole reasoning, which is pursued to some extent, is distinguished by its justness, and real penetration of the subject.—*De Resurrect.* p. 400.

Page 202.

Habak. ii. 2, 3. "For the vision is yet for an appointed time, but at the end it shall speak, and not lie. Though it tarry, wait for it." I have explained and applied this text in a Gospel sense, so far as I think it will justly bear that sense. I am aware indeed that others have pressed it much further, or rather have given it a different form. Bishop Chandler, in his valuable work, "The Defence of Christianity," has placed it among his "Twelve Texts, which *literally* and *singly* prophesy of the *coming* of the *Messias.*" (Defence, p. 132.) To justify his interpretation, he follows the other mode of version; "*He* shall speak : though *he* tarry, wait for *him*." The verb being impersonally put in the original, he would supply, as its personal subject, *the Messias.*

This interpretation, although it would favour my object, which is to shew the copiousness of prophecy in reference to the Messiah and the Gospel, I do not adopt. It is uncertain both in the reason, and in the form, of the text. It borrows too much from imperfect premises. And perhaps we sacrifice the true spirit of prophecy, as well as violate its letter, when we are intent on making every thing in it clear and express ; instead of being satisfied with its *general* allusions, as well as its direct notices, concerning the Gospel subject.

Eusebius cites a direct prophecy of the Messiah from another text of this same prophet; *viz.,* chap. ii. 13. "Thou wentest forth for the salvation of Thy people, even for salvation with Thine *anointed.*" Demonst. Evang. lib. iv. p. 189. But the passage is retrospective and historical, not predictive. The whole chapter, although, in our Version, entitled a *Prayer,* is more a devotional Hymn of *Praise;* and this *salvation of the anointed* is a *past* deliverance of God's chosen servants.

Page 273.

On the question concerning the consistency of the Divine Foreknowledge with Human Freedom, there are some opinions proposed by Archbishop King, in his Sermon on the subject, to which, notwithstanding the high sanction which that Sermon has received from the pen of Archbishop Whately, its recent editor, and from the praise and expressed approbation of Dr. Copleston, Bishop of Llandaff, I am unable to give my assent.

I was in error, however, in supposing that Dr. Whately approves Dr. King's hypothesis, as applied to the point in hand, *viz.,* the consistency of the Divine Foreknowledge with the Liberty of human actions. To this point Dr. Whately considers the hypothesis least applicable ; although this is the very difficulty which its author professes to solve by it. I am glad therefore to have Dr. Whately's judgment with me, in thinking that Dr. King's scheme of explanation is not tenable in this important question, nor calculated to afford us any assistance in treating it.

Dr. King, if I understand his hypothesis rightly, conceives some difference in kind, or " in properties and effects," between the *divine knowledge*, and *human;* by means of which difference the difficulty of the question he thinks may be relieved.

To my own mind it appears that the *essence* and *the effects* of *knowledge* must be held to be always the same; as I know of no ground either in Reason, or Scripture, for making a difference in it, in those respects.

One great difference there is, which we must admit to exist, between God's knowledge and man's; that is a difference ir their *origin.* Our stock of knowledge is raised upon the information of sense, a few axiomatic truths, inference, and testimony. Of the origin of God's knowledge we know nothing, except that it cannot be in our way, nor by these media. Perhaps it may not be a correct way of speaking, to say, that it *originates* at all. This is a mystery inscrutable to us.

Now the *certainty* of human knowledge is commonly grounded upon the *necessary* nature of the subject known. But it is plainly an inconsequence, to think that the *certainty* of God's knowledge is restricted within the same limits of subject; *viz.*, to things of a *necessary* nature. For since all our knowledge is in its origin wholly unlike to the intuition of God; since our media are not His; it is no more than reasonable to think that He has knowledge where we are ignorant; and that He has a certainty of vision where we see nothing. Our principles of knowledge are not His, nor therefore the scope of it, either as to things future, or any other of the objects of the intuition of His omniscient Mind.—Certainty of foreknowledge concerning free and contingent events never can belong to man by his own reason. When it is derived to him, as we have ground to believe it sometimes is, in prophecy, from God; then the certainty exists both in man and in God, and in neither disturbs or affects the freedom, or contingency, of the things foreknown. Knowledge, as knowledge, does not disturb or influence its subject.—If Dr. King had pressed the consideration of this difference in the *principles*, or the *faculty*, if I may so speak, of the Divine knowledge, instead of proposing a distinction " in its essence, or its properties and effects," I think his argument would have been more correct; and perhaps such a view of the question might have opened to us some mitigation of the difficulty belonging to it.

There is also a degree of *latitude* and *vagueness* in the opi-

nions which Dr. King has laid down concerning the *Moral At-*
tributes of God, which that author was far from intending to
be drawn to the favour of any scepticism, or unsettledness in
religious faith, but which I think is too liable to be drawn that
way. For my own part, I read his argument with an impression that such is the tendency of his doctrine, though most
remote from his design ; nor do I see how it can be effectually
defended against the objections, which, on this ground, were
made to it, when it was first published, by a most unfair writer,
Collins ; who, this once, seems to have had the advantage.
Thinking thus of it, I regret the approbation which it has received from a person, for whose learning, however, and acumen
in the investigation of truth, my respect is not diminished by a
difference of judgment in this instance,—Dr. Copleston.

Perhaps it is not impossible to suggest one cause, which,
probably, contributes its share to some erroneous, but certainly
inconsequent opinions, concerning the Divine Attributes. It
is this ; since *Infinites*, taken in their whole nature, are clearly
something above our comprehension, it comes to be thought that
we may assume almost any, or at least very arbitrary, notions,
respecting them. But Moral Infinites, as well as Mathematical ;
Moral Modes in their highest degree, as well as Modes of
Quantity in its unlimited extent ; are subject to some rules of
discourse, when we discourse of them at all ; and one rule is,
that in passing up the scale of the finite subject, in order to
approach the properties of the Infinite, we must pursue the
enlarged idea taken from the properties of the first, and not
adopt the contradictory, or any alien idea, to make the approximation to the Infinite in question.

Thus — they who have assigned to the Divine Justice or
Mercy, qualities, or operations, contradictory to, or alien from,
the highest and best notions of Human Justice or Mercy, have
sometimes appealed to the *infiniteness* of the Divine Nature,
and sought to defend their opinions by it. But that appeal is
unduly made. The infiniteness of that supreme excellence,
which is in God, renders the contradictory of the human virtues the less credible in Him. That infinity of perfection is,
indeed, an intense argument against the opinions so defended.
And such is the view which we are taught to take of the Divine
Nature, by Him who best knew its immeasurable perfections,

and how to direct us in our thoughts concerning it. "If ye then, being evil, know how to give good gifts unto your children, how *much more* shall your Father which is in heaven give good gifts to them that ask Him?" Matt. vii. 9, 10, 11.

Dr. King is clearly most opposite in his creed to those hard and perplexing tenets concerning the Divine Justice and Mercy, to which I have alluded. But his mode of argument seems to be that which lays a ground for those tenets, viz., the hypothesis, that the actual nature of the Divine Attributes is something different from our positive notions of the human virtues, and that our words and names are equivocal, or, which comes to the same effect, remotely analogous, when employed in the two subjects. A position which, I conceive, is introduced without a principle in the reason of it; and to the serious injury of our faith. Of any adequate and just comprehension of the nature and perfections of the Divine Being, we must believe not only the human, but every other finite mind, to be incapable. But this persuasion is exceedingly remote from the doctrine which I read in Dr. King's discourse. That doctrine threatens to take from us what I may call the Truth of our Faith in the contemplation of God: that Truth consisting in a real, though most imperfect, conformity of our ideas to their object. It is one of St. Austine's sayings which I should adopt, "*Rectissime dicitur homo* factus ad imaginem et similitudinem Dei ; non enim aliter *incommutabilem* veritatem posset mente conspicere.*"—De Vera Relig.*, cap. xliv.[g]

There is another Prelate of the Irish Church, a writer of a far more acute and vigorous intellect than Dr. King, Bramhall, who has expressed himself in the following sentence:—"The goodness, and justice, and mercy, and truth of God, are transcendent above the goodness, and justice, and mercy, and truth of men, *and of quite a different nature from them.*" As St. Austine said, "God is good without quality, a creator without indigence, everywhere without place, eternal without time[h]." This confession of the transcendent, exclusive, and even *different* character, of the Divine Attributes, is morally and substantially true. The absolute *transcendency* of the divine virtue makes it of a *different species.* But the same proposition

g A saying quoted from St. Austine by Malebranche.
h Bramhall, in his Controversy with Hobbes, Works, p. 741.

may become erroneous when put into certain forms of abstract reasoning. And Dr. King appears to have put the moral truth, thus expressed by that great writer, to this improper use.

But yet with regard to many of these inquiries respecting the Divine Nature and Attributes, I cordially agree in the sentiment of Dr. Copleston; and I have satisfaction in expressing that agreement, since in other points I am obliged to differ with him; the sentiment, that the confidence and arrogance of our reasoning ought to be repressed by a continual sense of the shortness of our faculties, and of the extreme imperfection and inadequateness of the ideas by which our knowledge is terminated. Incommensurate as our ideas are at best, when they are employed on this subject, and the communication of them embarrassed by the uncertainties of language, I think the silent meditation of private thought is here always more grateful than a protracted discussion; and I willingly retreat into that confession with which Hooker begins his admirable and exact discourse upon the Nature, Perfections, and Laws of God. "Dangerous it were for the feeble brain of man to wade far into the doings of the Most High; whom although to know, be life, and joy to make mention of His name, yet our soundest knowledge is, that we know Him not as He is, neither can know Him; and our safest eloquence concerning Him is our silence, when we confess without confession, that His glory is inexplicable, His greatness above our capacity and reach." *Eccles. Polit.* book i. sect. 2. Or, as the same thought is expressed, scarcely with less strength and beauty of words, by an older writer, a father of the Latin church, *O Maxime, de quo nihil dici et exprimi mortalium potis est significatione verborum; qui, ut intelligaris, tacendum est, atque ut per umbram Te possit errans investigare suspicio, nihil est omnino mutiendum.*—Arnobius *adv. Gent.* p. 17.

Page 308.

It has been thought by some persons, that the rejection and outcast state of the Jews, from the date of Christianity, involves a difficulty when taken as a subject of prophecy. It is said, they are strict adherents to the law of Moses; and upon that adherence depended their prosperity and welfare, according to the conditions of their covenant, and the tenor of prophecy. In their other judicial calamities, Idolatry was their crime. No such crime can be alleged against them under their last.   Thus it is argued.

The misapprehension in this point arises, as I believe, from want of attention to the actual tenor and language of prophecy.

It seems to be assumed, that adherence to their law and covenant, means nothing more than abstinence from Idolatry, or a formal attachment to the profession of their religion.   If we consider, however, how distinctly the divine judgments are threatened against them by the prophets for their failure of moral obedience to God's law, for their faithlessness in the love of it, and their violation of its chief commands, at the same time that they exulted in the name of their religion, and cried out, " The temple of the Lord, The temple of the Lord," we shall be led to make a more correct application of forewarning prophecy, and be satisfied that the whole of their later condition, in their apostasy from God's law, as well as in their rejection and sufferings, may perfectly correspond with what ancient prophecy had foretold of them.   The first chapter of Isaiah, in the view which it gives of God's government of His people, may suffice to shew what stress prophecy had laid upon substantial duties.   By Moses himself the love and fear of God had been made eminent in their conditions of obedience.

But when we demonstrate the inspiration of prophecy which is an argument with the unbeliever, it is less pertinent to allege the wickedness or moral corruption of a people as an element in proof of the fulfilment of a prophecy, so as to shew that for such particular moral corruption their sufferings have been their appointed punishment.

Degrees of national wickedness are not obvious and cognisable things to human observation.   External peculiarities are so.   If, therefore, those peculiarities obtain, and furnish a prophetic proof, that is sufficient for the conviction of the inquirer.

Again, it is an oversight to suppose that the inspiration of prophecy cannot be adequately demonstrated upon a separate member of a complex prediction.   The foretold *state* of the Jews, marked as it is by discriminating circumstances, affords of itself a complete basis of proof.

The Christian believer, however, when he takes the subject in hand for his own use, can easily supply the information required to illustrate this whole history. In the New Testament he finds the subject laid open in the discourses and remonstrances of our Saviour, which sufficiently attest the corruption and apostasy of the Jews, in their departure from the law of God, of which their enmity to Him was at once the greatest instance and the most condemning proof. Hatred to the Redeemer filled up the measure of their guilt. Unfaithful under God's first covenant, scornfully refusing the offer of the second, they were cut off from being God's people, and fulfilled prophecy in their doom.

THE END.

PRINTED BY JAMES PARKER AND CO., CROWN-YARD, OXFORD.

www.ingramcontent.com/pod-product-compliance
Lightning Source LLC
Chambersburg PA
CBHW032147110726
47902CB00003B/722